The Coronado Expedition to Tierra Nueva

The Coronado Expedition to Tierra Nueva
The 1540–1542 Route Across the Southwest

EDITED BY
Richard Flint AND
Shirley Cushing Flint

WITH AN INTRODUCTION BY
Carroll L. Riley

AND HISTORIOGRAPHICAL CHAPTERS BY
Joseph P. Sánchez

UNIVERSITY PRESS OF COLORADO

© 1997 by the University Press of Colorado

Published by the University Press of Colorado
5589 Arapahoe Avenue, Suite 206C
Boulder, Colorado 80303

All rights reserved
First paperback edition 2004

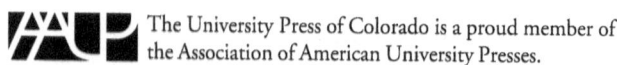 The University Press of Colorado is a proud member of
the Association of American University Presses.

The University Press of Colorado is a cooperative publishing enterprise supported, in part, by Adams State College, Colorado State University, Fort Lewis College, Mesa State College, Metropolitan State College of Denver, University of Colorado, University of Northern Colorado, and Western State College of Colorado.

Library of Congress Cataloging-in-Publication Data

The Coronado expedition to Tierra Nueva: the 1540–1542 route across the Southwest / Richard and Shirley Cushing Flint, editors.
p. cm.
Includes bibliographical references (p.) and index.
ISBN 0-87081-456-7 (alk. paper)—ISBN 0-87081-766-3 (pbk : alk. paper)
 1. Coronado, Francisco Vásquez de, 1510–1554. 2. Southwest, New—Discovery and exploration—Spanish. 3. Southwest, New—History—To 1848—Sources. 4. Southwest, New—Discovery and exploration—Spanish—Historiography. I. Flint, Richard. II. Flint, Shirley Cushing.
E125.V3C73   1997
979'.01'092—dc21
[B]
                                                                                            97-23539
                                                                                                 CIP

Chapter-opening pages include a detail of *Nueva Hispania Tabula Nova* by Girolamo Ruscelli, 1564, courtesy of the Virginia Garrett Cartographic History Library, Special Collections, the University of Texas at Arlington Libraries.

To
Nancy Marble,
geneaologist, historian, and museum director,
and
the late Jimmy Owens,
metal detector virtuoso.
Without whom archeological work at the Jimmy Owens Site
never would have happened.

Contents

LIST OF ILLUSTRATIONS	ix
PREFACE	xi
INTRODUCTION—*Carroll L. Riley*	1

Part I: Hypotheses and Evidence

1. A Historiography of the Route of the Expedition of Francisco Vázquez de Coronado: General Comments—*Joseph P. Sánchez*   25
2. The Coronado Documents: Their Limitations—*Charles W. Polzer, S.J.*   30
3. Coronado Fought Here: Crossbow Boltheads as Possible Indicators of the 1540–1542 Expedition—*Diane Lee Rhodes*   37
4. *Armas de la Tierra:* The Mexican Indian Component of Coronado Expedition Material Culture—*Richard Flint*   47

Part II: Precedents, 1538–1539

5. Pathfinder for Coronado: Reevaluating the Mysterious Journey of Marcos de Niza—*William K. Hartmann*   61
6. Cíbola, from fray Marcos to Coronado—*Madeleine Turrell Rodack*   84
7. The Search for Coronado's Contemporary: The Discovery, Excavation, and Interpretation of Hernando de Soto's First Winter Encampment—*Charles R. Ewen*   96

Part III: The Coronado Expedition, Compostela to Cíbola

MAPS OF THE REGION   112

8. A Historiography of the Route of the Expedition of Francisco Vázquez de Coronado: Compostela to Cíbola—*Joseph P. Sánchez*   115
9. Francisco Vázquez de Coronado's Northward Trek Through Sonora—*Jerry Gurulé*   124
10. The Relevance of Ethnology to the Routing of the Coronado Expedition in Sonora—*Daniel T. Reff*   137

11 An Archeological Perspective on the Sonora Entrada—*Richard A. Pailes* — 147

12 The 76 Ranch Ruin and the Location of Chichilticale—*William A. Duffen and William K. Hartmann* — 158

Part IV: The Coronado Expedition, Cíbola to Río de Cicúye

Map of the Region — 178

13 A Historiography of the Route of the Expedition of Francisco Vázquez de Coronado: Cíbola to Río de Cicúye—*Joseph P. Sánchez* — 179

14 Zuni on the Day the Men in Metal Arrived—*Edmund J. Ladd* — 187

15 The Geography of Middle Rio Grande Pueblos Revealed by Spanish Explorers, 1540–1598—*Elinore M. Barrett* — 195

16 Let the Dust Settle: A Review of the Coronado Campsite in the Tiguex Province—*Bradley J. Vierra and Stanley M. Hordes* — 209

17 The Coronado Expedition: Cicúye to the Río de Cicúye Bridge—*Richard Flint and Shirley Cushing Flint* — 220

Part V: The Coronado Expedition, Río de Cicúye to Quivira

Map of the Region — 234

18 A Historiography of the Route of the Expedition of Francisco Vázquez de Coronado: Río de Cicúye to Quivira—*Joseph P. Sánchez* — 235

19 Which Barrancas? Narrowing the Possibilities—*Donald J. Blakeslee* — 252

20 The Teya Indians of the Southwestern Plains—*Carroll L. Riley* — 267

21 "Por alli no ay losa ni se hace," Gilded Men and Glazed Pottery on the Southern Plains—*David H. Snow* — 287

22 A Large Canyon Like Those of Colima—*W. Michael Mathes* — 304

23 *Una Barranca Grande*: Recent Archeological Evidence and a Discussion of Its Place in the Coronado Route—*Donald J. Blakeslee, Richard Flint, and Jack T. Hughes* — 309

Concluding Remarks — 321
References Cited — 323
Contributors — 345
Index — 349

Illustrations

Figures

2.1	Title page, Castañeda's *Relación*	33
2.2	Folio 103v, Castañeda's *Relación*	34
3.1	Crossbow bolts	41
3.2	Copper crossbow boltheads from Santiago Pueblo and Pecos Pueblo	45
4.1	Young man leaving for war	49
4.2	Tenocha leaving Mexico City for Tierra Nueva, 1539	51
4.3	Tlaxcalan warrior with macana	52
4.4	Obsidian blade fragment, LA 54147, New Mexico	54
4.5	Mesoamerican columnar obsidian core and Mesoamerican prismatic blade	55
4.6	Texcoco point, Texcoco-type point (LA 54147), and Harrell point	56
6.1	Vicinity of Hawikuh, from south	88
6.2	Ruins of Hawikuh, near ridge	89
6.3	Dowa Yalanne from Mullen Canyon	90
6.4	Kiakima, center base of Dowa Yalanne	91
7.1	The Martin Site excavations	104
7.2	Objects from the Martin Site	107
12.1	Excavation of 76 Ranch Ruin, 1936	161
12.2	Room VIII, 76 Ranch Ruin, 1936	163
12.3	Mealing bins, Room IV, 76 Ranch Ruin, 1936	164
12.4	Room VI, 76 Ranch Ruin, 1936	165
12.5	Site plans, late Salado sites	169
14.1	Shu'la:witsi	193
16.1	Plan view and cross section of a tent dugout from LA 54147	212
16.2	Nails, a clothing hook, and a jack plate from LA 54147	213
21.1	Bowl rim forms, Espinoso Glaze-polychrome from LA 6455 and Pecos Glaze-polychrome	290

22.1	La Barranca Atenquique, Jalisco	306
22.2	Barranca near San Juan Espanatica, Jalisco	307
23.1	Blanco Canyon, Texas	311
23.2	Crossbow boltheads, Jimmy Owens Site, Floyd County, Texas	312
23.3	Crossbow boltheads, Hawikuh, New Mexico	313

Maps

1.	Northern Spanish America	xiv
2.	Zuni, New Mexico, showing location of archeological sites	87
3.	Approximate area of sixteenth-century Apalachee	102
4.	Compostela to Cíbola, Southern Portion: Nayarit, Sinaloa, Sonora	112
5.	Compostela to Cíbola, Northern Portion: Sonora, Arizona, New Mexico	113
6.	Reconstruction of routes to Tierra Nueva	138
7.	Archeological sites of the Río Sonora Valley	142
8.	Serrana Culture, sixteenth-century Sonora	149
9.	Sulphur Springs Valley area, Arizona	160
10.	Cíbola to the Río de Cicúye, New Mexico	178
11.	Sixteenth-century Cíbola	191
12.	Middle Rio Grande Pueblos, 1540–1598	198
13.	Pueblos of New Mexico based on the Enrico Martínez Map of 1602	205
14.	Principal previous hypothesized sites of Coronado's 1541 bridge, New Mexico	223
15.	Reconstruction of the Coronado expedition's route	227
16.	Río de Cicúye to Quivira	234
17.	Peoples of the Southwest and High Plains, 1540	268
18.	Road from Colima to Compostela, mid-sixteenth century	305

Tables

15.1	Pueblos Reported by Sixteenth-Century Spanish Explorers, Middle Rio Grande Subregion	196
17.1	Cicúye to Río de Cicúye Bridge Route Hypotheses	224

Preface

In 1539 and 1540 an imposing expedition was mounted in Spanish Mexico. Its objective was to bring into the orbit of Spanish colonial control a prosperous land far to the north. That region (stretching from modern Sonora to modern Kansas) was known to the Spaniards of the day as *la Tierra Nueva* (the New Land), in reference to its recent emergence into their awareness.

Conceived and organized by Spaniards, the massive expedition comprised an eclectic mix of people from the Old World and the New: Castilians, Portuguese, Italians, French, Germans, Africans, and even a Scot, accompanied and far outnumbered by Tlaxcalans, Mexica, Tlatelolcas, Tarascans, and other native people of New Spain. The indigenous people of la Tierra Nueva who met this heterogeneous expedition had neither solicited nor ratified the Spaniards' plans for them and their world. Nevertheless, the initial encounters between the peoples of the Tierra Nueva and the strangers from the south were usually not hostile, though perhaps cautious. Almost always, though, if the Spaniards and their cohorts decided to stay, conflicts festered and erupted.

For us at the end of the twentieth century the encounters in the Greater Southwest in 1539–1542 provide an instructive analog and counterpoint to frequently uneasy coexistence that has resulted from modern-day expansion of Western free-market commercial ideas, structures, and agents throughout the world. The similarities between sixteenth-century Spain and the late twentieth-century West are startling. Both represent highly commercial, bureaucratic, and litigious societies, self-assured (some would say arrogant) in their relentless efforts at worldwide hegemony. Hope for humanitarian outcomes of modern commercial empire-building make the study of the Old World–New World encounters that characterized the Coronado expedition especially pertinent today.

The minimum requirement for such study is to know where the encounters of 1539–1542 occurred and what peoples were involved. Surprisingly, the course followed by the expedition has remained largely unknown, uncertain, and ambiguous. In order to bring together the results of recent efforts to more precisely delineate the expedition's travel, a conference entitled "Where Did the *Encuentro* Happen in the Southwest?: Questions of the Coronado Expedition's Route in the Southwest, 1540–1542" was held at New Mexico Highlands University in August 1992. The papers presented at that conference form the core of this book. To them have been added half a dozen more recent essays, so as to include the results of the most recent work by historians, anthropologists, and geographers in defining the Coronado expedition route.

The Coronado Expedition to Tierra Nueva is a compendium of recent and exciting research. It lays out questions that we in the field are grappling with and suggestions that may lead toward their resolution. As a whole, *The Coronado Expediton to Tierra Nueva* represents the state of current research about the route of the Coronado expedition. Representing as it does the work of many individuals, there is not perfect accord among the various hypotheses and conclusions of this book. Indeed, there are several areas of active dispute. We have even made this explicit in Chapter 23, which deals with the Jimmy Owens Site in the Texas South Plains. Despite their lack of unanimity on all points, the authors are all serious and conscientious scholars, striving to illuminate a significant but shadowy period in the history of the Southwest.

The spelling of sixteenth-century Spanish names of persons and places and Spanish renditions of Native American words is one area in which the authors (and English speakers in general) sometimes disagree. For instance, one of Viceroy Antonio de Mendoza's chief rivals for exploration and settlement of the Tierra Nueva was Hernando de Soto. Following Spanish practice, many Southwestern scholars refer to his surname simply as Soto, while most Southeastern scholars refer to him as de Soto or De Soto. The sixteenth-century Spanish (and sometimes Italian and Portuguese) documents are the source of some of the variation in spelling. As examples, we have Melchior Díaz and Melchor Díaz; Alarcón and Alarçón;

Chichilticale, Chichilticalli, and Chichilticali. In this book we have not insisted on standardized spelling of such words. One exception is the name of the leader of the expedition to Tierra Nueva: Francisco Vázquez de Coronado, which is how he signed his name.

Both the conference that generated this book and the research work that it reports have been generously supported and encouraged by the Program for Cultural Cooperation Between Spain's Ministry of Culture and U.S. Universities; the New Mexico Endowment for the Humanities; New Mexico Highlands University; Wichita State University; the Southwestern Mission Research Center; the Coronado Trail Association; the Santa Fe Trail Association; the Coronado-Quivira Museum of Lyons, Kansas; the Rice County (Kansas) Historical Society, the Las Vegas/San Miguel (New Mexico) Chamber of Commerce, the Floyd County (Texas) Historical Museum, and the generous people of Floyd County, Texas, especially Joyce and QD Williams.

Not apparent in this volume, but integral to its success, is the work of Adrián Bustamante, Bernard Fontana, and Leigh Jenkins, who served as chairs and discussants for the sessions of the conference. At New Mexico Highlands University, Robert Mishler and Michael Olsen mustered the full support of their respective departments of Behavioral Sciences and History and Political Science. Volunteering their help at the conference were Linda Thayer, Mary Jo Whiteman, Susan Swan, Virginia Wilson, and Nancy Henry.

By the generous arrangement of Dr. José Ramón Remacha, Minister for Cultural Affairs at the Spanish embassy in Washington, D.C., the conference was enriched by the enthusiastic presence of Cultural Counselor Alvaro Alabart.

A special word of appreciation must be said about the late Dr. Waldo R. Wedel and Mildred Mott Wedel. Involved in research on the Coronado route for decades, they encouraged and participated in field investigations well into the 1990s. Representing them as their partner in research, as well as their son, Wally (Waldo M.) Wedel delivered preliminary findings of their continuing chain mail research at the 1992 conference. The passing of Dr. and Mrs. Wedel's enthusiasm and persistence is a loss to us all.

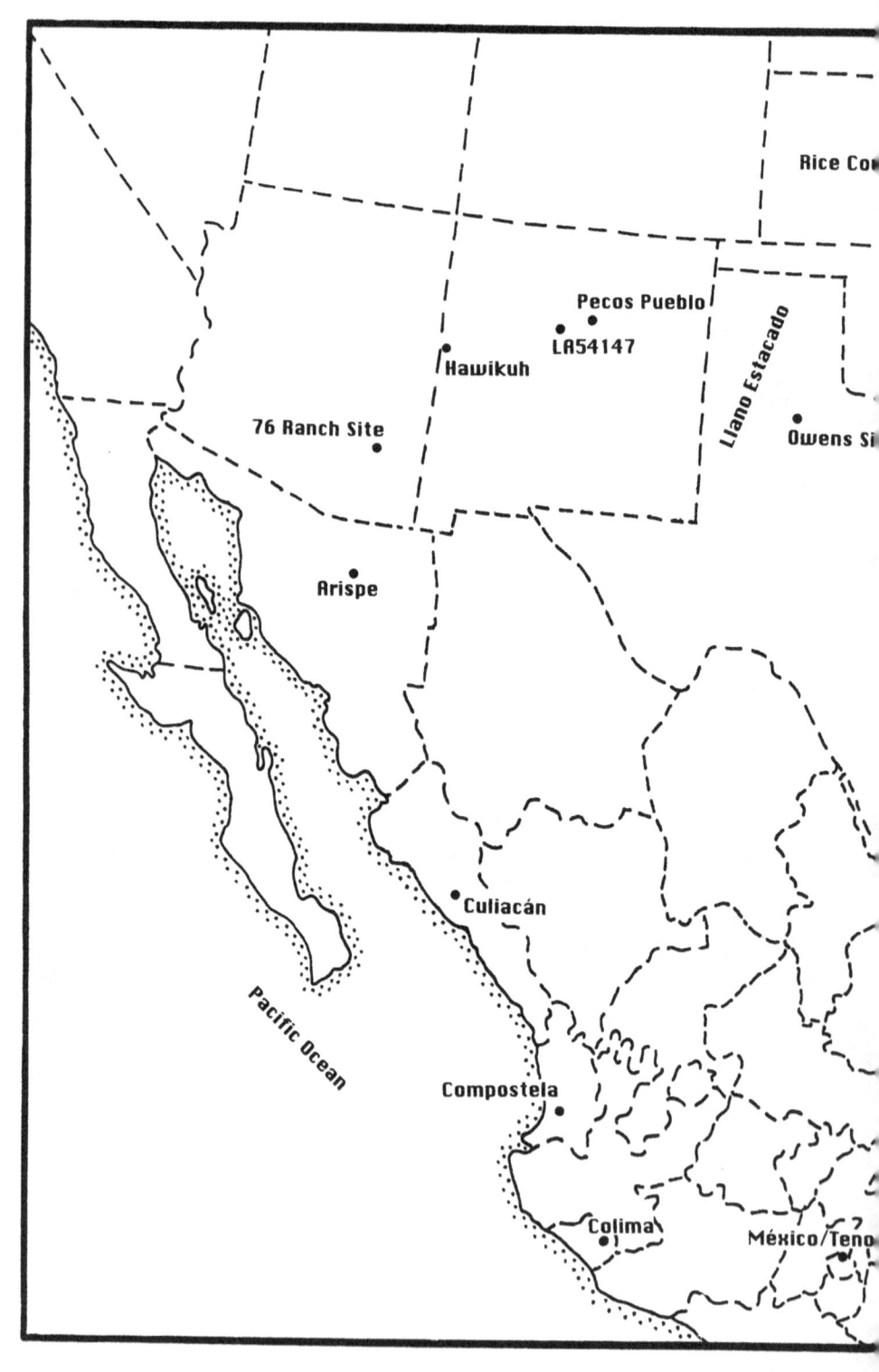

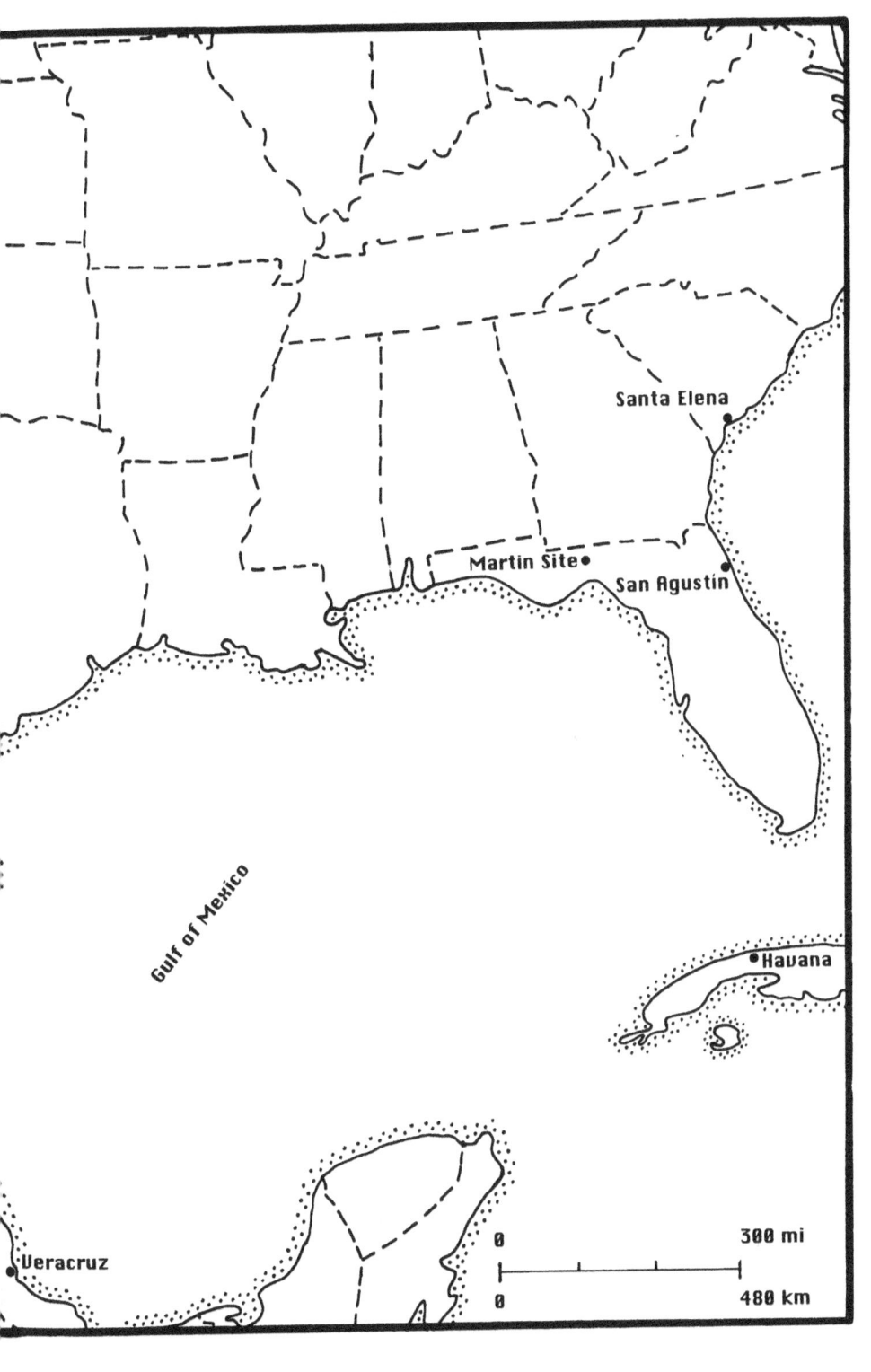

Introduction

CARROLL L. RILEY

Studies of the early Spanish period in the New World have become popular in recent years because of the celebration of the 500th anniversary of the first voyage of Christopher Columbus (1492–1992). It was in the spirit of this Columbus Quincentennial that a number of scholars met at New Mexico Highlands University, Las Vegas, New Mexico, August 21–23, 1992, to discuss Francisco Vázquez de Coronado and his exploration of the Southwest, 1539–1542.

In 1988 the United States Congress amended the National Trails System Act, thus allowing for a study to determine if the route of Coronado's expedition fell within the meaning of that act. The National Park Service (NPS) was directed to review the available documentation on the route and to search for new data. The NPS was charged with assessing a particular Coronado route in terms of eligibility for National Trail designation (Ivey, Rhodes, and Sánchez 1991: 1).

After considering the number of differing locations for Coronado's route suggested over the past century, the NPS recommended that further work be done on the route (Ivey et al.: 102–103), perhaps with emphasis not on a specific route but on a broad *corridor*. But the status of Coronado studies is such that even such a corridor cannot be drawn with any surety. The August 1992 conference at New

Mexico Highlands University was organized specifically to further this Coronado trail research. A number of experts on Coronado, and on Southwestern protohistoric studies generally, assembled at Las Vegas. A few of the participants discussed Coronado's trip up the west coast of Mexico, but the major concentration was on the route within the present boundaries of the United States.

Before talking about individual papers, let me sketch in broad strokes the history of the Coronado expedition. In order to properly understand this Spanish penetration of the Southwest it is necessary to review the events of the decade before Coronado (see also Riley 1995: 147–207).

By the late 1520s, Spanish forces, operating from their base in the Valley of Mexico, had overrun much of the west central portion of Mexico. The Tarascan kingdom in what is now Michoacán had collapsed and the Spaniards controlled the coastline from present-day Guerrero north into Nayarit. The period around 1530 saw an expansion northward from that region into southern and central Sinaloa. The Spaniards under their ruthless western commander, Beltrán Nuño de Guzmán, were in part following up on rumors of Amazon kingdoms, rich cities and provinces farther north. Guzmán pushed up the Sinaloa coast, establishing Culiacán in central Sinaloa. From that beachhead, in 1533, Diego de Guzmán, a relative of Nuño, led a slaving party northward as far as the lower Yaqui Valley, the very edge of the Greater Southwest.

During the next three years the Spaniards made a number of slave raids into the coastal country to the north. In the spring of 1536 one such slaving group met a four-person party led by Álvar Núñez Cabeza de Vaca. These Spaniards were the sole survivors of the Pánfilo de Narváez expedition which, some years previously, had attempted to travel by improvised boats from Florida to Mexico. The expedition was shipwrecked on the Texas coast and many of its members lost. Those who managed to reach shore gradually died from native hostility, disease, and starvation. Only Cabeza de Vaca and his three companions managed the long journey across coastal plain, mountain, and desert to west Mexico. Cabeza de Vaca and his group eventually worked their way into the heavily settled Sonora River region where they met friendly people and heard stories of contacts with northern peoples who lived in large apartment-like dwellings and who traded turquoise and "emeralds" (perhaps uvarovite garnet or possibly peridots) for tropical birds and their feathers.

Cabeza de Vaca's story, coming at a time when accounts of Pizarro's conquest of the gold-rich Inca Empire in South America were still fresh in Mexico, made a considerable impression on the Spaniards. The viceroy of New Spain, Antonio de Mendoza, planned a major expedition to the north. A final decision to launch such an expedition came when Hernando de Soto, a veteran of the Pizarro party in Peru, was given permission to explore the northern *terra incognita* entering North America from Florida. De Soto, with a party of six hundred, reached Santiago, Cuba, in May of 1538. A year later, with an augmented party, De Soto landed in Florida (see Chapter 7).

De Soto's activity spurred the cautious Viceroy Mendoza. In 1538 he had appointed the young courtier, Francisco Vázquez de Coronado, governor of the new province of Nueva Galicia on the Mexican west coast. At a time when the Peruvian conquistador was still in Cuba, on March 7, 1539,[1] Mendoza and Coronado sent a Franciscan missionary named Marcos de Niza northward to explore the unknown lands. Marcos had recently returned from Peru and the Pizarro conquests and could be expected to know gold and other riches when he saw them. A second Franciscan, fray Onorato, originally slated to go, fell ill shortly after the beginning of the expedition and was left behind. Continuing with Marcos, however, was a black slave, Esteban de Dorantes of the Cabeza de Vaca party, a most valuable member of the expedition because of his ability to pick up native languages and his experience with peoples of the region north of New Spain. With Marcos also were central Mexican Indians and Piman-speaking natives who had come south with Cabeza de Vaca three years earlier.

The route of Marcos and Esteban is a matter of some controversy. I consider that they stayed fairly close to the ocean until they reached the Altar-Magdalena drainage in northwest Sonora, then cut inward to the Upper Southwest (however, see Chapter 5 for another routing). Whatever the exact route, we do know that Esteban was sent on ahead and was killed outside one of the Zuni towns in west central New Mexico. Marcos *probably* reached Zuni before retreating to Mexico (see Chapters 6 and 14). At any rate, Marcos, on his return in August 1539, reported a rich urban confederation of the Seven Cities of Cíbola. Marcos did not mention gold at Cíbola, but Mendoza and other Spaniards clearly believed that something like the recently conquered Inca Empire was at hand.

A second expedition led by Captain Melchior Díaz was sent north in the fall of 1539. Díaz wintered in northern Sonora or southern Arizona and met Coronado's army on his return the following March. His report tended to confirm that of Marcos, especially as to the reality of Cíbola.

The Coronado expedition was an ambitious one. It contained some 350 Spaniards, more than two-thirds of them mounted. There were five Franciscans: three priests and two lay brothers. In addition there were perhaps 1,300 native soldiers from the Aztec, Tlaxcalan, and Tarascan areas, plus additional servants and slaves. With the party were some 1,500 horses and mules, large herds of sheep (probably in the thousands), and apparently a number of cattle. Pigs were also purchased for the trip (AGI Justicia 336) but it is unknown whether they went as salted-down pork or on the hoof, as had been true of the Diego Guzmán expedition seven years earlier. A separate sea expedition under Captain Hernando de Alarçón was to sail northward on the Gulf of California with supplies. The land party reached Culiacán on Easter Day, March 28, 1540. On April 22 Coronado went ahead with a vanguard of around eighty horsemen and some twenty to thirty foot soldiers. There were in addition a considerable number of Indian allies, plus black and Indian servants and slaves.

Coronado's advance party reached the town(s) and surrounding polity of Corazones, so named by Cabeza de Vaca, and spent several days exploring the small principalities of the Sonora River region. Resupplying himself, he moved on and reached the westernmost Cíbolan or Zuni town of Hawikuh on July 7. His route is much disputed. I have suggested that Coronado and his group followed the Sonora River north, then cut across the flat country east of modern Cananea to the upper San Pedro River drainage. The party went down the San Pedro and eventually swung north and east into the Gila River Valley. They followed the Gila to about the modern New Mexico state line, then forged northward again, following the San Francisco River. Eventually they crossed into the drainage of the Carrizo Wash, following it westward, and then turned north to the Zuni River (Riley 1992; 1995: 158). Certain other experts on the Coronado expedition, however, route Coronado to the east of my suggested trail in Sonora, and west of it in Arizona–New Mexico (for a survey of routes see Chapters 1, 8, 13, and 18).

After overrunning Zuni, Coronado sent out parties westward to explore the Hopi area and eastward to the Rio Grande. Western parties were sent partly in an attempt to locate the sea arm of the expedition. Alarçón in fact reached as far north as the junction of the Gila and Colorado Rivers but, finding himself still hundreds of miles from the land expedition, returned to Mexico. He planned to sail again in 1541, but the savage Mixtón rebellion in Jalisco, which broke out in April of that year, forced all Spanish attention onto this region of west Mexico. Alarçón's failure to resupply Coronado had serious consequences for the expedition.

A trading group from Pecos reached Zuni sometime after Coronado arrived there and a small party of Spaniards led by Hernando de Alvarado and the priest Juan de Padilla was sent east with them. Alvarado penetrated as far east as the High Plains, guided in part by a captive Pawnee Indian whom the Spaniards named "Turk." This man described to the Spaniards large Indian principalities with much sophistication and wealth off to the east. His accounts sound very much like chiefdoms of the Mississippi Valley, but Turk also claimed that there was a great amount of gold and silver in this eastern area, which the Spaniards understood was called Quivira.

Pressed for details, Turk was reported to have blamed the Pecos Indians for stealing some golden bracelets from him. Alvarado imprisoned Turk as well as the two Pecos leaders of the trading expedition, a young man called "Bigotes" (mustaches) and an older Pecos native whom the Spaniards referred to as "Cacique." These men may have been war society captains or possibly bow priests. In any case, they were part of the leadership structure at Pecos. The captives were brought back to the Rio Grande Valley where in the winter of 1540–1541 they worked out what I have named the "Pecos plot." It called for Turk to guide the Spaniards into the trackless reaches of the southwestern Plains and lose them.

At some point Alvarado advised Coronado to establish winter quarters in the Rio Grande Valley. Coronado's camp master, García López de Cárdenas, had been sent in late August in an unsuccessful attempt to reach the lower Colorado River. On Cárdenas's return, probably in mid-November, he was dispatched to the Rio Grande to prepare winter quarters. The body of the expedition, under its field commander Tristán de Luna y Arellano, finally reached Zuni a few days after the departure of Cárdenas. This main party had established the town of San Gerónimo de los Corazones in the Sonora Valley, a sort of halfway station so that Coronado could remain in contact with Mexico. Ordering Arellano to rest his group for twenty days before continuing to the Rio Grande, Coronado took thirty men and, with Zuni guides, marched east and south to the Piro region around modern Socorro (for another view, see Chapter 15). Sending one of his lieutenants to explore the southern Piro, Coronado himself went north, where, toward the end of the year 1540, he had a rendezvous with the other elements of his company. Cárdenas had settled on the province of Tiguex, the modern Tiwa, in the Albuquerque-Bernalillo region and had expelled the Indians from a town called Coofor (see Chapter 16).

The failure to meet with Alarcón and his ships with their supplies of food and warm winter clothing now became a serious matter. The desperate Spaniards forced the Indian towns to supply cotton garments and food. A series of violent reactions broke out in the twelve Tiguex towns. After some months of fighting, the Tiguex were scattered and their towns largely burned and looted. When Coronado launched his expedition to find golden Quivira on April 23, 1541, he left behind a ravaged Tiguex and a sullen Rio Grande Pueblo world. At the same time a small party under Pedro de Tovar was sent southwestward to San Gerómino de los Corazones to bring back part of the garrison there and to rendezvous with Coronado either on the trail or at Quivira. It was arranged that Coronado would leave crosses in prominent places to guide Tovar on his return from Sonora. Although Coronado was unaware of the situation, the Mixtón War was now raging far to the south in Jalisco.

Marching with virtually his entire party, plus slaves made in the Tiguex War of the previous winter, Coronado commanded 1,700 or more people and had with him large numbers of horses and sheep. Reaching Pecos, Coronado met with not-unexpected hostility. After a few futile days of attempted peacemaking, he went on, probably moving onto Rowe Mesa, then south to Cañon Blanco, and east to the Pecos River. Building a bridge over the Pecos, likely a little south of the juncture with the Gallinas River (see Chapter 17), Coronado quickly reached the bison herds of the western Great Plains. There he contacted two groups, the Querecho, ancestors of the eastern Apaches, and the Teya, linguistic kin to the Piro-Tompiro, as I believe. Reaching the featureless vastness of the Llano Estacado (Staked Plains), Coronado was led off to the southeast by Turk, fulfilling his part of the Pecos plot. A second Caddoan Indian, the Wichita native Ysopete, seems not to have been involved in the plot and warned Coronado that the Spaniards were off course.

At this point Coronado decided to send the bulk of the expedition back to Tiguex and with some forty men, most of them mounted, set off for Quivira. The two divisions separated at what the expedition called a great barranca. This was clearly one of the caprock canyons that cut into the east side of the Llano Estacado, perhaps Blanco Canyon. The main army marched back to the Pecos and then on into the Rio Grande Valley. Coronado with his party of horsemen moved north to Quivira, which was the Wichita region in the Great Bend of the Arkansas River in central Kansas. In my opinion they followed a trade route used by the Teya through extreme western Oklahoma, the area of the Wheeler Phase people (Riley 1992; 1995: 195; also see Chapter 20). Although neither man knew it, Coronado and De Soto, during the late summer of 1541, were both in the Arkansas River Valley, though De Soto was exploring the lower reaches of the river and Coronado traversed part of its middle course.

Finding no gold or other precious metal, Coronado rejoined the main party on the Rio Grande in September 1541. A short time later Pedro de Tovar returned from Sonora with dispatches that must have told of the Mixtón War. He also reported that the commander of the San Gerónimo outpost, Diego de Alcaráz, had endangered the garrison with brutal and ill-advised behavior. Tovar moved the site of the town upriver and then took about half of the soldiers with him as ordered. It left his link with the Spanish world woefully shorthanded.

The remainder of the Coronado expedition was an anticlimax. The general still believed that there was gold in Quivira and planned another expedition to that eastern region in 1542. However, events were now beginning to overtake the Spaniards and their dreams. The unknown outcome of the Mixtón War must have been a constant worry to Coronado. At this time the general also lost his main deputy, for López de Cárdenas had word that he had come into an important inheritance and left for Mexico.

After Cárdenas's departure, sometime around the beginning of the year 1542, Coronado, on one of his daily rides, had a saddle girth break and fell under the hooves of a companion's horse. The general was severely injured and was apparently unconscious for days. He had barely begun his recovery when Cárdenas returned with the terrible news that Alcaráz and a number of his men had been killed in a native uprising at San Gerónimo and the Spaniards no longer controlled the line of the Sonora River. This information led to a relapse on the part of the general and the decision to return to New Spain.

When Coronado left the Rio Grande in early April of 1542, several groups stayed behind. Father Padilla, in the far-fetched belief that a legendary Portuguese kingdom existed somewhere on the High Plains, led a small party back to Quivira. One of the Franciscan lay brothers, Juan de Úbeda, chose to stay and missionize Pecos. Various of the Mexican Indians, both Nahuatl and Tarascan speakers, also elected to stay in the Southwest.

Father Padilla lost his life at Quivira, but members of his party eventually escaped back to Mexico. Nothing more was ever heard of fray Juan de Úbeda, but a number of the Mexican Indians were still in the Southwest when Spanish expeditions of the early 1580s again reached that area. At least one Pueblo Indian woman returned with the Spaniards as a wife of a Spanish soldier. All in all, the Coronado expedition failed in virtually all its expectations. There remained a memory of the Upper Southwest and a number of documents described the approaches thereto. However, forty years later, when the Spanish crown next launched a party to explore the Pueblo world, it was from the northern interior of Mexico.

With this broad outline in mind, let me turn to the individual papers in this volume.

One of the conference participants, Albert H. Schroeder, a major figure in Southwestern archeology, and a friend to many at the Las Vegas conference, died in 1993. His paper for the conference, an account of Schroeder's own novel routing of Coronado in the Plains (Schroeder 1992; 1993), will not be included here. Three participants, Waldo R. Wedel, Kirk Bertsche, and Waldo M. Wedel, presented a paper on carbon-14 dating of a piece of chain mail that has been attributed to the Coronado expedition. The results from this interesting new approach to radiocarbon dating were equivocal and publication will be delayed, pending greater refinement of the methodology. After the conference several additional papers were solicited from interested scholars and these have been incorporated into this volume. The individual chapters are discussed in the remainder of this introduction.

Part I: Hypotheses and Evidence

Joseph Sánchez considers the route of Coronado as past experts have seen it, commenting on the varying interpretations and identifications in Chapters 1, 8, 13, and 18. Here, I shall treat all four segments of Sánchez's work as a unit. Sánchez was co-editor of the National Park Service report on the Coronado trail (Ivey, Rhodes, and Sánchez) so has been concerned for some years with the overall problem of the route. Sánchez draws on the materials in the National Park Service document but also cites later attempts to discover the route. He concludes that we may never discover the exact route and (as per his recommendation in the NPS document) suggests that perhaps we should think in terms of a corridor instead of a narrow trail. Sánchez does hold out the hope that future research in the various colonial archives and increased attention to the contact period archeology of the area will give us additional valuable data. He describes and analyzes various of the Coronado route proposals that have been made over the past century for one or the other segment of the trail.

Father Charles Polzer also discusses the complex and very important matter of documentation of the expedition. Polzer points out that no amount of reading about the expedition will really add much more to the delineation of the Coronado route. He quite correctly pleads for reconnaissance on the ground. Polzer also stresses that all of the documents of the expedition "with the exception of a couple of letters" were written after the journey was over, in some cases many years afterward. He points out another problem, that we are not clear as to what names in the documents actually *meant*. For example, when a given chronicler spoke of Corazones, did he mean town, a group of towns, or a province?

Polzer rightly says that we need to reconsider the documents, especially in terms of modern anthropological analyses of their content. The anthropological input of men like Bandelier and Hodge was fine for their day, but they are a half century to a century out of date and anthropology is now much more methodologically sophisticated.

Polzer generally does not commit himself on specifics of the route, though he argues (on the basis of extrapolations from latitude measurements) that the ruined town (and province?) of Chichilticalli was near the modern international border, rather than near the upper middle Gila River where many modern scholars place it. Polzer's essay is largely a plea for more extensive and sophisticated use of the documents and for associated archeology.

Dr. Polzer's cautionary notes are ones we all need to heed. I have one minor caveat with his statement about the time lapse between event and written documentation. In my opinion Dr. Polzer overemphasizes this point. Several crucial documents (the Coronado letter to Mendoza, the latter man to King Carlos I, Coronado to the king, the Marcos account, and the Alarçón account) were all written on-the-spot or within a few weeks after the events described. On the other hand, it is true that the most comprehensive of all the documents, the account of Pedro de Castañeda, was composed many years after the events of the expedition.

Introduction

The question of crossbow darts, usually called bolts or quarrels, is addressed by Diane Rhodes. As Rhodes points out, by Coronado's time the crossbow was in the process of being replaced by powder-driven weapons like the arquebus. Twenty-one crossbows are listed in the Coronado inventory, whereas none are given for expeditions to New Mexico in the 1580s and 1590s. It is of course possible that isolated, unrecorded crossbows may have been used in later expeditions.

All crossbow bolts in early New Mexico sites were made from copper rather than iron, the latter more commonly used in European crossbow boltheads. However, one of the thirty-plus boltheads found to date in the Llano Estacado *was* made of iron. It is known that Cortés utilized native metallurgical skills to produce copper boltheads (points) in his conquest of the Aztecs. It seems likely that such copper crossbow boltheads were still being produced twenty years later, in Coronado's day. In the Southwest, five copper boltheads have been found at Hawikuh, thus seeming to confirm Coronado's battle at that place. They have also been found at a scatter of sites in the Rio Grande Valley. Several come from Santiago Pueblo, one located in the chest of a skeleton on one of the room floors. There are also reports of boltheads from Pecos, Comanche Springs, and Piedras Marcadas (Mann-Zuris).

Crossbow quarrel heads in such numbers surely related to the Coronado expedition. The finds also would seem to indicate that Santiago Pueblo played an important role in Coronado's time, though whether it was Coofor, Moho, or another site altogether is still not clear.

With Richard Flint's paper we move to a more general analysis of the Coronado expedition. Flint asks, what do we know about the native components of the Coronado expedition through their material culture? To date, relatively few materials that relate to his force have been found in the Southwest, and most of those (boltheads, glass beads, lace tips, etc.) are European in manufacture. We know from the historical documents that a large number of central and west Mexican Indians, 1,300 or more, were with Coronado, and from equipment lists we are aware that even the Spaniards often used native equipment. Flint can find records of only a few actual artifacts from this period in the Upper Southwest. He points out a number of object classes that should be found in the Southwest specifically from the Coronado expedition. These would include obsidian, widely used in weapons and tools. There might perhaps be other lithic and metallic materials (such as sandal-making tools and *comales* (see also Chapter 16). It also seems likely that some native pottery was brought north, though none in any dependable context has as yet been found.

The inventory of material items now being compiled by Richard and Shirley Cushing Flint will be of great value to future contact period archeology in the Southwest. It will be a sort of handbook for what might be *expected* to appear in contact sites and give at least a preliminary indication of the provenance of such artifacts.

Part II: Precedents, 1538–1539

William Hartmann is interested not in Coronado as such, but in the pioneering effort of Marcos de Niza, sent by Coronado to the Southwest in the spring of 1539. Hartmann summarizes what little we know of the Franciscan friar's background, his service in Peru where he was elected *custodio*, his activities during the Coronado expedition, and the quiet life he led thereafter. Hartmann shows that the persistent rumors about gold and other wealth in Cíbola are the result of misunderstandings due to the powerful expectations about the situation in the north. He makes the perceptive observation that even if Marcos did exaggerate a bit (an accusation not proven), it was because he was so anxious to save souls in the new lands. Though Hartmann does not bring up this point, the early Franciscans in the New World believed that their conversion of the Native Americans, the last pool of heathen souls to be contacted, would hasten the second coming of Christ.

Much of the Hartmann paper is devoted to refuting the scurrilous attacks on Marcos's reputation by certain scholars, especially Carl Sauer and Cleve Hallenbeck. Hartmann demonstrates conclusively that these attacks have little or no substance and that the Marcos narrative is probably basically true. There still remains the task of interpreting the account in terms of a specific route for Marcos. Hartmann presents cogent arguments for his own routing of Marcos.

With Madeleine Rodack's paper we move northward to consider the identity of the original town reached by fray Marcos de Niza. Rodack summarizes what we know of the good friar and his trek northward to the Zuni area. She refrains from entering the long argument as to where exactly *were* various points on the Marcos trail. For example, the settlement of Vacapa has been located as far south as the Río Fuerte, as far north as the Altar-Magdalena Valley, and at several points in between.

Rodack's interest is in pinpointing the Zuni settlement that was seen by Marcos in 1539. That settlement has usually been identified as Hawikuh, the southwestern-most of the Zuni towns. Rodack argues, however, that the topography of Hawikuh is all wrong. Rodack and her husband Juel have extensively explored the region south and east of modern Zuni Pueblo. Drawing on this exploration, she argues that the Franciscan friar followed Mullen Canyon and from the north end of that canyon, looked across the flats to the town of Kiaki:ma that sits on the south slope of Dowa Yalanne, the Zuni sacred mountain.

Although less certain about the Coronado expedition, Rodack does list several factors in favor of Kiaki:ma being the town of Granada overrun by Coronado in 1540, though she remains equivocal on this identification. I might say here that

Rodack makes a good case for Kiaki:ma as the town visited by Marcos, but her identification of Kiaki:ma as *Coronado's* first Cíbolan town seems to me unlikely for reasons given by Edmund Ladd (see Chapter 14).

The final paper in this section takes us away from the Coronado expedition to the contemporary De Soto expedition. Charles Ewen directed excavations at the Martin Site, in the area of Anhaica, the main town of the Apalachee Indians, where De Soto spent the winter of 1539–1540. There have been attempts over a number of years to identify Anhaica, which was known to be somewhere near Tallahassee, the present-day capital of Florida. What seems to be Anhaica was discovered in 1987 in a residential area of Tallahassee about a mile from the capitol building. The site contained an assemblage of native materials but also Spanish olive jars and sixteenth-century majolica pottery. There were also chevron and Nueva Cadiz beads, a crossbow quarrel head, and five early sixteenth-century copper Spanish and Portuguese coins. A bone from a domesticated pig also suggests that the site is associated with De Soto since this is the first southeastern expedition known to have brought pigs as food sources.

For a study of Coronado, information on the De Soto expedition (covering as it does the same period of time) gives information on material culture—weapons, trade objects, especially beads, which should help in future identification of Coronado period finds. It also helps put the Coronado expedition into the perspective of the larger world of Hispanic North American exploration. The similarities in the two expeditions can be taken as given, but the differences are rather striking. Coronado ran a tightly planned and controlled expedition that opened a large segment of the Southwest to Spanish exploration and control by the end of the sixteenth century. By contrast, De Soto's party wandered aimlessly through the eastern United States, suffering steady attrition. Eventually, Luis de Moscoso led the tattered remnants of the expedition back to Mexico. The Spaniards were unable to follow up significantly on De Soto's explorations, and much of the area he traversed was eventually explored as *terra nova* by the English and French in the seventeenth and eighteenth centuries.

Part III: The Coronado Expedition, Compostela to Cíbola

The study by Jerry Gurulé is a most useful compilation of place names for the western part of the Coronado route. Some of these are well known and others, for example, the Señora Valley, relate only to the sixteenth century. This work of Gurulé's is a section of a planned, much larger work.

With Daniel Reff we turn to specific studies of the possible routes of Coronado through Sonora. Reff points out two main schools of thought about Coronado's Sonora route. The first, associated with Carl Sauer, among others, held that the general went up the Sonora Valley to the north-flowing San Pedro, eventually reaching the Gila. The second, largely pioneered by Charles Di Peso, routed the expedition up the Cedros River, then into the Nuri River drainage and on to the Yaqui River proper. Di Peso added the complication that from the Yaqui, Coronado's vanguard traversed the west loop of the Bavispe River while the main expedition, following a few months behind, went down the east loop of the Bavispe. Both segments then followed the Batepito River and then the San Bernardino River northward, crossing the present international border somewhat around modern Douglas, Arizona.

Reff accepts the routing of Sauer, who brings the Coronado party to Corazones in the Ures Basin and Señora north of the Ures Gorge. In defending this route, Reff cites the excavations and surveys of the Sonora Valley with their indications of large towns and large populations, very much as they were described in the sixteenth-century accounts of Castañeda and Obregón. He also points out that the Di Peso routing really does not fit the explorers' accounts, especially in terms of distances.

Reff poses an important question. Why did the Spaniards in the sixteenth century report such large and complex settlements while the Jesuits who reached Sonora in the next century saw scattered *rancherías* of Ópata and Pima Bajo Indians? He questions the belief by some modern scholars that the Jesuit accounts were necessarily more accurate or more honest than the sixteenth-century members of the Coronado and Francisco de Ibarra expeditions. In fact, statements from *both* periods were reasonably accurate. Between the time of Ibarra in the mid-sixteenth century and that of the Jesuit missionaries in the early seventeenth, this region of Sonora had been decimated by disease. The large towns noted by Coronado and Ibarra had dwindled to rancherías, and there remained only shattered remnants of the extensive populations of earlier times.

Reff's case is a strong one, combining as it does archeology and historical documentation. Reff himself was associated with the Rio Sonora Archaeological Project of the 1970s and so has firsthand experience in northeast Sonora. In addition, Reff, himself, has done extensive work on the timing and distribution of European diseases on the Mexican west coast.

Richard A. Pailes concerns himself primarily with the Sonoran background for the Coronado entrada. Pailes, the director of the Rio Sonora Archaeological Project, sketches the distinctive topography of northeast Sonora, the north-south–tending ranges with permanent streams in the fertile upper and middle valleys—important in prehistoric times as they are today. To the south, Coronado's route (and those of other Spanish explorers) is not in doubt for there is only a narrow corridor between the sierras and the coastal plain. Pailes believes that from the Fuerte River northward, the explorers were channeled inland along the Arroyo Cuchujaque to near modern Alamos and then along the Río Cedros. Farther north, a Río Sonora or Río Moctezuma route would be feasible, a Yaqui route somewhat less so.

Aboriginally, Pailes sees a widespread Río Sonora tradition with southern and northern branches. The southern Río Sonora peoples were influenced by the Mexican west coast cultures farther south. In the north, there developed hierarchical settlements and public architecture, the region of the Serrana or the Sonoran statelets. At some point in the past, Taracahitan peoples (in historic times including the Tarahumar, the Ópata, and the Yaqui and Mayo) spread along the live streams, reaching the Gulf of California in the lower Yaqui. In doing so, they split the Tepimans into a northern Piman enclave and a southern Tepehuan group. Pailes believes that the Serrana groups were Ópata and that these Indians were still expanding at the time of arrival of the Spaniards.

A number of years ago, I suggested (Riley 1979; see also Riley 1987: 48, 351) that the Ópatan Serrana civilization may have originated in Casas Grandes. This idea has been challenged by Doolittle (1988: 59), who thinks in terms of an in situ development of the Sonoran statelets. More recently, Phillips (1989: 390) has revived my Casas Grandes hypothesis. Pailes, however, points out that if the Serrana area chronology is correct, the statelets cannot be a remnant Casas Grandes population, though they may represent peoples indigenous to or related to the Chihuahuan region. Let me suggest another scenario in which the Serrana Culture and Casas Grandes both rose from a Chihuahuan/Mogollon base. However, around A.D. 1150–1200, Casas Grandes experienced a sudden and dramatic quickening that rapidly influenced the Sonora region, and was responsible for the sophisticated culture there. Whether, after the collapse of Casas Grandes, certain remnant populations made their way to the Sonoran valleys is still an open question.

Although Pailes's major excavation project in the Sonora Valley (the San José Site just north of Baviácora) covers over sixty acres, Pailes does not believe that it was a first-tier site. He suggests that the primary sites are situated under modern towns like Baviácora, Aconchí, and Arizpe. Like Reff, Pailes sees a basic collapse of the rich towns of the Sonora and other valleys in the decades between the Coronado and Ibarra entradas and the arrival of the Jesuits, a collapse due to epidemic disease.

The Duffen and Hartmann chapter on the 76 Ranch excavations represents a bit of archeological history. A large Salado town on this ranch, dating to the fourteenth and perhaps to the early fifteenth century, was believed by the archeologist Emil Haury and the historian Herbert E. Bolton to be the Chichilticalli of Coronado. The site is about ten miles southeast of Eagle Pass, which opens northward into the Gila Valley. One of the compounds that make up the large Salado Site on the 76

Ranch was partially excavated by William A. Duffen in 1936, the only scientific excavation on the site. Except for a small article by Duffen in 1937, nothing has been published previously on the 76 Ranch Site.

The authors include some of the original 1936 field notes on the site and discuss the incompletely known archeology. They then examine the various Coronado narratives for clues to Chichilticalli, including the occasional mentions of flora and fauna, and come to the reasonable conclusion that Chichilticalli could be identical with the 76 Ranch Site or with one of the other Salado towns in the general area. However, I rather doubt their statement that "being Nahuatl, even the name supports the idea that Chichilticale was on a significant trade route." As both Schroeder (1955–1956: 293–295) and I (Riley 1987: 126–127) have pointed out, the name Chichilticalli ("red house" in Nahuatl, the language of the Aztecs and Tlaxcalans) is a rather perplexing one. It is unlikely that the site *originally* had a Nahuatl name. However, given the numbers of Nahuatl-speaking Indians with Marcos and Coronado (and perhaps also with Díaz), a sixteenth-century Nahuatl renaming of the compounds with their red-plastered walls seems quite possible.

Part IV: The Coronado Expedition, Cíbola to the Rio del Cicúye

With Edmund J. Ladd we have a quite different perspective on the Coronado expedition. Ladd is an anthropologist who is also a member of the Zuni Tribe. Therefore, he looks at the Coronado *entrada* both from the viewpoint of a highly trained ethnologist and also that of a Pueblo Indian whose ancestors were involved in that invasion. Ladd gives us a scenario of probable events in the fateful years 1539 and 1540. In the spring of 1539 the black stranger, Esteban, arrived in Zuni. Ladd believes that the Zuni already had news of the Spaniards through traders. They were profoundly suspicious of these ruthless newcomers who were already spreading up the west coast of Mexico. Esteban was considered to be a spy for the approaching Spanish forces and, as a spy, he was set on and killed. Marcos, warned by fleeing members of Esteban's party of the latter man's death, made a hurried reconnaissance of one of the Zuni towns and returned to Mexico where, for reasons unclear, he exaggerated its size and wealth.

When Coronado arrived at Zuni in the summer of 1540, he interrupted the summer solstice cycle of ceremonies that must have been going on at just about that time (July 16 or 17 in the Gregorian calendar). The first skirmish with the Zuni came when Coronado's men interrupted a party of pilgrims moving toward or returning from the sacred lake Ko:thluwala:wa. The smokes observed by Coronado's party and considered to be signal fires were in reality part of a ceremony of the fire god. When Coronado arrived outside Hawikuh, Zuni priests put down a line of cornmeal across his path, indicating that the Spaniards should go no farther until the ceremonies were completed. The battle for Hawikuh was based on a series of misunderstandings, brought about by the Spanish ignorance of Pueblo customs and religion.

Ladd makes the interesting suggestion that the name "Cíbola" originated when Marcos met bearers of Zuni goods including bison hides. The Zuni word for bison is *si:wolo* and this was transformed into the name of the group. This is certainly a possibility, though we need to remember that the Zuni were well known in the Lower Pima and Ópata regions through trade contacts. To me it seems more likely that Cíbola is simply a Spanish attempt to pronounce *shiwana*, the Zuni name for their land. The term "Cíbola" was also picked up by Melchior Díaz in the winter of 1539, and Díaz (Hammond and Rey 1940: 157–158) specifically says that he got information from individuals (presumably traders) who had lived in the Zuni area "for fifteen to twenty years. I have learned this in many diverse ways, questioning some Indians together and others separately." Surely his informants knew the name of the region.

Aside from that minor objection, I consider Ladd's explanation of the activities of Esteban, Marcos, and Coronado to be extremely important. It allows us to make sense of events that are reported in a very distorted way in the Spanish chronicles.

The geographer Elinore Barrett turns her special expertise to examining the placement of various sixteenth-century pueblos in the middle Rio Grande Basin. She uses Spanish accounts, including Castañeda from the Coronado expedition, Gallegos from the Rodríguez/Chamuscado party, Luxán from the Espejo expedition, Castaño de Sosa's *Memorial*, and various of the Oñate documents. Barrett then matches information from those accounts with archeological information contained in the site files of the Laboratory of Anthropology, Museum of New Mexico.

Barrett believes that both the Tiguex and the Tutahaco towns, as listed by Castañeda from the Coronado expedition, were part of her Middle Rio Grande Subregion, extending from the lower Jemez River to the mouth of the Río Puerco. This conflicts with the idea of many scholars who consider Tutahaco to represent the Piro pueblos and thus extend well south of Socorro. I have recently suggested that not only is Tutahaco another name for Piro, but that the next entry on the Castañeda list, four pueblos "*por abajo del río*," were, perhaps, Manso towns (Riley 1995: 166). Although it seems to me that the balance of the evidence favors my position, that evidence is admittedly scanty and Barrett's placement of Tutahaco opens up a new way to look at Castañeda's account. It certainly must be taken seriously.

Barrett has worked out a series of intriguing relationships between the site names of late sixteenth-century Spanish explorers and actual ruins found by archeologists.

As base data, these will give us a clearer understanding, especially of Tiguex. She also makes the interesting suggestion that the Tiguex town of Puaray or Puala may have been moved a few miles to the north between 1583, when Espejo's men sacked and burned the settlement, and 1691, when Castaño de Sosa recorded it. Such a move, not too surprising considering Espejo's aggressive activities, would explain the discrepancy in distance reported by different Spanish parties.

In the late fall of 1540, the various divisions of the Coronado party moved into the Rio Grande Valley. The Spaniards took over a Tiguex village that they called Coofor, for which a number of locations have been posited, one of which is Santiago Pueblo (LA 326) on the west bank of the Rio Grande across from the south end of modern Bernalillo. Some years ago Bradley Vierra directed the partial excavation of site LA 54147 on the mesa a few hundred meters west of Santiago Pueblo. Here were found prepared floors of a campsite that clearly dates from the Spanish period because of the finds of bones of domesticated sheep. Excavation data suggest that the campsite was used during the fall and winter.

Vierra and Stanley Hordes, who did historical research on LA 54147, discuss the various expeditions (Coronado, Gaspar Castaño de Sosa, and Juan de Oñate) known to have brought domesticated animals into the Southwest during the sixteenth century. The evidence, including such items as crossbow boltheads, points strongly to the Coronado expedition. There were a number of metal objects, a broken obsidian blade from the Valley of Mexico, a projectile point of (probably) central Mexican origin, and what the excavators called "comales."

Vierra and Hordes suggest that Santiago Pueblo was either Coofor or the pueblo of Moho, destroyed by the Spaniards after a siege of some two months. If Coofor, it seems likely from Vierra's data that the campsite was used primarily (or totally) by Coronado's Mexican Indian allies. If Moho, this likely was part of the Spanish encampment surrounding the beleaguered town. My own educated guess (but I would not bet the farm on it) is that Santiago was Coofor and LA 54147 the campsite of some of Coronado's Indian auxiliaries (Riley 1995: 177–178). We badly need further excavation at the site to help resolve this problem.

Richard and Shirley Cushing Flint discuss their projected route for Coronado from the Indian town of Pecos in the Pecos Valley to the bridge built over the Pecos River. Although several previous analyses of the route have Coronado going down the Pecos River, the Flints point out that the Pecos Indians likely would have steered the expedition away from this route because of danger to native cornfields. In any case an easier route and one that would have avoided the apparently flooding river is over a natural ramp at Rowe, then down the gently sloping Rowe/Glorieta Mesa to the large Cañon Blanco. Water would have been available for humans and livestock on this route. In the spring, Rowe Mesa has numerous shallow ponds and the canyon itself is dotted with pools and, perhaps, even a small running stream. The bridge was built on the Pecos just downstream from the juncture with the Gallinas, the most important tributary on the upper Pecos River.

Part V: The Coronado Expedition, Río de Cicúye to Quivira

Donald Blakeslee's paper goes into the question of where Coronado might have ventured in the Caprock canyon country on the Texas Panhandle. In the spring of 1541 the Coronado party discovered two very large barrancas or canyons in the territory of Indians called Teyas. In the first of these, called "a large barranca like those of Colima," the Spaniards experienced a horrific hailstorm, one that destroyed much of their pottery. The second barranca, also called "large" (barranca grande) by Castañeda, extended two to three miles from bank to bank and here the army camped for a number of days. In the 1940s the historian Herbert E. Bolton identified the first barranca with Tule Canyon on the northeast edge of the Llano Estacado and the deep barranca with Palo Duro Canyon a few miles farther north and the northernmost major canyon of the Caprock group.

Blakeslee reevaluates these locations and also the Canadian River route of Albert H. Schroeder in terms of his reordering of the documentary sources, especially with a consideration of botanical distributions. He feels that both Bolton and (especially) Schroeder have the Coronado expedition going too far north. Blakeslee believes that possibly Blanco Canyon was the "large barranca" and that the main expedition returned to the Pecos by following Yellow House Canyon westward, crossing the almost flat region that divides the Yellow House from the Pecos drainage. Recent discoveries of copper crossbow boltheads and a chain mail gauntlet in upper Blanco Canyon suggest that this canyon was one of the areas visited by Coronado (see Chapter 23).

Part of my own chapter is, like that of Blakeslee, a survey of the route of Coronado. In the matter of routing, I substantially agree with Blakeslee. However, my primary task is to more clearly identify the Teya, that southern Plains group so important to Coronado. I make three major points about the Teya: that they are identical with the archeological Garza Culture; that they are the group called, from mid-century on, the Jumanos; and that they spoke a language similar to the Piro/Tompiro. Each of these three points has been suggested before, though I may be the first to weave all three into one fabric. I also argue for a route to Quivira that ran through the Wheeler Phase region of western Oklahoma, thus both avoiding the Querecho-controlled country farther west and utilizing the route between the Teya and their Wheeler Phase trading partners.

The chapter by David Snow approaches the Coronado problem from another angle, that of Pueblo trade wares in the southwestern Plains. In this wide-ranging critique, Snow perceptively points out the dangers of assuming a simplistic succession of glazewares in the Pueblo area. There seems to have been significant overlap of the various glaze types, an important factor for those using glazes as temporal markers on the southern Plains. Along these same lines, Snow doubts that site LA 54147 contained only Glaze E pottery (Vierra and Hordes, Chapter 16, concede this possibility). He also suggests that glazed pottery going into the Plains, whether by indigenous trade or brought by Coronado's expedition, must have served rather specialized purposes because of the awkwardness of transporting fragile pots.

W. Michael Mathes examines Castañeda's statement that the first barranca described by the Coronado party was "like those of Colima." Mathes points out that the principal route from the town of Colima to the crossroad Sayula region cuts through an area containing canyons that resemble Blanco Canyon in the Llano Estacado. He concludes that "there can be little doubt that Castañeda was describing Blanco Canyon."

As far as I know, no earlier writer has tried to match up Colima with Llano Estacado canyons. Mathes's chapter is an important bit of corroborative evidence for the scholars who believe Coronado's first canyon was Blanco. However, I must take issue with Mathes on his statement that there is "little doubt" in the matter. After all, Castañeda was writing twenty years after the expedition and his memory may have become muddled as to which canyon was which. Possibly, he saw other similarities that in his mind equated Colima with one of the northern canyons.

In the final chapter of this volume, Blakeslee, Flint, and Hughes discuss recent discoveries at Blanco Canyon on the eastern margin of the Llano Estacado, surely one or the other of the large canyons identified by Castañeda. Material found in the canyon includes both copper and iron crossbow boltheads, chain mail, horseshoes and nails, and Rio Grande glaze sherds, especially of Glaze E type. Other objects include a Mesoamerican-style blade and two sherds of unknown but possibly Mexican provenance. All of these objects can fit a 1541 date, and it does seem that Blanco Canyon was one of the areas in the Llano Estacado visited by Coronado. But was it the "*barranca grande como las de colima*" (the first barranca mentioned by the Spaniards) or was it the second "barranca grande"?

The evidence that Blanco Canyon was the first barranca has to do with marching time between the two barrancas. From the rather confused statement of Castañeda, it would seem that the Spaniards marched for several days. One logical routing, distance-wise, would take the expedition from Blanco Canyon along a well-known trail into the Palo Duro Canyon at the mouth of Cita Canyon. This is out of Teya (the archeological Garza) country and so would fit with Castañeda's statement that the army had reached beyond the last of the Teya rancherías (Hammond and Rey 1940: 239; see also Castañeda 1596: 83v), and his later comment (Hammond and

Rey 1940: 242) that, returning to the Rio Grande, the main party had to leave the barranca to get back into the Teya region.

I do have one problem with this routing. Even assuming that the second barranca lay beyond the cluster of Teya towns, it does seem to have been a location where the Teya felt comfortable. The Palo Duro area has settlements of the enemy Querecho (archeological Tierra Blanca) Indians, an unlikely place for the Teya to lead the Spaniards. Perhaps we should consider John Morris's (personal communication 1995; 1997: 100–101) suggestion that Coronado may have launched his Quivira expedition from farther down Blanco Canyon in modern Crosby County, Texas.

Clearly the Spanish expedition utilized Teya guides, and in fact Coronado, on his way to Quivira, sent back to the main expedition for a second set (Castañeda 1596: 86). If the trail led into Wheeler Phase country as I have argued (Riley 1991, 1995; Chapter 20), it probably would not have extended across an area settled by the Querecho, unless the Spaniards were mistaken about the enmity of the Teya and Querecho. From Teya country to the Wheeler Phase sites of western Oklahoma, a lower Blanco Canyon starting point might be logical, the route then skirting the Caprock canyons to the east.

The contention that Blanco Canyon was the second barranca relates to the distances marched by the expedition from the Rio Grande basin and the fact that the return route of the main unit would make the most sense if it were launched from Blanco Canyon. This is a cogent point. However, another argument involving Turk's intentions is less so. The authors suggest the possibility that Turk was in fact trying to lead the Spaniards to the relatively sophisticated Mississippian towns of the lower Mississippi River Valley. According to this line of reasoning, the "Pecos plot" never existed except in the imaginations of the Spaniards. Taking the Spaniards into the rich Llano Estacado would lead them into what—from Turk's point of view—was a food-rich area, so that he could hardly have been trying to "starve" them.[2]

This explanation does not convince me. The idea that Turk was tempting the Spaniards by a description of the rich Mississippian culture is hardly new; in fact, I pointed it out twenty-five years ago (Riley 1971: 304–306). It does not follow that there was no attempt to get rid of the Spaniards. Turk and his Pecos collaborators simply wanted to take the Spaniards somewhere distant from both the Pueblo and Pawnee lands. Given other considerations, such a route would necessarily be to the south or southeast. Failing that, the plan was to weaken the invaders, presumably by leading them off the rich Llano Estacado into the broken country to the south and east. Castañeda's account of this situation is quite matter-of-fact (Hammond and Rey 1940: 241–242). When challenged by the Spaniards about his "treachery,"

Turk told them that

> the people of Cicuye had asked him to take the Spaniards out there and lead them astray on the plains. Thus, through lack of provisions, their horses would die and they themselves would become so feeble that, upon their return, the people of Cicuye could kill them easily. . . . This, the Turk said, was the reason that he had misdirected them, believing that they would *not know how to hunt or survive without maize* [italics mine]. As to gold, he declared that he did not know where there was any.

Turk, according to Castañeda (ibid.) was speaking through the Teya guides, which suggests sign language, probably a communication system widespread in the south and central Plains. The Spaniards would by necessity have known this system after some months in contact with the Querecho and Teya, and it does provide for reasonably complex interchanges. Castañeda, incidentally, was not the only Spaniard to repeat the stories about Turk trying to lead the Spaniards to disaster. See also the account in the *Relación del Suceso* and the statement of Jaramillo in the Coronado period documents (Hammond and Rey 1940: 290–291, 301). During the mid-1540s investigation of Coronado's activities, several witnesses spoke of Turk's perfidious behavior. Juan de Zaldívar, for example, told how Turk followed instructions given him by the Pecos leaders to guide the Spaniards "where there wasn't any water or food so that they would all perish" (Walsh, 1993: 186–187). López de Cárdenas, in 1551 testimony, also describes Turk's leading the Spaniards astray in order that they "perish from hunger and thirst" (Hammond and Rey 1940: 363).

This book presents us with more questions than answers. In fact, the main value of the book is the framing and clarification of questions about early Spanish exploration in the Southwest. We need more documentary data, and especially more archeological work, directed at these queries. For example, we can now say something about the inventory of material objects carried by the Spaniards. Archeology on contact period sites should verify and clarify the kinds of objects listed, sometimes very vaguely, in the inventories. Such data should also allow us to increase our knowledge of the range of materials with Spanish parties in the Southwest.

Perhaps even more important is a consideration of the influences of central and west Mexican Indians in the Coronado and other early entradas into the Southwest. The Native American component of these parties was often very large, in the case of Coronado making up perhaps 80 percent of the total personnel. Many of the Indians with Coronado stayed in the Southwest and thus they continued to affect the native culture. We need archeological and documentary studies of the homelands of these visitors. With such knowledge we can begin to understand the range and depth of Mexican Indian contributions to Southwestern culture.

It may be that we will never completely delineate Coronado's trail, especially in Arizona and/or southwestern New Mexico and in the Plains. Even there, however, where the documentary evidence is so mixed and uncertain, further excavation may reveal important points of contact—note the recent dramatic finds of crossbow boltheads and other metal objects in the Blanco Canyon. And in the Rio Grande Valley, where the Spaniards spent much of their time between the late fall of 1540 and the spring of 1542, work like that of Vierra will slowly reveal the secrets of this earliest European history of the Greater Southwest and the first interaction between Spaniard and Native American in this great region.

Notes

1. All dates in this paper, unless otherwise noted, are Julian calendar.

2. The idea that Turk was heading for the Mississippi Valley is drawn from a perceptive paper by Mildred M. Wedel (1982), which uses my 1971 paper as a launching point. Wedel has a thoughtful alternative view of Indian-Spanish interaction in 1541. However, in my opinion the evidence really points in another direction.

PART I
Hypotheses and Evidence

CHAPTER 1

A Historiography of the Route of the Expedition of Francisco Vázquez de Coronado
General Comments

JOSEPH P. SÁNCHEZ

he route of the expedition of Francisco Vázquez de Coronado, 1540–1542, had for centuries intrigued colonial officials and explorers as it has perplexed modern-day historians and archeologists. Although historical documentary sources report extensively about the expedition, exact details of the route are few, vague, and sometimes contradictory. Archeological evidence is scant, for the expedition left few physical traces. Even when found, Spanish colonial artifacts can seldom be dated precisely and, given the intense Spanish activity throughout the Greater Southwest, especially between 1540 and 1680, they are extremely difficult to identify in relation to each of the expeditions of the period. Ethnohistoric evidence is likewise vague and confusing, for the sedentary and semi-sedentary Indian groups encountered by the Vázquez de Coronado expedition have experienced considerable movement since 1540. The tribes of the Great Plains, for example, abandoned sites in migrating from one locale to another or were driven out during the Indian Wars by the United States Army in the nineteenth century. Pueblos, on the other hand, were abandoned and new ones built or new pueblos emerged as a result of consolidation. To add to the obscurity of such places on our modern maps, their names changed or were forgotten. So too, in many instances, were Spanish tribal designations lost in time. Topography,

botany, ethnohistory, archeology, linguistics, and toponymy are some of the factors used by historians and archeologists to analyze the data related to the expedition's route. Still the route is elusive.

With few exceptions, however, theories about the route have been presented as fact by several researchers, but proof for hypothetical conclusions concerning the actual line of march by the expedition will never be satisfactorily attained. The purpose of this historiographical overview of the expedition of Francisco Vázquez de Coronado, 1540–1542, is to examine the data in the literature concerning the route, so that future researchers and interested readers may express their theories with the wisdom of those who came before them, and so that they may be able to provide a reasonable alternative to the route or even a corridor designating a line of march between certain known places visited by the expedition. The scholarship of the selected literature examined herein focuses on one specific problem: the tracing of the route of the expedition. It should be noted that the literature surrounding the expedition is massive. However, the selections contained in this study are representative of the issues that surround the location of the route.

The expedition of Francisco Vázquez de Coronado was the first major European exploration to penetrate the interior of the present United States. Exploring from Compostela on the west coast of Mexico, northward through Sonora, eastern Arizona, across central New Mexico to the Rio Grande, the expedition moved eastward across the Texas Panhandle, marched through Oklahoma, and reached the Great Bend of the Arkansas River in central Kansas.

Narrative accounts of the expedition describe its many encounters with the native inhabitants and contain a wealth of information about certain societies and their cultures while they were still in a pristine state of development. Likewise, descriptions of the flora and fauna and other natural resources were written by these explorers. They were the first Europeans to describe the Grand Canyon of Arizona, the large herds of buffalo on the Great Plains, the name we give today to the vast treeless plains that stretch from the Arctic coast to South Texas and from eastern New Mexico almost to the Mississippi River. The expedition members noted mountains, valleys, rivers, saltbeds, lakes, forests, and other topographical features including the Continental Divide, the watershed that separates rivers flowing toward the Pacific Ocean and the Gulf of Mexico or the Atlantic.

During the period 1539 to 1545, two other expeditions, one led by Hernando de Soto who explored from Florida to Texas, and the other commanded by Juan Rodríguez Cabrillo, who sailed up the California coast as far north as Cape Blanco in Oregon, aided Spanish officials in evaluating the widest geographic expanse of North America from coast to coast. Indeed, the Spaniards were the first Europeans to leave a written record of their deeds in North America, thus beginning a literary heritage about a large geographic area from California to Florida.

The traditional consensus regarding the route, however, is that it lies close to that proposed by A. Grove Day and Herbert Eugene Bolton. Both men popularized portions of the route through western Mexico, Arizona, New Mexico, Texas, Oklahoma, and central Kansas. Although the route they proposed is not the object of this analysis, it plays an important role in the historiography of the expedition led by Francisco Vázquez de Coronado. The Bolton-Day route is presented herein with other issues related to the expedition's route through a large portion of North America.

In recent years, nonetheless, researchers have debated portions of the route proposed by Day and Bolton and some have even gone as far as to propose new ones. There are reasons for the disparities between some of the hypotheses. Day and Bolton dealt with the larger picture of the route. They were able to connect known places visited by the expedition with theories explaining how it reached them. Later researchers, concerned only with portions of the route, began to discover other hypothetical alternatives by concentrating on specific topographical and cultural features in certain areas believed crossed by the expedition. It should be noted that Day and Bolton actually tested their hypothetical routes on the ground, as have other researchers. Unlike Day and Bolton who visited the Spanish colonial archives in Spain and Mexico, plying their skills in reading the original manuscripts of the expedition, some of the early writers on the route lacked access to the documentation and used translations that precluded certain perspectives about what the expedition had seen. Other writers, it is apparent, lacked geographical knowledge about the areas traveled by the expedition or did not read carefully the sources available to them.

A. Grove Day (1940: 227) might just as well have written about the entire route when he penned his thoughts about the expedition's effort on the Great Plains:

> It is impossible to locate with precision, four centuries later, the trail of Coronado's army from the Rio de Cicuye to the province of Quivira. Landmarks on the vast Staked Plains that they traversed are few; in fact the general was not far wrong when he wrote to his king afterward that there was "not a stone, not a bit of rising ground, not a tree, not a shrub, nor anything to go by." Furthermore, the reckonings of direction in those days were clumsy. Consequently the wake of the army in 1541 on the ocean of prairie has forever vanished, even though its point of departure and ultimate landfall are known with some degree of certainty.

There are known references to the route. Among them are obvious points on a given map: Mexico City; Compostela; Culiacán; Zuni Pueblo; the El Morro–Malpais area; Acoma; the Tiguex-Albuquerque-Bernalillo area; the Rio Grande Pueblos from Isleta to Taos; the Pueblos outside the Rio Grande Valley, Zia to the west, Galisteo to the east, and Pecos Pueblo; as well as the location of some pertinent Quiviran sites in central Kansas. There are known topographic elements to the route whose specific points of reference are vague, such as the Fuerte, Mayo, and Sonora River Valleys, the Pecos River, the caprock of the Llano Estacado, the Canadian and Arkansas Rivers, the Palo Duro and Tule Canyons of the Llano Estacado, and the area of the Buffalo Plains reached by the expedition. There are places such as Chichilticale, Cona, and Tabas that may never be known. There are vast areas where the expedition's route is still to be determined with precision, such as northern Sonora, the *despoblado* of southern and eastern Arizona, and the Oklahoma Panhandle. Ethnographic data may also be derived from the documentary sources, but anthropological and archeological interpretive data and skills are required to arrive at conclusions, which in some instances are at best debatable.

That there are no final answers to the precise location of the route is not a pessimistic conclusion, but an optimistic observation based on the historiographical hope that more data must be gathered and analyzed before a comprehensive hypothesis regarding the route can be formed and tested. Historians have offered their best efforts to date by locating pertinent documents, weaving narratives and analyses, proposing hypotheses, and popularizing the expedition's endeavors four centuries after the event. There are, however, documents and maps related to the expedition that are yet to be found. Indeed, since Bolton published his "definitive" history of the expedition in 1949, historians have made few research efforts for new documentary sources. The colonial archives of Spain, Mexico, and Peru may one day yield such secrets. Archeology may hold the key to unlocking the secrets the earth holds regarding the route. Because of possible archeological discoveries related to the expedition, archeologists offer the best hope for future studies. The recent discovery of a sixteenth-century Spanish campsite near Bernalillo, New Mexico (Chapter 16), and another possible campsite in Floyd County, Texas (Chapter 23), are indicative of such possibilities.

Given the advancing technology of the Space Age, it is likely that, futuristically, an interdisciplinary effort between humanists and scientists may one day result in identifying more sites related to the expedition, thereby contributing precise locations of segments of the route until an acceptable line of march is brought to light. Even if an exact route that can be considered a "trail" cannot ever be established, a corridor along the line of march is the probable product of future research. It would seem that in the best of all cases, the corridor would include precise locations along certain segments; in other cases, the corridor would include a ten to fifty-mile-wide swath in which the route would be included. In any case, those who have spent their careers analyzing the available documentation and archeological evidence have contributed much to our understanding of the expedition and its observations of the interior of North America. They have given us much to consider in the future discoveries yet to be made. For now, we should be grateful for what we have and what we know about the route.

CHAPTER 2

The Coronado Documents
Their Limitations

CHARLES W. POLZER, S.J.

y comments here are an attempt to refocus our current approach in solving the Coronado expedition problem. It is dysfunctional to speak of the Coronado trail any longer; I would rather speak of the Coronado expedition, which is a much more meaningful concept.

I delight in the historiographical overview that Dr. Sánchez provides here and the comprehensiveness of his historiography. I suspect that his bibliography includes all the articles written about Coronado since Herbert Bolton's book, which would be a useful thing to see in print. It is worthwhile to realize the tremendous number of people who have discussed the Coronado expedition and have theorized about its route and perhaps some of the more specific places it passed through. But no matter who has speculated about what, it all comes down to which few documents we actually have, and they are not much. What Dr. Sánchez presents throughout this volume makes it plain that there is not only a lack of unity in what the experts and the documentary historians have done, but nearly a cacophony of interpretation.

Often when I talk about Coronado's route it becomes apparent all over again how confusing are the dates and places, and east and west, and north by needles and south of canyons, and who knows what else. Consequently, I have come to the strong conclusion that the most important way to handle the Coronado expedition problem is to do it on the ground. I don't think that you do it at the desk. I insist that archeology is not done by reading reports on ceramics. It is done on the ground. When we look at ambiguous archeological reports (frequently developed with no relevant focus) in order to psyche out the number of sites of Indian pueblos or of types of villages or their distributions, it is clear that new archeological reconnaissance is the only way we have to work out the archeological and documentary discrepancies. And the only way to do that is to start in the south and work north. It is a terrible disservice to begin in the north and go south. That was Bolton's problem: he came from the north always asking where Coronado had come from to the south. He should have started in Compostela. He would have changed his ideas rather dramatically.

Reconnaissance, though, must be guided by the sixteenth-century documents, which brings me to my subject: the limitations of those documents. In the first instance, all of the documents, or nearly all of the documents, that we deal with in the Coronado expedition (with the exception of a couple of letters) are summaries written significantly after the expedition took place or, better said, after the expedition failed. "Failed" because they did not find the gold, or the cities, or the vast numbers of sophisticated Indians that they could enslave, or other ready-to-hand resources. As a result, the accounts depend on distant memory. We don't have diaries. We don't have any *day-to-day* account of where the expedition went or what it did. We have only summary reminiscences, records such as "We spent two days going there and we stayed at this one place."

There is, in addition, the terrible trouble of place names. One of the major things that the historian or anyone using the documents has to confront in guiding oneself archeologically is that the place names are not always site specific. For example, you might think that the expedition was certainly *in* the village of Yaquimi (Hammond and Rey 1940: 250) or Lachimi (Hammond and Rey 1940: 164) and then you realize that Pedro de Castañeda and Coronado were not always talking about a village. They were often talking about complexes of villages. They were sometimes talking about the pattern in which these people lived.

All of us who have worked in the Southwest for many years know that there was not a great capital city. We may be able to point to Casas Grandes as a trading hub, but by and large the cities or, I should say, settlements that we know about were almost, but not quite, ephemeral. They shifted; they changed; they migrated. And obviously they never lasted very long because today we often cannot find even the traces of these places archeologically. What I'm suggesting is that the naming of places is an extremely difficult problem. Sánchez discusses later the valley of Señora or Sonora. Most people make that equivalence. But when the sixteenth-century chroniclers speak of Señora they always have the expedition leave the valley of Señora and go over to another valley, a day and a half away. It is always a different place. That means that they were now in a different place, a different drainage system. Which one were they in at any given time? I don't know, and I can't tell from the written word; it has to be worked out on the ground—going north!

Likewise, consider the problem of Corazones. What does the name signify? It is the name of a village, a complex of villages, and a whole province. The expedition could have been all over the map and still have been in Corazones. What term was in actual use in the minds of the persons writing down their reminiscences? A terribly difficult problem. Charles Di Peso tried to answer that question. He tried to line out who used what name about which place. And it is pretty hairy once the expedition gets north of Culiacán. It is extremely difficult. We see in the documents themselves this critical problem of what the names could actually mean and what they might actually refer to.

The next problem is that all through the documents the authors are constantly changing their focus. What do I mean by that? I mean that in one sentence they may use a narrow focus by minutely describing a village to which they came, the food they ate, the houses they saw, and how many days they had traveled. And in the next sentence you find them using an enormously wide-focus statement, saying that this place is where the coast turns west, although they were a long way from the coast when they were in this village. So, what was going on in the mind of the writer? We have to devise a new mind-set to really understand what these men were saying.

Castañeda's narrative tells us that Chichilticale is located essentially where the coast turns west (Hammond and Rey 1940: 251). Now Chichilticale was inland at least ten days' travel, according to Coronado's letter to Viceroy Mendoza (Hammond and Rey 1940: 165). Taken together, what could these statements have possibly meant? When you stand back and remember cumulatively what Castañeda or Coronado may have been saying in their writing, you can see that there was a distinct macrofocus at work. They zoomed their mental lens back and forth, zeroing in on detail and pulling back to describe vast regions.

One of the things that seems evident but nobody talks about is navigational devices. Nobody talks about latitude. The men of the Coronado expedition were obviously measuring latitude because they knew exactly how far north Hernando de Alarcón sailed and they knew where they were in relation to that latitude. So they knew that if they followed along this line of latitude they would link up with the head of the Gulf of California, as we call it today. They were obviously measuring latitude; they were making maps based largely on latitude. And then they combined ideas of how far north they were or wanted to be with east and west variations. So,

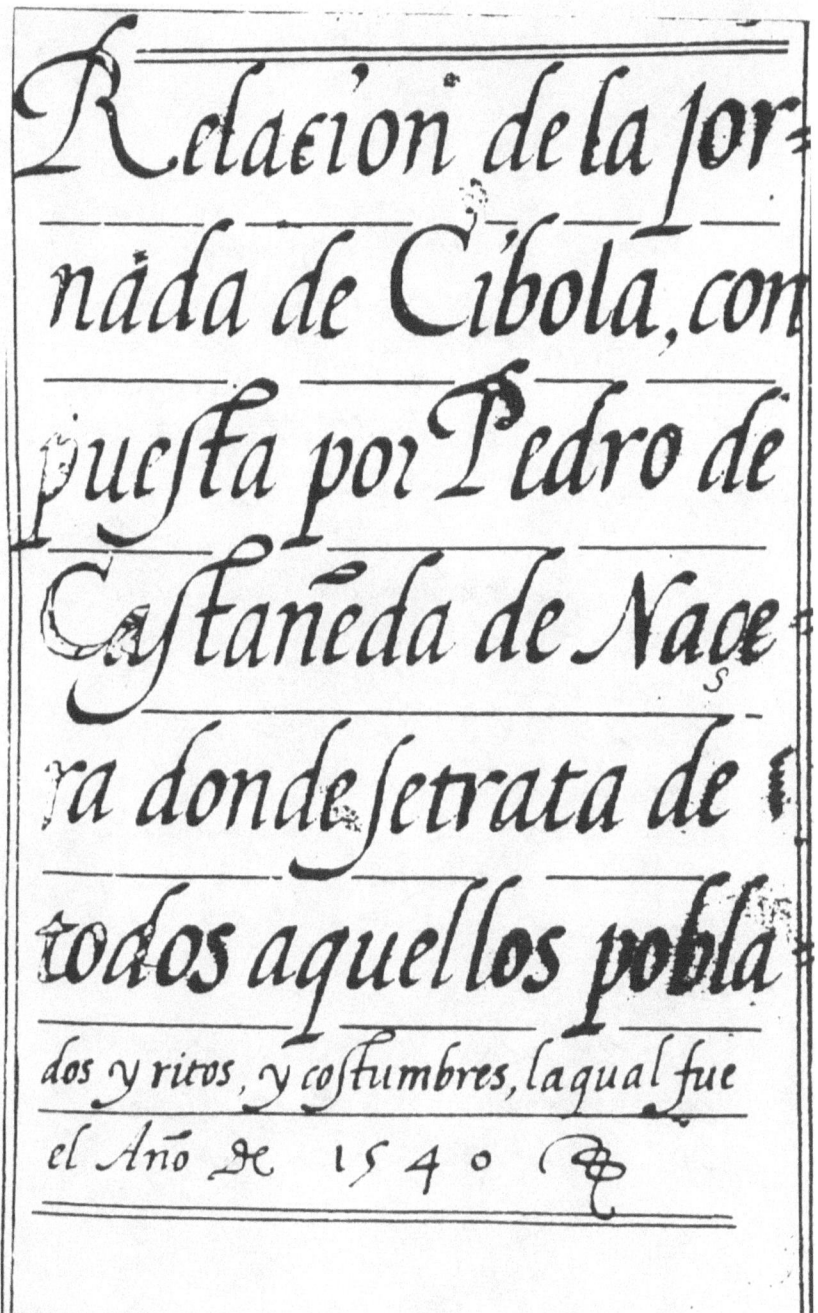

Figure 2.1. Title page, Castañeda's Relación. Rich Collection (no. 63) Rare Books and Manuscripts Division, The New York Public Library, Astor, Lenox and Tilden Foundations.

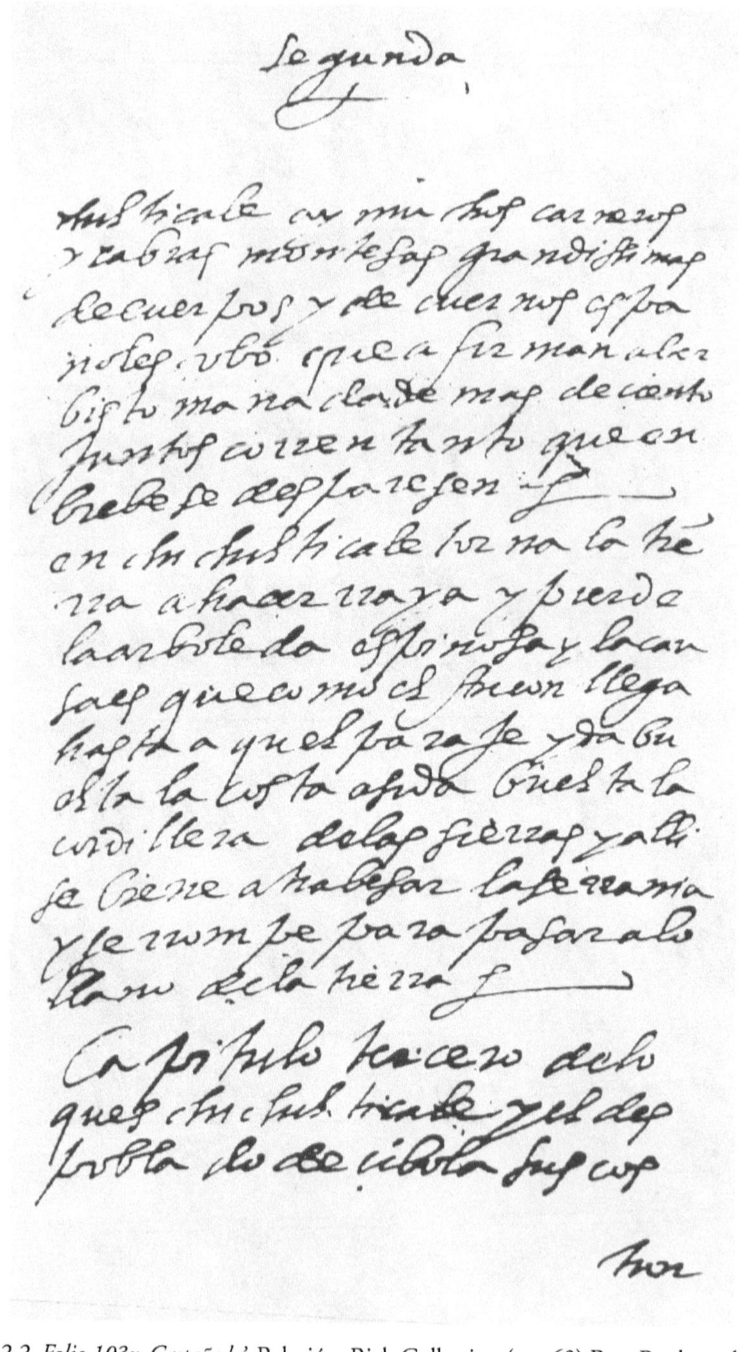

segunda

Ausi tiene en mis boscarneros y cabras montesas grandissimas de cuerpos y de cuernos españoles. ubo que afirman aber bisto manada de mas de ciento Juntos corren tanto que en breue se desparesen §

en sin chus ticable bz na la tie rra a hacer uaya y pierde la arboleda espinosa y locan saes que como el Inuern llega hasta aquel paraje y da bu elta la bosta apida Pues ta la cordillera de las sierras y alli se biene a trabesar la sierra nia y se rompe para pasar alo llano de la tierra §

Capitulo tercero delo ques sin chustiable y el des pobla do de cibola sus cos

tum

Figure 2.2. Folio 103v, Castañeda's Relación. Rich Collection (no. 63) Rare Books and Manuscripts Division, The New York Public Library, Astor, Lenox and Tilden Foundations.

Castañeda's and Coronado's comments become quite meaningful. They aren't just saying Chichilticale is "kind of up here." No, it is precisely at this latitude where the coast turns west in the Gulf of California. Now, if that is the case, where does Chichilticale wind up? Very close to the current international border between Arizona/New Mexico and Sonora/Chihuahua. It would not be on the Gila River, which is the most commonly posited place for Chichilticale, the beginning of the despoblado, for most historians. If Chichilticale is on the Gila, the latitude measurement becomes really skewed when compared to the western turn of the Gulf coast.

The macrolanguage that the chroniclers used when they were talking about the rivers raises another problem. Castañeda counted five rivers, following the expedition up the Gulf of California coast (Hammond and Rey 1940: 249–250). That works until you get to the Yaqui River. All the rivers came out of the mountains and flowed out toward the west. So, going north, the expedition crossed a series of rivers. But depending on how far east or west it was when the expedition came to the Yaqui River, it could have crossed the river or gone up it. And that's the one river that really does flow north, then south, then west. Did they go "up" the Yaqui? Or "down" it? Who knows? Di Peso liked to think that the expedition shifted into the mountains. He may be right because there are routes that do that.

My point is that we haven't trained ourselves to be in tempo with this modulation between macrolanguage and microdescription. And I suggest that the only way we can interpret what is being said in these documents is to test it out on the ground. You will find out that a certain reconstruction doesn't make sense when you are in a particular topographical region or sector. And so we have to go through a whole new rethink for the Coronado expedition. I think it would be good for all of us, with all due apology to Dr. Sánchez, to take his and everyone's bibliography and burn them. Because if you follow all that stuff, you are bound to get confused. Albert Schroeder was a great person and had some great ideas, but I think that we have to stop paying attention to him and his zeroing in; we have to back off and do the job all over again. Not because he is wrong, but because we don't know who is right. The limitations of the documents are such that they leave so much open to interpretation that you and I are bound to become very confused when we try to put it all together. If we insist in our own work on the primacy of archeological reconnaissance, we are doing the best job we can with respect to the Coronado expedition problem.

One fellow who gets lost in the Coronado expedition story is Melchor Díaz. He was all the way to Chichilticale long before Coronado. As you remember, Coronado sent Díaz up there to scout the whole situation out. So there he sat at Chichilticale, waiting for Coronado. We never talk about that. He was obviously already in the present U.S. If Melchor Díaz could have gotten to Chichilticale as he did, he had to have known the territory pretty well. He had, after all, been working out of Culiacán for some time. It was Melchor Díaz who came back from Chichilticale to the forces just outside Culiacán and then in a few days was sent off to the head of the Gulf of California to meet Alarcón, which he was very late in doing. He had to know that route as well. He had to know how far east and west he was, and he had to know the latitudes where he was. We haven't talked much about this. I'm not saying that we have any solutions. I am saying that if you pay critical attention to the documents there are a lot of details that are there that are not microdetails; they are macrodetails. And they begin to point to different ways of interpreting and different ways of evaluating what we see in the documents.

I was in the New York Public Library not so awfully long ago and ordered a microfilm copy of the Castañeda narrative and the *Relación del Suceso* from the Rich Collection. Those are the ones reputedly used by George Winship in his 1896 transcriptions. I realized that we don't have available to us, except for Hammond and Rey's work (1940), a really thoroughgoing critical edition of the original Spanish documentation of the Coronado expedition. We don't have it readily at our fingertips. We need, I think, a lot more work in the area of critical editions of primary documents of exploration. It is the only way to find how to use the documents that are there. I'm just appalled when I look at the secondary literature. We don't have any solid anthropological annotation of Castañeda or anybody else. Everything goes back to what knowledge derives from Adolph Bandelier or Frederick Hodge. It isn't that Bandelier and Hodge were wrong; I just think that the field of anthropology, and the field of ethnology in particular, has advanced very far beyond the studies of these early giants. An up-to-date annotation of the currently known Coronado documents would be a tremendous contribution, which in turn would help out archeological field reconnaissance. We need a much more richly annotated set of original documents. I continue to insist on the critical importance that these documents have and the tedious work that it is to drag information out of them. Meanwhile, we must remember that the documents, by themselves, do not and cannot tell us all we want to know about the Coronado expedition.

CHAPTER 3

Coronado Fought Here
Crossbow Boltheads as Possible Indicators of the 1540–1542 Expedition

DIANE LEE RHODES

Introduction

lthough historic records document the 1540–1542 Coronado expedition across the Southwest and the Great Plains, the search for tangible archeological evidence of the entrada has been frustrating and often fraught with controversy. A number of factors contribute to the tenuous nature of the archeological resources. The expedition was a onetime event whose short-term camps left few permanent traces upon the landscape. The passage of four and a half centuries and subsequent settlement and development have obliterated all but the most durable or most isolated artifacts and features related to the entrada. Later Spanish exploration and colonization brought similar cultural materials into the New World, confusing the search for artifacts directly associated with Coronado. Dating methodologies traditionally used for archeological resources are often inadequate when applied to metals and, in the past, there was a strong tendency for researchers to disregard "intrusive" metal or bone in what were assumed to be prehistoric sites. Trading and seasonal movements of American Indian groups redistributed artifacts, and possible ethnographic evidence relating to the entrada has been poorly researched. Researchers are left with a few known sites such as Hawikuh and Pecos and with a limited repertoire of possible diagnostic artifacts

such as glass beads and metal pieces to help identify the expedition's route and activities.

Coronado's presence at Hawikuh (Zuni), Pecos, and pueblos along the Rio Grande is documented in the expedition narratives. Because archeologists have found crossbow boltheads (dart points) in association with contact-period Indian artifacts at several of these New Mexico sites, it has been suggested that the boltheads may be diagnostic of the Coronado expedition (Vierra 1989: 218, 227). The following discussion examines this possibility.

Historic Use of the Crossbow

By the 1500s, the crossbow had been in use for several centuries and was a favored weapon of the early Spanish explorers of the New World. A strong military crossbow with a steel bow was able, at fair range, to penetrate with a sharp-headed bolt armor that was in use at the time. The point-blank firing range was sixty to seventy yards (Byron Johnson, personal communication 1992).

There are dozens of references to the use of the crossbow by Hernán Cortés in his conquest of Mexico two decades before Coronado. Cortés's army is known to have been supplied with "a large quantity of balls and arrows" from Spain and the Antilles (Clavigero 1807: 159). Using guns and crossbows, the Spaniards "cleared the terraces" of the Indian villages as they swept through Mexico (Clavigero 1807: 103). Francisco Pizarro sailed from Panama in 1524 with a small band of men described as crossbowmen. Records note that bowmen were included in the muster lists of both Juan Rodríguez Cabrillo and Coronado, and are known to have accompanied the expedition led by Hernando de Soto.

There are other references to use of the crossbow in early journals. Distances were often expressed in terms of the length of crossbow shots (Peterson 1956: 7). During Pánfilo de Narváez's expedition, pieces of metal from the crossbows were used to manufacture nails to construct boats.

Spanish narratives document the presence of the *ballestas* and *ballesteros* (crossbows and crossbowmen) on the Coronado expedition, and mention use of crossbows at the Zuni towns, along the Rio Grande during the long cruel winter of 1540–1541, and at the stalwart pueblo of Pecos. The narratives also document the use of crossbows on Coronado's journey across the buffalo plains. Here the

> Spaniards discovered a collection of animal bones as wide as the distance a crossbow could shoot, a *tiro de ballesta*. The plains were so flat that wherever a man placed himself, he could see the sky around himself for the distance a crossbow could shoot. And in one time of siege, the Spaniards captured the roofs of some houses . . . getting off good shots with crossbows . . . (Strout 1958: 793).

History also documents the decline in crossbow use as Europe's Middle Ages ended and, by Coronado's time, the crossbow was rapidly being superseded as a military weapon by the arquebus and other firearms. As De Soto and others were to learn, the power of the crossbow could not compensate for its lack of speed. An Indian could shoot off three or four arrows in the time that a bowman could load and fire once. By the early 1530s, during the capture of Cuzco, Francisco Pizarro had only about a dozen crossbowmen among his followers.

Crossbows are not mentioned in the documents of any expeditions to New Mexico after Coronado's: those of Francisco Sánchez Chamuscado (1581), Antonio de Espejo (1582), Gaspar Castaño de Sosa (1590), and Juan de Oñate (1598) (Flint 1992: 126–138). And, as Richard Flint has noted, "The imminent obsolescence of the crossbow may be indicated by the fact that during the 1540 muster of the Coronado expedition *arquebuces* outnumbered ballestas by twenty-five to twenty" (Flint 1992: 137–138).

The situation seems to have been similar elsewhere in Latin America. For instance, "crossbows are known to have been among the principal weapons of the De Soto expedition, but they were not in general use when the Spanish returned to the Florida panhandle in the seventeenth century" (Ewen 1989a: 116).[1]

Thus it has been suggested that Coronado was the last of the Spanish explorers to bring crossbows into New Mexico. Inclusion of twenty crossbows in Coronado's muster when they were rapidly declining in use elsewhere probably reflected the eclectic nature of this privately financed and outfitted expedition.

Technology of the Crossbow

The Spanish used three types of crossbows—the *ballesta de gafa*, the *ballesta de armatoste*, and the *ballesta de cranequin* (Johnson 1988: 9). These types were differentiated by the way the bow was armed, the first being cocked with a lever, the second a windlass, and the third a rack and pinion device.

The bow itself was usually of steel or horn with a string of hemp or flax fixed to a stock of straight-grained wood. The strength of the bow was enough to require leverage, provided in the case of the common military crossbow by a detachable goat's foot lever, so called because of its shape. The lever worked by hooking its claws over the center of the bowstring. The prongs were then placed over the top of the stock with the ends resting upon a transverse iron pin. Holding the crossbow in a level position with the left hand, the lever could be pulled towards the bowman with the right hand.[2] After the bowstring was stretched taut by use of the lever and hooked over the nut, the projectile—the crossbow bolt—was placed in the groove. Pressure on the trigger released the nut which revolved and in turn released the bowstring and the arrow.

In Europe, crossbow boltheads or points varied in design and size depending upon their specific function and place of manufacture.[3] However, because the recovery of spent military bolts and arrows could never be counted on and immense numbers were needed, bolts used in warfare were generally of a simple design.

Most commonly used military crossbow boltheads of European manufacture were of ferrous metal capable of piercing armor. For example, a ferrous specimen owned by the Albuquerque Museum was made with a diamond-shaped head (and a ferule joint that exhibits the overlapping so common in early hand-forging techniques). The stocky cylindrical shaft measures roughly 31 cm in length, and tapers toward the butt, terminating in a flattened end. It has two flights or rounded wood feathers. Together the wooden arrow and ferrous point measure 39 cm long (Figure 3.1).

These bolts and shafts were shorter and heavier than arrows for longbows. The wooden shafts were fairly uniform and were usually tapered forward. "The gradual preponderance of weight towards its point was necessary . . . in order to give the proper balance" (Payne-Gallwey 1903: 17). The bolts used for military service were often winged with thin strips of wood, leather, skin, or horn.

The Crossbow and the Coronado Expedition

Based on the factors discussed above, it is suggested that Coronado's entrada was probably the only major Spanish expedition into what is now New Mexico and Texas to utilize the crossbow in significant numbers. As previously mentioned, quarrels have been found in archeological deposits of this time period in several pueblos in New Mexico. Recently, investigations in the Blanco Canyon region of Texas have unearthed a number of quarrels associated with glazed ceramics and other indicators of Euroamerican and Native American contact.[4] All of the boltheads recovered in the Southwest are of similar design.

Crossbow boltheads have been found at a number of sites in North America thought to date to the mid-1500s: at Hawikuh, at several pueblo sites along the Rio Grande, at Pecos in New Mexico, and in the southeastern United States at San Felipe, at the Martin Site in Tallahassee,[5] and at the colonial capital of La Florida, Santa Elena. The New Mexico specimens resemble old-fashioned metal pen nibs (a hollow cylinder with one pointed end) measuring between 3.5 and 5.0 cm in length (Ellis 1957: 209; Vierra 1989: 145; and South et al. 1988: 103–108). These artifacts are similar in form to those found in the southeastern United States but the manufacturing methods of both differ from European military weaponry of the time.

There are differences in materials as well. The boltheads found in the Southeast are of ferrous metal; the ones from the Southwest are copper.[6] It appears that

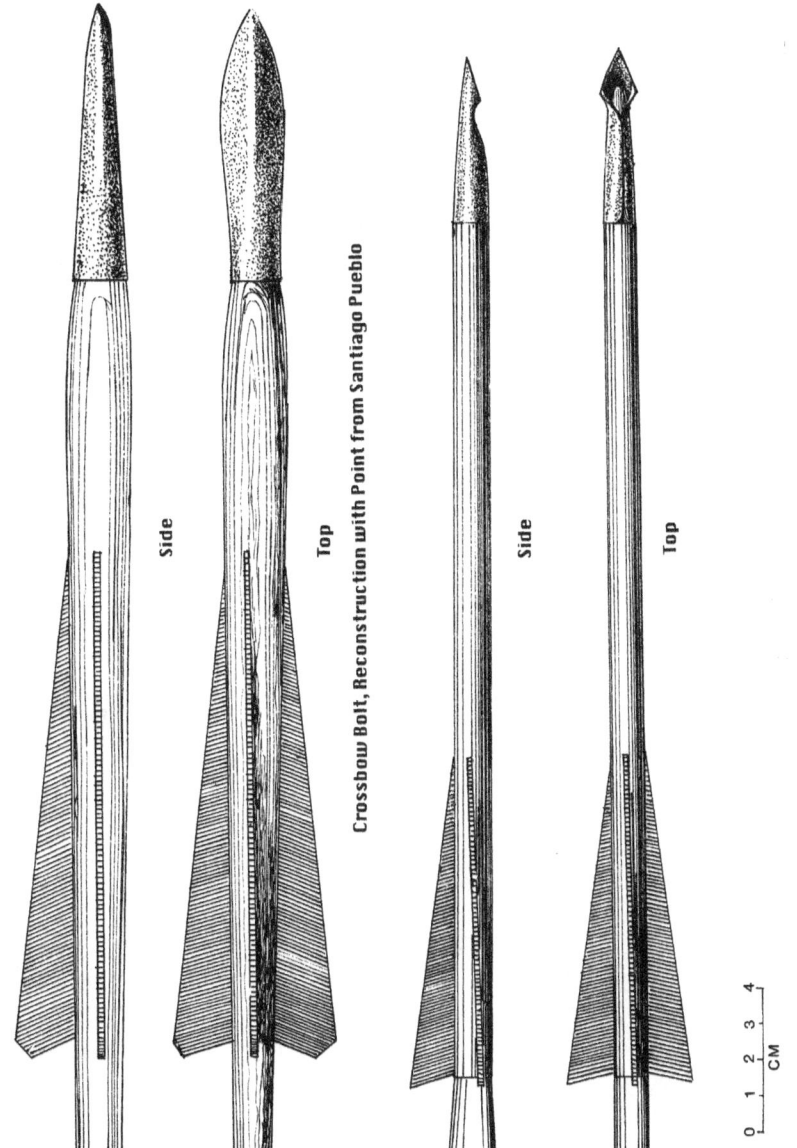

Figure 3.1. Crossbow bolts. Drawing by Don Carlisle.

these differences may be a result of manufacture in New Spain or with materials and technologies from New Spain. Just twenty years prior to the Coronado expediton, Cortés took advantage of local indigenous copper craftsmen to produce quarrels during the siege of Mexico. He issued a circular order to the various Texcoco districts in the basin of Mexico

> to send him each within the space of the next eight days, eight thousand arrow heads made of copper; also an equal number of shafts, of a particular wood. By the expiration of the given time the whole number was brought, executed to a degree of perfection which exceeded the pattern. Captain P. Barba who commanded the crossbowmen ordered each of his soldiers to provide themselves with two cords and nuts, and to prove the range of their bows . . . (Díaz del Castillo 1927: 320–321).

The speed with which these bolts were produced was remarkable and it is also noteworthy that the "degree of perfection . . . exceeded the pattern." Some Spaniards asserted that the Native American coppersmiths had discovered the secret "of giving copper a temper equal to that of steel . . . and that the copper equalled the ancient arms [of Greeks and Romans] . . . in hardness" (Clavigero 1807: 368).

In producing the quarrels for Cortés, the Mexican Indians were working with familiar metals and techniques, but with patterns introduced by the Spanish. The skill of the native smiths and the quality of their products are further illustrated by Bernal Díaz del Castillo who wrote:

> the Indians . . . brought with them highly polished copper axes with painted wooden handles . . . and we thought that they were made of inferior gold, and began to barter for them, and in three days we had obtained more than six hundred, and we were very well contented thinking that they were made of debased gold . . . but it was no good . . . for the axes were made of copper . . . and there was a good laugh at us, and they [the Indians] made great fun of our trading (Díaz del Castillo 1956: 28).

Arthur Woodward cites Díaz del Castillo and notes that "it stands to reason that others [copper crossbow bolts] could have been made by the same craftsmen for the Coronado expedition eighteen years later. After all, steel was not needed to penetrate unarmored Indian bodies" (Ellis 1957: 211). Woodward also describes the armor-piercing iron quarrels and suggests that "the same form would be followed when made in copper" (Ellis 1957: 212).

While many of the quarrels were undoubtedly made in what is now Mexico and carried northward by Coronado's expedition into New Mexico, additional raw materials may have been brought along to manufacture boltheads as needed. Díaz del Castillo noted that "Cortés ordered the crossbowmen to get ready all the arrows they possessed and to feather them and fix on the arrow heads, for on these expeditions we always carried many loads of materials for arrows and over five loads of arrow heads made of copper, so that we could always make arrows when they were needed" (Díaz del Castillo 1927: 505).

In Alfred Kidder's classic *Artifacts of Pecos* (1932), he describes the metal artifacts found in the 1915–1925 excavations. Two hundred twenty-nine artifacts were of copper or bronze and, of these, 132 were sheet scraps and fifteen rolls of sheet metal. According to Kidder: "More than half of the collection consists of small, irregularly shaped scraps of *thin sheet metal*, varying from the size of a fingernail to that of the palm of one's hand. Their edges are sometimes cut as with a sharp instrument, . . . sometimes roughly torn. They are apparently wastage produced when wornout copper or brass kettles . . . were cut up for the manufacture of ornaments or implements" (1932: 308).

Although unlikely, it is conceivable that some of these copper scraps at Pecos came from the production of crossbow quarrels.

Of the two copper quarrels found in the Pecos excavations, Kidder described one as a projectile point (arrow point) of sheet copper whose base was bent to enclose the shaft (Kidder 1932: 306–308; Figure 3.2g). The copper appears to have been cut in triangular form before shaping (Ellis 1957: 210).[7]

Later excavations at the East Mound, Room 1, at Pecos uncovered a small flat piece of copper described as an attempt at making an arrowpoint measuring 2.5 cm by 3.3 cm in size.[8] Rooms 64 and 69 also yielded copper artifacts, one defined as a scraper, the other as shaped like an arrow.[9] These roughly triangular pieces of thin sheet metal are similar to the basic form of a crossbow bolt before the socket is completed.

Several copper crossbow boltheads were found by Frederick Hodge during his excavation of Hawikuh Pueblo (Hodge 1918). However, his site report fails to mention these items. According to Eulalie Bonar, assistant curator at the National Museum of the American Indian, the Hawikuh collection includes five boltheads.[10] It is only recently that these have been identified as boltheads (see Figure 23.3).

Other cupreous quarrels were found in the archeological site known as "Bandelier's Puaray" or Santiago Pueblo (LA326) when these pueblo ruins near Bernalillo were excavated jointly by the University of New Mexico and the School of American Research in 1934 (Ellis 1957: 209).[11] This pueblo may have been Coronado's winter camp, known as Alcanfor/Coofor (Vierra 1989: 3). According to Vierra (1989: 12) one of the boltheads "was located in the chest of a skeleton found lying on the floor of a room in the south wing of . . . [Santiago] pueblo. The individual presumably died from the wound. . . . A second bolthead was recovered from an adjacent room."

The Santiago specimens, most of which are currently held by the Museum of New Mexico in Santa Fe, were described by Bruce T. Ellis in 1957. Another quarrel described by Ellis is presumed to have come from either "Puaray" or from the nearby pueblo of Kuaua during the 1934 joint excavations (Ellis 1957: 209–210). Its present whereabouts is unknown.

Possible crossbow boltheads were also found at Comanche Springs (Vierra 1989: 137). Diligent search at the University of New Mexico's Maxwell Museum has failed to locate them. Unverified reports suggest that quarrels were also found at Piedras Marcadas, a large pueblo located on the west edge of present-day Albuquerque.

Description of Boltheads and Evidence of Production Methods

Examination of five crossbow boltheads from the New Mexico pueblos and interviews with metalsmith Brian Anderson from Taos, New Mexico, have revealed differences and similarities among the artifacts as well as the manufacturing techniques used. The technology used to produce the copper boltheads was relatively simple. The mined ore was refined, probably using a wood charcoal fire. The liquid metal was run into ingots or blocks, perhaps weighing from two to five pounds, that could be handled easily by the craftsmen. Working with readily available tools such as a metal hammer, anvil, and tongs, the ingot was hammered into a bar or into thin flat sheets. The temperature of the hot copper had to be just right or it would behave like wet clay; however, the copper can also be worked cold. Once the ingot was reduced to a workable size, the crossbow boltheads could be produced.

The boltheads found at Santiago exhibit two different manufacturing techniques. Artifacts a and e (Figure 3.2) were of copper bar stock that may have begun as a cube measuring about a centimeter square. The bar was repeatedly hammered and annealed to produce quadrilateral tips on the point end while the bases were hammered flat and thin to create a fan-shaped section that could be cut and rolled to form the socket or ferule, by which the head would later be attached to the shaft of the dart (Brian Anderson, personal communication 1992; Ellis 1957: 210). In other words, the bar was pinched just above what was to become the socket, then the socket was spread out.

After the socket was formed, the bolt was cut off the bar using a chisel and the tip was hammered into a pyramid shape (Figure 3.2a and 3.2e). Using quarter turns, the smith would have formed the point, turning it over to true it. There is no way to determine whether the socket was rolled before or after creation of the point. The shaping of the quarrel could be done while being held with tongs, or could be finger held because, after the metal is set up, the work could also be done cold. In cross section, points a and e form a solid pyramid in shape that looks somewhat similar to the iron points from Europe and the southeastern United States.

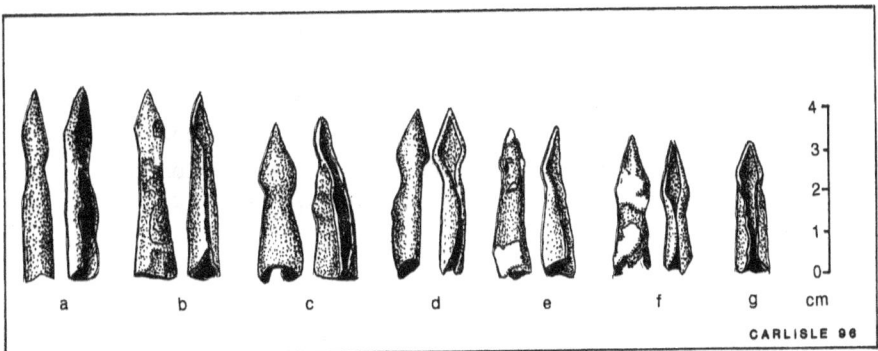

Figure 3.2. Copper crossbow boltheads from Santiago Pueblo and Pecos Pueblo. Drawing by Don Carlisle.

Three of the quarrels (artifacts b, c, and d) were made from a fairly thin sheet of copper that had been rough hammered to the approximate desired thickness. The piece was then trimmed into triangular blanks. Next, the base or socket area was thinned to less than one-half as thick as the point of the triangle. The points were then forged into a rectangular cross-section after the socket was rolled. Rolling of the socket was probably done by turning the bolt and tapping it to bend it over a wedge or edge. During the forging process the tip of the triangular point was laid on the anvil and tapped along the edges to harden, thicken, and true the point. The Indian craftsmen may have been using some sort of shaft to determine the diameter of the ferule. However, variations suggest the operation could also have been accomplished by "eyeballing" each individual item.

Major variations among the boltheads are due primarily to differences in skill and technique among smiths. For example, close examination of artifact c shows chisel cuts along the edge of the socket/ferule (Figure 3.2). Artifacts b and c are fairly straight and well formed with parallel socket edges, suggesting they took little additional work to true. Artifact d shows a "curl" where the metalsmith tried to correct a skew in the metal by working from both directions.

Color and texture differences between the two types are also apparent. The items made of bar copper exhibit a different color and appear to be somewhat more deteriorated. These variations, however, may also be due to site conditions such as heat, cold, moisture, soil pH, or conservation techniques. Or, the working techniques and amount of forge hardening may have created differences in metal hardness or variations within individual points. The metal may have come from different sources, or may contain different percentages of impurities. Further analysis is needed to understand these variations.

Some metal artifacts found in the American Southwest may represent crossbow boltheads recycled for use by historic Indian tribes; for example, some of the artifacts described by Kidder for Pecos. Also, Ellis (1957: 214) describes "a small piece of sheet copper rolled in the form of a slim cone 3.83 cm long, tapering from .4 cm to .7 cm in diameter . . . resembl[ing] the metal 'tinklers' commonly used as thonged ornaments on recent Western Apache baskets, and on Apache, Navaho, and Pueblo dress and ceremonial dance equipment."

Conclusion

Tantalizing evidence from sites such as Santiago Pueblo and the recently discovered Jimmy Owens Site in Texas strongly suggests that crossbow boltheads produced in the New World and found in context with sixteenth-century American Indian artifacts may be diagnostic of the Coronado entrada. However, because of the relatively small sampling and the lack of accurate provenience for most of the known boltheads, much more work is needed. Such analytic research should include artifacts and sites in Mexico, examination of ethnographic accounts, more sophisticated analyses of base materials, and revisiting of archeological collections across the Southwest.

Notes

1. Some authors (Jack Williams, personal communication 1991) suggest use of the crossbow may have persisted well into the seventeenth century in isolated parts of the New World frontier despite declining popularity elsewhere.

2. This description is taken from records of the Albuquerque Museum. These records describe a goat's foot lever, a companion piece to the museum's crossbow which was made in Portugal.

3. The *Old English Dictionary* notes the use of the word *quarrel* for boltheads as early as A.D. 1225 and defines the term as "a short, heavy, square-headed arrow or bolt, formerly used in shooting with the crossbow or arbalest" (1971: 2384). According to Woodward (Ellis 1957: 212), "the crossbow bolts were often referred to as 'quarrels' after an old French word meaning 'square' because the heads were square in shape, blunt rather than sharpened, and with a top surface resembling the top of a molar tooth."

4. Researchers currently working on the Texas investigations include Donald Blakeslee of Wichita State University and Richard Flint of the University of New Mexico. See Chapter 23.

5. Some authorities suggest that this was De Soto's first winter encampment, Anhaica, which was occupied from October 1539 to early March 1540 (Ewen 1989a: 112–116).

6. Of the boltheads recently found in Texas, all but one are of copper (Flint, personal communication 1995).

7. This artifact is part of the collections at Phillips Academy in Andover, Massachusetts.

8. Specimen 16, number 1.

9. Artifacts BM32/33 and BM82/35.

10. Numbers 8/6601, 8/6602, 8/6603, 12/4536, and 12/4945.

11. These crossbow boltheads are housed at the Palace of the Governors in Santa Fe.

CHAPTER 4

Armas de la Tierra
The Mexican Indian Component of Coronado Expedition Material Culture

RICHARD FLINT

ince 1990, Shirley Cushing Flint and I have been engaged in determining what equipment, utensils, and supplies may have been carried by members of the Coronado expedition. Our goal has been to determine whether archeological remains of the Coronado expedition are likely to be distinguishable from those of other Spanish expeditions of the sixteenth century. Definition of a material culture inventory distinctive to the Coronado expedition makes it easier to identify archeological sites that are associated with the expedition. For example, the pattern of Coronado expedition material culture that we have thus far identified made it possible for us in summer 1994 to conclude with considerable confidence that a relatively small assemblage of artifacts recently unearthed in the South Plains of Texas probably originated with the Coronado expedition. The particular array of artifacts from the South Plains is diverse enough to strongly suggest that their source is a campsite of the expedition in the area (see Chapter 23), rather than more random indigenous trade of exotic items. Confident association of sites with the expedition should, in turn, allow archeological investigation of many of the questions raised by or inherent in the documentary and traditional accounts of the expedition.

As but one example of such questions, there is whether the people of the Tiguex pueblo of Arenal (in the modern Bernalillo, New Mexico, area) ever returned to and rebuilt their town after being forced to abandon it under attack from the Coronado expedition during the winter of 1540–1541. The documents cannot answer that question because it isn't known precisely where Arenal was, though several scholars have outlined possibilities and have adduced documentary evidence to support them. Which of the numerous pueblo ruins in the Albuquerque-Bernalillo area was the one the Spanish called Arenal?

However, we are now convinced that certain objects were carried only by the Coronado expedition (of all those that came to the Upper Southwest). Their recovery now would make it possible to say with some assurance that the Coronado expedition probably had contact with places where those objects occur in significant number and variety. Ultimately, it may be possible to define a social geography of the Rio Grande Pueblos in the mid-1600s and correlate it with the Spanish documents of the Coronado expedition. Then perhaps we can say, "Such and such a place was Arenal." At that point the question of Arenal's reoccupation after 1541 would reduce to one of archeology's bread-and-butter issues, dating and occupation sequences. An answer to the question concerning Arenal's reoccupation would be one indication of just how much and how lastingly the Pueblo people were affected by the first coming of Europeans to the Southwest.

In defining the probable material culture inventory of the Coronado expedition, our method has been simple, but laborious. We have compiled many lists of what the Europeans themselves said they were carrying, not only members of the Coronado expedition, but also those of twenty-five other Spanish expeditions of the sixteenth century in the Western Hemisphere, from Christopher Columbus in 1492 to Sebastián Vizcaíno in 1602. In addition, we have tried to read between the lines of what the expedition members wrote, to suggest other goods that they did not write about, but which, nevertheless, they probably carried. Furthermore, to supplement these documentary material culture catalogs, we have added sixteenth-century items that have been recovered archeologically in North America.

What has emerged is a large, but still partial, listing of gear that Spanish expeditions of the sixteenth century probably had with them: equipment of mining and prospecting, military hardware, trade goods, clothing, cookware, and items from twenty-three other functional categories. We have also compared the gear of the various expeditions. (See Flint 1992.) With respect specifically to the Coronado expedition, we are now confident in saying that, indeed, there are some objects that probably were carried into the Upper Southwest exclusively or primarily by the Coronado expedition. Diane Rhodes (Chapter 3) provides basic information about one of those items, copper crossbow boltheads (or dart points).

Besides the boltheads, the short list of objects associated distinctively with the Coronado expedition includes: 1) crossbow parts and accessories, 2) short copper

Figure 4.1. *Young man leaving for war*, after Codex Mendoza, *sixteenth-century Mexico*.

or brass aglets (lace tips), 3) Nueva Cadiz glass beads, 4) sheet brass Clarksdale bells and their cast harness bell counterparts, and 5) obsidian-edged swords and lances. All of these are European-made goods except the last, obsidian-edged weapons. This brings me to the subject of this chapter, items that probably accompanied the Coronado expedition, but were part of the cultural tradition of Indians from central Mexico.

Perhaps the most neglected element of encounters between native peoples of the Southwest and the Coronado expedition is the host of Mexican Indian allies that accompanied the expedition. Although the leadership and organization of the Coronado expedition were definitely European, much of its character and "infrastructure" derived from those Mexican Indian allies. Pedro de Castañeda (Hammond and Rey 1940: 200) reported that "some eight hundred Indians of New Spain" were recruited to join the expedition, and Francisco Vázquez de Coronado, himself, testified in 1547 at Viceroy Antonio Mendoza's *residencia* (Aiton and Rey 1937: 314) that 1,300 Indians, more or less, participated voluntarily in the expedition to the Tierra Nueva of Cíbola and Quivira. On the basis of the expedition's 1540 muster roll and other documentary sources, it is estimated that the European membership of the expedition was about 350. Thus, whichever figure for number of Mexican Indians may be more accurate (800 or 1,300), it is clear that the membership of the expedition was predominantly Mexican Indian.

There is no evidence that European equipment was provided to the Indian allies. Therefore, a large share of the material carried by the expedition from Mexico was undoubtedly of indigenous make and design. In order to suggest items of material culture that Mexican Indians carried with them on the expedition, it is necessary to determine which native groups were represented in the expedition. Herbert Bolton (1949: 57) suggested that Mexican Indian allies "were enlisted in Mexico City and in the pueblos along the road to Compostela, many of them being from the province of Michoacán." More recently, Carroll Riley (1974: 28) proposed that of the hundreds of Mexican Indian allies reported by Mendoza and Vázquez de Coronado, "300 seem to have been from the central Mexican area [the Basin of Mexico]—the rest being, presumably, from west Mexico."

Direct evidence regarding precisely where the Mexican Indian allies came from is slim in the sixteenth-century documents. Juan de Jaramillo (Hammond and Rey 1940: 306) specifically mentioned a Tarascan Indian (that is, from Michoacán) and two possibly from Jalisco. Riley (1974: 30), citing fray Pedro Oroz's 1585 report on the religious province of New Spain, referred to another Indian member of the expedition from Tlatelolco (now within Mexico City). These few Indian individuals were all associated with the Catholic friars that comprised a distinct segment of the expedition. As such, they may not be representative of the bulk of Mexican Indian allies. Without supplying information on his precise place of origin, a native leader from central Mexico called Luis de León is mentioned in an *interrogatorio*, prepared by Viceroy Mendoza in 1547, as having participated in the expedition (Hanke 1976: 70). With more precision, the *Codex Aubin* (Monjarás-Ruiz et al. 1989: 268) recorded a group of Tenocha (Aztecs) leaving the Mexico City area for the "*yancuic tlalpan*," new lands, in 1539. (See Figure 4.2.) Almost certainly, this represents part of Coronado's company of allies. How many people were included in this group was not recorded. In 1582, Diego Pérez de Luxán (Hammond and Rey 1966: 184) reported that the Espejo expedition met at Zuni "Mexican Indians, and also a number from Guadalajara, some of those that Coronado had brought." Thus, it seems safe to say that most, if not all, of the Coronado expedition's Mexican Indian allies came from Nahuatl-, Tarascan-, and Caxcán-speaking areas of central and west Mexico. Importantly, there was broad similarity of material culture throughout these areas in the mid-1500s.

Unfortunately, the Spanish chronicles of the Coronado expedition are usually silent even as to the presence of the Indian allies and more so as to their roles and appurtenances. Nevertheless, their presence and participation were of major importance to the expedition and the native Southwestern peoples that it met. The relative tranquility of the expedition's sojourn in the Southwest (from a European viewpoint) resulted primarily from the reluctance of native peoples of the Southwest to engage the Europeans and their formidable allies (Flint 1991). The reputation of Mexica, Tlaxcalans, and Tarascans as fearsome warriors probably preceded them into the Southwest. That reputation, combined with their large numbers,

Figure 4.2. Tenocha leaving Mexico City for Tierra Nueva, 1539, after Codex Aubin.

would have rendered the Coronado expedition an overwhelming force, particularly when confronting the independent and relatively small Pueblo and Plains groups of the Southwest.

Thus, the character of the Coronado expedition and its inventory of goods must have been decidedly Mexican Indian. There is minimal documentary evidence specific to the Coronado expedition concerning items of Mexican Indian material culture that may have accompanied the expedition in the Greater Southwest. As Bolton (1949: 69–70) wrote, "The Indian allies doubtless carried their native implements of war, including cotton armor. Just what these weapons were, we are not informed [by the sixteenth-century documents], but it may be surmised that they included bows and arrows, clubs, spears, light javelins, and slings—all of which had been in use by the Aztecs and Tarascans at the time of the Spanish conquest." Most assuredly, the Coronado expedition's Mexican Indian allies were equipped very similarly to the central Mexican Indians whom Viceroy Mendoza enlisted to put down the Mixtón Revolt in Jalisco, while Vázquez de Coronado, the province's governor, was away in the north in 1541. Mendoza's allies wore padded cotton armor and bore elaborate insignias (including headdresses, pennants, and feather-decorated shields). And they carried weapons such as slings, lances, and *macanas* (obsidian-edged swords) (Vázquez 1866: 307). Indigenous Mexican military gear was certainly present in abundance with the Coronado expedition, since not only the Indian allies, but also nearly all the European members of the expedition, were carrying such articles.

Figure 4.3. Tlaxcalan warrior with macana, after Lienzo de Tlaxcala, *sixteenth-century Mexico.*

Probably as important as military gear, both to the expedition at the time and for purposes of archeological study of the events of the expedition, are the food preparation, domestic, and personal baggage brought by the Mexican Indian allies. That assortment of utensils, furnishings, and clothing formed the technological base that made the expedition possible. Many of the activities that supported the huge group of people and animals that constituted the expedition were likely performed in great measure (or perhaps exclusively) by the Mexican Indians. There is documentary evidence that they guarded livestock for the expedition (Hammond and Rey 1940: 225). They fed and clothed themselves and maintained their own gear and transported it. In all likelihood, they also did much, if not all, of such work for the European members of the expedition, as well. The vast majority of the equipment employed by the allies was doubtless their own; that is, items from their home cultures.

It seems surprising, therefore, that so little Mexican Indian material culture has been recovered archeologically from possible Coronado expedition sites (Hawikuh, Pecos Pueblo, Santiago Pueblo, Kuaua, LA 54147, and the Rice County, Kansas, sites). A combination of nonlocation and nonrecognition of places occupied or passed through by the Indian allies, though, has resulted in their present invisibility in the archeological record. That invisibility seems even more complete than in the documentary record and is part of the archeological invisibility of the expedition as a whole. That larger absence from the archeological record has stemmed from ignorance and lack of interest on the part of many archeologists. In the teens, twenties, and thirties, when the major excavations were done at Hawikuh, Santiago, and Pecos, for instance, interest was overwhelmingly in the native cultures alone. That is exemplified by Frederick Hodge's treatment of European objects unearthed during his 1917–1923 excavation of Hawikuh. "No detailed description of Spanish artifacts was made in the field notes, but their presence in the fill of each level was noted" (Smith, Woodbury, and Woodbury 1966: 79). Even today, the significant collection of European objects from Hawikuh has not been analyzed. Lack of awareness of the presence of Coronado's Indian allies, even among researchers familiar with the Coronado documents, has probably resulted in failure to segregate many items of possible central Mexican origin from artifact assemblages of the Upper Southwest.

As a first approach toward delineating the inventory of Mexican Indian material culture associated with the Coronado expedition, we have reviewed sixteenth-century Spanish accounts of central and west Mexico, post-conquest Mexican painted books, and reports of modern archeological work.

Six objects of Mexican Indian material culture that have been recovered from sixteenth-century contexts in the Upper Southwest and areas immediately adjacent all relate to the same technology. A fluted, columnar obsidian core, found in Beckham County, Oklahoma (Bell 1959), and five obsidian blade fragments (one recovered from LA 54147, near Bernalillo, New Mexico [Vierra 1989: 121], and four from the Padre Island shipwrecks of 1554 [Arnold and Weddle 1978: 287–288]) all derive from the protohistoric and early historic blade-flaking tradition of central Mexico. In both the Mexican and Tlaxcalan cultures of the period, production of such long, narrow obsidian blades was highly developed. The blades, *navajas*, were used in multiples to form the cutting edges of swords (macanas) and lances. Several long blades were glued (with glue made of sap, sand, and blood [Gómara 1964: 152]) into slots cut into the margins of the wooden blanks of swords and lance points. The blades also served in a number of other tools, including razors (Feldman 1978: 29). (See Figures 4.4 and 4.5.)

As Paul Tolstoy (1971: 271) observed, in the late Aztec culture fully 95 percent of all blade cores were obsidian (*ixtle*). According to Tolstoy's description (1971: 274), archeologically recovered central Mexican blade cores have smooth platforms and are usually longer (often considerably) than they are wide. The blades themselves are long and prismatic and exhibit a prominent bulb of force. Some of the sources of central Mexican obsidian are mineralogically distinctive enough to have allowed identification of the material of the LA 54147 blade fragment as Pachuca obsidian from northeast of Mexico City (Vierra 1987a: 9).

If, as was probably the case, Mexica, Tlaxcalan, or Tarascan swords and lances (or similar ones recorded from the region between Jalisco and Culiacán [Beals 1932: 140]) saw appreciable use by members of the Coronado expedition, one would expect to find significant numbers of broken obsidian blades at sites where battles took place (as at Cíbola and in the Tiguex area).

With inclusion of obsidian-edged weapons in this list of articles specific to the Coronado expedition, I am suggesting that by the time of the 1580 Chamuscado/

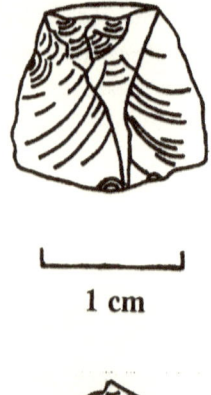

Figure 4.4. Obsidian blade fragment, LA 54147, New Mexico; plan, above (after Vierra 1989); cross-section, below.

Rodríguez entrada into the Upper Southwest the use of obsidian blade technology was so much diminished in central Mexico that weapons in that tradition are unlikely to have accompanied that expedition or any later ones. Blade production may have continued in central Mexico in "great congruence with the previous late Aztec industry" well into the seventeenth century (Cressey 1975: 107), as Pamela Cressey concluded on the basis of study of three colonial-era sites of the Teotihuacan Valley. And certainly the mid-sixteenth-century tax records for the Coyoacan market (in the Mexico City area) document the vending of obsidian blades at that time (Anderson, Berdan, and Lockhart 1976: 138–149). I suggest that although domestic use of blades did persist for a considerable time, use of obsidian-blade weapons probably declined rapidly as more and more iron was imported into New Spain. As Marc Simmons and Frank Turley (1980: 14) remarked, "[Spanish] blade makers had first claim on the bar stock that trickled in from Spain, because production of weapons was deemed by [Hernán] Cortés to be of uppermost importance." Steel swords and lances were much more durable than ones with obsidian edges (though obsidian blades were much sharper when new). Thus, within several generations, obsidian-edged weapons were probably rarely used, if at all.

Other lithic materials likely to be preserved at sites of sixteenth-century Mexican Indian presence include projectile points, *manos* and *metates,* and possibly stone comales. For instance, a projectile point similar to Texcoco points of protohistoric central Mexico (both side and basally notched) was found at LA 54147 (Vierra 1989: 122). (See Figure 4.6.) If other such points have been recovered previously in the Upper Southwest, they may have been attributed to any of "various protohistoric groups," including Puebloans (ibid.).

Regarding central Mexican metates, Tolstoy (1971: 288) wrote, "evidence for the Postclassic period suggests the continued predominance of the quadrangular slab metate, usually tripod, with legs that are conical." Small metates of this type may well be expected on Coronado expedition sites.

As Vierra and Hordes argue (Chapter 16), the sandstone "comal" (griddle) fragments recovered from dugout structures at LA 54147 appear to be of central Mexican design rather than being indigenous Southwestern products. This, despite the fact that the sandstone from which the LA 54147 comales are made is appar-

Figure 4.5. Mesoamerican columnar obsidian core, above; *Mesoamerican prismatic blade,* below *(after Tolstoy 1971)*

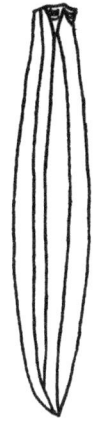

ently local (Vierra 1987a: 5) and that central Mexican comales of the period were traditionally ceramic. Bernardino de Sahagún (1961: 10: 83) recorded in the sixteenth century that Aztec clay workers sold "hard fired" comales "which ring." Thus, it would appear that the comales from LA 54147 are central Mexican in design, but made from local materials, an expedient adjustment to compensate for absence of *comal* artisans in the Coronado expedition, lack of appropriate clay sources in Tiguex, or lack of time to produce the traditional ceramic griddles. But whether or not the comales from LA 54147 can be conclusively demonstrated to be Mexican, many comales must have been used by the Coronado expedition's Mexican allies. Many of those must have been broken or abandoned and some of their remains ought to be present at a number of locations in the Southwest.

Even in the unlikely event that ceramic comales did not accompany the expedition, many other ceramics must have. In the Mexico City region at the time of the expedition, the predominant indigenous ceramic wares were Aztec IV and Aztec Polychrome. As described by Robert Chadwick (1971: 252–254), Aztec Polychrome (Texcoco Black/Red) is characterized by interiors "painted brilliant cherry red or bright brown" and exteriors with black decoration on cherry red or black and white on cherry red. Three-legged bowls were common in both Aztec IV and Aztec Polychrome. These bright tripod vessels ought to stand out in Southwestern ceramic assemblages, if, indeed, they were carried by the Coronado expedition. And, as pointed out above, ceramic comales at least started the expedition's journey.

There is also the problem of transportation of bulk items, particularly food and water. Castañeda (Hammond and Rey 1940: 206) wrote that the residents of Culiacán shared their "abundant food supplies" with the Coronado expedition, so that "not only was there plenty to use there but also to take along." In what sort of containers was that supply transported? The contemporary documents are silent on this point. However, the protohistoric Mexica (Aztec) *pochteca* (long-distance merchant) tradition included wicker backpacks and hampers that could have been adapted for use on horses and mules. For liquids, such as oil and wine mentioned by Vázquez de Coronado (Hammond and Rey 1940: 176), skin bags and ceramic vessels were surely employed. The ceramic vessels, probably supplementing a meager supply of

Figure 4.6. Texcoco point, central Mexico, top (after Tolstoy 1971); Texcoco-type point, LA 54147, New Mexico, middle (after Vierra 1989); Harrell point, Texas, bottom (after Turner and Hester 1985).

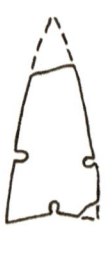

Spanish olive jars, would have been of indigenous make. Such jars could have come from central or west Mexico and may have included shell-tempered wares from the Culiacán area, as described by Sauer and Brand (1932: 33).

Throughout the sixteenth century, many members of Spanish expeditions were shod in *alpargates* (hemp sandals), which were also being worn in Spain at the time (Anderson 1979: 83). Despite that, documents of only a few expeditions refer to alpargates and the documents of the Coronado expedition are *not* among those that did. However, significantly, several expeditions originating from Mexico, both before and after the Coronado expedition, did use alpargates (those of Hernán Cortés, Beltrán Nuño de Guzmán, and Francisco de Ibarra). Also, alpargates are not mentioned for expeditions after the 1560s. I suggest that at least some of the European members of the Coronado expedition wore such sandals and most of the Mexican Indian allies also did. Many, if not all, of those sandals were likely of Mexican manufacture.

While examples of sixteenth-century alpargates are unlikely to survive to the present, awls used in their manufacture and repair probably do. Certainly, with the thousands of miles members of the Coronado expedition walked, repair of old footgear and manufacture of new would have been vital. Thus, discarded broken sandal-making tools are to be expected at Coronado expedition sites. Sahagún (1961: 10: 74) recorded the traditional use of copper awls by Mexica sandal makers. Such awls or their European or ad hoc replacements are likely to be recovered from Coronado expedition sites.

These few items are only the beginning of a list of what goods the Coronado expedition's Mexican Indian allies brought with them and contributed to the expedition's inventory. One of the critical needs, if the Coronado expedition material culture inventory is to be thoroughly defined, is for much more in-depth study of the material culture of Mexican Indians of the sixteenth century. In particular, it is very important to determine in what way and at what rate the prevailing material culture inventories of Tlaxcalans, Mexica, and Tarascans were altered during the sixteenth century. The changes those groups went through as a result of sudden, sustained, and often violent contact with Europeans and Africans were so extreme and so rapid that it may be possible to seriate their material culture inventories on the basis of very small time intervals (perhaps decades). This, in turn, would permit accurate relative dating of archeological assemblages including such material. That ought to facilitate detailed archeological scrutiny of separate episodes of subjugation, accommodation, and resistance of Old and New World groups in the Greater Southwest.

PART II

Precedents, 1538-1539

CHAPTER 5

Pathfinder for Coronado
Reevaluating the Mysterious Journey of Marcos de Niza

WILLIAM K. HARTMANN

"Critics . . . have a habit of hanging attributes on you themselves—and then when they find you're not that way accusing you of sailing under false colors . . ."
—ERNEST HEMINGWAY (1985: 111)

Introduction: Marcos de Niza and the Coronado Expedition

A curiosity of Southwest history is that the man who authored the first purposeful account of Arizona/New Mexico exploration and laid claim to the first eyewitness written descriptions of the Zuni pueblos (Cíbola) has been branded a liar by most twentieth-century historians. Marcos de Niza was a Franciscan priest praised by his superiors for his good reputation and whose report launched the mammoth Coronado expedition to the north from Mexico, but who is commonly labeled a fraud. Many historians and popular accounts claim he never even made it north of the present international border during his 1539 journey of reconnaissance.

To take some examples, A. Grove Day (1940: 30) calls Marcos the "mystery man . . . of the American southwest." Cleve Hallenbeck (1949) labels him "the lying monk," one of the "Munchausens of history." The *Arizona Highways* account of Coronado's journey by Stewart Udall (1984) not only casts doubt on Marcos for reporting gold in Cíbola, but refers readers to a sidebar about Marcos labeled "A Monumental Liar." An official National Park Service guide to the Spanish expeditions of 1539–1543 (Lavendar 1992) says, "It seems likely that he did turn back . . . at some distance from Cíbola [and] concocted a tale out of the descriptions he had heard. . . ." In these views, the fate of the entire Coronado expedition can be traced to a hoax perpetrated by Marcos de Niza.

The controversy over Marcos raises fascinating questions, not only about the origins of the Coronado expedition, but about the man himself, considering his profession as a priest. Not much is known of his life; we remain ignorant even of his birthdate (Chavez 1968). He was respected early in his career, at least in ecclesiastic circles. He came to the New World in 1531 and was elected an officer of his order in Peru, whence he came to Mexico in 1537. At that time, he stayed in the house of his bishop, Juan de Zumárraga, who wrote in April 1537, "this father is a great religious person, worthy of credit, of approved virtue, and of much religion and zeal, and whom the friars in Peru elected custodio" (Wagner 1934: 198).

In 1539 the viceroy, Antonio Mendoza, chose him to make the northward search for the rumored northern empire. The minister provincial of New Spain signed a certification of Marcos's *Relación*, saying that Marcos was "esteemed by me and my brethren of the governing deputies . . . learned, not only in theology, but also in cosmography [and] in the art of [navigation] . . ." (Hallenbeck 1949: 36). Fray Angelico Chavez (1968: 12, 75) remarks that Marcos was elected third provincial of the Holy Gospel Province after his return from Cíbola, making him a high-ranking member of the clergy in Mexico and senior priest on the Coronado expedition. A month or so after Coronado reached Cíbola, Marcos returned to Mexico, apparently something of a broken man. His term of office finished in 1543. Correspondence in 1546 with Bishop Zumárraga suggests a lonely life at Xochimilco, outside Mexico City. He requested a stipend of wine which the bishop provided. He was said to be ill from the strains of the expedition; in 1554 he was reportedly living on the coast at Jalapa in Veracruz, crippled; he died March 25, 1558.

There are important archeological and ethnographic motivations for reexamining Marcos's case. The written records of the 1530s and 1540s have been all but ignored in archeological studies because a) the Marcos diary is controversial, b) the Cabeza de Vaca/Marcos/Coronado routes are uncertain, and c) the 1530s and 1540s fall in a gap of modern academia, between archeology and history. However, there has been steady progress, over decades, toward identifying locales of the Coronado expedition (for example, see Wedel 1942; Ellis 1957). If such discoveries can be duplicated in Sonora or southern Arizona, it may soon be possible to interpolate positions along the whole route of Coronado and perhaps of Marcos himself. To the extent that sites along the routes of Marcos's and Coronado's expedition can be located and correlated with the diaries, the eyewitness observations become very much more important as ethnographic data on the nature of the early historic Southwest.

Background to the Expeditions

The circumstances and records of Marcos's journey have been recounted elsewhere in great detail (Bancroft 1889; Bandelier 1981; Winship 1990; Wagner 1934; Sauer 1932, 1937, 1941; Bloom 1940, 1941; Hallenbeck 1949; Cushing 1979; Hartmann and Hartmann 1972; Hartmann 1989), and I give only a brief overview here.

Four elements combined to foster belief in a rich native empire north of Mexico. 1) Even as the Spanish began exploring the New World, there were rumors of a wealthy polity, Seven Cities of Antilia, supposedly founded in the New World by bishops who escaped the Moors' advance up the Iberian Peninsula during the Middle Ages (Hallenbeck 1949). 2) Hernán Cortés had conquered the Aztec empire in 1519–1521 and Francisco Pizarro conquered the Inca empire in the 1530s; it was natural to assume other empires awaited plunder. 3) In 1531–1536 Beltrán Nuño de Guzmán and Diego de Guzmán explored and raided for slaves along Mexico's west coast as far north as the Fuerte and Yaqui Rivers and heard stories from natives about wealthy cities to the north. Coronado's chronicler Pedro de Castañeda states that "the way we first came to know about the Seven Cities" was a native informant in Nuño de Guzmán's possession in 1530, who reported that as a boy he had gone with his father, a trader, across a desert wilderness to "seven very large towns," comparable to Mexico itself, where his father had traded fine feathers for ornaments and "large amounts of gold and silver" (Winship 1990: 99; Undreiner 1947: 432). 4) Álvar Núñez Cabeza de Vaca and three companions, after a shipwreck on the Gulf of Mexico coast and years of wandering across Texas and the Southwest borderland, arrived in Spanish Mexico in the spring of 1536 with stories of a rich empire somewhere north of their route.

After Cabeza de Vaca arrived in Mexico City, the viceroy of New Spain, Antonio Mendoza, began making plans for an expedition to the north. Meanwhile, priests, including Marcos himself, were complaining to the authorities about the excesses and atrocities that had occurred during the recent Peruvian ventures and cautioning against a repeat in the north.

Mendoza's task by 1537 was to control the unruly adventurers who were chomping at the bit for a conquest of the north and to ensure that the final venture came in the name of the Spanish crown, not rogue commanders like the Guzmáns. His first effort was to assess the veracity of the rumors as secretly as possible so that he could make and control the plans. His interest in secrecy is spelled out in the original orders that he wrote to Marcos, "if . . . you find some large settlement . . . you shall send information by Indians or return yourself to Culiacán. Send such information with all secrecy, in order that whatever is necessary can be done without commotion, because in bringing peace to the country which may be found, we look to the service of Our Lord and the good of the inhabitants" (Hallenbeck 1949: 11).

The Problem of Marcos's Reputation During His Lifetime

The main charge against Marcos in his lifetime was that he led everyone astray by falsely claiming riches in Cíbola and/or along the route. This is a paradox because his *Relación*, or report, certified in Mexico City after his trip on September 2, 1539, is sober and *nowhere mentions gold in Cíbola!*

At the outset, we can dispose of some of the later claims about Marcos's exaggerations; they stem from an aberrant historical phenomenon. Wagner (1934: 211n) notes that booksellers of the 1500s were accustomed to inserting their own material in authors' texts to make them sell better, and that editions of Marcos's *Relación*, such as an Italian edition published by Ramusio in 1556, interpolate many claims of gold in Cíbola and other exaggerations. Such widely disseminated corruptions of Marcos's work explain the persistence of Marcos's early reputation for exaggeration. Such editions are still on library shelves and continue to be cited. This explains some modern false charges, but does not explain the problems in 1540.

As for whether Marcos turned back near the Arizona-Sonora border and simply fabricated his final march to Cíbola, we have direct contrary evidence. Melchior Díaz was sent north in November 1539 to check Marcos's findings. He wintered for perhaps two months in the last villages in southern Arizona or in the adjacent region called Chichilticale, from which Estevan and Marcos left for Cíbola. He interviewed the villagers and confirmed Marcos's general description of Cíbola, including details of Estevan's death there. Díaz's report (reproduced by Viceroy Mendoza; compare Winship 1990), while it does not mention Marcos by name, surely would have commented, if Marcos himself had never reached these villages or had turned back from there. Díaz also affirmed that in Cíbola "they have turquoises in quantity, though not so many as [Marcos] said" (Hammond and Rey 1940: 159). While this suggests that Marcos (or the secondhand rumors) spoke overenthusiastically, it does *not* say that Marcos lied, as might be expected if the modern critics were correct.

To understand the mind-set of the 1540 Coronado expedition, we need to examine more closely what Marcos did say when he returned to Mexico City from his Cíbola expedition in the summer of 1539. As is well known, Marcos's companion, the dark-skinned Moor, Estevan, arrived at Cíbola/Zuni several days ahead of Marcos and was killed, along with some of the native guides from the Chichilticale region. Marcos therefore never entered Cíbola and stated in his *Relación* only that he saw it covertly from a distance before returning to Mexico. Contrary to most implications, his written description of Cíbola from a distance is curt, sober, and can be credited as literally accurate.

When news leaked out in Mexico City in the late summer and fall of 1539 that Marcos had actually found a major northern trade center, the population was agog.

There are eyewitness accounts of rumors flying in Mexico City about gold, jewels, and a fabulous pagan empire. My interpretation is that these rumors originated in exaggerations of what Marcos had said, among an excited populace already primed to believe in a fabulous empire to the north.

Do we have direct evidence that Marcos himself propagated these rumors? Very little. A secondhand account by a friar writing on October 9, 1539—weeks after Marcos returned from Cíbola—reports that Marcos told him about the trip (Wagner 1934: 223). While most of this account attributes reasonably accurate statements to Marcos, it does say that "the friar himself told me this, that he saw a temple of their idols the walls of which, inside and outside were covered with precious stones; I think he said they were emeralds." Marcos is unlikely to have said this about Cíbola since he did not claim to have entered the town; it may have been a misunderstanding of something Marcos said about turquoise in an Arizona or Sonora shrine (Marcos did repeatedly report turquoise there, and the Hohokam of 150 years earlier were famous for their turquoise mosaics). Later reports by Coronado expedition members Díaz and Castañeda (Winship 1990) confirm that natives along the Coronado route built huts as shrines to sacred objects. Reports of shrines and objects of turquoise in the valleys on the way to Cíbola would probably have been correct.

An even more important account, probably a secondhand account based on conversations with Marcos, is a letter written by Marcos's friend and sponsor, Bishop Zumárraga, on August 23, 1539. Zumárraga says nothing about gold or jewels in Cíbola or elsewhere (Wagner 1934: 223):

> Fray Marcos has discovered another much larger [country] 400 leagues beyond where Nuño de Guzmán is. . . . Many people are moving to go there. The marqués [Hernán Cortés] pretends that the conquest of it belongs to him but the viceroy takes it for the emperor and desires to send friars ahead without arms and wishes the conquest to be a Christian and apostolic one and not a butchery. The people are more cultured in their wooden edifices of many stories and in their dress. They have no idols, but worship the sun and moon. They have only one wife and if she dies they do not marry another. There are partridges and cows which the father says he saw, and he heard a story of camels and dromedaries and of other cities larger than this one of Mexico . . .

The rumored "cows," mentioned also in Marcos's *Relación*, refer to bison, whose skins had been shown to Marcos. The lack of claims of gold and jewels proves that Marcos himself was not trumpeting fabulous riches. Zumárraga's assertion of wooden multistory houses (instead of the correct statement of stone multistory houses) suggests Zumárraga had not had time to become completely familiar with Marcos's story, thus suggesting that this August 23 account is a very early record of what Marcos was saying when he first arrived in Mexico City. The mention of worshiping the sun and moon suggests Marcos brought back additional ethnographic information not in the *Relación*. At Zuni, the sun priest made solar observations to calibrate the calendar, which was based on the solstices (Cushing 1979: 116–117). Moreover, Zuni had a summer solstice ceremony that would have occurred around June 12 on the Julian calendar Marcos was using—only two to three weeks after Marcos arrived.[1] Preparations may have been under way and Marcos was probably told about the ceremony.

Incidentally, the last line of the letter supports Adolf Bandelier's suggestion (Bandelier 1981: 100) that Marcos compared Cíbola not with the mighty Aztec city of Tenochtitlán, but rather to "this (Spanish city) of Mexico," and thus rebuts the modern ridicule leveled at Marcos for saying that Cíbola was bigger than Mexico City.

The strongest testimony for Marcos mentioning gold comes from a thirdhand witness. A deposition in Havana on November 12, 1539, came from a man who said that his son-in-law was a barber who shaved Marcos after his return and that the friar, while being shaved, had spoken about his discoveries (Winship 1990: 21). "After crossing the mountains the friar said there was a river and that many settlements were there, in cities and towns, and that the cities were surrounded by walls, with their gates guarded, and were very wealthy, having silversmiths, and that the women wore strings of gold beads and the men girdles of gold and white woolen dresses. . . ." This report is consistent with other reports and Marcos's own *Relación*, except for the specifics about gold. A thirdhand interpolation about gold is possible if, as reported by Castañeda, Nuño de Guzmán's native informant in 1530 had already been alleged to have spoken of gold in the north. It appears that Marcos's report was simply assumed in the streets to be congruent with preexisting myth of a rich northern empire.

To sum up, there is little direct evidence that Marcos himself made serious claims of gold in Cíbola or on the route. It makes little sense to believe that if Marcos saw gold ornaments or publicly claimed firsthand knowledge of gold and fabulous wealth in Cíbola, he would omit this both from his report to the viceroy and from his conversations with Zumárraga. It makes more sense to assume that a fullblown phantasm of a gold-paved Cíbola blossomed on the streets of Mexico City in September 1539. My guess would be that Marcos was a man inclined to put an optimistic gloss on things; he may have been personally inclined to believe that once the Spaniards entered Cíbola, they would find some treasures, as he had seen in Peru and Mexico. Even if he was willing to say so privately, he apparently did not stress this with Zumárraga and was circumspect in his official and public statements.

Nonetheless, wild rumors about Cíbola did take Mexico City by storm. The churches reportedly preached a crusade (presumably in order to save the souls of the heathens), and people clearly thought Marcos had reported a bejeweled city of gold. Some people demonstrably were informed only through rumor; Castañeda, for example, always speaks of Marcos's trip as if more than one friar had reached the north country, proving that even members of Coronado's expedition didn't get Marcos's story straight. Marcos started with a companion priest, who promptly fell ill and gave up the trip. The whole affair is one of the most classic cases in history of unfounded rumor being reinforced by a preexisting paradigm.

By the spring of 1540 a full-blown expedition was organized. Díaz's party returned from Chichilticale and met the freshly organized company between Compostela and the jumping-off point of Culiacán. Castañeda tells us that Díaz reported in secret to Coronado but the report leaked: it supported what Marcos had written in his *Relación*, but did not confirm the hoped-for riches along the way or in Cíbola. This disappointed the Spaniards. Castañeda says that "Marcos, noticing that some were feeling disturbed, cleared away these clouds, promising . . . that he would place the army in a country where their hands would be filled, and in this way he quieted them" (Hammond and Rey 1940: 205). Had Marcos himself been convinced by this time, and did he publicly promise gold? Or did he just give a good pep talk? Castañeda does not quite tell us. Marcos's private motivations, like Eusebio Kino's in the next century, may have been primarily to move the Spanish frontier to the north, in order to save souls.

As the Coronado expedition moved on toward Cíbola in 1540, more attacks were leveled against Marcos for misleading everyone. When the soldiers actually entered Cíbola and found the plazas paved with dust instead of gold, "such were the curses that some hurled at Friar Marcos that I pray God may protect him from them," reported Castañeda (Hammond and Rey 1940: 208). Marcos left Cíbola in disgrace with a return party for Mexico, probably in August with Díaz (Bancroft 1889: 46). Writing on August 3, 1540, a few weeks after Cíbola fell, a disappointed Coronado reported to the king that doubts about Marcos had surfaced even before the army reached Chichilticale, because the road was rough and had to be widened. It is interesting to note that while disparaging Marcos, Coronado actually verifies Marcos's report that there were preexisting roads, that is, a trail system.

In the same letter Coronado recounts (about eight to ten weeks after the fact) that when they reached Chichilticale the expedition members were disillusioned because they thought Marcos had said Chichilticale was about a day from the sea. Coronado himself calls it the "port" of Chichilticale and apparently had conceived an idea (from Marcos, he says) that it was only five leagues, or one day, from the coast; he was disgusted to learn from natives that Chichilticale was ten or fifteen days inland. This has been widely interpreted as evidence of some deception by Marcos and his complete lack of knowledge of the terrain. However, Marcos's alleged claim of a one-day distance does not agree with what Marcos himself wrote in his *Relación*. Here, he vaguely describes eight days of travel from the coastal region to the last village before Chichilticale. Adding the two days from the village to the Chichilticale ruin itself (see Chapter 12) gives a total of roughly ten days or a bit more, exactly congruent with the natives' report!

So why did Coronado claim that Chichilticale was going to be a port only one day from the sea? Why hadn't Díaz straightened this out during his winter stay there? The answer, though incomplete, seems to point back to Mendoza, not Marcos. Cabeza de Vaca repeatedly spoke of his attempts to reach the "South Sea" (the Pacific and Gulf of California). At one point, his party was given a copper bell reportedly originating north of their route, in a region with permanent houses, and Cabeza de Vaca then remarks "and we believe that this [place] must be the Southern Sea" because they had heard that the area toward the coast was prosperous (Pupo-Walker 1993: 92, 94). Cabeza de Vaca also spoke of the town of Corazones, on his route, as a gateway to the coastal provinces. All this he imparted to Mendoza, who must have concluded that an arm of the sea ran inland, somewhere north of Cabeza de Vaca's route. Mendoza wrote in his instructions to Marcos to "inquire always . . . about the coast of the sea" because "some arm of the sea may enter the land" in the northern country (Hallenbeck 1949: 10). Although Marcos was able to stay within some days of the coast for most of his northward route, he accurately reported that the seacoast eventually turned westward, away from the route. Nonetheless, Mendoza sent a fleet to supply Coronado, expecting harbors where the expedition could be contacted. Castañeda tells us that Alarcón's ships had many soldiers' personal baggage (Winship 1990: 105).

Chichilticale, being at the latitude of the head of the gulf, would have been the last chance for the expedition to meet the ships and get their supplies and possessions. Clearly, an assumption of the expedition, from Mendoza downward, was that the ships would be contacted at one of the harbors or ports, and Marcos had no doubt confirmed the view that his route was only a few days inland at many points. The dismay reported by Coronado was thus the pain of abandoning that erroneous preconception and the last hope of linking up with supplies, not the result of face-to-face confrontation in which Marcos defended an erroneous one-day figure. Had Marcos been confronted directly with this at Chichilticale, he surely would have defended his *Relación*, not a figure of one day. Yet Coronado (adroitly?) assigned Marcos the blame when the preconception turned out not to be true.

To dismiss the claims against Marcos in his lifetime merely as a result of the problems of the expedition and the debacle at Cíbola seems attractive, except for one thing. After Marcos returned to Mexico City in 1539, Cortés left for Spain to argue his claim to the north country to the king, and, apparently on June 25, 1540 (Winship 1990: 21, 72n6), before Cortés could have known that Cíbola was not a rich empire, he accused Marcos of being a well-known exaggerator. This is the only such charge we have that was written before the Coronado venture failed. Cortés states in this deposition that:

> [Marcos in 1539] went by land in search of the same coast and country . . . I had discovered, and which it was and is my right to conquer. And since his return, the said friar has published the statement that he came within sight of the said country, which I deny that he has either seen or discovered . . . everything which the . . . friar says . . . is just the same as what [the] Indians told me, and in enlarging upon this and in pretending to report what he neither saw nor learned, the said Friar Marcos does nothing new, because he has done this many other times, and this was his regular habit, as is notorious in the provinces of Peru and Guatemala . . . (Wagner 1934: 220)

Here is serious evidence against Marcos's credibility. Before anyone knew any other reasons to attack Marcos, Cortés made the same charge that later historians make: Marcos lied; he exaggerated; he never saw Cíbola. This seems to me the strongest part of the case against Marcos. Of course, Cortés is not denying that Cíbola is rich; he wants to conquer it. He merely wants to discredit Marcos in order to establish his own supposedly prior claim to the conquest. Cortés says he could provide proof of the last statements, but as Winship (1990: 22) points out, "so far as is known the charge was never substantiated."

It comes down to assessing the reliability of Cortés versus Marcos. It is hard to side with Cortés. Clearly, he had self-interest more glaringly uppermost than Marcos did. But there is a secondary reason for distrusting Cortés that has not been argued previously: in the mid-1530s, Marcos and Bishop Zumárraga wrote scathing attacks on the conquerors because of their treatment of the Incas in Peru. Indeed, on this basis, Marcos emerges as a constant defender of the native Americans and comes off as a hero by standards of modern sociopolitical sensitivity. After the conquest of Peru, Marcos made an affidavit of uncertain date, published by Bartolomé de las Casas in Seville in 1552. It speaks of the benevolence of the Peruvian natives and details atrocities against them by the conquistadors, blaming their resistance on their mistreatment by the soldiers (Las Casas 1992: 115–118).

Similarly, in the 1537 letter in which Bishop Zumárraga praises Marcos's abilities, Zumárraga writes that he is trying to persuade the king to put a halt to atrocities against natives throughout the New World. He says he believes that Mendoza (Cortés's rival) is the man to do it. Las Casas, priest-historian who published the testimony of Marcos about Peru, was said to have been at least acquainted with

Marcos (Wagner 1934) and also to have attacked Cortés concerning violence against the Indians (Las Casas 1992: 58–64). From these documents we have a clear picture of Marcos, Bishop Zumárraga, Viceroy Mendoza, and Las Casas, reinforcing each other as early as 1537 in attempts to publicize and stop atrocities committed during conquest. It is no wonder, then, that conquistadors like Cortés tried to discredit Marcos, a star witness against them.

The Reputation of Marcos with Modern Historians

The reaction of modern historians deserves critical attention, but a detailed critique is beyond the scope of this chapter. A deluge of criticism came in the 1930s and 1940s with the work of Henry Wagner, Carl Sauer, and Cleve Hallenbeck. Basically, they studied the route and concluded that Marcos did not have time to do what he said he did. A widespread conclusion, mentioned above, was that Marcos got no further than the present Arizona-Sonora border region and then made up the rest of his report from the descriptions of his native contacts.

There is some poor scholarship involved here. Some of it I call the Hemingway syndrome, after the quote at the beginning of this chapter. Critics of Marcos have a striking tendency to hang attributes on him or his route and then, when they find that things are not that way, accusing him of flying under false colors (a secret conspiracy with Mendoza to falsify the data is theorized by Sauer and Hallenbeck).

For example, both Sauer and Hallenbeck discuss routes from Culiacán to Zuni that seem to them the most reasonable ones to follow. Their routes are relatively far inland at the latitude of the Gulf of California's north end. Then they attack Marcos for saying that he made a side trip to the gulf, because they say he is too far inland! At the same time they attack him for not following his instructions to stay close to the coast! This is the classic Hemingway syndrome: assign Marcos what route *you* think he should have taken, and then attack him as a liar when the evidence suggests he did something different. Concluding a critique of this sort, Sauer (1937: 287) writes, "It is time that the story of the discovery of the Seven Cities by Fray Marcos be classed where it belongs, as a hoax devised in the interests of Mendoza's *Realpolitik*. [Marcos] was sent out to establish as strong a claim as possible for Mendoza against Cortés . . ."

To take another example, Hallenbeck (1949: 44) says that "not even such sinewy men as Kino and Garces . . . ever averaged as much as 20 miles a day" in this area. Then he adds insult to injury by saying they "were quite different from the aging Marcos." Later (1949: 50) he says, "16 miles a day would not have been too much to expect of the old friar." These are amazing passages because none of Marcos's biographers knows his date of birth, and Hallenbeck offers no evidence of his age. The historian, Father Charles Polzer, speculates that Marcos was in his forties in 1539, based on his career and the dates when he took his orders and was elected provincial (Charles Polzer, personal communication 1992). Kino, in contrast, made most of his heroic journeys in the far harsher southwest Arizona deserts in his mid-fifties, and was sixty-one when he led a party to the rugged Pinacate volcano summit!

Hallenbeck (1949: 65) joins Sauer in a bizarre claim that Marcos ignored his instructions from Mendoza: "While Marcos had been instructed to send back reports on the country as he advanced, there is not even a suggestion that he did so. . . . His utter disregard for most of his instructions is . . . obvious." On the contrary, as I will demonstrate, there is virtual proof in a letter of Coronado that Marcos *did* send back reports and these solve the problem of the return timescale that so vexes Sauer and Hallenbeck.

As another example, Hallenbeck (1949: 84) asserts that "Marcos was *not* instructed to visit the coast [emphasis Hallenbeck's]." This is a misleadingly literal claim at best, since Mendoza spends a whole paragraph ordering Marcos to seek information about the coast, and tells Marcos to leave markers on the shore "if you come to the coast," especially marking "situations suitable for harbors" (Hallenbeck 1949: 10). Contrary to Hallenbeck's implications, Mendoza clearly regarded coastal information, in support of a maritime expedition, as a primary goal of the reconnaissance.

Aside from the unconvincing nature of their arguments, the proponents of a Marcos/Mendoza conspiracy, and even those who simply call Marcos a liar, seemingly did not think through their own theory. If Marcos knew he had lied and if he had not even reached Arizona let alone Cíbola—and, indeed, if it could so obviously not be done in the time he reported—why would he agree to turn around and accompany Coronado and the full-scale expedition all the way back to Cíbola? As soon as he reached the area where he had not traveled, he risked catastrophic exposure at every step. If Marcos returned to Compostela only about thirty-six days or less after claiming to have seen Cíbola, as Wagner and Sauer posit, instead of the minimally required forty-three to fifty days, wouldn't Coronado discover this blunder during the journey to Cíbola? After all, Coronado personally knew when Marcos returned, hence his total travel time. The only other writer to emphasize this point, to my knowledge, is Ernest Peixotto in an obscure but beautiful 1916 travel book, where he comments, "Fray Marcos accompanied the expedition as guide and adviser, thus showing that he really believed in the stories . . ." (1916: 68).

Worse yet, if Marcos turned back near the Arizona border, as Sauer and Hallenbeck conclude, how would he have expected to keep Díaz (who wintered at Chichilticale in 1539–1540) and Coronado from finding this out from the local villagers of that area? Marcos's *Relación* said that thirty chiefs and native bearers from this region had gone with him to Cíbola, following Estevan's party, an easy falsehood to expose, had it been a falsehood. Had it been a hoax, why not say that only a few obscure natives went along?

Instead of a refutation, Díaz confirmed Marcos's remark that when Marcos returned, the natives in this region were angry over the deaths of some of their comrades in Cíbola, along with Estevan. Díaz says that the natives received him, with "coolness" and "mean faces" (Hammond and Rey 1940: 160), that the Cíbolans had told them to kill any advancing Christians or at least send word of their arrival.

It is not unprecedented in human nature to construct an elaborate hoax or to claim riches in a city you've never seen, but it does seem against human nature to construct a hoax and then turn around and lead an armed group of your fellows the very next year to the people who witnessed your deceptions, especially if your lie is so grossly obvious as Sauer and Hallenbeck would have us believe.

New Light on Prehistoric Trade Routes and Regional Interactions

Various early authors, including Karl Lumholtz in 1902 and Hallenbeck in 1949, commented on evidence for ancient trade routes that stretched from the Valley of Mexico to New Mexico. Nonetheless, archeological evidence of highly developed prehistoric pochteca trading networks, involving organizations carrying out trade from Mesoamerica to the pueblos, was considered something of a breakthrough in the 1970s (Di Peso et al. 1974). Carroll Riley (1975), in the same vein, documented evidence that Cíbola/Zuni, specifically the pueblo of Hawikuh (the one first reached by Coronado) was a hub of a north-south trade network, a conclusion eminently consistent with Marcos's report. Lack of appreciation of the full extent of such commerce explains the tendency of earlier historians to treat Marcos more as an explorer of uncharted wildernesses than as the first European to be led north on a centuries-old trade route. Such writers ignore Marcos's own testimony that his enthusiastic native allies carried his burdens ahead on the trail and made camps for him at traditional campsites.

All the eyewitness testimony from the time, from Cabeza de Vaca through Guzmán, to Marcos and Díaz, indicates that natives from mid-Sonora northward were very familiar with Zuni, because members of their tribes had visited, traded, and worked there. Marcos's description of the roads, native knowledge of precise travel times along the route, his reports of well-used camps in *despoblados* (unpopulated areas) along the route, and the widespread knowledge of Cíbola are important records of regional political economy only 150 years after the collapse of Hohokam culture; they need better integration into current archeological theorizing about late prehistoric social structures.

How Far Could Marcos Travel in a Day?

Are Marcos's required travel times plausible? He gives a fairly detailed account of his trip north, indicating the number of days when he rested in villages and the number when he was on the road. For Marcos's average rate of travel northward, we have a distance of 1,029 road miles (as opposed to airline miles) from Culiacán to Zuni (Hallenbeck's figure, 1949: 46), covered in about forty-five to fifty-four days of cumulative northward travel (not counting his rest days, and depending on details of his side trip to the sea); this gives an average of 19 to 23 miles per day.

Marcos gives almost no detail of his return trip, once he espied Cíbola and fled to the south, except that he says he continued fleeing 10, 8, and 10 leagues on the first three days after he emerged from the despoblado into the Chichilticale region, because the villagers there, who had been friendly, were now hostile owing to the debacle at Cíbola.

Marcos's league is believed to be about 2.5 to 3.1 miles (Undreiner [1947] favors about 3.0 miles; Hallenbeck [1949: 46, 98, 100] favors 3.1 miles; Rodack [in Bandelier 1981] favors 2.6 miles). This gives perhaps 21 to 31 road miles per day, for three consecutive days of flight at what Marcos indicates was an unusually rapid rate for him. Marcos would not have reported these rates if they were considered impossible by his contemporaries. In my own tentative reconstruction of his hasty return to Culiacán, which follows, I allot forty-four days of travel, requiring a sustained average of 23 road miles per day.

The question is: Are these average rates of 19 to 23 miles a day, with peak rates up to about 31 miles a day, plausible? Several lines of evidence, beyond the scope of this paper, indicate that the answer is yes.

From ancient and modern accounts of hikers, I conclude that Marcos, who had walked all his life, could easily handle 17–20 miles a day in rough country and, say, 22–25 miles per day in smoother country for sustained marches, and that he averaged 25–33 miles per day for at least some days at a time when in a hurry. With this background, it remains only to calculate whether Marcos could have done what he said he did.

The Return Journey: The Critical Test

In most odysseys dramatic attention is usually focused on the outward journey, not the return (the Homeric odyssey itself being the ironic exception). Yet, as pointed out by Wagner (1934) and Sauer (1932, 1937, 1941), the timing of the return journey is crucial to the whole issue of Marcos's veracity, because less time was available for the return. For this reason, I have constructed a detailed hypothetical chronology of the return, to test whether it can fit the time constraints; if not, Marcos's whole story collapses.

The key to the most plausible reconstruction is the likelihood that Marcos sent native messengers back to Coronado in advance of his own arrival, as, indeed, Viceroy Mendoza explicitly instructed. As first pointed out by Bloom (1940), this helps resolve some time pressures created by letters of Coronado and Cortés, which indicate receipt of preliminary news from Marcos. These letters are dated July 15, 26, and August 6, 1539. Native messengers could have brought news sent by Marcos either before he reached Cíbola, when he discovered the "good country" of northern Sonora and southern Arizona, or after he reached Cíbola and started home. This news could have arrived weeks before Marcos did in the first case, and days before Marcos's own hurried return in the second.

Ironies abound here. Sauer (1941: 239) says he cannot understand this suggestion—a peculiar statement, as it solves his whole problem. Hallenbeck (1949: 85), without evidence, attacks Marcos for disobeying his orders by *not* sending back native messengers.

Strangely, virtual proof that Marcos sent native messengers to Coronado exists, but has gone unremarked by these authors. This proof exists in a well-known letter from Coronado to Viceroy Mendoza, written during Marcos's journey, and dated March 8, 1539 (Hammond and Rey 1940: 42–44). This letter mentions the "marvelous" progress of Marcos's venture, and then says, "with this letter I enclose one I received for your lordship from the said padre. The Indians tell me they all adore him . . . He says that he will write to me when he finds good country." It is clear from the context of this letter that Marcos had started some weeks before and that Coronado has already received an early letter back from him and expects more letters.

Armed with evidence that Marcos utilized messengers, we can analyze the return journey. Sauer (1937: 286) states correctly that "a definite date of return has not been established." To resolve this, Wagner (1934), Sauer (1937), and Bloom (1940) introduce various letters, including a letter to the king dated July 15, 1539, by Coronado in Compostela, reporting "the grandeur which Fray Marcos relates of the land" (Sauer 1937: 286) and that the king will hear more about it from Marcos and from Mendoza. This letter can be interpreted to indicate that a message from Marcos (not Marcos himself) has arrived at Compostela by July 15. It reported on the good lands in northern Sonora and/or on information gathered about Cíbola itself. Suppose it was sent from the last villages (in southern Arizona) before Marcos entered the twelve to fifteen-day despoblado, a logical and prudent place for Marcos to dispatch news to his sponsors. The time between Marcos's northward passage through southern Arizona until, say, July 10 is about sixty-seven days and the distance to Compostela is no more than 1,100 road miles (Hallenbeck's figure, 1949: 46), giving about 16 miles a day for the message's rate of travel, a plausible rate for the native messengers. By July 26, a letter of Cortés written in the Mexico City area (Wagner 1934: 213) indicates that similar preliminary news of Marcos's progress (perhaps from even earlier messengers?) has reached him; he is writing to Mendoza to ask that when Mendoza hears news from Marcos, Mendoza should let Cortés know.

There would seem to be no problem here. Yet, by neglecting the possibility of messengers arriving ahead of Marcos, Wagner concludes that *Marcos himself* had arrived in Compostela and not around July 15, as might be suggested by the date of Coronado's letter, but rather on July 1! This in turn leaves only about forty days according to Wagner's calendar for Marcos to cover the 1,320 miles from Cíbola (May 22 till July 1; Wagner places Marcos at Cíbola about May 22; I would make it more like May 25). This gives an average sustained rate of at least 33 miles per day. Wagner concludes that Marcos couldn't have done this, and thus couldn't have left from Cíbola and therefore never reached Cíbola. With similar logic, Sauer (1941: 239) also concludes Marcos was in Compostela by July 1, and Hallenbeck (1949: 63) has him there by July 4.

The alleged discrepancy in the return date, advocated by Wagner, Sauer, and Hallenbeck, is the foundation for the whole modern attack on Marcos—the claim that he did not have enough time to have reached Cíbola. The simple idea of Marcos using messengers appears to demolish the problem.

In contrast to the charges that Marcos engaged in hysterical exaggeration, it is important to note that the phrases attributed to Marcos in the letters of July 1539 are remarkably restrained. Coronado at Compostela on July 15 refers to news of "so fine a land" and "the grandeur . . . of the land" (Sauer 1937: 286), while Cortés on July 26 refers to rumors of "a good country" (Wagner 1934: 213). These phrases fit not the Wagner/Sauer/Hallenbeck scenario of a Marcos arriving on July 1 or 4 and trumpeting gold and jewels, but rather a scenario in which Coronado has received messages of a positive discovery of a good land (northern Sonora), and in which this news has leaked through the grapevine to a few of the other key players, such as Cortés. Phrases such as "the grandeur of the land" match the descriptions of the well-populated, irrigated borderland valleys that Marcos used in his own *Relación*.

Bloom (1940) makes another important assertion: Coronado's letter of July 15 refers to Estevan in a way proving that Coronado did not yet know that Estevan was dead. Coronado (Hammond and Rey 1940: 47) writes:

> I charged [the Indians] to take Fray Marcos and Estevan, a Negro, to the interior of the land . . . The viceroy bought the Negro for this purpose from one of those who escaped from Florida. His name is Estevan. They [the Indians] did so, treating them very well.

> ... the Lord willed that they should come to a very fine country, as your Majesty will see by the report of Fray Marcos and by what the viceroy is writing to you, and inasmuch as he is doing so I shall not go into details ...

This hardly seems like the report of an official who has been talking to Marcos for two weeks and has learned that Estevan is dead, as claimed in the Wagner/Sauer/Hallenbeck reconstructions.

In summary, the totality of evidence suggests that Coronado received a message somewhat before July 15 that Marcos had found a good country and would soon return. Coronado, not knowing how long he would have to wait for Marcos, then includes the news in his letter to the king about larger issues of the provinces, and instead of second-guessing Marcos's final report, prudently says that further details will come from Marcos and the Viceroy themselves.

Based on the arguments developed here, I have constructed a preliminary timetable of Marcos's journey, concluding that Marcos sent several messengers back to Coronado and Mendoza, and that he left Cíbola on May 25, 1539, reaching Culiacán about July 8, after about forty-three days, Compostela about July 22 (fifty-seven days), and Mexico City about August 20. A certification about Marcos's trip was prepared August 26, 1539, and his *Relación* was notarized on September 2. This covers the period when rumors of riches to the north began to fly in Mexico City.

The Northward Journey: The Location of Vacapa

Having concluded that the timing of the return trip is plausible, we can now turn our attention to two specific problems associated with the northward portion of Marcos's reconnaissance, which has a schedule less tight than the return journey.

A key problem is the location of the important town named Vacapa, where Marcos found himself moving inland. Marcos says it was 40 leagues inland (about 105 trail miles, perhaps closer to 84 air miles) and he stayed for more than a week while his messengers reconnoitered the coast.[2] Vacapa is important because his specified departure date (April 7, the day after Easter) fixes the time line for the rest of the trip. Also, three *jornadas* (or day's marches) north of Vacapa were the villages where Estevan received the first descriptions of Cíbola.

The site of Vacapa is very controversial and it becomes a fulcrum of various theories. (See Maps 4 and 5.) Bandelier (1981: 73) suggests the word is Pima. In history books, the town is amazingly mobile: various authorities have placed it all over Sonora from between the Río Fuerte and the Río Mayo on the south border of the state (Sauer 1937: 280; Hallenbeck 1949: 51) to mid-Sonora (Bandelier 1981: 74); and even to the Trincheras region of the Río Magdalena in the north (Bancroft 1889: 29; Oblasser 1939: 6, 9; Undreiner 1947: 437; Reff 1991: 72). In particular, by insisting that Vacapa lies close to the modern village of Vaca close to the present Sinaloa-Sonora border, Sauer gets Marcos's journey off to an extraordinarily slow start. By the time he leaves the Sauer/Hallenbeck Vacapa, Marcos would have used thirty-one of his available seventy-six total elapsed days to Cíbola (41 percent of his available time) covering only about 21 percent of the travel distance. Not surprisingly, Sauer and Hallenbeck run out of time for him to complete the journey and then accuse him of lying (the classic Hemingway syndrome). At the other extreme, archeological evidence of trade indicates that it is absurd to think that knowledge of Cíbola only began three days north of Las Trincheras; furthermore, that location requires Marcos *not* to hear of the head of the Gulf when he is near it at Las Trincheras, but inexplicably to travel much further (as far as the Gila–Salt River valley, according to Oblasser [1939: 15–17] and Undreiner [1947: 452–456]) before he hears of it, which makes no sense.

Marcos's own testimony places Vacapa in the middle of his trip. He tells us (Hallenbeck 1949: 18) that from a river valley two days beyond, it was thirty jornadas to Cíbola, that is, thirty-two jornadas from Vacapa to Cíbola. But he also tells us it was fifteen jornadas across the mountainous despoblado from the Gila River to Cíbola, placing Vacapa seventeen jornadas south of the Gila. In terms of proportions, then, we might assume the distance from Vacapa to the Gila should be 17/15 or 1.13 times that from the Gila to Zuni. Because the native travel rate on the easier land south of the Gila might average 22 to 25 miles a day instead of the 16 miles a day in the mountains north of the Gila (calculated from the reported fifteen days across the latter 235-trail-mile despoblado [Hallenbeck's reported mileage, 1949: 46]), we can make a correction that the Vacapa-Gila air distance would be 22/16 to 25/16 higher than that, or about 1.6 to 1.8 times the Gila-Zuni air distance. Placing Vacapa at this distance from the Gila, and about 84 to 105 miles inland, puts it in the region from the middle Yaqui River near Sayopa or the upper Mátape River, some 35–80 miles southeast of Ures, to the area on the Sonora River west or east of Ures.

Ures is widely considered to be the approximate location of the town of Corazones, or Hearts, first described by Cabeza de Vaca, and later used as a major camp by Coronado's expedition (compare Hedrick 1978). Important clues about the location of Vacapa come from Cabeza de Vaca's account of Corazones. He says (Pupo-Walker 1993: 104–106) that they reached this area after traveling west seventeen days "through plains and . . . high mountains" and came out in a prosperous region where villages had permanent houses of earth and houses of reed mats; in this area they traveled 100 leagues among well-clothed and well-fed people with earth and mat houses, where they gave him cotton blankets, beads, coral from the coast, turquoises, and five ceremonial "emerald" arrow points traded by them for plumes and parrot feathers, from people to the north who lived in towns with "very large houses."

Cabeza de Vaca's description of Corazones resembles Marcos's description of the beautiful, irrigated valley reached by Marcos two or three days north of Vacapa, where Estevan first met the people who knew of Cíbola. Marcos reports on the first day that he arrived in that valley (the third day after leaving Vacapa) that he encountered many Indians who traded for turquoise and buffalo hides in Cíbola. About five days farther on in this valley Marcos describes the irrigated town where he was given a feast including deer meat. This echoes Cabeza de Vaca's description of his feast of deer hearts at Corazones. Again, the implication is that Vacapa is a few days south of the Corazones/Ures area.

Additional clues come from following the linear sequence of events along the route. The first town Marcos mentions is Petatlán, but he spends little time on its location or any details of its vicinity. As Marcos confirms, this area had been partially abandoned due to the Guzmáns' slave raiding in the early 1530s, and may have been on the Río Sinaloa (Hallenbeck 1949: 49; Reff 1991: 26, 30n). I infer that Marcos's sketchiness about this region, which has puzzled many readers and led to charges of obfuscation, is because the first part of the region was already explored. Riley (1987: 49, 78) notes that Guzmán found Spanish artifacts being traded throughout the Río Sinaloa–Fuerte–Mayo zone as early as 1533, and that the language group was reportedly the same from the Sinaloa to the lower Yaqui Valley. Of the road a few days north of Petatlán Marcos says, "I saw nothing worthy of being placed [in my report]" (Hallenbeck 1949: 16). In Marcos's mind, the account of his adventures begins when he arrives in terra incognita where the Christians were unknown.

Then Marcos tells us he passed over a four-day despoblado, which apparently began some days north of Petatlán. In the country north of the despoblado, beginning three days south of Vacapa, Marcos encountered a new language group and refers to having to work with interpreters, which also suggests that he reached a region north of the lower Yaqui. Here, he says, the natives "had no knowledge of Christians because they have no dealings with those below the despoblado" (Hallenbeck 1949: 17). Three days farther among those people he came to Vacapa. This is the first major town that Marcos identifies or stops at after leaving Petatlán. If Guzmán's men had raided on the lower Yaqui, it seems likely that people all along the Yaqui drainage might have known of the Christians, which might place Vacapa somewhat farther north or in the Mátape valley (about 60 air miles south of Ures/Corazones).

All of this accords with the statements about the limits of Spanish probing in the 1530s. According to different accounts of the Cabeza de Vaca party, either one day or 30 leagues (three to four days) south of Corazones (about 15 to 80 miles), the party encountered an Indian who wore a necklace including a Spanish buckle and nail, the first signs they saw of the Spaniards. The Indian said the artifacts had come from heaven and had been brought by strangers with beards. Thus, one to four days south of Corazones in 1536 was the geographic limit of knowledge of Christians as encountered by Cabeza de Vaca; and three to seven days south of Vacapa was the limit as encountered by Marcos in 1539. The general testimony thus shows that Corazones and Vacapa were within the same general region, perhaps on different drainages, a matter of some days apart, just as in my reconstruction.[3]

Vacapa cannot be at Ures/Corazones itself, because people during Marcos's week-plus stay in Vacapa did not report about Cíbola. The clues so far constrain Vacapa to the middle of the route within a few days in some direction from Ures/Corazones.

Vacapa may even be west of Ures/Corazones since 1) Marcos was trying to stay near the coast (on the Río San Miguel?), 2) Cabeza de Vaca's party came to their Corazones "gateway" from the mountains to the northeast, 3) at Vacapa Marcos realized he was moving away from the coast, and 4) Marcos doesn't mention Corazones, which Estevan (who was with Marcos until Vacapa) would have recognized (having come through it with Cabeza de Vaca). In other words, Marcos and Estevan probably did not pass specifically through Cabeza de Vaca's and Coronado's Corazones, but a day or more on the coastal side of it.

Another independent argument that Vacapa is somewhere near Corazones comes from Castañeda. His narrative jumps about in time and place, but he tells about the founding of the semi-permanent army camp at Corazones, tells about explorations toward the Colorado River by Melchior Díaz, and then returns to the body of the expedition as it leaves Corazones to pursue Coronado and his advance guard (Winship 1990: 111, 113). At this point, he mentions "a province called Vacapan" where soldiers ate the natives' prickly pear preserves and fell sick. Castañeda's next sentence says, "After this they continued their march, until they reached Chichilticale." The story (written years after the events, raising the possibility of some geographic confusion) suggests that Vacapan was connected in Castañeda's mind with the area of Corazones and implies Vacapan was either an area visited by the Spaniards in the vicinity of Corazones or was the first province north of Corazones. While it seems unlikely that Marcos's Vacapa could be north of Corazones, Castañeda's story (written years later) confirms that the name was used near there.

For what it is worth, the natives in the valley of Vacapa called Marcos "Sayota," which he said meant "man from heaven"; the upper Yaqui valley has a village named Soyopa on modern maps, about 65 miles southeast of Ures. "Mátape" itself is a name suggestive of "Vacapa." Bandelier, writing in the 1880s, also chooses the

Mátape Valley, about 40 miles south of Ures, as the best site for Vacapa and says that the original spelling was Matapa, even closer.

To conclude, I am inclined to place Vacapa within a few days of Ures, probably south (on the Río Mátape) and/or west of Corazones. Marcos probably traveled not up the Sonora Valley itself, but a valley to the west, closer to the coast. Vacapa could even have been on the lower Río San Miguel, west of Corazones.

The Problem of the Side Trip to the Head of the Gulf and a Solution

Marcos's claim to have made a side trip to reconnoiter where the Gulf Coast turns west (the north end of the Gulf) has especially troubled historians. A factor in this trouble is the Hemingway syndrome. Both Sauer and Hallenbeck start out by reconstructing a reasonable route from Culiacán to Cíbola, indeed the route that Coronado probably did take. In this view, Marcos headed up the Río Sonora Valley or the Río Bavispe Valley or even farther east. Such reconstructions then fall victim to the Hemingway syndrome; the authors complain mightily that Marcos was too far from the sea to have made the side trip!

The answer is that Marcos followed not Sauer's or Hallenbeck's instructions, but Mendoza's. He stayed a bit farther west on his northward journey, still trying, as he says, to gain information about the seacoast. In fact, contrary to Hallenbeck's complaints, Marcos specifically mentions several times that he felt his mission was to get information about the coast. He mentions explicitly three days south of Vacapa (Hallenbeck 1949: 17) that he will investigate a certain eastward valley only during his return because on the northward journey he is concentrating on the coast and "my instructions are not to depart further from it." In Vacapa, he fretted that he was moving inland, and delayed his trip to send parties out to the coast.

I suggest that Marcos traveled through this region west of Corazones and west of the Coronado expedition's 1540 route, probably traveling up the Río San Miguel (Kino's approach about 160 years later), about 30 miles coastward from the Río Sonora. Marcos might even have traveled up the drainage farther westward, now traversed by railroad from Hermosillo to Benjamin Hill.

Contrary to Mendoza's hopeful speculation that the sea might turn east and provide a route toward the putative northern empire, Marcos learned from natives two valleys north of Vacapa that the coastline turned west. Marcos decided to try to verify this.

As all students of this matter have commented, Marcos's report of his side trip to the west is frustratingly vague, perhaps to gloss over the fact that he could not reach the water's edge in a reasonable amount of time. The Gulf Coast actually turns west in an extraordinarily dry and desolate region bordered in part by the Gran Desierto dune field. Marcos obviously could not explore that region. He is usually said to have reported the latitude where "the coast turns to the west very abruptly" as 35 degrees, but it is actually at about 31.5 degrees. This seems to be a serious error for someone reportedly skilled in navigation, but Cortés's sea captain, Francisco de Ulloa, reported the end of the Gulf to be at 34 degrees and other Spanish latitude measurements of the period also were systematically too high, by an average of a degree (Ives 1975). Interestingly, however, Madeleine Rodack (personal communication 1994) located copies of two original versions of the *Relación* obtained for her in Spain; she points out that while one version appears to say "treinta y cinco" (35), the other clearly reads "treinta y mas," or a little over 30. Coronado, in a letter of August 3, 1540, cites Marcos as having said that "the port of Chichilticale" was at 35 degrees (Hammond and Rey 1940: 165). Chichilticale itself was closer to 33 degrees, but Coronado may have been referring to the head of the Gulf and a corrupted copy of Marcos's *Relación*. If "treinta y mas" was the original wording, and "treinta y cinco" was a scribe's error, then Marcos's measurement is within about a degree of the truth and another charge against Marcos evaporates!

My solution to the problem of Marcos's seaward trip relies on a comment in Kino's diaries. Some 154 years after Marcos, Eusebio Kino was faced with exactly the same problem. Due to the failure of Coronado's expedition, the north country had been forgotten, and knowledge of the north end of the Gulf had been lost. Kino tried to find out, all over again, if the coast turned west. In 1693 and 1694, when Kino was just beginning to work on the problem, natives took him on a trip to the mountains west of Caborca, where they showed him the coastline and told him that it turned west in the distant northwestern haze.

With this bit of history added, the details of Marcos's side trip at last make sense. When Estevan left Vacapa, Marcos instructed him to stay on the westernmost possible route that would still go north toward Cíbola. Perhaps they both ascended the San Miguel; Marcos says he was following Estevan at this point. For about nine or ten days in this valley he encountered turquoises and cow (bison) hides traded from Cíbola and was told of "the grandeur of the land" of Cíbola. At a "fresh, cool . . . irrigated" town the people wore turquoise and cotton and much-prized "cowhides," and they served him the feast of deer meat and other foods, mentioned above, and offered him turquoises, bowls, and other things (Hallenbeck 1949: 23).

Archeological evidence fits either the Sonora or San Miguel river valley. The Sonora Valley was very well populated with irrigated towns, according to archeological evidence (Sauer and Brand 1931; Doolittle 1988), and the San Miguel was so fertile and populated that Kino chose it as his main mission headquarters for the Pimería Alta. Beatrice Braniff C. (1978) gives a preliminary assessment of the San Miguel, indicating the strong role the valley played. Her Map 3 indicates ten missions in post-contact times on the Río Sonora drainage and nine on the slightly shorter length of the San Miguel, suggesting equivalence in native population (Braniff C. 1978: 71).

Marcos then says he crossed a four-day despoblado to a well-populated valley where he got definite news that the coast turned west. He decided to go see it. He had been saying that he was following Estevan's route until this point, but in the passages after the four-day despoblado he does not say so.

In my reconstruction, which differs from most, but follows part of Kino's journey for the same purpose 154 years later, Marcos turned four days west through the hills from the northern San Miguel River and came out on the Río Magdalena between present-day Magdalena and Trincheras. Just as they relayed to Kino, the natives of this area told him that the coast turns west beyond the mouth of that river, and foreshadowing Kino, Marcos spent several days traveling down that well-populated valley toward the mountains west of Caborca, where he could have viewed the coast in the distant haze. Whether he got that far, before being convinced of the Gulf's end, is uncertain, but he at least made a probe to the west. He said he "saw" (became convinced?) that the coast turned west, but even the vaunted Kino stretched the truth by reporting that he could confirm the Gulf's end visually from the top of the Pinacate Mountains. About a week later, Marcos was back on Estevan's path and makes his next mention of encountering messengers from Estevan, possibly along the San Pedro River.

Summary and Speculation on Marcos the Man

This work rebuts half a century of claims that Marcos's reconnaissance of the Cíbola route is obviously impossible because of lack of time and that Marcos is easily exposed as "the lying monk." Historical studies that have branded Marcos a fraud and conspirator in a grand scheme of Mendoza's appear to be flawed. New archeological understanding conforms with Marcos's report of well-established trade routes from Sonora to Cíbola. While we wish that Marcos had added more detail to his *Relación*, the *Relación* does not contain demonstrable falsehoods of consequence. It was ordered by Mendoza as a report on what Marcos learned about the north and the relation of the coastline to possible Cíbola routes; it meets those requirements, albeit sketchily. Much more may have been filled in verbally. A second, missing document, which Marcos said included names of islands and villages west of Vacapa, may also list villages all along the route.

Marcos may have been a somewhat credulous individual, energetic and too willing to base conclusions on what he already believed, and his reporting may have been biased by a greater interest in souls than in geographical or ethnological documentation, but his *Relación* appears to be an earnest attempt to recount his journey.

It is noteworthy that he credits his native informants when he did not observe something personally and he notes that their descriptions of the route ahead always turned out to be true.

Areas of future research, which might clarify Marcos's *Relación* and tie down points on the Marcos/Coronado routes include: 1) determination of the date of Passion Sunday as used by Marcos, to clarify when he reached Vacapa; 2) archeological surveys near Ures and along the Río Sonora to confirm the location of Corazones; 3) interviews with Arizona and Sonora ranchers to gain better information on distribution of artifacts from the Coronado era; 4) inclusion of instructions to look for copper crossbow boltheads and other diagnostic Coronado expedition artifacts during archeological surveys on the Río Sonora, San Pedro River, in the Sulphur Springs Valley, and elsewhere in the area of possible Coronado routes (volunteers instructed to look for Hohokam and other prehistoric material are apt to miss Coronado artifacts during otherwise valuable surveys); 5) excavation at the (fast-disappearing) remains of ruins that might be candidates for the Coronado campsite of Chichilticale; 6) searches in Spanish and Mexican archives for more documents from the Coronado period, specifically Marcos's missing list of islands and villages and the map of the route that Coronado sent with his letter of August 3, 1540, from Cíbola. Confirmation of even a single Coronado camp in Sonora or Arizona would go a long way toward confirming other parts of the routes used in 1539 and 1540 and hence greatly increase the value of the ethnological data included in documents of that period, which in turn would improve our understanding of Native American life in the modern border area 150 years after the Hohokam collapse.

Notes

1. All dates cited here are in Marcos's Julian calendar, not our present calendar.

2. Many critics have him stay more than two weeks in Vacapa, cutting down on his road time. As Madeleine Rodack and I have pointed out at the Gran Quivira Conference in 1995, there is some evidence that the period he cited from Passion Sunday to Easter reflected one week in his calendar, not two as in some modern liturgical calendars, giving him an extra week on the road from Culiacán to Vacapa.

3. Contrast this approach with Sauer/Wagner/Hallenbeck, who place Vacapa well within the area of Guzmán's probing, and then accuse Marcos of lying about his observation that he had reached an area where Indians did not know of the Christians, several days before reaching Vacapa. Sauer (1941: 240) remarks on the "mendacity" of this claim, saying it is "a compound falsehood." Wagner (1934: 204) more charitably attaches a footnote saying, "This was incorrect. Spaniards from Culiacán had passed through this country previously." Hallenbeck (1949: 82) says, "That is a lie, direct and obvious." Instead of manifesting the Hemingway syndrome so petulantly, it seems preferable to accept Marcos's observation and apply it to the problem.

CHAPTER 6

Cíbola, from Fray Marcos to Coronado[1]

MADELEINE TURRELL RODACK

ad it not been for fray Marcos de Niza, the Coronado expedition might never have taken place. Coronado set out for Cíbola only because fray Marcos's report inspired the viceroy to seek more information on that area.

The story of the seven rich cities in the north had been bandied about for some time, especially since the days of Beltrán Nuño de Guzmán, who had heard of these cities from the son of a native trader. Álvar Núñez Cabeza de Vaca, during his long westward odyssey after his shipwreck in Florida, had also heard rumors of their existence. So Viceroy Antonio de Mendoza was motivated to send a scouting party to make an attempt at locating them.

His choice of fray Marcos, already an experienced traveler, accompanied by the black slave Estevan, who had been with Cabeza de Vaca and was presumably familiar with the peoples of the north, was a most intelligent one. So, when Marcos, Estevan, and a large group of Indians set out from San Miguel de Culiacán on March 7, 1539, there were high hopes that the golden cities would be found.

After checking the coast as far as the Río Yaqui, which he most likely followed, along with its northward tributary, the Río Tecoripa, Marcos stopped to celebrate Easter in a town called Vacapa. This may have been in the area of either today's

Suaqui Grande or Tecoripa, forty leagues from the coast, as he says. From there he sent Estevan northward to gather what news he could of the famous cities. Within four days he received word that these cities not only existed, but were well known among the local populations. There were supposedly seven, all under one ruler, and the first was called Cíbola. So the friar set out to join Estevan as quickly as possible.

However, Estevan, feeling his newfound freedom, was impatient and did not wait. Marcos, nevertheless, continued on, gathering Indians who joined him along the way. He was now obviously being led by people who had traveled that road before.

In one village he met a man who even said he was a native of Cíbola. He had fled from there because of some trouble with "the person whom the lord placed there in Cíbola, because that lord of these seven cities lives and has his seat in one of them which is called Ahacus, and in the others he had placed people who govern in his name" (author's translation of Marcos's *Relación*). Let us remember those words later. The man also said that Ahacus was the largest of the villages.

Arriving probably somewhere slightly west of today's Cananea, Marcos, having given up all hope of catching Estevan and traveling light with only part of his retinue, presumably took time out to make a side trip to the west to check stories of a westward turn of the coastline. This he most likely viewed to some degree from the Cerro Alamo near Caborca. Returning to join the bulk of his followers, he probably went up the San Pedro River. Though fray Marcos's route is still generally controversial, after this point it becomes even more so and has considerable bearing on the identity of the village of Cíbola that he saw.

Marcos had been told that just before reaching Cíbola he would enter a *despoblado*, an uninhabited area, which it would take him fifteen days to cross, which he indeed did enter on May 9. Twelve days later he met an Indian from Estevan's group. The man was exhausted and brought him sad news. Estevan, one day away from Cíbola, had sent messengers ahead with a gourd that he carried and a string of rattles and two feathers, one red and one white. This had been his custom when traveling with Cabeza de Vaca, presumably showing that he came in peace, and he was always well received. This time, however, it didn't work. The man "appointed there by the ruler" became angry and said that if Estevan and his companions approached they would all be killed (author's translation). But Estevan ignored this and continued on his way. He and his entourage were intercepted and imprisoned overnight in a house outside the town, stripped of all their possessions, and given neither food nor drink.

The bearer of sad news told Marcos that the next morning he had been thirsty. He managed to slip out of the house to drink at a stream that ran nearby. From there he saw the people of the town chasing Estevan and his followers, shooting arrows at them, and he saw that Estevan and many others were killed. He escaped by going *up the stream* and *crossing it* to join fray Marcos.

Marcos, with great difficulty, persuaded his followers to proceed and they soon encountered several other Indians who confirmed the bad news. They had escaped by playing dead and managed to steal away at nightfall.

Marcos felt, however, that, in spite of all this, he must at least *see* Cíbola, so he convinced two of the chiefs and a few Indians to accompany him. They finally came within sight of the village. Marcos describes it thus in his *Relación*: "It is situated in a flat area at the base of a rounded height. It is a beautiful village, the best that I have seen in these parts. The houses are as they had been described to me by the Indians, all of stone, with terraces and flat roofs, from what I could see from a height where I placed myself to view it" (author's translation). He erected a rough cross where he stood and took possession in the name of the emperor. After which he left in great haste to join his followers and traveled back to report to the viceroy.

The question that becomes apparent is: what village did fray Marcos see? Archeologists and historians all agree that Cíbola was located in the area of present-day Zuni, New Mexico. Vestiges of six pueblos dating from fray Marcos's time do exist there. No seventh has ever been found. But there are certainly six. Which one of them could he have seen?

The four largest pueblos are Hawikuh, about fifteen miles southwest of the present town of Zuni; Halona, practically on the site of Zuni pueblo; Matsaki, a fairly large place east of Zuni near the Zuni River; and Kiakima at the base of Dowa Yalanne, a prominent elevation commonly called Corn Mountain. The other two are much smaller: Ketchipawa, on a high plateau southeast of Hawikuh and invisible from the valley, and Kwakina across the river, about halfway between Hawikuh and Halona. (See Map 2.)

In the 1910s and 1920s the eminent archeologist Frederick W. Hodge conducted extensive excavations at Hawikuh. He came up with the theory that Hawikuh was Marcos's Cíbola, in spite of the fact that Adolph Bandelier, back in the 1880s, had maintained that it was Kiakima. Bandelier was a close friend of Frank Hamilton Cushing, who lived for some time at Zuni and had even become a member of the tribe. While visiting him, Bandelier had explored the area extensively on foot and was thoroughly familiar with the country. But for some reason Hodge's theory caught on, and today many historians and archeologists equate Hawikuh with Cíbola, even using the names interchangeably. Nevertheless, a close examination of the terrain and a study of documents relating to Cíbola point strongly toward Bandelier's theory.

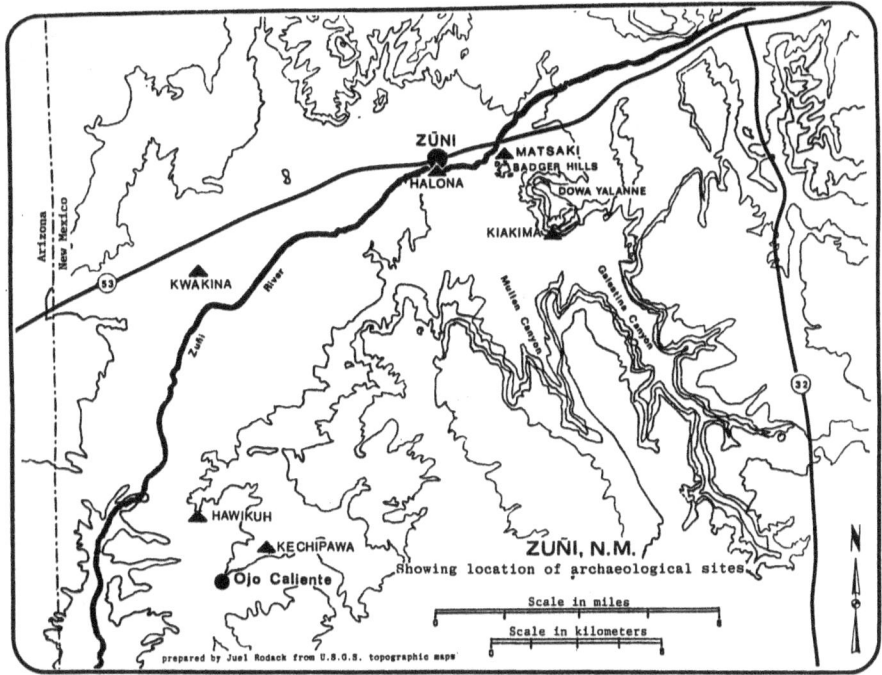

Map 2. Zuni, New Mexico, showing location of archeological sites.

The main clue to Cíbola's location is, of course, fray Marcos's description in his *Relación*. The original Spanish reads *"en un llano a la falda de un cerro redondo"* (AGI 1539). This has usually been translated as "in a plain on the slope of a round hill." It is true that "llano" can mean "plain," but it also indicates merely any level area. "Falda" means "skirt" and implies the lower part of a slope or "near the base." "Redondo" does indeed mean "round" or "rounded." And "cerro" is often equated with a hill. But if dictionaries are consulted it is clear that it is something larger than a mere hill. For example, one dictionary says: "A rise of land of considerable elevation in proportion to its area, steep, of earth or rocks." Another says: "A usually rocky—or craggy—and steep elevation."

In view of this, let us consider Hawikuh. The ruins from fray Marcos's time are on a little ridge that blends so completely into the surrounding country that it is barely visible. They lie on top of the ridge, which is hardly more than sixty feet high. There *are* ruins at the base but they date from other times. It hardly fits Marcos's description.

In addition, if fray Marcos "placed" himself on a height from which to view it and if he came up the Zuni River as Hodge claims, he would have had to cross a

Figure 6.1. Vicinity of Hawikuh, from south. Photo by Juel Rodack.

large wide open area where he could easily be seen from the village. The only real heights are on the far side of Hawikuh, all the way across the valley. He would have had to pass right in front of the pueblo to reach them. North of Hawikuh the land slopes up from the Zuni River and eventually drops off at one end. If he followed that slope he would have been highly visible from the pueblo. Exposing himself in either of these ways would seem unlikely in view of his fear of being seen.

Kiakima, on the other hand, stands on an essentially flat bench at the base of Dowa Yalanne, which appears oval in contour. It is a steep, rocky, craggy elevation over 600 feet high. Thus the ruins are on a mainly level talus near the base of an impressive rounded "cerro."

Fray Marcos was struck by the beauty of the pueblo. The setting of Kiakima is certainly more imposing than that of Hawikuh, which does not have particularly striking surroundings. Approaching from the south, Kiakima is in fact most impressive, almost breathtaking indeed, at certain times of the day. The cliffs of red sandstone rising behind the ruins give an effect, even today, of tall structures that add to the grandeur of the scene.

Let us now return to the Indian who went to the stream to drink. In the case of Hawikuh, this would presumably be the Zuni River, which is at some distance and

Figure 6.2. Ruins of Hawikuh, near ridge, center. Photo by Juel Rodack.

running between high banks at this point. A man drinking in the stream could not have seen what was happening at the village. Of course, Hodge points out, there are irrigation canals in the neighborhood of Hawikuh. These were indeed mentioned by Diego Pérez de Luxán who visited the area with Antonio de Espejo in 1583. They are still there. However, whether drinking at the canals or at the river, the man would eventually have had to follow the river *downstream* rather than *up* to join Marcos.

But did Marcos come up the Zuni River? There are many approaches to Zuni. He could have come from the south. From the San Pedro River he could have traveled eastward, crossing the Gila near Clifton at the present Arizona–New Mexico line, and proceeded directly north, led by Indians who had joined him along the way and who knew the route. This would take him through a mountainous area that might well have been a despoblado since the villages tended to cluster in the valleys and open agricultural areas. He would then reach the high rolling country cut by canyons that descend directly to Zuni. There are two such canyons: Galestina Canyon and Mullen or, as the local people call it, Pié Canyon. My husband Juel and I received permits from the Zuni authorities to explore this area on foot and did so on more than one occasion. We never had the opportunity to go all the

Figure 6.3. Dowa Yalanne from Mullen Canyon. Photo by Juel Rodack.

way to the very tip of Galestina from below, but the country above indicates that there may well be a possible approach from there. The exit from Galestina, however, approaches Kiakima from a side perspective and the village, from that angle, would probably not have been as full or appeared as impressive as in Marcos's description, unless he traveled a long risky distance along the cliffs opposite in order to view it directly. This approach seems unlikely since, again, it would make him more visible.

Mullen (Pié) Canyon, however, is a much better candidate. There is a trail going through it that is used by the Zuni today to reach the high country. The canyon has springs in it, pools, and a stream that runs through it. Even if Coronado came this way later with his horses, he would have had no problem. The descent is relatively easy and at the bottom Marcos would have had a direct view of Dowa Yalanne with Kiakima on a rise at its base.

Marcos says he viewed the pueblo from a height. The high country from which the canyon descends forms an arc out from the canyon's mouth and curves away opposite the village. Marcos could have followed around to his right in the shelter of these heights and climbed the ridge directly opposite the pueblo from behind. From there he could easily view it, believing that he had not been seen. Of course,

Figure 6.4. Kiakima, center base of Dowa Yalanne. Photo by Juel Rodack.

it is most likely that he *was* seen. The Indians surely were on the lookout after Estevan's arrival, but they were not basically a warlike people and Marcos, with his handful of followers, posed no threat. There was no real need to attack him if he did not approach. So they observed his movements closely and simply let him go.

The stream from Mullen Canyon joins a stream from Galestina Canyon in the valley at a point just below the village. The area is now silted over, but we know that things were much more humid in those days and there was more water in the rivers. The thirsty Indian would indeed have had to go *upstream* and cross over it, as he says, to go through Mullen Canyon to the despoblado where fray Marcos was. The trail in the canyon today is in fact on the far side.

One other argument in favor of Kiakima is Zuni tradition. A story reported by Cushing states that in the days of their ancestors, the Zuni said, "when roofs lay over the walls of Kiakimé, when smoke hung over the housetops and the ladder rounds were still unbroken . . . one day, unexpectedly, out of Hemlock Canyon [the Black Mexicans] came, and descended to Kiakimé." Their ancestors, they said, chased the intruders, throwing their war clubs, killing many, and it was then that "the black Mexican, a large man with Chilli lips, was killed right where the stone stands down by the arroyo of Kiakimé" (Cushing 1979: 174).

I have not yet found anyone in Zuni today who can identify Hemlock Canyon by name, though they agree that it could well be Mullen. There is, however, a plant called "aconitum" related to the hemlock that grows on the slopes throughout the area. It is a flat weedlike plant, barely noticeable, but at some point in history it may have provided a local name for the canyon.

The arroyo of Kiakima is now crossed by the tribal road that runs through the valley. At that point lies an extremely large "stone." It no longer stands because the stream banks have eroded away and it has fallen over or perhaps the building of the road dislodged it, but it is still there. When we visited the area a wrecked car had crashed against it. Though not very picturesque, it gave some idea of dimension. So there lies the stone still today, larger than a car, and undoubtedly a landmark when it was standing erect high on the bank above.

Hodge deprecates this story by saying that nobody can believe Indian traditions. He cites others, sometimes incorrectly, trying to show that they are unbelievable. However, this is Zuni oral history and there is no reason to disbelieve it simply because it is often expressed in more imaginative terms than our more straightforward attempts to record our history. It certainly should not be brushed aside in such a cavalier manner as does Hodge. Incidentally, note that the black Mexicans "descended" to Kiakimé. It would be hard to descend to anywhere if Marcos came up the Zuni River.

Finally, let us go back to the man from Cíbola whom fray Marcos had met along the way. This man mentioned that he was fleeing from the lord whom the ruler had placed to represent him in Cíbola. He also said that the ruler lived in Ahacus—hence not in Cíbola. Now Hodge, who insists upon equating Cíbola with Hawikuh, also says that Ahacus was Hawikuh. But, if the ruler lived in Ahacus, hence Hawikuh, and placed a representative in Cíbola, then Cíbola could not have been Hawikuh. Remember, too, that the chief who became so angry when he saw Estevan's gourd was, according to the Indian who escaped, the man whom the ruler had placed there to represent him. It was not the main village.

There are other arguments in favor of Kiakima, but it is not possible here to analyze them all. Suffice it to say that Hodge's theory of Hawikuh does not fit the facts and should not be so readily accepted in spite of Hodge's importance as an eminent archeologist. So I submit that not Hawikuh, on top of a low ridge, but Kiakima, near the base of an impressive cerro, was the village that fray Marcos saw.

But what about Coronado? It has generally been assumed that he approached the same way as fray Marcos and visited the same village that he described. However, in spite of references to Marcos leading him, Coronado was probably led in fact by local Indians as Marcos had been. A change of route might indeed seem quite logical since he had horses and much livestock with him. Fray Marcos was entirely on foot and had no animals. Coronado quite likely followed river valleys when he could, and might well have come up the Zuni River, in which case he would indeed have come upon Hawikuh first. However, the approach from Mullen Canyon would not have been impossible for him since it is not steep. And the route through the mountains along the New Mexico–Arizona line would have hardly been more rugged than negotiating the Salt River Canyon or the Mogollon Rim, as some theories claim he did.

Let us consider the available evidence. First, let us assume that Coronado did go up the Zuni River and stopped at Hawikuh. This would indeed account for his complaint, in a letter to the viceroy, that nothing is like what fray Marcos described (Hammond and Rey 1940: 170). But, if that is so, we might have expected Marcos to defend himself by pointing out that it was not the same place. Of course, perhaps he did, but the reports we have come from Coronado and his men who were definitely prejudiced against Marcos and might not have reported his protests. Thus, it is not impossible that they were in fact at Hawikuh.

Another possible argument on the Hawikuh side of the roster is the statement by Francisco de Escobar, who visited the area with Juan de Oñate in 1604. He says categorically that the main pueblo was called Sibola by the Spaniards and Havico by the Indians (Hammond and Rey 1953: 1014). But please note that, by 1604, the other pueblos were falling into decay and had become less important. Escobar himself goes on to say that all the others together by that time had a total of less than 300 houses (ibid.). So it is quite possible that the group name "Cíbola" had become attached in the Spaniards' minds to the then main village, which by that time was quite likely Hawikuh. However, when all villages were active it might still have been Kiakima!

The strongest argument in favor of Hawikuh is perhaps the mention in the *Traslado de las Nuevas* of Coronado's four-league trip to "see a rock where the Indians were wont to fortify themselves" (Hammond and Rey 1940: 181). This rock would seem offhand to be Dowa Yalanne. However, this is an area of "rocks," of isolated mesas and prominent points. Dowa Yalanne is not alone. Nevertheless it is one of the most impressive. If this were the rock, however, Coronado would not have had to travel four leagues to see it if he was already at Kiakima at its base.

However, on the other side of the coin, another hard-to-contest argument is that Coronado mentions in a long letter to the viceroy that a town "nearby" was "somewhat larger than this," and another "about the same size" (Hammond and Rey 1940: 171). There is only one town near Hawikuh, Kechipawa, which was one of the smallest. However, near Kiakima is Matsaki, which *was* larger, and Halona, which might have been close to a similar size.

Coronado called the place "Granada" in honor of the viceroy's birthplace, but also because it resembled the Albaicín, a district of that city in Spain. Nothing, however, could resemble the Spanish city less than Hawikuh. Spanish Granada is in mountainous country, with actual cliffs in the Albaicín district. The cliffs of Kiakima resemble it much more. This would seem to favor Kiakima!

Coronado and Pedro de Castañeda, Coronado's unofficial chronicler, seem to disagree as to the nature of the terrain. Coronado states that "the country is all level and nowhere shut in by high mountains" (Hammond and Rey 1940: 172). Whereas Castañeda, who was with him, says that the area was "a valley between sierras that rise like boulders" (Hammond and Rey 1940: 252). Hawikuh might fit Coronado's description, though he says "country" and might have been referring to the area in general. He did, in fact, once describe Cíbola as "a group of towns." However Castañeda's description fits Kiakima perfectly and could not possibly describe Hawikuh.

Finally, Coronado mentions in one of his letters to the viceroy that Estevan was "killed here" (Hammond and Rey 1940: 177). This would seem to imply that he was at the same place as Marcos. Thus, if Estevan was killed "where the stone stands at the arroyo of Kiakimé—if you accept Zuni oral history, or Cushing's reporting of it—this would mean Coronado was at Kiakima. However, Coronado may only have meant that Estevan was killed in the general area.

There are other references that could apply to either pueblo and so aren't really very helpful:

Coronado mentions a nearby spring. Both villages have one.

Coronado mentions good grass and pasture a quarter of a league away. This exists at both villages.

Luxán, with the Espejo expedition, states that a book and trunk left by Coronado were found "here." But no specific town is mentioned and we cannot be sure which town Espejo was in. He himself speaks of Cíbola as a "province," which he said was called "Zuni or Cíbola" (Hammond and Rey 1966: 183–184). So it could be either.

So, to sum up, where does that leave us? Probably not far from where we started, with questions still unanswered. We still have little to go on that is positive. However, in the case of fray Marcos, his description so perfectly fits Kiakima and his approach is so probable and demonstrable, that it is almost impossible to accept the theory of Hawikuh. In Coronado's case the facts are admittedly less clear, though there is no absolute reason to assume that he was at Hawikuh. Some points seem in Kiakima's favor.

Again, there are a number of other considerations pro and con, but a complete analysis would go beyond the space available here. Hopefully new documents will someday be discovered. More archeological work is definitely needed. Little major excavation has been conducted in the area since Hodge's day. As with most other theories relating to Coronado's route, much is inconclusive. However, it is clearly wrong to categorically equate Cíbola with Hawikuh based on the evidence presently available. To perpetuate this as an established fact is historically incorrect.

So, in the last analysis, we must accept the fact that the Coronado route as a whole, including the identity of Coronado's Cíbola, cannot yet be positively established. However, the clues must still be examined even more closely. Continued consultation and discussion between scholars can be most useful, and possibly that needed piece of the jigsaw discovered by one may fit with another discovery and hopefully lead to more definite conclusions.

Note

1. An earlier version of this chapter appeared in 1983 as "Cíbola Revisited" in *Southwestern Culture History: Papers in Honor of Albert H. Schroeder*, Anthropological Papers No. 10, The Archaeological Society of New Mexico, Albuquerque. Portions of it are reprinted here by the kind permission of the Society's Publication Committee.

CHAPTER 7

The Search for Coronado's Contemporary
The Discovery, Excavation, and Interpretation of Hernando de Soto's First Winter Encampment

CHARLES R. EWEN

Introduction

nhaica Apalache, the Indian village that housed the army of Hernando de Soto during the winter of 1539–1540, has long been sought by archeologists and historians researching that ill-fated expedition. As is so often the case in archeology, the actual discovery of this site was a fortuitous accident. Thus, the finding of the site required little effort on our part. Demonstrating the association with the De Soto expedition proved to be far more challenging. To fully appreciate the discovery, it is essential to understand the importance of this site to those researching the De Soto entrada, in particular, and the contact period in general.

Four hundred and fifty years after the De Soto and Coronado expeditions through the southern United States, the importance of these events needs to be reevaluated. Are we merely interested in where the conquistadors went? Is the purpose of our research to validate the historic claims of assorted municipalities and roadside attractions? Surely not, though it is often easy to lose sight of our true goals.

For many scholars in the Southeast, tracing the route of De Soto transcends the desires of local chambers of commerce or the placement of historic markers along highways. A statement of the real importance of this research was published more than a decade ago.

> ... an accurate reconstruction of the route will enable us to advance greatly our understanding of the aboriginal people of the Southeast. It will provide archeologists with more chronological precision than they now possess, and this will allow them to do more precise descriptive and comparative work.... Moreover, by combining the information in the De Soto documents with archeological information, we can gain at least some insight into the internal structure of the Southeastern chiefdoms, as well as some understanding of the kinds of relationships which existed between chiefdoms (Hudson et al. 1984: 75).

The situation is analogous to NASA's moon program, for which the destination was actually secondary to the trip itself. It is what was learned along the way that ultimately proved to be really important. The hoopla of events such as the Columbus Quincentenary makes this easy to forget.

While many individuals have been involved in contact period research for much of their academic careers, many more have recently jumped on the bandwagon. This is not necessarily a bad thing, as long as studies of the sensational aspects of the Discovery and its consequences don't preclude serious inquiry into the day-to-day activities of the average individual among both the native groups and the Europeans. This was certainly our intent at the De Soto winter encampment site. The De Soto saga served as the "hook" that caught both the popular and scholarly attention, and while they were funding that research we painlessly gathered information about the local residents at the time of contact. A brief synopsis of De Soto's expedition to La Florida will put the archeological investigation in its proper context.

Historical Background

Hernando de Soto was born in 1500 in the Extremadura region of western Spain. Born the second son of noble parents, De Soto shipped out at an early age to seek his fortune in the New World. There he demonstrated a keen military sense and diplomatic ability and quickly rose through the ranks. So successful was he, that by the age of thirty-one he had become one of the chief lieutenants of Francisco Pizarro and was a key figure in the conquest of the Inca empire. His efforts in Peru brought him wealth equivalent to several hundred thousand dollars (Varner and Varner 1980: 4n), but not complete satisfaction.

De Soto desired hereditary titles and estates. Pizarro was justly wary of this valuable, but exceedingly ambitious man. After the conquest of the Inca, De Soto quickly surmised that he would not receive an important appointment in Pizarro's administration and turned his attention elsewhere, while he still had a head to do so. He petitioned the crown for lands to govern in either South or Central America but was denied. The king had other plans for De Soto as is evident from this royal letter dated April 20, 1537.

> Inasmuch as you, Captain Hernando de Soto, set forth that you have served us in the conquest, pacification, and settlement of the Provinces of Nicaragua and Peru, and other parts of our lands; and that now to serve us further, and to continue to enlarge our patrimony and the royal crown, you desire to return to those our Indias to conquer and settle [from] the Province of Río de las Palmas to Florida, the government whereof was bestowed on Pánfilo de Narváez, and the Provinces of Tierra-Nueva, the discovery and government of which was conferred on Lucas Vázquez de Ayllón . . . I bestow on you the conquest of those lands and provinces . . . (Swanton 1985: 76).

The offer was readily accepted. Álvar Núñez Cabeza de Vaca, one of four survivors of the Narváez expedition, was approached to serve as guide. Not surprisingly, he could not be persuaded to join the new undertaking. Undaunted, De Soto assembled the youngest, best equipped, and most disciplined army to sail to the New World.

The expedition set sail from its staging point at Havana, Cuba, on May 18, 1539, and made landfall off the west coast of Florida a week later. By the end of the month, the Spaniards and their supplies were being off-loaded, presumably in the vicinity of Tampa Bay (Jerald Milanich, personal communication). Besides more than 600 men and two Spanish women, the expedition included over 200 horses, a herd of swine, a couple of mules, and specially trained attack dogs (probably greyhounds and/or mastiffs).

De Soto established a base camp and left a force of about a hundred men to hold it. Meanwhile he and the body of his expedition marched inland and then turned north. They were able to maintain a good pace despite the difficult terrain and hostile native encounters. In the area around the town of Cale (in north central Florida) two Indians were captured. "One told the governor that seven days away by trail there was a very large province of much more maize that was called Apalachee . . ." (Hann 1988d: 13). De Soto set out in search of it with part of his force.

By the first of October, De Soto was at the Aucilla River, which marked the eastern boundary of the Apalachee Province. He met some resistance there, but when the Apalachee saw that they could not prevent the Spanish crossing they fell back. The Spaniards advanced and found the town of Ivitachuco in flames. Pressing on, they reached the principal village of the Apalachee Province, Anhaica Apalache, on October 6.

The village had been abandoned and so "the field master, whose duty it [was] to assign and provide lodging, lodged everyone round about this settlement" (Hann

1988d: 21). Garcilaso de la Vega (Varner and Varner 1980: 184) describes the village as "consisting of two hundred and fifty large and good houses." De Soto, himself, moved into the cacique's residences, "which were located on one side of the town and as royal dwellings had advantages over all the others" (ibid). It was at this point that De Soto decided that his company needed to stop, reconsolidate its forces, and plan where to go next. Again, Garcilaso de la Vega provides the fullest description.

> Having noted that cold weather was setting in, since it was already October, he felt it wise to discontinue his exploration for the year and to winter in the province of Apalachee where provisions were abundant. . . . With such ideas in mind, he ordered his men to collect all possible supplies and build many new houses in addition to those that the town already afforded, so that there might be comfortable quarters for his entire army. And then for greater security, he had the place fortified to the extent that he felt was necessary (Varner and Varner 1980: 193–194).

De Soto and his men hoped to rest and recover their strength before pressing on after the riches they were sure must lie before them.

The time spent at the winter encampment was anything but restful. For nearly five months the occupiers were besieged at Anhaica. Infuriated over the loss of their village, the Apalachee harassed the Spaniards at every opportunity. According to De Soto's private secretary, Rodrigo Ranjel, "they burned the settlement on two occasions and they killed many Christians with ambushes on some occasions. And although the Spaniards pursued them and burned them, they never showed any desire to come to peace" (Hann 1988c: 11). In short, no one left the camp alone or unarmed. The first Christmas mass celebrated in La Florida could not have been very festive.

By the following spring, the Spaniards were ready to move on. Reports of gold to the north gave the expedition a direction in which to travel.

> Wednesday, on the third of March of 1540, the governor set out from Anhaica Apalache in search of Yupaha [the reputed location of much gold]. He ordered that all his [men] should be provided with maize for sixty leagues of uninhabited territory. The horsemen carried their maize on their horses and those on foot on their backs because the Indians he had for work, most had died with the hard life that they had endured that winter, naked in chains (Hann 1988d: 25).

The campaign would eventually claim the lives of half the expedition and its leader, Hernando de Soto. Three years later, the battered remnants limped into a Spanish outpost in northern Mexico.

Archeological Background

SEARCH FOR ANHAICA

Anhaica Apalache did not cease to exist when De Soto's reduced force decamped in March 1540. The Apalachee returned to re-occupy their violated homes, while the Spaniards marched to their fate. When Spanish missionaries returned nearly a century later, they encountered a community of such importance that they founded a mission in its midst, San Luis de Xinyaca (Hann 1989: 78–80). In 1656, the mission was relocated approximately five miles to the west and Anhaica faded from memory.

The site of Hernando de Soto's first winter encampment has been sought by cartographers, historians, and archeologists for many years. Since the pioneering attempts of Guillaume de l'Isle in 1718, researchers have pursued a variety of alternative routes. The evidence, however, has been very meager with very little agreement between scholars on any spot along De Soto's itinerary.

John R. Swanton chaired the United States De Soto Expedition Commission, which produced the first systematic study of the route in 1939. Based on geographic descriptions of De Soto's chroniclers and the distances that they reported traveling from place to place, Swanton placed the location of Anhaica in the Tallahassee area.

> The position of Iniahica [Anhaica] is fixed with reasonable accuracy by estimating the distance from the Aucilla River probably covered in two days' march. We should expect this to be not less than 20 nor more than 40 miles, and the distance from the Aucilla River to Tallahassee is, in fact, about 31 miles, which is not much greater than the distance in leagues given by Garcilaso, about 11 leagues or 28.6 miles. The country around Tallahassee is indicated clearly though the exact spot may have been on the site of Tallahassee itself, at the site of the later mission of San Luis de Talimali slightly west of Tallahassee or the mound group on Lake Jackson somewhat to the north. Judging by the distance to the sea . . . one of the first two sites is the most likely, and Tallahassee has more remains of the aborigines while the location of San Luis suggests that it was selected by the Spaniards with an eye to its defense (Swanton 1985: 158).

Despite the certitude of all researchers that the first winter encampment was located in Tallahassee, no trace of the site was recognized, even after a century of urban development and land clearing.

The next serious attempt to locate Anhaica was made by Louis Tesar during the bicentennial archeological survey of Leon County. Building on Swanton's rather vague parameters, Tesar reexamined the documentary and cartographic evidence and attempted to reconcile this information with known archeological sites. Tesar (1980: 301–304) rejected the suggestion that the Lake Jackson mound group was the site, noting that the chroniclers' diaries mention neither the mounds nor the large lake in their description of the village. He also recognized that excavations at Lake Jackson produced no sixteenth-century Spanish artifacts. He rejected the San Luis mission site west of Tallahassee on the same grounds. Of Swanton's earlier candidates, this left the city of Tallahassee itself, which Tesar attempted to more closely define.

An important clue to the search neglected by previous researchers was a description of how the site of Anhaica should appear in the archeological records. Tesar (1980: 303) presumed, based on the documentary record, that

> division of the village into identifiable sections is characteristic of large Apalachee villages. . . . In this respect, it is noted that the results of the Leon County Survey indicated that possible simultaneous occupation of several adjacent finger ridges [occurred] in the Tallahassee Red Clay Hills area in the northern half of the county. If such an interpretation is correct, then the dwelling sites on these ridges should be considered as part of a single dispersed village with each ridge serving to divide the whole into apparent parts.

This distinction is important since separate, but adjacent, ridgetops are usually assigned separate site numbers. Such assignments would mislead scholars using the site files and make the delineation of a large site such as Anhaica difficult.

At the time he wrote, Tesar knew of no site that fit the criteria for Anhaica. He believed he could, however, narrow the area where the site was likely to be located. Based on the De Soto chroniclers' narratives and location of known historic trails, Tesar (1980: 345–346) felt that "the most likely area for the De Soto wintering site was in the area north of Lake Lafayette, east of Lake Jackson, and south of Lake Iamonia." In fact, this area is very close to where Anhaica was later discovered.

Jeffrey Brain of the Peabody Museum examined the evidence that had accumulated up to 1981 and tentatively placed the site near Lake Lafayette. He noted optimistically that although the site had not yet been found, the chances for discovery were good. He stated:

> the possibilities are fairly well circumscribed and within the scope of a realistic program of archaeological research. Furthermore, the stay was a lengthy one by the entire army, and many buildings and fortifications were constructed that should be manifest in architectural features contrasting with native constructions. Finally, only in its first year, the army was still well accoutered and recently resupplied from its base camp at the landing. It might be expected that discarded artifacts would be relatively abundant compared to subsequent stages of the journey (Swanton 1985: xxiii).

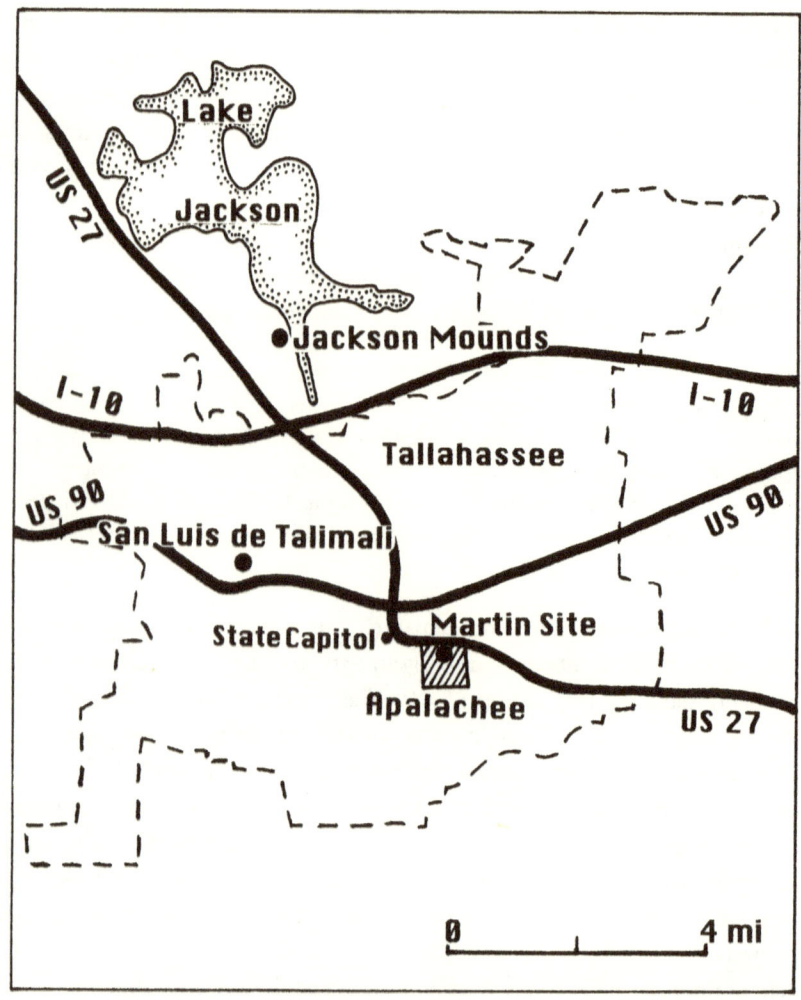

Map 3. Approximate area of sixteenth-century Apalachee.

Such was the state of the search for Anhaica in the middle of the 1980s. The parameters of the search were suggested as well as certain criteria against which all claimants would be judged.

The next player in the De Soto drama was B. Calvin Jones, an archeologist with the Florida Bureau of Archaeological Research. Jones had been conducting research on the Florida mission system for two decades. He had discovered the sites of possibly nine of these missions (Jones and Shapiro 1987). On March 11, 1987, he thought he had another to add to the list.

Jones had suspected for some time, based on historic documents, that a mission had existed on a ridge nearly a mile east of the capitol building. However, since the property was located in an old, residential neighborhood, there seemed to be no opportunity to test this hypothesis. The situation changed dramatically in early 1987 when construction began on an office complex on the ridge in which he was interested. Jones, after examining the area disturbed by bulldozers, asked the developers if he could put in a couple of test excavations. Fortunately (or foolishly, depending on your perspective) they agreed.

The first pit revealed Spanish olive jar sherds, leading Jones to believe that the mission he sought had been located. But this exciting discovery created the first of a series of dilemmas. There was no money in the budget of the Bureau of Archaeological Research to mount a large, unanticipated field project. Further, the site was threatened with imminent destruction through development activity. Negotiations with the developers resulted in a two-week delay in construction, allowing Jones to hastily assemble a crew of volunteers to conduct salvage excavations.

Mobilizing the volunteers, Jones was able to open several units and recover an impressive array of artifacts. The material assemblage was puzzling, though. The artifacts recovered tended to predate the seventeenth century, and the tin-glazed Spanish majolicas and the aboriginal ceramic types that characterize Spanish missions in north Florida were largely missing from the collection. The aboriginal ceramics that were found tended to immediately predate the Mission Period (1635–1704). It became apparent that the site (named the Martin Site) represented Spanish contact prior to the seventeenth century.

The possibility that the Martin Site might be associated with De Soto inflamed the interest of the local community and caused the Bureau of Archaeological Research to reassess the situation. The first requirement was confirmation of the site's significance before announcing the discovery of the long-sought site of Hernando de Soto's first winter camp. To this end, a professional archeological crew was brought over from a nearby project, on an interim basis, to assist in the excavations. By the end of April, the Bureau managed to acquire limited funding and a delay in construction to allow the excavations to continue. I had just received my Ph.D. from the University of Florida (I graduated on a Saturday and started work on Monday) and joined the project at this time as codirector.

The project remained in the field until late December 1987, stretching the budget and the patience of the developers to the limit. The Institute for Early Contact Period Studies of the University of Florida provided the majority of the funding through its contracts with the Florida Department of Natural Resources, though a great many other individuals and businesses contributed to the effort. One of the most gratifying parts of the excavation was the cooperation of the developers. Initially, the Tallahassee Development Corporation and Mad Dog Design and Construction agreed to only a two-week delay in construction to allow some salvage archeology to be done. This eventually expanded into a full-scale excavation lasting eight months. Throughout all the inconvenience and aggravation, the developers demonstrated extraordinary cooperation and contributed greatly to the preservation of the site. The additional field time allowed the recovery of evidence confirming the site's association with De Soto.

The Evidence for Anhaica

The Hypothesis

When a professional crew was hired to conduct the excavations at the Martin Site the working hypothesis was that this was the site of the first winter encampment of De Soto's expedition. Thus, the primary goal of this project was to test that hypothesis. Clearly there was early Spanish material at the site, but could it be definitively tied to De Soto? There was the possibility that these artifacts might represent other early contact: material recovered from shipwrecks, evidence of the 1528 Narváez expedition, or an altogether unrecorded Spanish presence. To rule these alternatives out, it was necessary to define what evidence would be needed to test the hypothesis.

The documentary evidence, if the hypothesis were true, should not contradict the characteristics of the site's location. That is, if the narratives had mentioned that Anhaica was in the midst of a mangrove swamp on the banks of a major river (which they did not), then this would have tended to negate the Martin Site's identification as Anhaica. The documents were also used to determine what physical evidence of the expedition might appear in the archeological record.

Artifacts are an obvious and important category of evidence but they must be used judiciously. The presence of a sixteenth-century Spanish artifact on a site does not necessarily mean that De Soto slept there. Beads, coins, tools, and other objects are very portable items that could easily have been carried far from their original point of deposition. A good indication of a Spanish encampment would be large numbers of sixteenth-century artifacts in contexts that suggest loss or disposal rather than ritualistic burial of a prized item. Also, in the case of the Martin Site, generic sixteenth-century artifacts do not distinguish a Narváez site (1528) from a De Soto site (1539–1540). The artifacts must have a tightly dated *terminus post quem* (coins, for example) or be peculiar to the De Soto expedition.

The artifact assemblage should be predominantly aboriginal and these aboriginal artifacts should date to the early sixteenth century. The Spaniards spent less than six months in this populous Apalachee village so it is unlikely that their impact on the total artifact assemblage would have been very great.

The Search for Coronado's Contemporary

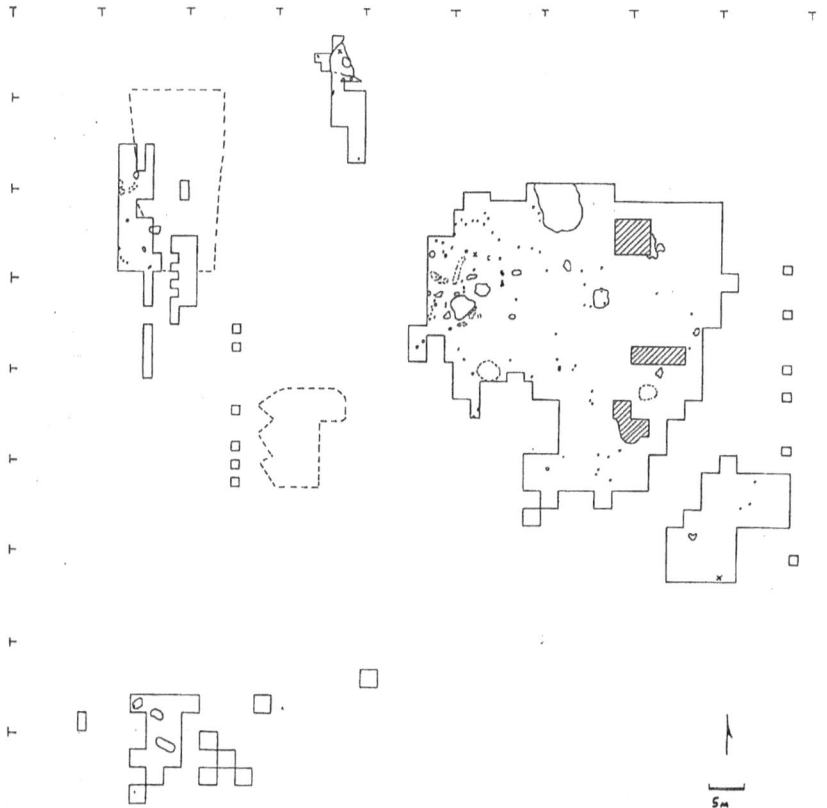

Figure 7.1. *The Martin Site excavations.*

Finally there is the village itself. It is described as a large village of over 250 houses which the Spaniards expanded and fortified in some way (Varner and Varner 1980: 184, 193–194). The Martin Site would have to be a part of a large Apalachee village to qualify as the site of Anhaica. Evidence of European building techniques (sawn timbers, nails, anomalous floorplans) amongst the aboriginal structures would constitute solid evidence for the De Soto encampment. So, how does the Martin Site shape up?

The Tests

Aboriginal artifacts account for 90 percent of the material assemblage. The majority of the ceramics recovered are late Fort Walton types (A.D. 1450–1633) including: Lake Jackson Plain, several varieties of Fort Walton Incised, and a punctated variety that appears to be unique to the site. The aboriginal assemblage is what one would expect with the interpretation of the site as being part of Anhaica.

Spanish ceramics at the site consist mainly of olive jar fragments. Ubiquitous to Spanish sites in Florida and the Caribbean, the utilitarian olive jar can be distinguished chronologically on the basis of rim type and vessel form. Identifiable rim fragments from the Martin Site can be classified as the Early type with date ranges of A.D. 1490–1650. Also recovered were such sixteenth-century majolica types as Columbia Plain (A.D. 1492–1650), including a pre-1550 green variant, and Caparra Blue (A.D. 1492–1600).

Beads of European manufacture have been one of the primary tools for tracking the route of De Soto through the Southeast. A faceted amber bead, a dozen faceted chevron beads, and a single Nueva Cadiz bead recovered at the Martin Site are good sixteenth-century marker artifacts. All of the abovementioned bead types have been found at other sites thought to be associated with the De Soto expedition. Several blown glass beads were recovered from the Martin Site. These were difficult to date with any certainty and may in fact be modern. However, a bead of similar manufacture was found at the Poarch Farm Site in northern Georgia, which has also been associated with the De Soto expedition.

Iron artifacts make up a significant portion of the European items in the Martin Site assemblage. Dozens of wrought nails of various sizes and types are present in the material assemblage. One unusual type has also been reported from a site in New Mexico possibly associated with the Coronado expedition (LA 54147). (See Chapter 16.) A crossbow quarrel is the only example of sixteenth-century weaponry recovered. The crossbow was the principal weapon of De Soto's expeditionary force, but had become obsolete when Spain returned to the panhandle in the seventeenth century. Another example of military hardware, but in a defensive class, were the many pieces of chain mail armor. Initially the fragments of twisted iron wire were difficult to identify. The function of these links became clear when a corroded patch of interconnected links was found. A chronicler of the De Soto expedition related that the Spaniards discovered, during their time in the Apalachee territory, that their mail was incapable of stopping arrows and so was "thrown aside" (Varner and Varner 1980: 236).

The most exciting artifacts in terms of popular appeal and as a chronological tool were five copper coins. These were found scattered across the site and appear to have been deposited as a result of loss. Two of the coins were Spanish maravedis; the other three were badly corroded but appear to be Portuguese *ceitils*. All the coins date to the early sixteenth century, though one of the ceitils may be even earlier. They were coins of little worth to the Spaniards of that time and so may have been brought along incidentally or as trade items.

All of these items place the site in the early sixteenth century, but could not distinguish between the expedition of Pánfilo de Narváez in 1528 and that of

Hernando de Soto eleven years later. True, the documents associated with the expeditions place Narváez closer to the coast than the Martin Site (compare Hann 1988b), but these descriptions are sketchy at best. The blown glass beads that had also been reported from other parts of the route of De Soto were found in disturbed contexts and may not be of a sixteenth-century type after all. Fortunately, just before the close of the 1987 field season, a discovery of a unique item strengthened the claims that the site was the De Soto encampment.

The shattered maxilla of a pig was unearthed during the excavation of one of the sixteenth-century structures. (See Figure 7.2.) This is significant because it is recorded that a herd of swine accompanied the De Soto expedition. There is no record of pigs on the earlier Narváez expedition. While Narváez was in the Apalachee Province, he and his men were reduced to eating their horses (Hann 1988b: 18). De Soto, determined not to share the same fate as his predecessor, brought along a herd of live pigs to accompany the entrada. In fact, it was De Soto who introduced pigs to the Southeast.

The chronicles associated with the expedition describe the site of the first winter encampment as being in the principal Apalachee village of Anhaica. Given the hierarchical settlement pattern of the Apalachee, one would expect large villages to be widely spaced geographically with intervening areas occupied by smaller hamlets or individual farmsteads (Scarry 1994: 160). A survey of properties surrounding the Martin Site confirmed that it is part of a large Late Fort Walton Indian village (Ewen 1989b). There are no other sites that qualify as far as size, location, and chronological association for identification as Anhaica.

Summary and Conclusions

A great deal of time and effort by a great many concerned parties went into the work at the Martin Site. Donated time and materials, by both professionals and amateurs alike, far exceeded that which was actually paid for out of the project's meager budget. Was it all worth it? What qualities does the Martin Site possess that made its excavation imperative?

The significance of the Martin Site has been widely recognized. A century of searching for the first winter encampment was finally successful, even if accomplished by accident. The *New York Times* (May 19, 1987) referred to the discovery as 'the crowning achievement of recent scholarly efforts to determine more precisely the route of the De Soto expedition." The late Gary Shapiro, looking at the site from a different perspective, felt that it "opened the door to a new understanding of the Apalachee and many other native cultures that have long since vanished" (1988). Actually, the Martin Site is significant for both these and a number of other reasons.

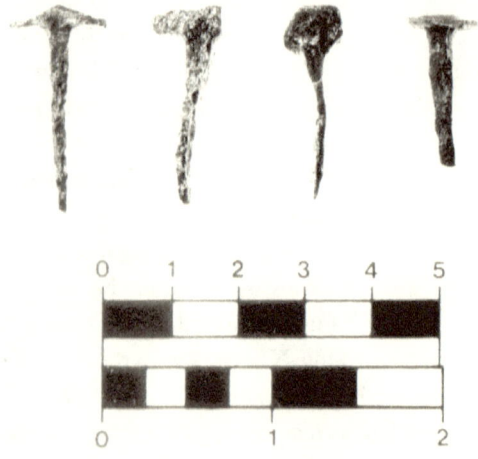

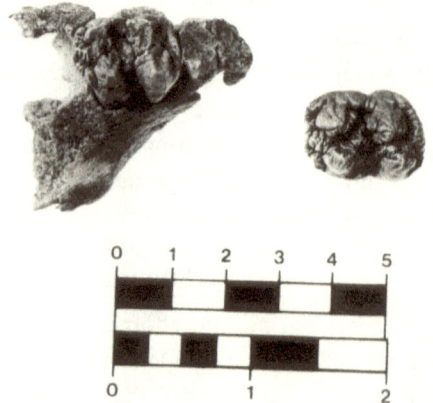

Figure 7.2. Objects from the Martin Site: nails, pig maxilla and teeth, and indigenous ceramics (next page). Photo courtesy of the Florida Division of Historic Resources.

Historically, the De Soto expedition was Spain's most ambitious exploratory venture into North America. A force of over 600 young, highly trained, and well-equipped Iberians spent four years traveling through ten states of the modern southeastern United States. During this time, De Soto and his men met, traded, and fought with scores of indigenous groups of various sizes and social complexity.

The conquistadors induced much in the way of directed change of the aboriginal population to meet their desires. The native inhabitants of the New World presented a challenge to these ambitions, to be overcome by negotiation, intimida-

Figure 7.2 (continued).

tion, or warfare, whichever was most expedient. The native responses varied with the particular circumstances: alliance, resistance, or flight. However, it has been suggested that the biological consequences of European contact eventually rendered the native responses moot.

European diseases are hypothesized to have had a severe impact on the native population in terms of population loss and accompanying social upheaval (Dobyns 1983; Ramenofsky 1987; Smith 1987). The extent of this impact has not been well established and the hypothesized devastating pandemic has been recently brought into question (Burnett and Murray 1993; DePratter 1994). The idea that the aboriginal cultures of the historic period are only a dim reflection of those that had evolved prior to the "discovery" of the New World by Europeans is certainly amenable to further investigation. The Spanish missionaries, who followed De Soto a century later, *may have* encountered an aboriginal culture greatly changed from that in existence at the time of first contact. Data recovered from the Martin Site's sixteenth-century component permit an examination of the Apalachee as they were at contact, before any alteration would have occurred.

From an archeological perspective, the De Soto encampment site represents a solid chronological anchor for refining the local ceramic sequence. As Shapiro (1988) points out, "excavations at this site tell us *for the first time* [emphasis his] what pottery styles were prevalent in Apalachee around the year 1539." This information can then be used to seriate other Apalachee sites with a more precise, absolute date rather than an approximate, relative date.

Spanish artifacts recovered from the Martin Site have been used for comparative purposes by other De Soto researchers elsewhere in the Southeast and now by Coronado researchers. Links of iron mail, first identified at the Martin Site, have subsequently been identified at the Tatham Mound (Jeffrey Mitchem, personal communication). Since the Martin Site is the only agreed-upon De Soto campsite, the artifacts recovered from it have become the standard for comparison. It is now virtually impossible to do any research on the De Soto entrada without referencing the Martin Site.

The discovery and excavation of the Martin Site is a tremendous educational tool. It is a sad fact that Spain's role in the history of the United States has received such short shrift in contemporary history textbooks. Most elementary and secondary school texts devote no more than a paragraph to the nearly 500-year Spanish presence in the American Southeast. Hernando de Soto, when he is mentioned at all, is credited only for "discovering" the Mississippi River.

When I began I suggested that the research on De Soto's route could be likened to the Apollo missions to the moon, in which the discoveries made and accomplishments derived in the course of getting there provided far more insight and benefit than the actual landing. We are coming closer to a goal enunciated earlier by Charles Hudson: "that an accurate reconstruction of the De Soto route will enable us to draw a social map of the sixteenth-century Southeast. We would like to be able to locate specific, named societies and towns on specific rivers and creeks. Such a map could be used as a baseline from which to move backwards in time" (Hudson et al. 1984: 75).

In our efforts to reconstruct the route of De Soto, we have been forced to consider a number of ancillary issues concerning the distribution and organization of indigenous populations, prehistoric as well as historic trails, past environmental conditions, material culture studies, epidemiological studies, and so on. I expect the same for Coronado route reconstructions. The knowledge gained from this research represents a truly significant accomplishment, whatever the outcome of the route reconstruction efforts.

PART III

The Coronado Expedition, Compostela to Cíbola

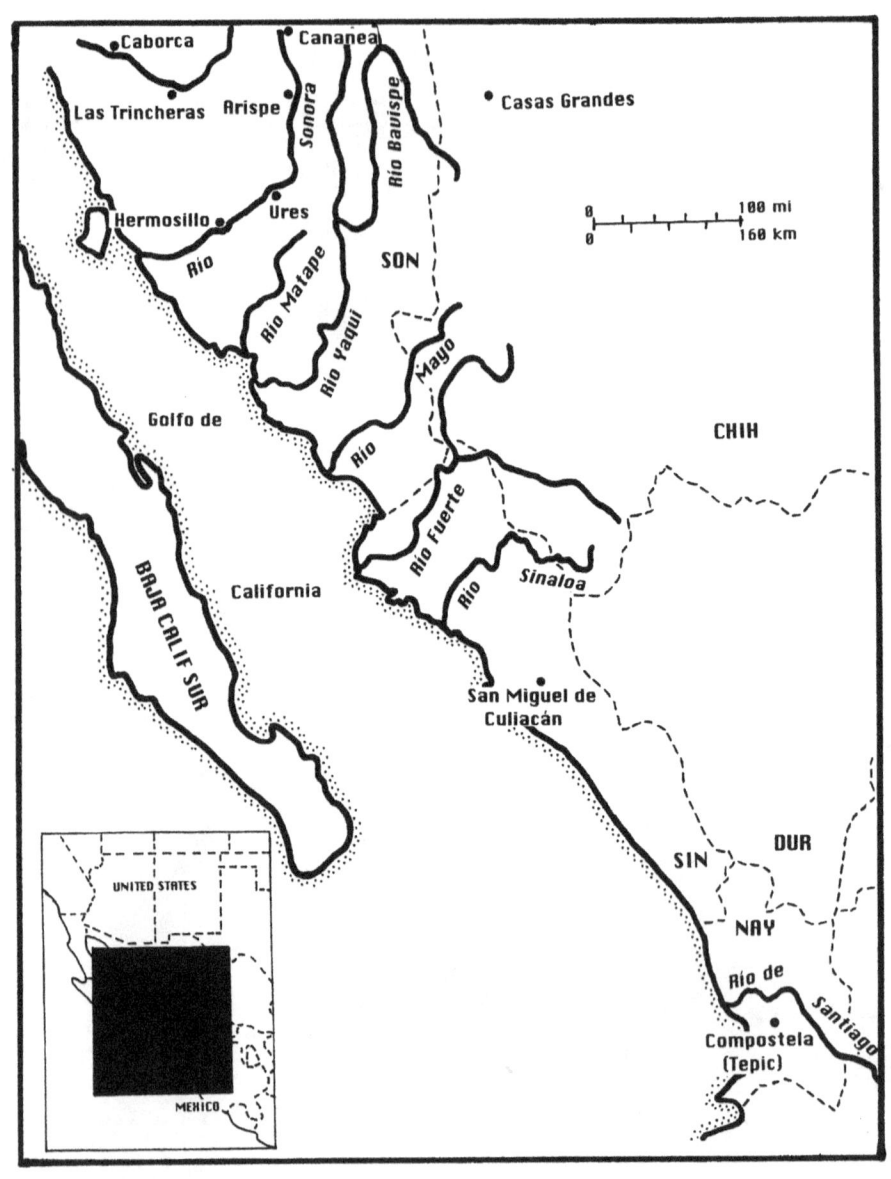

Map 4. Compostela to Cíbola, Southern Portion: Nayarit, Sinaloa, Sonora.

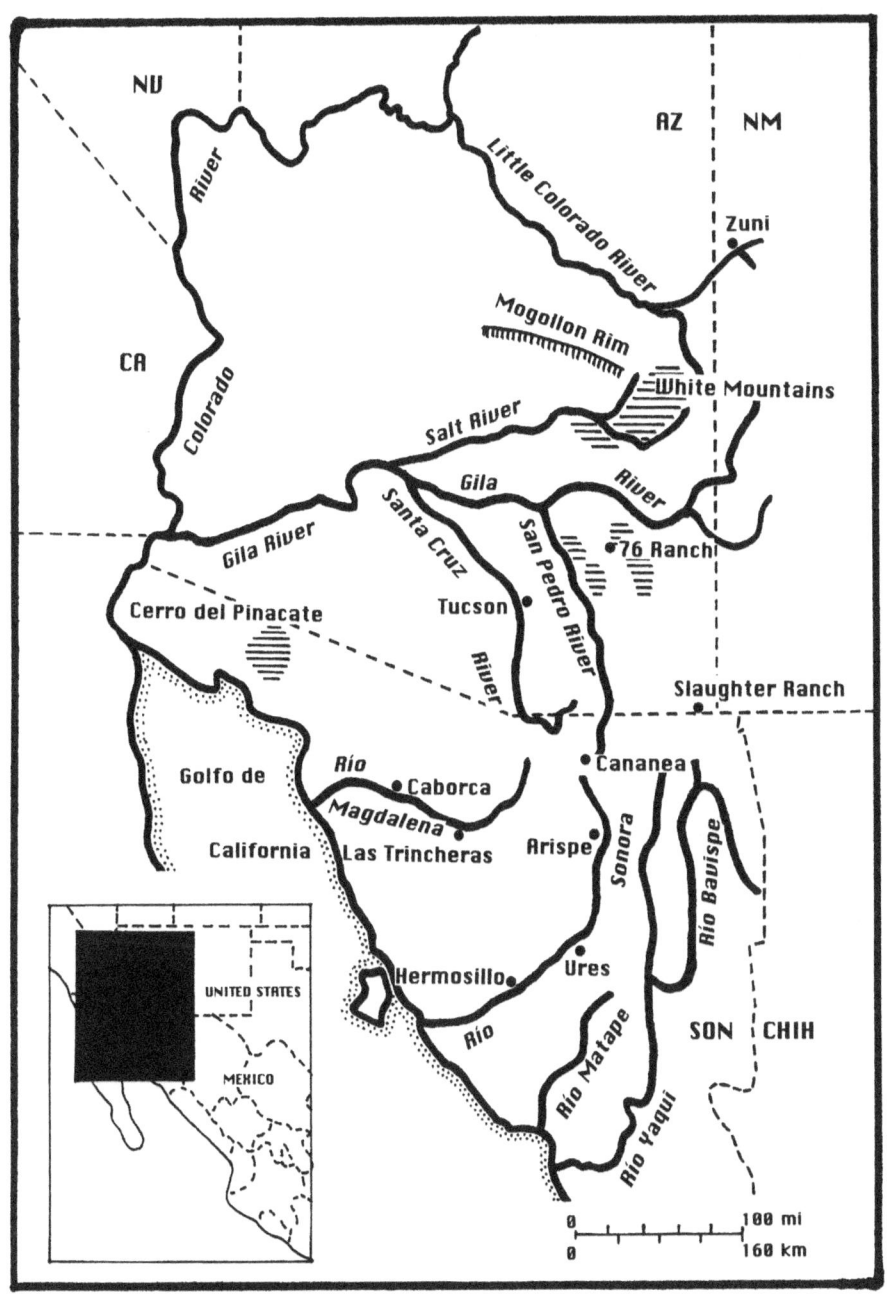

Map 5. Compostela to Cíbola, Northern Portion: Sonora, Arizona, New Mexico.

CHAPTER 8

A Historiography of the Route of the Expedition of Francisco Vázquez de Coronado
Compostela to Cíbola

JOSEPH P. SÁNCHEZ

The Sonora-Arizona Connection

he single most important leg of the expedition is that from Compostela through Sonora. Without a fundamental understanding of that portion of the route it is impossible to determine exactly where the expedition entered present Arizona and what direction it took beyond that point. The literature suggests two viable points through which the expedition passed upon entering present Arizona: the San Pedro and San Bernardino River Valleys. Because the route from Compostela to either of those two points is vague, a third line of march, one farther east, is possible. A fourth alternative, a western route through the Santa Cruz Valley, has been discounted in recent years by scholars. In any case, finding the location of the expedition's entry into the present United States depends wholly on determining the route taken through Sonora.

Although Herbert Bolton and A. Grove Day presented a route through Sonora based on observation and analogy of their readings of the documents and what they perceived to be on the ground, Charles Di Peso approached the problem by utilizing available archeological data and pertinent historical documentation. The historical problem lay in part with the lack of identity of rivers in Sonora for the early Spanish period. Di Peso wrote, "when modern historians attempt to correlate present-day names, such as Yaqui or Sonora River, with names used by early explorers, who had no maps and often were inconvenienced by a lack of interpreters and who used such terms as Yaqui and Señora, then distances and travel times are sacrificed and misconceptions are bound to arise. As mentioned, a league was accepted as being a specific distance, and wherever possible was used to determine distances between points" (Di Peso et al. 1974: 37). By comparing the accounts from various expeditions, Di Peso arrived at a certain determination of place names in Sonora. For example, he determined that the first river crossed by Vázquez de Coronado was the Río Evora de Mocorito. Using the Villa de San Miguel de Culiacán as the beginning point, his methodology involved comparing terminology and distances or time of travel reported by Diego de Guzmán, nephew of Beltrán Nuño de Guzmán (1533); Álvar Núñez Cabeza de Vaca (1536); Marcos de Niza (1539); Vázquez de Coronado (1540); and Francisco de Ibarra (1565); sources that agreed on the sixteenth-century location of Culiacán and on the historic name of the Río Evora de Mocorito.

Testing his hypothesis to determine that the first river was indeed the Mocorito, Di Peso discovered that Vázquez de Coronado's Río Petatlán, the first river north of Culiacán, matched with Guzmán's Petatla and Marcos's Petatlán. So too, he determined, the Río Petatlán had been renamed Río San Sebastián de Ebora during Ibarra's time. Hence evolved the modern name Río Evora de Mocorito. Next, following the same methodology, Di Peso concluded that the second river crossed by the expedition was the Río Sinaloa, for Vázquez knew it by Guzmán's old name "Río Cinaloa." But here Di Peso noted a discrepancy that he resolved by accepting Guzmán's and Vázquez de Coronado's "Río Cinaloa." Guzmán also referred to the Río Sinaloa as the Río Santiago and Ibarra called it the Río Petatlán. The third river, the Río del Fuerte, was known by Guzmán as the Río San Miguel as well as the Río Mayomo; by Vázquez de Coronado as Arroyo de los Cedros; and by Ibarra as the Río Cinaro. The variations, explained Di Peso, were inconsequential because their singular locations were determined by Indian settlements along them, and their names were constant. Besides, he argued, the distance between them was a controlling factor, for the explorers had given estimated figures of time taken to travel between them and/or measurements in leagues. Vázquez de Coronado went so far as to have a man count the steps between the expedition's daily campsites (Hammond and Rey 1940: 240).

For Di Peso, locations of Indian settlements along the rivers or their tributaries were of paramount consideration. For example, on the first river was the village of Mocorito, on the second Guasave and Sinaloa de Leyva, and on the third El Fuerte. The fourth river, Río del Mayo, had an Indian town called Conicari. Guzmán called this river Río San Francisco de Yaquimi or simply, Río Yaquimi; Vázquez de

Coronado referred to it as Lachimi; and Ibarra said it was the Río Mayomo or Río Mayonbo. On one of its tributaries north of Conicari was Tesocoma, referred to by Guzmán as Nebame, by Cabeza de Vaca as Corazones, and by Vázquez de Coronado as Corazones. And finally, north of Corazones was the Río Yaqui, whose tributary Coronado knew as Río de Senora or Señora and Ibarra as Río Oera. Ibarra knew the Río Yaqui as the Río Yaquimi. Crossing to another tributary of the Río Yaqui, the expedition came to the Indian village of Guisamopa, known to Vázquez de Coronado as Ispa. Beyond there, and still on the Río Yaqui drainage, near the Arroyo Babaco, was Vázquez de Coronado's Suya or Ibarra's Senora.

Di Peso's analysis could very well be the key to the historical conundrum concerning Vázquez de Coronado's route through Sonora. By following the documentation almost to a fault, Di Peso determined that the route of Vázquez de Coronado veered northwestward to the Río Bavispe and its confluence with the Río Batepito, which he followed to the Río San Bernardino that originates in southeastern Arizona considerably east of the San Pedro River. Di Peso made a strong case for the expedition crossing into Arizona at present Slaughter Ranch not far westward from the Arizona–New Mexico border. He concluded that the expedition entered New Mexico, crossing into the Animas Valley through Antelope Pass, and then straddled the Arizona–New Mexico boundary until reaching Zuni Pueblo. Di Peso wrote,

> Padre de Niza, Melchior Diaz, and Coronado's troops all traveled along this section of the old Acoma road seeking Cíbola. From the Río Batepito junction the army may have gone N by NW up this river to the San Bernardino junction, 43 km., and then up the San Bernardino in a northerly direction, keeping the Sierra de San Luis on the right (E), to the vicinity of the modern Slaughter Ranch, another 17 km. Next they would have continued up the San Bernardino Valley, traveling NE past the site of present-day Rodeo, New Mexico, and keeping the Chiricahua Mountains on the left (W) and the Peloncillos on the right (E), finally arriving at what is now called Antelope Pass in the latter range, an additional 65 km (Di Peso et al. 1974: 100).

Earlier, in 1872, Brigidier General James H. Simpson, one of the first to attempt to trace Vázquez de Coronado's route in southern Arizona, had assumed that the Spaniards had entered the present United States through the Santa Cruz Valley, stopping at Chichilticale, which he reckoned to be Casa Grande on the Gila River, and then turned northeast across the Pinal and Mogollon Mountains to Zuni. Simpson's account, filled with errors, suggested the westernmost theory of the expedition through Arizona. His discussion of the route across the Mogollon Rim, however, lacks substantive detail (Simpson 1871: 329). The notion persisted for almost seventy years, however, and in 1939, archeologist Charlie Steen suggested that fray Marcos de Niza's preliminary expedition in 1539 had entered Arizona through the Santa Cruz River Valley and turned northeastward somewhere between Tucson and Phoenix, entering the mountains probably beyond Florence near the Salt River (Steen 1939). Marcos was one of the guides of the Vázquez de Coronado expedition in 1540.

Other scholars contended that the expedition entered Arizona through the San Pedro River Valley because it was most compatible with Spanish documentation and topography, being the easiest route northward. Frederick W. Hodge argued that the expedition traveled north along the Río Sonora and entered Arizona through the San Pedro River Valley, then crossed the Pinaleno Mountains over Railroad Pass, followed the San Simon Valley to a point near present Solomonsville and the Gila River, south of the present White Mountain Apache Reservation (Hodge 1895: 142–152). Hodge's route took the expedition on a directly northeastward path to the Zuni River. Of this portion of the route, Hodge's explanation, likewise, lacks sufficient detail for analysis. The debate over the location of the expedition's crossing into Arizona from Sonora was only beginning. Hodge had raised a point that would cause much speculation concerning the San Pedro River Valley hypothesis.

In 1947 George J. Undreiner reexamined fray Marcos de Niza's journey to Cíbola and proposed that Marcos had entered Arizona on April 13, 1539, by following a route north along the Pima road about fifteen miles east of Lochiel soon after which he reached Quiburi, a Sobaipuri village on the San Pedro River. Three days later, the friar visited Baicatcan, another village on the San Pedro, which Di Peso had dated pre-1698. Herein was the riddle. Pedro de Castañeda, chronicler of the Vázquez de Coronado expedition, stated that after visiting a certain Indian town, the expedition encountered a four-day despoblado (desert) north of there. Undreiner pointed out that in his preliminary expedition of 1539, Marcos, probably at Baicatcan, or at least at Quiburi, learned that two more days of travel would bring him to a despoblado that would take four days to cross. He contended that fray Marcos, after two days of travel, had reached the northernmost Sobaipuri village on the San Pedro and that it was probably near Aravaipa Creek (Undreiner 1947: 415–486).

On that same point, Albert H. Schroeder responded to historians who had suggested that Vázquez de Coronado's expedition went down the San Pedro River in southeastern Arizona, and, on the basis that Juan de Jaramillo, another chronicler of the expedition, indicated that the expedition turned east, had routed Marcos and Vázquez de Coronado either up Aravaipa Creek or east from the Tres Alamos region (See Bandelier 1881: 1; 1892, pt. II: 407; Winship 1896: 387; Bolton 1949: 105; Sauer 1932: 36). Schroeder wrote,

If the former route is accepted it would imply that the portion of the middle San Pedro River more than two days travel south of the junction with the Aravaipa, would not have been occupied, since it would then be within the four-day despoblado. This is the very area in which Di Peso has suggested, on the basis of archeological evidence, that occupation may have been unbroken from late prehistoric into historic (1690s) times. Thus, the old routes appear to be in error (Schroeder 1955: 265).

In support of Hodge's hypothesis, Schroeder defends Marcos, commenting that "the evidence presented herein not only indicates the good father was telling the truth, but that Coronado and his chroniclers knowingly supported much of his relation pertaining to the trip through this area" (Schroeder 1955: 267). Thus, Schroeder casts his lot with the San Pedro River Valley entrance hypothesis.

Chichilticale

The debate surrounding the San Pedro River Valley entrance is tied to the location of Chichilticale. Of Chichilticale, Vázquez de Coronado wrote, "I rested for two days at Chichilticale, and there was no chance to rest further, because the food was giving out" (Hammond and Rey 1940: 166). In his account Pedro de Castañeda reported, "the land changes again at Chichilticale and the thorny trees disappear. The reason is that since the gulf extends as far as that place and the coast turns, so also the ridge of the sierra turns. Here one comes to cross the ridge and it breaks to pass into the plains of the land" (Hammond and Rey 1940: 251). What was Chichilticale? At times the documents refer to it as a valley; at other times it appears as a mountain range, a port, or even a despoblado, and finally, as a place or a village. Vázquez de Coronado and Melchior Díaz mentioned the "people of Chichiltcale" (Hammond and Rey 1940: 165). After careful consideration, Di Peso concluded that it was south of the Arizona-Sonora border closer to the Río Batepito and the San Bernardino Valley. He wrote, "ruins which might be ascribed to those of the 'red house' of Chichilticale occur up and down the San Bernardino Valley, and the Stevens Ranch Site contains pottery fragments which indicate a trade relationship with the N and the Little Colorado" (Di Peso et al. 1974: 100). By placing Chichilticale in that area, Di Peso suggested that north of the confluence of the San Bernardino River Valley was a fifteen-day despoblado.

Di Peso's analysis is fairly thorough and deserves lengthy quotation:

De Niza did not mention "Chichiltacale" in his narrative, but Coronado, in his letter to Mendoza . . . did, and said that it was "fifteen days journey distant from the sea, although the father provincial had said that it was only five leagues distant and that he had seen it . . . [and] which the father said was at thirty five degrees. . . ." Either Coronado referred to the journal of place names and locations which de Niza had mentioned (Baldwin 1926: 206) or he was given this information verbally by the priest while on the trail E of Bacadehuachi. The latter had previously scouted out the coast and mentioned the fact that the coast turned W at latitude 35 degrees. It would seem that Coronado's "port of Chichilticale" was that referred to by de Niza after crossing the second despoblado of four days. De Niza mentioned entering a town at the end of this trip in which he was given food. Coronado, in turn, questioned the Indians of Chichilticale (Hammond and Rey 1940: 165) and was told that "they go to the sea for fish, or for anything else that they need, they go across the country, and that it takes them ten days. . . ."

Melchior Díaz, who was sent to check de Niza's report, spent the winter in Chichilticale and said it was 220 leagues from Culiacan (Bolton 1949: 87). Using the proposed routing, this distance would have taken him by way of the Bavispe, a distance of 221.3 leagues. In this Castaneda confirmed the distance (Hammond and Rey 1940: 198).

Castaneda (ibid.: 212, 251–252) wrote that the priests (de Niza and his party) named Chichilticale because of an abandoned mud fortress which had been built by people who broke away from Cibola and which was later destroyed by folk who hunted and lived in rancherias without permanent settlements. He went on to say that the gulf extended as far as this area and turned W at the head of the Gulf of California, which it does on the latitude several minutes above 31 degrees N. This latitude falls across the San Bernardino Valley.

Melchior Diaz attested to the cold (ibid.: 157). Although he did not mention Chichilticale directly in his letter to Mendoza, he spoke of the despoblado which separated him from Cibola and recounted his interview with the Cibolans of Chichilticale, who, after Esteban was killed advised the people of that town not to respect the Christians but to kill them (ibid.: 160).

Schroeder correctly surmised the critical need to define the location of Chichilticale because, for one of many reasons, it determined where the expedition went next. He countered any argument that suggests that Chichilticale lay south of the Arizona-Sonora border by stating, "the ethnological traits reported by the early Spanish who recorded their travels of 1539 and 1540 through Arizona point to the Yavapai as the people who occupied the area on the north side of the four-day despoblado, where Chichilticale was located. Internal evidence within these early documents also indicates that Fray Marcos and Coronado followed the San Pedro to its mouth, not just to Tres Alamos or Aravaipa on the San Pedro, and that from there they crossed the Gila and went over to the Salt River as Undreiner suggests" (Schroeder 1956: 32). Schroeder is emphatic about the significance of this point, writing, "thus, the Yavapai remain as the only possible group, separated by four days' travel, that bordered the Sobaipuri on the north in 1539 and 1540" (Schroeder 1956: 33). Furthermore, in contrast to Di Peso's and Hodge's routes from Arizona to New Mexico, he proposed that after departing the mouth of the San Pedro River, the expedition proceeded down the Salt River "almost to the mouth of Tonto Creek, then up Salome Creek and over the north end of the Sierra Anchas and then generally northeast over the Mogollon Rim across to Zuni. There is little or no evidence to indicate they went east from the San Pedro at Tres Alamos or via Aravaipa Creek and then across the present day San Carlos Apache country to Zuni. Such a trail would necessitate a route directed to the north or north-northeast, rather than northeast as the documents state" (Schroeder 1956: 32).

Carroll L. Riley and Joni L. Manson also agree, without specifying their argument, that Chichilticale was in southern Arizona or New Mexico (Riley and Manson 1983: 349). Riley, on the basis of historical, anthropological, and botanical evidence revolving around linguistics, argued that the location of Chichilticale was at one of two probable locations: one on the lower Salt River, the other on the upper Gila River (Riley 1985, 1995:157).

From the Despoblado to Cíbola: The Arizona–New Mexico Riddle

Having crossed the despoblado, the anonymous writer of the *Relación del Suceso* (Hammond and Rey 1940: 284) commented that "the entire route up to within fifty leagues of Cíbola is inhabited, although in some places at a distance from the road." This and other commentary by the members of the expedition are open to interpretation. The route to Cíbola from the despoblado is fraught with a dearth of information, leaving the researcher often with little more than his imagination. The most accepted route of the expedition through Arizona is that proposed by Herbert E. Bolton. Since 1949, the Bolton route has gained in venerability, partly because of his scholarly influence and partly because his trek in field research rivaled that of Francisco Vázquez de Coronado's epic march across a large portion of North America. Bolton built on the work of earlier researchers and was probably influenced, although he denied it, by A. Grove Day's work, which was published in 1940.

Day favored the Sonora Valley as a probable point from which Arizona was reached. Furthermore, he opted for the San Pedro River route, specifying that Vázquez de Coronado had entered Arizona through a plain extending to the headwaters of the San Pedro River near present-day Naco. Somewhere near there, he explained, was the point of departure for crossing the despoblado. Day went on to propose that the expedition crossed the Gila and Salt Rivers by means of an old Indian trail, and then proceeded through the White Mountains to the upper drainage of the Little Colorado near St. Johns to the Zuni River. Although Day did not specifically tell how the expedition crossed the area, he deferred to the work by Carl Sauer and George Winship for his information.

Like Day, Bolton relied on Winship and other sources to define his proposed route, which he then set out to prove through his fieldwork. Generally, Bolton's route has the expedition leaving Culiacán, from where they followed the coastal plain, veering northeastward between the Gulf of California and the Sierra Madre Occidental, crossing rivers until they reached the Sonora River Valley. From there, deduced Bolton, they entered Arizona through the San Pedro River Valley. The Bolton route placed the expedition's point of departure through the despoblado near Benson, Arizona, from where it marched northeast through the Galiuro Range and crossed the Aravaipa Valley, passing through Eagle Pass between the Pinaleno and Santa Teresa mountains. The line of march through the despoblado ran along the Gila River, crossing it at present-day Bylas, after which it forded the Salt River near Bonito Creek. Next, Bolton proposed that they continued northward, crossed the White River near Fort Apache, and ascended the Mogollon Rim by following small streams before emerging on the Little Colorado River near its confluence with the Zuni River. Shortly, the expedition reached Hawikuh (Bolton 1949: 108–117).

The route has been accepted by some historians, modified by others, and contested by yet another group of researchers who offer their own conclusions markedly different from Bolton's. Researchers, namely Robert M. Wagstaff, have criticized the Bolton proposal by noting that the distances traveled by the expedition do not conform with Bolton's conclusions. Also, Bolton's identification of rivers, which often appear to be juxtaposed to fit the narrative, are misleading. Although Wagstaff did not adequately support the discrepancies he cited, Di Peso attempted to propose an alternative route in which he accounted for rivers and distances.

Employing the same methodology as he had on the rivers in Sonora, Di Peso suggested that the expedition traveled from Antelope Pass to Cíbola, meandering in and out of Arizona and New Mexico until they reached Cíbola. Di Peso argued that from Antelope Pass the expedition crossed into New Mexico, then veered northwest into Arizona passing present-day Duncan, Guthrie, and Clifton northward beyond the San Francisco River to Stray Horse Creek, which it crossed, following the Blue River into New Mexico. Passing through Luna, New Mexico, Di Peso's proposed route placed the expedition near Spur Lake from where they followed a line, almost straight north across Carrizo Wash and beyond the west side of Zuni Plateau to the Zuni River before reaching Cíbola (Di Peso et al. 1974: 102).

Preceding Bolton, Carl Sauer's interpretation of the route through Arizona is traced from the San Pedro River to a point north of Benson, around the Galiuro Mountains into the upper basin of Aravaipa Creek north to the Gila River by way of Eagle Pass between the Pinaleno and Santa Teresa Ranges. Following the San Carlos River, the expedition turned northeast, crossing the Natanes Plateau and the Black River, to a point on the White River near present-day Fort Apache, from where Vázquez de Coronado passed near present McNary. From there, they crossed the Colorado Plateau to the Little Colorado River, thence to the Zuni before reaching Hawikuh (Sauer 1932: 36–37).

Riley and Manson retraced the expedition from San Miguel de Culiacán, first through the eyes of the Marcos de Niza preliminary exploration of 1539, then through the sources of the Vázquez de Coronado expedition. Reanalyzing Marcos's route of 1539, they concluded that he reached "a settlement called Vacapa in the Altar-Magdalena drainage of northwestern Sonora" (Riley and Manson 1983: 348). They proposed that Marcos had taken the westernmost path through central Sonora, and traveling north, he had entered Arizona "at some point in the lower San Pedro or perhaps Santa Cruz valley" (ibid.). More recently, Riley has concluded that Marcos's entry into Arizona was by the San Pedro (Riley 1995: 153).

Also in 1539, Melchior Díaz led a scouting party from Culiacán to northern Sonora and "the ruin of Chichilticale in southern Arizona or New Mexico, but did not try to cross the mountains to Cibola." (Riley and Manson 1983: 349). The two events influenced the route Vázquez de Coronado would take north to Chichilticale. According to Riley (1995: 157–159), one year after fray Marcos's travel, the full-blown expedition led by Vázquez de Coronado pursued a more easterly course, once it entered modern Arizona. In this reconstruction the expedition followed the Gila and San Francisco Rivers east and northward along the present Arizona–New Mexico state line, eventually crossing to Carrizo Wash, which led to the Zuni River and Cíbola.

Riley and Manson (1983: 350) make the point that the existence of aboriginal trails linking Zuni, Sonora, and ultimately Mesoamerica was known to the Indian guides of fray Marcos, Díaz, and Vázquez de Coronado. That is the key to understanding where the expedition entered Arizona, and it subsequently influenced the direction taken after Chichilticale, as well as the route the Spaniards took after they had established themselves at Zuni.

As a result of their study, Riley and Manson clarify that the valleys of the Santa Cruz River, the San Pedro River, and the San Bernardino River were part of a major trade network, which was also utilized by explorers associated with the expedition of Vázquez de Coronado.

CHAPTER 9

Francisco Vázquez de Coronado's Northward Trek Through Sonora

JERRY GURULÉ

ertinent place names are a primary concern for historians, archeologists, and others interested in Coronado's route from Compostela, Mexico, to the Great Bend of the Arkansas River. To find a fixed route has been persistently elusive, but nonetheless, certain fixed place names can be verified and given reliable coordinates. Of course some place names are more difficult to verify than others.

What follows is an excerpt from an unpublished manuscript entitled the *Historical Dictionary of Place Names Associated with the Expedition of Francisco Vázquez de Coronado, 1540–1542,* by Joseph P. Sánchez, Jerry L. Gurulé, and William Broughton. The purpose of the *Historical Dictionary* is to offer researchers a guide that may help them develop reasonable alternatives for the route Coronado took. The place names mentioned come from prominent works done by earlier researchers in the field. The principal works from which the place names were taken are: Adolph F. Bandelier's *The Discovery of New Mexico*; Herbert E. Bolton's *Coronado, Knight of Pueblos and Plains*; *Coronado's Quest: The Discovery of the Southwestern States* by Arthur Grove Day; *Land of the Conquistadores* by Cleve Hallenbeck; *Narratives of the Coronado Expedition 1540–1542* by George P. Hammond and Agapito Rey; "The Narrative of the Expedition of Coronado by Pedro de

Casteñeda," in *Spanish Explorers in the Southern United States 1528–1543*, edited by Frederick W. Hodge and Theodore H. Lewis; and finally "The Coronado Expedition, 1540–1542, by George Parker Winship, in the *Fourteenth Annual Report of the Bureau of Ethnology, 1892–1893, Part I.*

In order to make the *Historical Dictionary* easily comprehensible, it is divided into four major sections: "Mountains, Ridges, Hills, Canyons, Valleys, Plains, and Passes"; "Rivers, Creeks, Dams, and Other Bodies of Water"; "Pueblos and Other Related Places"; and "Other Geographical References and Peculiarities." The place names that occur in each of the four major sections are alphabetized for easy reference. Whenever possible, longitudinal and latitudinal coordinates are given for each place name. At the end of each place name entry, the author, page, and/or note number are given from the works cited above. The page reference for each citation allows the researcher to cross-reference, compare, and contrast the individual place names cited by each major author and, in cases where the physical location is not known, more easily hypothesize about their possible location. For the purpose of this publication only the entries pertinent to Sonora, Mexico, are listed.

This portion of the *Historical Dictionary* begins with a valley called the Abra, in Sonora. The Abra's description is seen through the eyes of fray Marcos de Niza, who later accompanied Coronado on his expedition. As would be expected, many of the valleys and canyons that are mentioned correspond to rivers that flow through these topographical features. The Río Mayo, for example, passes through the Mayo Valley. The same is true for the San Pedro and the Señora Valleys through which, respectively, the San Pedro River and the Río Sonora run.

Many of the settlements that appear in the *Historical Dictionary* were in valleys and along the many rivers that were mentioned, such as Bacoachi and Banámichi, both in the valley of the Río Sonora. These features become important, of course, with the reasoning that any large expedition would follow the path of least resistance. Two other main factors to consider are supplies of water and food. Hospitable settlements along river valleys would be favored stops on the way north.

The San Pedro Valley lies along a route often chosen on the trek northward. It is thought to be one of the possible routes fray Marcos de Niza took into the southern part of what is now Arizona. Adolph Bandelier argues that if fray Marcos had followed the Sonora Valley he would have naturally connected to the San Pedro Valley. Opinions vary, but this route is often hypothesized as the most likely one to have been followed.

This selection from the *Historical Dictionary*, like the complete work, is meant not only to show where there is agreement, but also to emphasize differences in interpretation by major writers and researchers on Francisco Vázquez de Coronado.

With review and analysis of the work of the major writers mentioned above and utilization of the work that follows, it is hoped that a better understanding of the possible routes may emerge.

Sonora

MOUNTAINS, RIDGES, HILLS, CANYONS, VALLEYS, PLAINS, AND PASSES

Abra: 27°14'N 109°6'W. A Spanish word meaning a gorge, dale, or valley. Used by fray Marcos de Niza and others to denote the valley of the Río Mayo which lies just south of modern day Ciudad Obregón, Sonora. The mouth of the Río Mayo lies at Punta Santa Lugarda at 26°45'N 109°49'W. Quoting fray Marcos, Herbert E. Bolton writes, "at Rio Fuerte, where the natives called him Sayota, 'Man from Heaven,' Fray Marcos learned that a few days beyond, 'where the chains of mountains end,' there was a level opening (abra) with much land and very large settlements of people who wore cotton garments, and had vessels, nose and ear pendants, and sweat scrapers, all made of gold. This was news indeed! The abra thus described was at Mayo River and the people of whom he heard lived in villages along the banks of that stream" (Bolton 1949: 26). Bolton further writes: "Fray Marcos was now in the fertile valley of the Mayo River, of whose settlements he had heard when he was near Fuerte River. Here, evidently about at Conicari, in compliance with his instructions, Marcos 'erected two crosses and took possession.' The friar now understood the Abra to be the opening of Mayo Valley toward the east. 'Since this Abra leads away from the coast,' he writes, 'and my instructions were not to depart from there, I decided to leave it for the return, when it would be possible to see it better.' The attractions of the Abra had faded beside the scintillating news of Cibola" (Bolton 1949: 29). Again, Bolton traces the activities of Marcos in the Abra by writing: "He was informed that the Abra was peopled for many days' journey toward the east. 'But I did not risk entering it, since it seemed to me that someone must come to settle and rule this other land of the Seven Cities and the kingdoms which I name, at which time the Abra could be better explored, without putting my person in jeopardy and thereby failing to give a report of what I had seen. So I only saw, from the mouth of the Abra, seven fair-sized settlements, and somewhat distant a valley below, very fresh and of very good land, whence came many smokes.' This would imply that he had ascended an elevation to obtain a view. 'I heard that in it there is much gold, and that the natives of the Abra make it into vessels, and ornaments for the ears, and paletillas with which they scrape themselves to remove the sweat; and that they are people who do not permit those of the other side of the Abra to trade with them. Here . . . I erected two crosses and took possession of all this Abra and valley.' This, as he confesses, was a somewhat long-range exploration and a tenuous 'possession' of the Abra" (Bolton 1949: 37). Bolton 1949: 26, 29, 37, 99, 100, 108. See Arroyo de los Cedros.

Arroyo de los Cedros: 27°14'N 109°6'W. A tributary stream entering the Río Mayo from the north at the village of Conicari, Sonora. This was the rendezvous point between Coronado and the Díaz party, which was exploring the Abra. In his account, Captain Juan de Jaramillo writes: "Upon leaving the said valley of Culiacán, we came to a river called Petlatlán, which must be about four days' journeys distant. We found these Indians friendly, and they gave us a small amount of food to eat. From here we traveled to another river called Cinaloa. There must have been about three days' journeys between these two rivers. At this place the general sent ten of us with horses to travel lightly by forced marches until we came to the Arroyo de los Cedros, and from there to enter an opening in the sierras on the right side of the road, and to see the sierras and what there was behind them. If we needed more days than we were allowed, he would wait for us at the said Arroyo de los Cedros. Thus it was done, and all that we found there was some poor Indians settled in a few valleys in the manner of rancherias. The land was sterile. The distance from the river to this arroyo must be an additional five days' travel" (Hammond and Rey 1940: 296). The translators identify Jaramillo's Petlatlán and Cinaloa rivers as the Sinaloa and Fuerte rivers, respectively. Bolton identifies Arroyo de los Cedros as "the stream which joins Mayo River at Conicari." And he interprets the route as follows: "From there they were to enter the opening 'at the right of the road,' described by Fray Marcos, 'to see the sierras and what there was behind them.' If [Melchior] Díaz needed more time than that specified for the reconnaissance, Coronado was to await him at the Cedros, which was on the direct road to the north" (Bolton 1949: 99). Bolton states that the distance from the Fuerte River to the Cedros where it joins the Mayo is approximately seventy miles. Bolton 1949: 99, 100; Day 1940: 100, 101, 338–339 n5; Hammond and Rey 1940: 296; Winship 1896: 584.

Cañada Ancha: 30°55'N 110°9'W. According to Bandelier, Cañada Ancha is one of the three places in the Sonora River Valley north of Mututichachi that offers suitable space for village sites. It is probably a location visited by fray Marcos de Niza. Bandelier 1981: 79.

Cananea Plain: See Cananea. A grassy plain extending approximately from Bacoachi on the upper Río Sonora to the headwaters of the San Pedro River west of the Dragoon Mountains in Arizona. Day 1940: 331 n18, 339 n11.

Corazones, Valle de los: See also Ures, Ures Canyon, Ures Basin. Exact location is unknown. Usually it is thought to be near Ures, Sonora, 29°26'N 110°24'W. Also thought to have been situated in the vicinity of Mátape, Sonora, 29°7'N 109°58'W (Bandelier 1890) or near Yécora, Sonora, 28°19'N 108°58'W (Alegre 1956). Bandelier 1981: 51, 53, 54; Bolton 1949: 115, 148, 151; Day 1940: 102, 131, 132, 326 n13.

La Tescalama: 27°12'N 108°52'W. La Tescalama is in western Mexico and north of Los Mochis. Hammond and Rey write: "at Corazones in the Sonora Valley, about where the river emerges from the canyon known locally as La Tescalama, the army settled down to await orders from Coronado." Hammond and Rey 1940: 20.

Mayo Valley: See Río Mayo. Bolton 1949: 99, 108.

San Pedro Valley: 32°14'N 110°19'W, Source: 31°47'N110°13'W. This valley lies along the route often chosen to the north country from the interior of Mexico. It is most often associated with one of the most likely possible routes taken by fray Marcos de Niza. The San Pedro River that runs through the valley connects the northern part of Mexico with Arizona. The argument according to Bandelier is that if fray Marcos de Niza followed the Sonora Valley up he would have naturally come through the San Pedro Valley. Fray Marcos of course would return north with the Coronado Expedition. Bandelier 1981: 37, 80, 89–90; Hammond and Rey 1940: 16.

Senoquipe: See Sinoquipe.

"Señora" Valley: See also Río Sonora. The Spaniards knew it as "the valley of Señora" but its true native name was Sonora. Day describes the valley as "the next basin upstream on the Sonora River from that of Ures, in which Corazones lay, and . . . separated from it by a long and narrow gorge" (Day 1940: 102). Jaramillo had this to say: "we went to another valley made by this same arroyo. It is called Señora. It is also irrigated and has more Indians than the others, and the settlements and food are of the same type. This valley must extend six or seven leagues, more or less. These Indians, at first, were friendly, but not later; on the contrary, they and those they could assemble around there became our bitter enemies. They possess poison, with which they killed several Christians. They have sierras on both sides that are not very productive" (Hammond and Rey 1940: 297). Day 1940: 102, 103; Hammond and Rey 1940: 297.

Sierra de los Ajos: 30°57'N 109°54'W. These mountains just south of Arizona are located between Cananea and Fronteras in the state of Sonora. Bandelier mentions the mountains as one of the obstacles fray Marcos may have faced on his northward trek. Bandelier 1981: 79.

Sierra de San José: 31°16'N 110°2'W. Very near the Sierra de los Ajos, in the state of Sonora, Mexico, this range is found between Naco and Cananea. Like the Sierra de los Ajos, the Sierra de San José was mentioned by Bandelier as another of a series of impediments that caused delays and detours for fray Marcos. Bandelier 1981: 79.

Sinoquipe (Gorge): Sinoquipe: 30°10'N 110°12'W. This gorge in northwestern Mexico is approximately eighty miles south of the Arizona border. Day refers to the "twelve-mile gorge of Sinoquipe" as being passed by Coronado on the way to Arispe before reaching Ispa. Sinoquipe, however, is a populated place that lies in the valley of the Río Sonora. Parts of that valley become narrow in some places, but many side canyons also enter it. It is difficult, therefore, to ascertain exactly which feature Day means by the "gorge of Sinoquipe." Bolton also writes of the "deep and narrow gorge of Senoquipe" and says "swinging eastward now to avoid the fearsome gorge of Senoquipe and the Ópata settlements farther down Sonora Valley, Coronado reached Batuco . . ." Bolton 1949: 104, 151, 348; Day 1940: 104.

Sonora River Valley: See Río Sonora. Bandelier 1981: 37, 78, 80.

Sonora Valley: See Río Sonora. Bolton 1949: 90, 97, 103–105, 114, 150, 151, 169, 175, 187, 192, 194, 196, 235, 317–319, 348, 402; Day 1940: 131, 158, 160, 165, 273, 287, 293, 299, 364 n5, 365 n10.

Suya Valley: NF GNIS.[1] Day writes of Coronado and his men continuing through the Suya Valley after passing through Sinoquipe Gorge, then Ispa: "then, at the northern end of the right fork of the Sonora, they found, 'forty leagues farther toward Cíbola,' the valley of Suya, which was to become the third and final site of the town of San Gerónimo" (Day 1940: 104). Hammond and Rey also mention the valley many times in their translation of Castañeda's account, who locates the valley as forty leagues from Señora. In the Suya, Castañeda says, the town of San Hierónimo was founded (Hammond and Rey 1940: 250). Bolton 1949: 321, 322, 323, 324, 325, 347; Day 1940: 104, 105, 222, 268, 273, 292, 319; Hammond and Rey 1940: 233, 250, 266, 268–270, 293.

Ures Canyon (Basin): See Ures. Bolton 1949: 151; Day 1940: 102, 132, 326 n13.

Yaqui Valley: See Río Yaqui. Bolton 1949: 12.

RIVERS, CREEKS, DAMS, AND OTHER BODIES OF WATER

Cedros River: See Río Cedros.

Cocoraqui River: 27°5'N 109°59'W. A stream near Ciudad Obregón, Sonora. Cited by Hammond and Rey as being Castañeda's Teocomo River. Hammond and Rey 1940: 250n.

Río Altar: 30°39'N 111°53'W. Rising in the Sierra Madre Occidental of Sonora near the United States border, the Río Altar flows generally northeast to southwest until it joins the Río Magdalena. Day suggests that Melchior Díaz traveled up the valley of the Río Altar to Sonoita. Day 1940: 349 n24.

Río Bavispe: 29°15'N 109°11'W. Bandelier 1981: 37.

Río Cedros: 27°14'N 109°6'W. A river of Sonora, Mexico, flowing into the Río Mayo at Conicari. Cited by Bolton as the location of the Abra, into which Coronado sent Melchior Díaz and fifteen men on a route reconnaissance. Also mentioned as being ascended by Tristán de Luna y Arellano on his way to Corazones with the livestock, supplies, and main body of Coronado's army. Castañeda says that, "the army, which had remained in charge of Don Tristán de Arellano, set out following the route of the general. They were all burdened with provisions, their lances on their shoulders, and all on foot in order that the horses could be loaded. After considerable labor they reached, by stages, a province which Cabeza de Vaca had named Corazones. . . ." (Hammond and Rey 1940: 209). Hammond and Rey think that the Río Cedros offered access to the Río Yaqui and thence to Soyopa. Bolton 1949: 30, 99, 100, 101, 150; Hammond and Rey 1940: 16, 209.

Río Chico: 28°10'N 109°25'W. Mentioned by Day as a link between the valleys of the Río Cedros and the Río Yaqui. Day 1940: 101.

Río Mayo: 26°45'N 109°47'W. One of the principal rivers of northwestern Mexico. The Río Mayo rises in Chihuahua and flows southwest through Sonora to the Gulf of California. Hammond and Rey say that Castañeda referred to it as the Boyomo. It is mentioned by many commentators as part of Coronado's route because its valley joins the Arroyo de los Cedros at Conicari and is probably the Abra of Castañeda. Bandelier 1981: 47n; Bolton 1949: 11, 26, 29, 37, 99, 100, 101; Day 1940: 82, 100, 101, 110, 294, 330 n6, 339 n5; Hammond and Rey 1940: 16, 250n.

Río Moctezuma: 29°9'N 109°40'W. Also known as the Soyopa. The Río Moctezuma of Sonora is part of the Río Yaqui system. It is mentioned parenthetically by Bandelier and Day. Bandelier 1981: 47n; Day 1940: 365 n10.

Río Mulatos: 28°33'N 108°50'W. A Sonoran river that is part of the Yaqui system. It is said that the approaches to the Río Mulatos were occupied by the Jovas. Bandelier 1981: 61 n39.

Río San Pedro: 32°59'N 110°47'W. A river of Sonora and Arizona. This stream is probably the one called the Río Nexpa by the Coronado party, according to Day and Hammond and Rey. Traversing Cochise County, the San Pedro becomes a tributary of the Gila when they join near Winkelman in Pinal County. The San Pedro is thought by several interpreters to be part of Coronado's route into Arizona. After leaving Arizpe, Jaramillo says, "one goes from here in four days over a despoblado to another arroyo, which we understood was called Nexpa. . . . We continued down this arroyo for two days; leaving the arroyo we went to the right in two days' travel to the foot of the cordillera, where we learned that it was called Chichilticalli" (Hammond and Rey 1940: 297). Bolton 1949: 317; Hammond and Rey 1940: 297; Hodge 1907: 371n.

Río Santa Cruz: 33°19'N 112°14'W. A small stream of Sonora and Arizona that, like the Río San Pedro, may have been used as a route north by Coronado and even, according to Winship, may have been the Río Nexpa. Bandelier transposes the Río Santa Cruz and the Río San Pedro in his chapter on fray Marcos de Niza. Bandelier 1981: 80, 80n; Winship 1896: 387.

Río Sonora: 28°48'N 111°49'W. Also known as the Río Señora and the Senora River. It rises on the plateau of Cananea in Sonora near the United States border and flows generally southwest for 250 miles through Arizpe and Ures. Often shrunken during dry seasons, the river can reach the sea in years of heavy rainfall. Bolton and Day feel that the valley of the Río Sonora was the major corridor to the north for the Coronado expedition. Bandelier 1981: 47n, 78, 79, 83 n33, 85; Bolton 1949: 10, 11, 30, 32, 83, 102–105, 148, 150, 154; Day 1940: 102–105, 110, 132, 168, 189, 267, 316, 326 n12, 331 n14, 339 n11, 357 n20; Hammond and Rey 1940: 16; Winship 1896: 386–387.

Río Yaqui (Yaquimi, Yaqui River): 27°37'N 110°39'W. A river in Sonora formed in the Sierra Madre Occidental by the Río Bavispe and other tributaries. It flows about 200 miles generally southwest to enter the Gulf of California south of Guaymas. Day holds that the Río Yaqui was part of Coronado's route through Sonora. Bandelier 1981: 54; Bolton 1949: 6, 11, 37, 101, 102, 144, 150; Day 1940: 82, 101, 167, 330 n11, 348 n22; Hammond and Rey 1940: 16, 164n, 296; Hodge 1907: 376n; Winship 1896: 386, 515, 553, 584.

Pueblos and Other Related Places

Arizpe: 30°20'N 110°10'W. Arizpe lies about seventy miles south of the Arizona border in northern Mexico on the edge of the Río Sonora, in the Senoquipe Valley. "Coronado followed the regular trail northward by way of Arizpe and Bacoachi into the San Pedro Valley, proceeding along its course for several days before striking Chichilticalli near the Gila River" (Hammond and Rey 1940: 16). Jaramillo says, that "from here we continued in general along the said arroyo [the Señora Valley], crossing its meanderings, to another Indian settlement called Ispa. It must be one day's journey from the confines of the last one. . . . One goes from here in four days over a despoblado to another arroyo, which we understood was called Nexpa" (Hammond and Rey 1940: 297). Bolton 1949: 104; Hammond and Rey 1940: 16, 297; Winship 1896: 515, 585.

Babiácora: 29°43'N 110°9'W. Babiácora or Baviácora is in northwest Mexico in the state of Sonora, sixty-five miles northeast of Hermosillo. A municipality in the Judicial District of Arizpe, originally an Ópata village. A Jesuit mission was founded in Babiácora in 1639. Bolton refers to Jaramillo's account when he speaks of the fertile valley from Babiácora to Senoquipe. Bandelier uses its location to place the Valle de los Corazones. Day follows the same argument. The settlements there were more populous than any the expedition had seen. Bolton 1949: 104; Bandelier 1981: 53; Day 1940: 103.

Bacanuchi: 30°39'N 110°16'W. In northwest Mexico, Bacanuchi is situated on the Río Bacanuchi. One of the Ópata settlements south of Cananea. Bacanuchi and Bacoachi are both approximately twenty miles from Arizpe. According to Bolton, Coronado may have stopped in Bacanuchi. He speculates as to which fork of the Sonora River Coronado may have taken. Bolton 1949: 105.

Bacapa, Sonora: NF GNIS. This location, supposedly northeast of the Gulf of California, is perhaps one of fray Marcos de Niza's stops. According to Madeleine Rodack, Bacapa is now associated with Quitovac. Bandelier 1981: 35, 74n.

Bacoachi: 30°38'N 109°56'W. In northwest Mexico Bacoachi is situated on the Río Sonora and is seventy-five miles southeast of Gales. A settlement charged to Diego de Alcaráz was eventually moved to Suya near what is today Bacoachi. Hammond and Rey 1940: 16, 268n.

Bacuache, Bacuachi: See Bacoachi. Bolton 1949: 105, 318.

Bacuachi: (Probably Bacoachi, 30°38'N 109°56'W). A village in the valley of the Río Sonora that was apparently once inhabited by the Ópatas. Bandelier and Day place it on the route of fray Marcos de Niza. Bandelier 1981: 78–79, 83 n33; Day 1940: 331, 339, 355.

Banámichi: 30°1'N 110°10'W. Another of the Ópata villages in the valley of the Río Sonora that Coronado may have visited. Day says that the "Señora" Valley extends from Babiácora to beyond Banámichi and was well suited for settlement. Banámichi is located at the mouth of the Cañada Mole. Bandelier 1981: 78; Day 1940: 103.

Batuco: NF GNIS. Friendly Indians at Batuco supplied Coronado with provisions on his march southward. As to its location, Day writes: "there were two Sonora towns of this name, but the one meant by Castañeda was probably that on the Río Moctezuma not far above its junction with the Aros and about twenty-two miles east of Ures. It would therefore seem that Coronado avoided the Suya and Sonora valleys on his return route by descending the Moctezuma, the next watershed to the east" (Day 1940: 365 n10). Bolton 1949: 348; Day 1940: 293, 365 n10); Hammond and Rey 1940: 273n; Winship 1896: 537.

Cananea: 30°57'N 110°18'W. See Cananea Plain. Cananea is in northwest Mexico in Sonora and is forty-five miles east-southeast of Nogales, Arizona. Before reaching Cíbola Coronado had to cross the plains east of Cananea. Bolton 1949: 32, 105.

Conicari, Conicarit: 27°14'N 109°6'W. Conicari is approximately twenty-two miles from Navojoa in western Mexico. Fray Marcos had sparked the interests of Coronado about this region, although Mendoza remained skeptical. The report of gold and large settlements in the area caused Coronado to send Melchior Díaz to explore. "They were to go by forced marches to Arroyo de los Cedros, the stream which joins Mayo River at Conicari" (Bolton 1949: 99). Today Conicari sits on the edge of a lake formed by the Macuzari Dam. Bolton 1949: 29, 99.

Corazones (Town of Hearts): 29°26'N 110°24'W. Álvar Núñez Cabeza de Vaca and his companions so named the town because as they passed through they were given six hundred dried deer hearts, turquoise, and emerald arrowheads (Hallenbeck 1950: 16). The coordinates for Corazones are the same as those for Ures, reflecting the general belief that they were in the same vicinity. There is some disagreement though, as Di Peso suggests that Corazones may have been in the upper drainage of the Río Mayo, while others opt for an area near the present town of Yécora. Bandelier thought it was near the village of Batuco (Bandelier 1981: 47n). This was the first Spanish settlement in the Sonoran territory established by Tristán de Luna y Arellano. In 1540 Coronado rested here for several days, then continued on his northward journey. In his *Relación* Juan de Jaramillo describes the place as "the arroyo and pueblo called Corazones, so named by Dorantes, Cabeza de Vaca, Castillo, and the negro [sic] Estebanillo. They gave it this name because they were given, as a customary present, hearts of animals and birds to eat. The distance to this pueblo of Corazones must be about two days. There is an irrigation arroyo here, and the climate is warm. Their houses consist of huts. After setting up the poles in the shape of ovens, although much larger, they cover them with mats. For their food they have maize, beans, and calabashes, in abundance, I believe. They dress in deerskins. As this place seemed to be a suitable one, an order was issued to establish a town here with some of the Spaniards who were coming in the rear. They lived here almost until the expedition failed" (Hammond and Rey 1940: 296–297). Bandelier 1981: 47n, 53; Bolton 1949: 10–11, 30, 93, 101–104, 106–107, 147, 149–152, 256, 323, 325, 348; Day 1940: 10, 12, 38, 49, 102, 131, 291, 293, 326, 338; Hallenbeck 1950: 16, 31; Hammond and Rey 1940: 20, 28, 164, 209, 250–251, 277, 278, 296–297, 363; Hodge 1907: 108, 115n, 301, 347, 372, 376; Winship 1896: 392, 484, 515, 534, 537, 553, 572, 585.

Corodéhuachi: NF GNIS. According to Bandelier, Corodéhuachi is the former name of Fronteras, Sonora. In that case, its location would be about 30°57'N 106°30'W. Bandelier says the site is on one possible route that fray Marcos de Niza may have taken to Cíbola. Bandelier 1981: 83 n36.

Fronteras: See Corodéhuachi.

Guagarispa: NF GNIS. It is mentioned in a footnote by Winship in his translation of Castañeda. His reference is to the work of Henri Ternaux-Compans entitled *Voyages, relations et mémoires originaux pour servir à l'histoire de la découverte de l'Amérique, publiés pour la première fois en français.* Ternaux writes, "Upatrico, Mochila, Guagarispa, El Vallecillo . . ." (Winship 1896: 515 n8). Since Ternaux also translates Castañeda, the names seem to correspond to Winship's, that is: Upatrico is Comupatrico, Mochila is Mochilagua, Guagarispa is Arispa, and El Vallecillo is Little Valley. Winship's Spanish transcription is "u patrico, mochilagua y arispa, y el uallecillo . . ." (Winship 1896: 449). From this we can deduce that Guagarispa is Arispa. An alternative spelling of Arispa is Arizpe. See Arizpe. Winship 1896: 515.

Huépac: 29°54'N 110°10'W. Huépac is located seventy-five miles northeast of Hermosillo on the Río Sonora. First Cabeza de Baca, then later fray Marcos de Niza, gave an account of this Sonoran valley that encompasses what is now modern Huépac. Bolton 1949: 30, 104, 151.

Mátape: 29°8'N 109°58'W. This settlement is sixty miles east of Hermosillo and fifteen miles west of Novillo Reservoir in northwestern Mexico. Three days after crossing the arroyo at Rebeico Coronado reached another arroyo probably at Mátape (Bolton 1949: 101). Bolton 1949: 11, 101, 150; Day 1940: 330 n13, 339 n8; Hammond and Rey 1940: 16.

Mochila or Mochilagua. NF GNIS. One of the Indian villages in the Río Sonora Valley that is described by Castañeda in his narrative. Hodge 1907: 347; Winship 1896: 515.

Mututicachi (Motuticatzi): 30°45'N 109°59'W. A Sonoran village, Bandelier says, eleven miles north of Bacuachi, where the Sonora River goes underground for a distance. It is part, he thinks, of fray Marcos de Niza's route to Cíbola. Bandelier 1981: 78, 83 n33.

Ponida: 28°57'N 109°10'W. A settlement cited by Bandelier as having been occupied by the Jova Indians. Bandelier 1981: 61 n39.

Quitovac: 31°32'N 112°42'W. A village in Sonora that according to Rodack may have been Eusebio Kino's Bacapa. Bandelier 1981: 35, 74n.

Satechi: NF GNIS. Another place in Sonora that Bandelier claims was occupied by the Jova Indians. Bandelier 1981: 61 n39.

Sonoita: (Sonoyta) 31°51'N 112°50'W. A town on the Arizona-Sonora border and State Route 85. In describing the journey of Melchior Díaz into the area, Day surmises that Díaz probably traveled from the valley of the Río Altar through Sonoita and thence to the Camino del Diablo. Bolton 1949: 169; Day 1940: 349 n24.

Soyopa: 28°46'N 109°39'W. A municipality in Sonora on the Río Yaqui. Day says that Coronado's advance party probably forded the Yaqui River near Soyopa. Hammond and Rey say that Coronado's route followed "the east bank of the Yaqui to Soyopa." Bolton 1949: 11, 101, 348; Day 1940: 339; Hammond and Rey 1940: 16.

Ures: 29°26'N 110°24'W. See also Corazones. A city and township in Sonora. It is usually associated with the Indian village that the Spaniards knew as Corazones and which later became San Gerónimo de los Corazones. Hammond and Rey hold that the route north that passes through present-day Ures was the most commonly traveled one. Bandelier 1981: 47n; Day 1940: 102, 132, 326 n13, 364; Hammond and Rey 1940: 16.

Yécora: 28°20'N 108°58'W. In discussing the location of Corazones, Rodack says that one of the sites that has been suggested is "near the Sinaloa-Sonora border, around the present town of Yécora." Bandelier 1981: 47n.

Other Geographical References and Peculiarities

Frailes, Rock of the: (Cerro Frailes) 22°46'N 103°15'W. Bolton says, "from Fuerte River, Coronado and his train followed behind Díaz, past Vacapa, past the famous rock of the Frailes who still look down upon the old trail . . ." (Bolton 1949: 101). Bolton 1949: 101.

Janover-Achi: (Genoverachi) 30°53'N 110°9'W. A location in the valley of the Río Sonora. Bandelier says that it is one of only three places which offer sufficient space suitable for village sites. This area is just southeast of Cananea between that city and Bacoachi. Bandelier 1981: 79.

Mochopa: NF GNIS. A location in Sonora given by Bandelier as having been occupied by the Jova Indians. Bandelier 1981: 61 n39.

Sonoytac: NF GNIS. Bandelier writes, "emerging from the mountains of Sonoytac or Altar." Although no Sonoytac can be found, the Sierra de Sonoyta is located in a position that would agree with the text. It is assumed, therefore, that Bandelier's Sonoytac is actually Sonoyta. Bandelier 1981: 79.

Tiburon Island: 29°N 112°23'W. An island off the coast of Sonora about seventy-five miles west of Hermosillo. It is about thirty miles long and eighteen miles wide. It was populated by the Seri Indians, some of whom apparently met the Coronado party on the mainland near Corazones. Bolton 1949: 151; Day 1940: 330 n4; Winship 1896: 554.

Note

1. Not found in the Geographical Names Indexing System.

CHAPTER 10

The Relevance of Ethnology to the Routing of the Coronado Expedition in Sonora

DANIEL T. REFF

his chapter focuses on the routing of the Coronado expedition in Sonora. As we all are aware, there has been considerable scholarly debate over Coronado's route, owing to the vagueness of the chronicles with respect to the expedition's itinerary. At present, there appear to be two principal schools of thought with respect to routing of the Coronado expedition in Sonora (Map 6). The older of the two schools, led by Carl Sauer (1932), has held that Coronado traveled through the middle and upper Río Sonora Valley to the headwaters of the Río San Pedro, subsequently turning to the northeast and to Cíbola. The second school, founded by Charles Di Peso (Di Peso et al. 1974), has held that Coronado traveled farther inland, principally up the Río Bavispe, to the Río San Bernardino, and then north along the Arizona–New Mexico border to Cíbola.

Here I evaluate these different routes, particularly the Río Sonora route favored by Adolf Bandelier, Herbert Bolton, Sauer, and others. I pay particular attention to the explorers' ethnographic observations and their degree of fit with ethnohistorical and archeological data. Basically, I conclude that the chronicles of the Coronado as well as other expeditions are remarkably consistent with archeological and other evidence of a large and sophisticated Ópata population in the Río

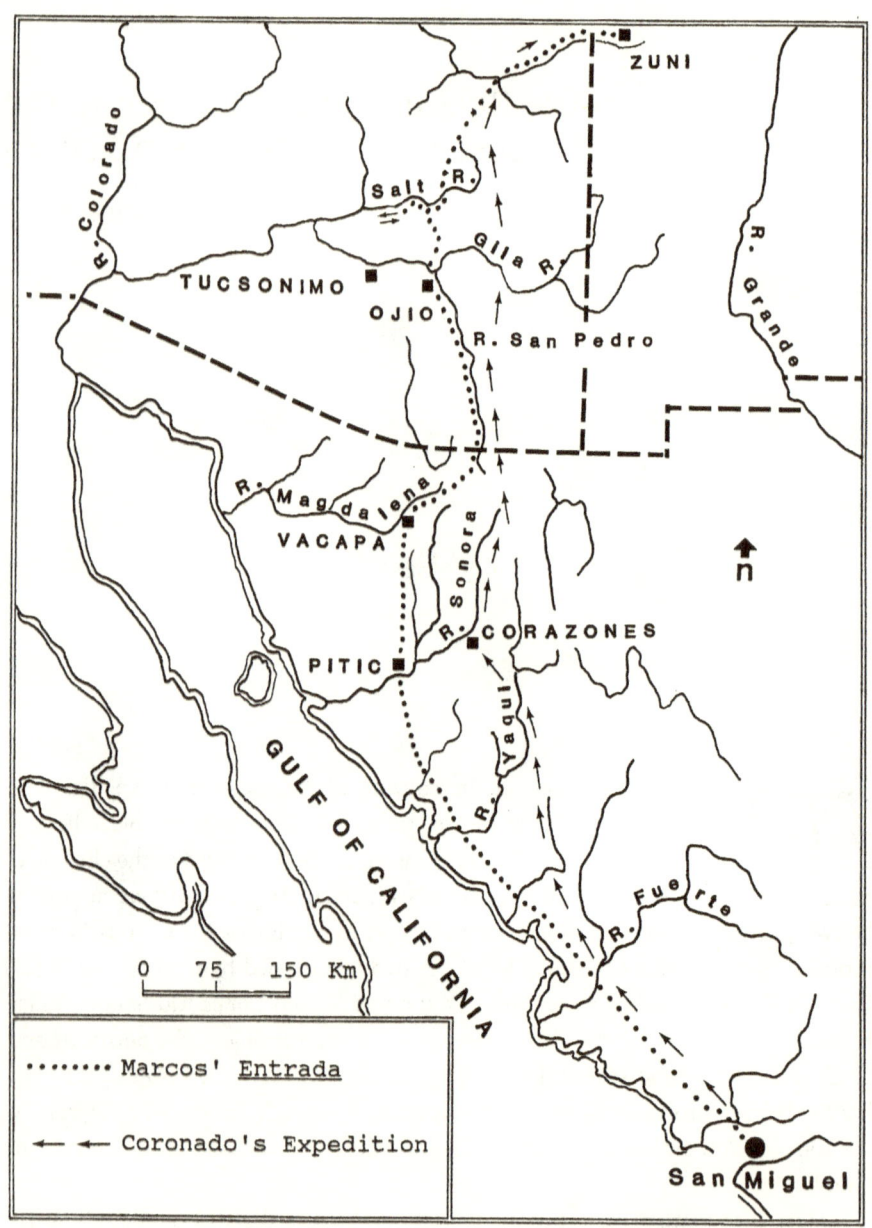

Map 6. *Reconstruction of routes to Tierra Nueva.* By Daniel Reff.

Sonora Valley. This finding is significant for reasons that go beyond a determination of Coronado's route.

Specifically, the exploration chronicles often have been devalued as a source of data on native life in the Greater Southwest. Scholars continue to point out that the explorers were not social scientists,[1] and accordingly, their comments on native life are ethnocentric, exaggerated, or were composed to defame or defend the explorers' actions (see, for example, McGuire and Villalpando 1991: 170). Although the chroniclers of the Coronado expedition clearly were not social scientists, formal social science education does not render observers free of bias, ethnocentrism, imprecision, and ulterior motives (Clifford 1988). Anthropologists in this regard have been lulled into a false sense of security with respect to the "accuracy" of modern ethnographic texts, as opposed to texts generated by pre-anthropology observers (Thomas 1989).

Another important reason why the explorers' comments have been held suspect is that often the explorers' characterization of aboriginal culture was contradicted, in whole or in part, by the later Franciscans and Jesuits (Reff 1991; Upham 1982). The missionaries in the 1600s generally reported much smaller native populations as well as less complex native societies. This lack of correspondence between the explorers' and missionaries' writings has contributed to doubts about the reliability of the explorers' accounts. Again, many have assumed—if only implicitly—that the missionaries, because they were religious, were trustworthy, whereas the explorers, because they were "soldiers of fortune," were apt to lie to enhance the importance of their efforts on behalf of the crown (see, for instance, Mecham 1927: 157; Simmons 1979: 192).

In the second part of this chapter I explore the reasons for the discrepancy between the explorers' and later Jesuits' descriptions of what the explorers referred to as the Señora Valley. Briefly, Jesuit and other colonial documents indicate that Old World diseases spread in advance of the mission frontier during the late sixteenth and seventeenth centuries. Diseases such as smallpox decimated many native populations during the interlude separating the time of the explorers and the founding of the first missions. Thus, the fact that the explorers' comments are seemingly at odds with the later observations of the missionaries reflects disease and its consequences, not the explorers' predilection to lie or exaggerate.

The Sonoran Routing

In reconstructing the route of the Coronado expedition, early theorists, such as Bolton (1949) and Sauer (1932), were convinced that Coronado's expedition departed the villa of San Miguel de Culiacán and followed the foothills of southern Sonora to the Middle Río Yaqui (see Map 6). It has been generally assumed that the expedition crossed the river at Sayopa, and proceeded in a northwesterly direction to the Río Sonora and the village of Corazones, which had first been visited by Álvar Núñez Cabeza de Vaca and his party in 1536. At Corazones Coronado established his first base camp of San Gerónimo. In 1932, Sauer specifically argued that Corazones was about eight miles above present-day Ures, near the modern settlement of Puerto del Sol.[2]

From Corazones, Coronado's expedition traveled ten leagues, through what Juan de Jaramillo (Hammond and Rey 1940: 297) described as a "sort of small gateway"—apparently through the *barranca* below present-day Mazocahui—into the Río Sonora Basin proper. Members of Coronado's, as well as of Francisco de Ibarra's later expedition in 1565, referred to the basin as the "Señora Valley." There Coronado established a second base camp, which Sauer believed was located near present-day Baviácora. From the Sonora Basin proper, Coronado's expedition continued up the Río Sonora to modern-day Bacoachi, or what was referred to as the "Suya Valley." There, a third base camp was established, which was destroyed in 1541. From the headwaters of the Río Sonora, Coronado's expedition is believed to have made its way to the headwaters of the Río San Pedro.

The arguments proffered by Sauer and other proponents of a Sonoran routing of the Coronado expedition generally were accepted until the early 1970s, when Charles Di Peso outlined an alternative routing of Coronado's expedition and that of other explorers. Di Peso's reconstruction was prompted by his discovery of a prehistoric trade route that extended from Casas Grandes to Sahuaripa (Di Peso et al. 1974: 37n). Di Peso believed this trade route still was functioning in the sixteenth century and was used by Cabeza de Vaca and later explorers, including Coronado. Di Peso went on to suggest that the settlement of Corazones, visited by Cabeza de Vaca and Coronado, was located in the middle Cedros Valley. Di Peso argued that the "Señora Valley," where Coronado's second base camp was located, was in the Nuri Chico Valley. Finally, Di Peso believed Coronado's third base camp (San Gerónimo III), in the Suya Valley, was near the confluence of the Río Batepito and Río Bavispe—near modern Colonia Morelos. From there, Coronado purportedly continued north to the Río San Bernardino and then over Antelope Pass, en route to Cíbola.

Di Peso's analysis, when it appeared in 1974, generally was well received. Although it is not possible here to pursue a full critique of Di Peso's many assumptions and propositions, I think it is important to note that his analysis suffers from many of the same problems that have plagued other attempts to make sense of the explorers' itinerary (Brand 1978; Hedrick 1978; Reff 1981). For instance, a major problem with most reconstructions is the frequency with which theorists have had to stretch or shrink the distance of a league to accommodate the estimates in the

Spanish journals (Di Peso et al. 1974: 77–78). Di Peso himself had difficulty making his proposed route fit the explorers' accounts. For example, while the chroniclers failed to indicate precisely the location of Corazones, they did suggest that it was roughly halfway between Culiacán and Cíbola. Thus, Coronado reported that his vanguard took thirty-five days to reach Corazones and another forty-one days to reach Cíbola. Pedro de Castañeda commented that Corazones was "down the valley of Señora," which he indicated was 150 leagues form Culiacán (Hammond and Rey 1940: 162–165, 250, 284). Finally, the author of the *Relación del Suceso* stated that the Valley of Corazones was 150 leagues from the Valley of Culiacán and an equal distance from Cíbola. The location of Corazones postulated by Di Peso, namely the modern Rancho Tesocoma in the middle Cedros Valley, is only 110 leagues from Culiacán.

In point of fact, neither Di Peso's nor Sauer's rendering of the exploration chronicles is totally satisfactory. While no ancillary documents apparently have surfaced in recent years that explicitly deal with the explorers' routes, recent ethnohistorical and archeological research have produced new data with which to interpret and evaluate some of the explorers' ethnographic observations. These data also help address the question of where the encounter occurred in Sonora. In what follows I focus specifically on the explorers' statements regarding native settlement systems, warfare, and socio-political organization and their fit with archeological and other historic data.

Chroniclers of the Coronado and other expeditions invariably described Señora as a densely populated valley. This was indicated in both relative and absolute terms. Jaramillo, for instance, noted that the Señora Valley "has more Indians than the others" (Hammond and Rey 1940: 270). Castañeda commented that "Señora is a river and valley thickly settled" (Hammond and Rey 1940: 250). Elsewhere, Castañeda implied that the Señora Valley was the largest of a group of native provinces, the smallest of which had ten or twelve pueblos.[3] It should be noted that Castañeda as well as other explorers such as Baltasar de Obregón (Hammond and Rey 1928) and Cabeza de Vaca (1944) used the term "pueblos" as opposed to "*ranchos*" or "*aldeas*," implying relatively large settlements.[4]

Although the chroniclers of the Coronado expedition said little more about the size and location of pueblos, Obregón, who accompanied Ibarra's expedition in 1564, reported that expedition marched for four short days in the Señora Valley, finding most of it populated, with towns three and four leagues apart, containing 100 or more "terraced houses of reed matting" (Hammond and Rey 1928: 163–164). Obregón reported that the town of Guaraspi, which is apparently the same town as Ispa mentioned by Jaramillo, had 600 houses laid out along well-planned streets (Hammond and Rey 1928: 173–175).

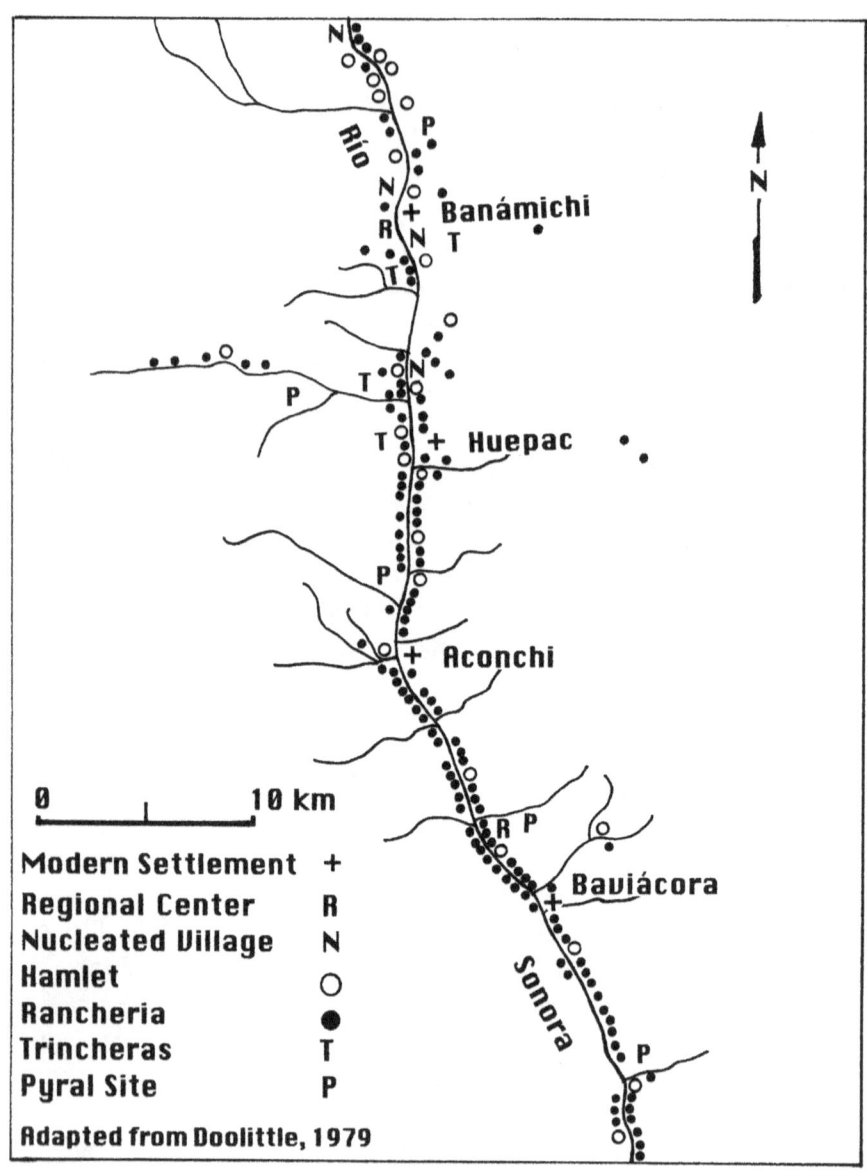

Map 7. Archeological sites of the Río Sonora Valley. By Daniel Reff.

Obregón's observations, as well as Castañeda's and Jaramillo's from the Coronado expedition, are entirely consistent with the results of an intensive archeological survey of the Río Sonora Basin, which was conducted in the mid-1970s (Doolittle

1979; Pailes 1978, 1980; Reff 1981). The survey, which was directed by Richard Pailes from the University of Oklahoma, disclosed some 227 sites, 162 of which were habitation sites, on mesa tops overlooking the floodplain of the Sonora River (Map 7). Excavation of some fifty-nine structures indicated that the Ópata lived in surface structures of puddled adobe as well as pithouses well into the early historic period. This finding is consistent with observations by Obregón and Cabeza de Vaca regarding native use of houses of mud and others of cane matting.

In describing Señora, the Spaniards noted not only the presence of a large population, in the aggregate, but also a hierarchical settlement system, composed of villages, towns, and rancherías. The 162 habitation sites that were identified through survey in the Sonora Basin were classified into four groups on the basis of size (areal extent), numbers of structures, and the presence or absence of special architectural features. Two sites in the middle Sonora Valley have been termed regional centers because they are large, nucleated, architecturally complex sites with public architectural features. The San José Site, just north of Baviácora—where Sauer believed one of Coronado's base camps was located—has over 125 visible structures and encompasses an area of twenty-five acres. The site of Las Delicias, located on the west bank of the Río Sonora near Banámichi, has been severely eroded, but nevertheless covers an area in excess of sixty-one acres, with an estimated 200 structures. To the north and south of these regional centers are nucleated villages with an excess of eighty-five structures as well as still smaller rancherías and hamlets (Doolittle 1979; Pailes 1978, 1980; Reff 1981).

At the two regional centers in the Sonora Basin as well as a third settlement with close to 100 structures, called La Mora, we identified and, in one case, partially excavated a court-platform structure. The court-platform structure at the San José Site consisted of two elevated, parallel, elongated platforms, about a meter high and two meters wide in their present condition. These platforms are joined at each end by a cross wall, creating an enclosed plazalike area measuring forty-five by twenty-eight meters (Doolittle 1979; Pailes 1978, 1980). Although the function of these public architectural features is unclear, Castañeda noted with respect to the Señora Valley that "the dignitaries of the pueblos stand on some terraces which they have for that purpose and remain there for one hour, calling like town criers, instructing the people in what they are to do" (Hammond and Rey 1940: 250). Elsewhere, Castañeda noted that the dignitaries or elites kept royal eagles as a symbol of authority. This observation is consistent with Jesuit reports from 1619, some ten years before the Jesuits established a permanent mission among the Ópata. At this time, a group of caciques, bearing a gift of three eagles, visited Father Diego de Guzmán who was working among the Nébome along the lower Río Yaqui (Reff 1991: 63).

As noted previously, Castañeda implied that the Señora Valley was the largest of a group of related native provinces, the smallest of which had ten or twelve pueblos that "were toward the Sierras." Castañeda recalled the names of some of these provinces, including "Comu, Patrico [Cumupas, Batuco], Mochil, Agua, Arispa [Arispe], and Vallecillo. Castañeda's comments here agree nicely with Obregón's later account of a conspiracy to plunder the Ibarra expedition, which was hatched by elites in Señora Valley together with Ópata-speakers of Guaraspi (Arizpe), Cumupas, and what appears to have been Guasabas (Hammond and Rey 1928: 162–195). It is significant that when the Jesuits first began working among the Guasabas Ópata in 1647, Father Marcos del Río noted that the *vezinos* of Gusavas were related by marriage to those of Cumupas, Sonora, and other Ópata living to the west (AGN 1647).

The inhabitants of Señora and related provinces were described by the explorers as a highly militaristic people. Both Coronado's and Ibarra's expeditions engaged the Señorans in battles. Castañeda, as well as Obregón, reported the presence of defensive retreats or fortifications (Hammond and Rey 1940: 232). Obregón also noted that the inhabitants of Señora used a pyral communication system for military and other purposes. The archeological evidence from the Sonora Valley again confirms these reports. In particular, four large defensive works were found in the Sonora Basin. In all cases they consist of extensive breastworks of stone and are located at the edge of a high mesa overlooking the valley. Along with these defensive works, five unusual sites that suggest an intravalley pyral communication system were located. Each of these sites consists of a single low, circular structure of stone, approximately two meters in diameter, and is situated at the edge of a high mesa overlooking the valley. Importantly, these pyral sites are spatially discrete from habitation sites and are located such that each is in view of the next to the south, north, or west.

In general, the explorers' observations conform quite well with archeological and other data that point to the middle Sonora Valley as being one and the same as the Señora Valley mentioned in the chronicles. It should be pointed out that this conclusion also was reached by two prominent Jesuit historians, who were missionaries in Sonora during the seventeenth and eighteenth centuries. Specifically, both Andrés Pérez de Ribas (1944: 2: 186), who completed his *Historia* in 1644, and Cristóbal de Cañas[5] (Documentos 1857: 625), who authored the *Estado de la Provincia de Sonora* in 1730, explicitly equated the Río Sonora Valley with the Señora Valley discussed in the exploration chronicles.

The Ethnohistorical Implications

Determining the explorers' routes is an intriguing historical problem, particularly now when our attention necessarily has been drawn to the age of exploration by the recent Columbus Quincentenary. Determining where the explorers went also is important in making sense of the protohistoric period. After all, Coronado and other explorers were the first Europeans to observe and comment on native life. As noted at the outset, anthropologists frequently have ignored or questioned the reliability of the explorers' ethnographic observations. Again, this neglect is partly related to the fact that the explorers often were contradicted by the later missionaries. Missionaries like Eusebio Kino in the late seventeenth century made little or no mention of settlements such as Corazones or "kingdoms" such as Totonteac and Marata. Indeed, the Jesuits characterized many areas of northwestern Mexico in terms of small rancherías (Spicer 1962; Reff 1991).

In the past decade I have worked extensively with Jesuit *anuas* as well as other documents from the sixteenth and seventeenth centuries. Much to my surprise, I discovered that the Jesuit materials, in particular, are replete with references to disease and epidemics (Gerhard 1982; Reff 1991). The historical records, for example, indicate that smallpox, measles, typhus, pneumonia, and other maladies reached epidemic proportions in 1593–1594, 1601–1602, 1607–1608, 1612–1613, 1617, 1623–1625, and on numerous occasions during the decades that followed (Alegre 1956–1960; Pérez de Ribas 1944; Reff 1991). The destruction wrought by these epidemics is reflected in the annual report that Father Juan Lorencio submitted toward the end of the epidemic of 1623–1625. In his report, Lorencio noted the epidemic killed over 8,600 natives in Sinaloa and Sonora alone (AGN 1635: 137). Perhaps of greater importance with respect to the explorers' accounts is the fact that the Jesuit materials make clear that groups such as the Ópata of the Sonora Valley were devastated by Old World diseases prior to the establishment of Jesuit missions (Reff 1991: 168–180). In point of fact, maladies such as smallpox spread far in advance of the mission frontier.

It is not surprising, therefore, that there is a lack of correspondence between the explorers' and missionaries' accounts. This is precisely what one would expect, given the evidence of disease. Although the changes wrought by disease often went unobserved by Europeans, we know that infectious diseases such as smallpox and measles have their greatest impact on large, nucleated settlements. Significantly, archeological data indicate that the three largest settlements in the Río Sonora Basin were abandoned sometime around the turn of the seventeenth century (Reff 1981). This inference is supported by Jesuit reports that the Ópata were living in dispersed rancherias when the Jesuits reached the Sonora Valley in 1638–1639 (AGN 1639; Pérez de Ribas 1944: 2: 187). Gone were the large towns that the explorers reported a century earlier and which archeological evidence indicates existed as early as the thirteenth century (Pailes 1978, 1980).

Conclusion

In conclusion, the archeological evidence from Sonora, together with historical data, support the idea that Coronado and other explorers traveled through the middle Sonora Valley. Both archeological and historical data also confirm many of the explorers' comments regarding a large and sophisticated Ópata population in the Río Sonora Valley in the early 1500s. Finally, there is considerable evidence that Old World diseases profoundly impacted the Ópata during the interlude separating the explorers and later missionaries, specifically during the first quarter of the seventeenth century. As we have seen, the Ópata were not the only native group to be negatively affected by smallpox and other introduced diseases. The evidence of disease is another reason to reexamine our assumptions about the exploration chronicles and the protohistoric period. Too often in the past we have assumed that many of the "problems" of interpreting the exploration chronicles are due to the explorers themselves, specifically their lack of integrity or ethnocentrism. I have come to believe that the explorers did not lie or exaggerate as much as we think. What we perceive as exaggeration, particularly statements regarding large and complex societies, is a reflection, at least in part, of disease-induced reductions in population that followed Coronado and other explorers.

Notes

1. Undoubtedly asides like those in Castañeda's account, which relate how Coronado and many of his men were convinced that the Devil had appeared to a soldier named Trujillo (Hammond and Rey 1940: 206), have cast a shadow of doubt on the "objective" faculties of the explorers.

2. Following Sauer, Corazones would have been a Pima Bajo settlement, bordering on the lands of the Ópata. This is consistent with Juan de Jaramillo's and Pedro de Castañeda's comments that natives from Corazones fought with the Spaniards against the people of Señora, when the latter attacked the main body of Coronado's army under Diego de Alcaráz (Hammond and Rey 1940: 232, 269).

3. "Around this province [Señora], toward the Sierra, there are large settlements forming separate small provinces. They are composed of ten or twelve pueblos" (Hammond and Rey 1940: 250).

4. Spaniards in the sixteenth century were very conscious of settlement-size distinctions for both legal and ideological reasons (Gibson 1964: 32; Nader 1990; Pagden 1982: 97–98).

5. Luis González (1977) has convincingly argued that Cañas is the author of what previously was referred to as the "anonymous" *El Estado de La Provincia de Sonora*.

CHAPTER 11

An Archeological Perspective on the Sonora Entrada

RICHARD A. PAILES

rcheology has somewhat limited potential in dealing with the Spanish entrada in Sonora. The routes taken by the explorers in their journeys through Sonora are by no means certain and the conquistadors did not remain in one place long enough to make much of an impact of the kind that would leave archeological evidence. Even Coronado's supply base, the initial location of which was purportedly the town named by Álvar Núñez Cabeza de Vaca as Corazones, was moved several times during the relatively brief span of the Coronado expedition. Thus, it is unlikely that direct evidence of the Spanish presence in Sonora in the sixteenth century will be found, unless by serendipity.

Nevertheless, archeological data in combination with ethnographic, linguistic, and historic data can contribute indirectly to a number of problems concerning the Spanish entrada. Questions that potentially can be addressed by archeology include the following:

1) The actual routes of the explorers. By comparing late archeological data (protohistoric) with descriptions provided by the various chroniclers of the entrada, we might narrow the alternatives to a few most likely routes. Also, with remarkable luck, we might even identify specific places, although never with certainty.

2) The identification of indigenous peoples encountered by the explorers or confirmation of such identification made through other sources and knowledge of their cultures. Archeology can both confirm and add to the chroniclers' descriptions of the peoples of Sonora in the sixteenth century.

3) The impact of Spanish contact on the native cultures during its first eighty to one hundred years, by contrasting the protohistoric archeology with the historic data for the contact period.

The routes of the earliest Spanish penetrations into and through Sonora, from the north by Cabeza de Vaca and from the south by Melchior Díaz, Vázquez de Coronado, and Francisco de Ibarra, took place through the eastern half of the state (Di Peso et al. 1974: 37–120; Sauer 1932), in what has been described geographically as the Serrana zone by Braniff C. (1978). The route of fray Marcos de Niza is more uncertain, but Undriener (1947) has made a convincing argument that Marcos followed the coast northward at least as far as the mouth of the Río Sonora before turning inland and that he never entered the Serrana Province either on his outward journey or his return.

Two environmental features of this eastern half of Sonora are significant here. First, the topography features a series of mountain ranges aligned on a north-south axis with corresponding intervening valleys and water courses. Second, the streams are live year-round (see Map 8).

The Río Sonora is a live stream above Ures, while downstream under natural conditions it is absorbed by the desert before reaching the sea. East and south of the Río Sonora the streams are live and reach the sea under natural conditions.

In contrast, the topography of central and northwestern Sonora consists of isolated ranges separated by broad alluvial basins (Dunbier 1968). The rivers, consisting of the lower Río Sonora and its western tributary, the Río San Miguel, and the Río Concepción with its tributaries, the Altar and Magdalena, are ephemeral streams flowing intermittently only during rainy seasons. Hence, as has been noted frequently in the past (see, for example, Pailes 1980; Sauer 1932), the valleys of eastern Sonora provide a natural corridor of north-south travel and it is generally understood that it was through this zone that the explorers traversed northwestern Mexico.

Although the mountains of the Serrana appear substantial, in reality they do not present significant barriers to east-west travel until the escarpment of the sierras is reached east of the western arm of the Río Bavispe. The area as a whole represents a unified cultural province as well as a geographic one and is ethnographically, linguistically, and archeologically distinguishable from central and northwestern Sonora (Pailes 1973; Riley 1987). The distribution of Taracahitan speakers

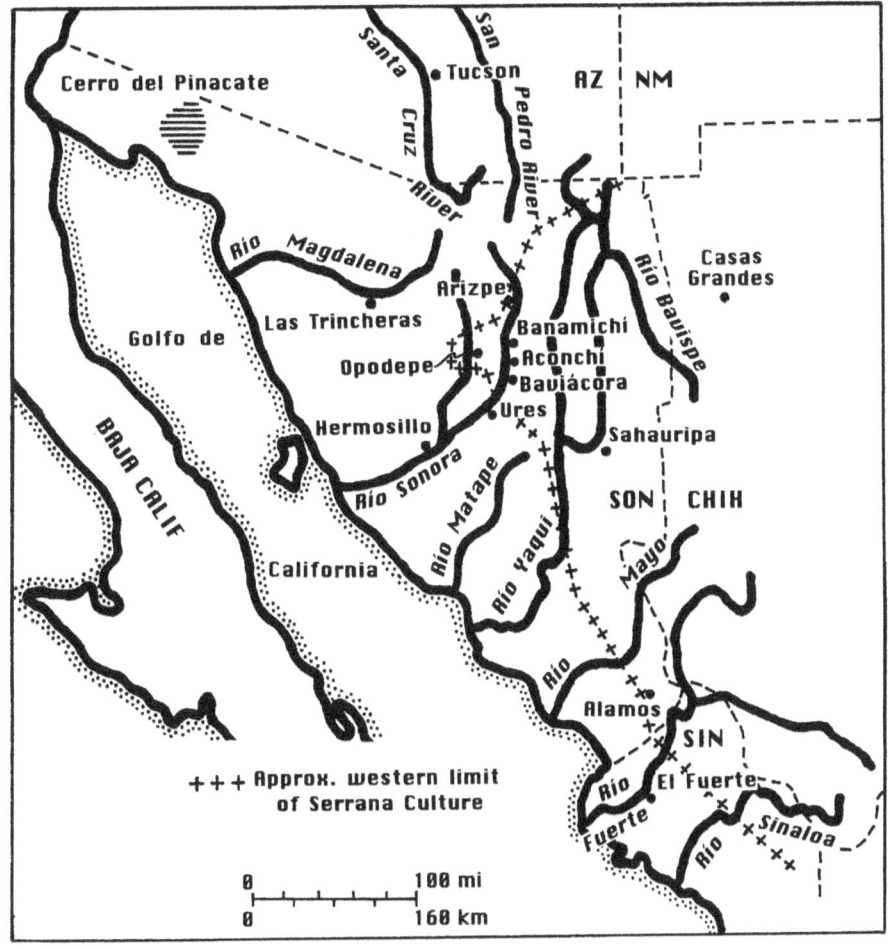

Map 8. Serrana Culture, sixteenth-century Sonora.

in Sonora, consisting of the Tarahumara, Ópata, Eudeve, Warihio, Yaqui, and Mayo, conforms almost exactly to the distribution of live streams, and the only area where Taracahitans reached the sea is in the south along the Río Yaqui, Río Mayo, and Río Fuerte, all live streams to the coast (Sauer 1934). Conversely, with the exception of the Pima Bajo enclave in east-central Sonora, the distribution of the Pima is confined to the dry northwest deserts where intermittent streams prevail.

The southern portion of the explorers' routes through Sonora is not much in doubt. Sonora is shaped like an inverted triangle. In the south, the sierra is virtually within hailing distance of the coast and there is little room for alternative routes.

Upon reaching the Río Fuerte, it is almost certain that the explorers continued northward along the Arroyo Cuchujaqui, a tributary of the Río Fuerte, passing through the vicinity of modern Alamos, and on to the Río Mayo at a point where they could cross the river and continue northward following the Río Cedros (Beals 1932: 148 n51; Sauer 1932: 34).

Our knowledge of the routes north of the upper Río Cedros is less than certain. Various routes of Coronado's entrada that have been suggested from time to time include: 1) crossing from the Río Yaqui to the Río Sonora near La Puerta del Sol and, after negotiating the barranca of the Sonora, following that valley northward; 2) continuing up the Yaqui to the Río Moctezuma, and thence up that tributary and across a low divide to the Río Fronteras; 3) crossing over from the Río Cedros to the Río Sahuaripa, thence northward to the Río Yaqui, and its tributary, the Río Bavispe, and north up the Bavispe; and 4) variations of any of the above (Di Peso et al. 1974: 37–120; Sauer 1932).

Each of these routes has advantages and disadvantages. The Bavispe is the least likely because of the difficulties of travel. The Río Sonora route is favored by most scholars for reasons too detailed to go into here, although I see no reason why the Río Moctezuma would not be equally likely. With the exception of the Río Sahuaripa and a small portion of the middle Río Yaqui and the Río Sonora below the barranca, that is at Puerta del Sol, all of these routes are encompassed by the distribution of Taracahitan speakers. This includes the Mayo and Warihio in the south, and the Ópata and related Eudeve and Jova in the north.

Archeologically we find throughout eastern Sonora prehistoric traditions that show strong evidence of having been derived from a common cultural core. The earliest representation of these traditions was by Monroe Amsden, who in 1928 identified a prehistoric cultural tradition in the upper Río Sonora Valley, which he named the Río Sonora Culture. Subsequent research by Gordon Ekholm (1939, 1940, 1947), William Wasley (personal communication and field notes on file at the Centro Regional-INAH, Hermosillo, Sonora), and Pailes (1973, 1976a and b, 1980, 1984) has determined that sites comparable to Amdsen's finds are distributed throughout the eastern Sonoran valleys with sufficient similarities to link the entire eastern portion of Sonora to a common cultural base (see Map 8).

The term *traditions* is used in the plural because certain differences between north and south can be recognized and, to some extent, between east and west in the northern part. These differences might form the basis for defining local branches in terms of archeological cultural unit classification, but at this time it is best not to venture beyond speaking in general terms of a Serrana culture with northern and southern branches, without being too precise on drawing a line between them. Elements they hold in common include:

1) Rectangular surface structures with foundations of stone embedded in an adobe matrix. In the south there appear to be two temporally distinct versions: an earlier group of sites located on high hilltops with very crude stone architecture and a later series of sites in the valley bottoms. The latter are larger sites, but the known architectural remains consist only of stone foundations in the form of multiple rectangular outlines.

2) By late prehistoric times a community hierarchy of a few large sites or central places and numerous smaller satellite villages. In the northern branch a four-tiered system can be distinguished in the Río Sonora Valley, where most archeological research has been focused.

3) The use of water diversion devices, such as check dams and weirs, and ditch irrigation on the floodplains of river valleys and large tributary arroyos.

4) A brown ware pottery with textured exterior designs as the primary locally made decorated variety. These designs consist of incised and punctated geometric patterns that are similar throughout the area. In the northern branch we also find some design patterns that are absent from the south, including the use of red paint in combination with incised motifs, and some incised motifs that seem to be earlier in the northern ceramic sequence and entirely absent in the south.

   Less frequently found are sherds of a paint-decorated red-on-brown variety. Both the red-on-brown and the textured pottery are crudely reminiscent of southern Mogollon pottery characteristic of northwestern Chihuahua, in particular Convento Incised, Casas Grandes Incised, and Playas Red Incised (Di Peso et al. 1974), as well as the more northerly Mogollon type, Alma Incised (Haury 1936). Conversely, this ceramic tradition contrasts sharply with the ceramics in neighboring areas to the north and west and is not at all comparable to the earlier Hohokam textured pottery.

5) There are several other generalized similarities between the northern and southern branches that would require too much detail here, such as the manufacture and use of three-quarter-grooved axes, similarities in flaked-stone-tool industries, similar basin-and-trough metates, and the practice of breaking metates. (Throughout the area metates are consistently found broken, with one half absent, and rarely are whole metates found).

Significant differences also occur. In the southern branch there is evidence of influences from farther south, in the form of modelled ceramic spindle whorls, ceramic cylinder stamps, stone idols, and the use of flat-slab metates with overhanging manos characteristic of the Sinaloan cultures and of Mesoamerica in general (Ekholm 1942: 107; Tolstoy 1971: 288).

The northern branch, on the other hand, has a greater variety of architecture, although this difference may be an artifact of research. In the north are found large pithouses occurring both before and contemporaneously with surface structures of adobe; multiple-room surface structures; public architecture in the form of platforms bordering rectangular enclosures; and ball-courts, including at least one recorded T-shaped court (Pailes 1980).

Other elements associated with the northern branch include hilltop features that suggest components of a pyral signal system; numerous modelled and engraved stone discoid spindle whorls; ceramic female figurines; rectangular, engraved stone shaft abraders; copper tinklers; and the use of turquoise, which was obtained from sources in New Mexico.

Finally, virtually all the trade pottery consists of various Chihuahuan polychromes, indicating that the strongest external ties were with the southern Mogollon in northwestern Chihuahua.

Most of our current knowledge of the northern Serrana cultures comes from the upper Río Sonora Valley in its northern branch. Only minimal survey and test excavations have been conducted in neighboring valleys to the east and south, the results of which indicate essentially similar patterns in pottery, architecture, and settlement. In the Río Sonora Valley three phases have been defined, representing a sequence of development beginning with small moderate-sized-pithouse villages and culminating in a hierarchical settlement and community pattern featuring regional centers and the domestic and public architecture mentioned above (Doolittle 1988; Pailes 1984). Relative to the Spanish entrada, only the late phase is discussed here.

Pithouses continue in use alongside surface structures. These were up to a meter and a half deep and up to five by eight meters in area (forty square meters). The floor was raised approximately thirty centimeters above the bottom of the pit. The crushed remains of noticeably large pottery vessels are found in these structures, and in one excavation an abundance of charred hulled corn was recovered. These data suggest that the pithouses may have served as storage facilities. In addition, modelled and engraved spindle whorls are predominantly associated with pithouses.

Jean Johnson (1950: 14–15) reports that the Ópata maintained special subterranean structures where women wove basketry and cloth fabrics. According to Johnson's Ópata informants, the underground rooms were necessary to maintain the proper humidity for the weaving materials. A raised floor might well have contributed to humidity control and would also be important for storage facilities.

The elaboration of spindle whorl design and their frequency of occurrence suggest that weaving was an important activity, and elsewhere it has been postulated that a principal concern during this phase was the production and trade of cotton products (Pailes 1984). Riley (1987: 76–88) has noted the frequent references to cotton in the explorers' accounts.

Domestic surface structures usually consisted of a single room, although two- and three-room structures are not unusual. These structures are identified by their foundation remains, which consist of hard adobe footings approximately twenty to thirty centimeters thick, into which flattish stones or rocks have been embedded on edge. No postholes are found associated with these structures, indicating that the walls must have been of some solid material, which could only have been adobe. The thickness of the walls makes it unlikely that these structures were more than one story high. Occasionally foundations are found up to forty centimeters thick and in only two excavated sites were foundations found that suggest the possibility of multiple stories. No foundations suggestive of more than one story have been found at the San José Site, which has been the focus of research in the Río Sonora Valley and which appears to have been a regional center.

In northeastern Sonora the Río Sonora Culture and its Serrana variants appear in the upper Río Sonora Valley, the Río Moctezuma and Río Fronteras Valleys, the western arm of the Río Bavispe, a small portion of the middle Río San Miguel, and tributaries of these streams. These localities correspond to the statelets of the Serrana Province identified by Riley (1987) as the Señora, Guaraspi, Cumupa, Sahuaripa, and Batuco. Farther south, a variant of the Serrana Culture has been found in the Río Cedros Valley, where Riley identifies the Oera statelet.

To the west, in north central Sonora, is found the Trincheras Culture, so named for the numerous hillside terraces that characterize many sites in the area. Equally characteristic, however, are hilltop stone enclosures of crude boulder construction, which are found in the eastern half of the Trincheras Culture distribution. Typically, Trincheras sites are found in areas of *malpaís* (lava flows), on hills and terraces littered with basaltic rocks and boulders of all sizes, making simple walking difficult without a trail. This is the case in the Río Sonora Valley, where the malpaís is apparent in aerial photos, and the distribution of known Trincheras sites conforms almost exactly with the malpaís.

Sites consist of man-made clearings in the malpais where the rocks have been removed, frequently being piled up to form borders around the cleared area. On slopes the rocks have been deposited on the downhill side, forming the foundations for crude terraces. An additional common feature is rectangular enclosures crudely constructed of malpaís boulders, such as at the Batonapa Site immediately south of present-day Banámichi in the Río Sonora Valley.

Another group of sites might also be associated with Trincheras in the Serrana, although this is still uncertain. These are sites that contain low piles of rocks forming small rectangular aprons of platforms of from fifteen to twenty square meters, reminiscent of Tepehuan house platforms (Riley 1969). Most such features occur as minor components in sites that are predominantly attributed to the Serrana Culture. However, one site near Arispe consists entirely of fourteen such features.

A full range of similar Trincheras sites is known from the Río Moctezuma to the east, and Doolittle (personal communication) has identified a rock wall enclosure about thirteen kilometers east of the Río Sonora Valley that may be a Trincheras site. Immediately southeast of the town of Moctezuma, in the Río Moctezuma Valley, a large area of malpaís occurs in which several such sites have been recorded, although not yet published, including a relatively large site immediately across the river from the modern town of Moctezuma, on the northwest edge of the malpaís.

The core of the Trincheras Culture is in the Altar and Magdalena Valleys, with the distribution of Trincheras sites extending into southern Arizona and as far east as the Río Moctezuma (Sauer and Brand 1931). Equally characteristic of the Trincheras Culture are rockwall enclosures commonly situated on hilltop prominences. These features are generally considered to have been defensive in function. It is therefore significant that, in comparison with the Trincheras Culture distribution taken as a whole, Sauer and Brand (1931) describe sites with defensive characteristics in the San Miguel and Altar Basins, but not to the west in the Río Seco Basin.

It has been postulated that the Ópata, and the Serrana Culture in general, were related to the Chihuahuan cultural province, which is essentially Mogollon (Pailes 1973, 1984). Similarly, Riley (1979) has suggested that the Ópata were a remnant Casas Grandes population.

This idea is disputed by Doolittle (1988: 52–56), who argues for an in situ development of the prehistoric populations in the Río Sonora Valley. However, Doolittle demonstrates only that the population of the late phase *could* have resulted from in situ internal growth, based on the ratio of arable land to population and the rate of population increase as determined by settlement sizes.

It has long been recognized that the Taracahitan linguistic division of Uto-Aztecan represents a relatively recent intrusion separating the previously continuous distribution of Pima-Tepehuan speakers (Sauer 1934: 82) and it should not be surprising if we find archeological evidence of such a movement. Using glottochronology, Swadesh (1967: 98) has estimated a minimum time of eight centuries for the separation of Papago and Tepecano. While this technique is often viewed with skepticism, it is noteworthy that his age estimate is not out of line with our radiocarbon and obsidian hydration dates for the appearance of the Serrana cultural pattern.

I consider it not coincidental that the distributions of live streams, Taracahitan speakers, and Serrana Culture are in almost perfect conformity, the pattern broken only by the Yaqui and Mayo on the coastal plain of southern Sonora and the Pima Bajo between Mátape and Sahuaripa.

Thus archeological, ethnographic, and linguistic evidence supports the hypothesis that the Ópata (and the Río Sonora Culture as described for southern Sonora) represent an intrusive group from the east and that they were still in the process of expanding westward at the expense of the Pima when the Spanish arrived and unknowingly prevented further expansion. If this hypothesis is correct, they would not be a remnant group from Casas Grandes as Riley has suggested, since their presence in Sonora appears to predate the collapse of Casas Grandes. Rather, they would represent an expansion of peoples either indigenous to the Chihuahuan Province or somehow related to those who were.

A comparison of the archeological data with the accounts of the conquistadors reveals a lack of conformity regarding the descriptions of architecture and the size of principal towns. For example, Cabeza de Vaca and others described Corazones as having houses of cane mats, which have not been found archeologically, but which ethnographically are more characteristic of the hot country. Pedro de Castañeda (Riley 1987: 53) describes Corazones as being "down the valley of Señora." Perhaps the original Corazones was located below the barranca that separates the upper Río Sonora, occupied by Ópata, from the lower Río Sonora, occupied by Pima. If Corazones were near Ures or Puerta del Sol, it would have been in Pima territory and the country of mat and cane houses.

In the Serrana, however, the accounts are much different. Riley (1987: 74) cites Baltasar de Obregón as describing small towns with 100 to 200 houses and large towns with 500 to 600. Guaraspi is said to have had 600 to 700 terraced adobe houses and stone-and-adobe temples. No such architectural features have been found in the Río Sonora Valley, nor have our brief surveys encountered anything like such towns in the other Serrana valleys. According to the site hierarchy as presently defined, there were two regional centers in the Río Sonora Valley during the late phase, the San José and Las Delicias del Sur Sites. Neither of these shows evidence of having over 200 houses, if indeed they had even that many, and neither provides evidence of foundations that would be indicative of terraced, multistoried, multiroomed structures.

Given the prehistoric settlement data for the late phase in the Río Sonora Valley, if the locations of the modern towns were not also occupied prehistorically, they would represent glaring anomalies in the site distribution pattern. Furthermore, given the locations of the modern towns in respect to topography, water supply, and proximity to arable land and major tributaries, their favored locations would have been just as attractive in the past as they are today. It is possible, if not probable, that the sites that have been identified archeologically as regional centers, such as the San José Site, are really second-tier sites, and that the primary sites are precisely where the modern towns are today and for the same reasons. In effect, to find Corazones II and III, it would be necessary to excavate the plazas of Baviácora, Aconchí, and Arizpe.

Finally, it has long been observed that there existed a large disparity between what the conquistadors reported and what the Jesuit fathers found sixty years after Ibarra (Reff 1991). In 1627 Father Pedro Méndez entered the lower Ópata country and by 1636 missions were being established in the Río Sonora Valley. The Jesuit fathers found no large pueblos, no large town-dwelling population cultivating well-kept irrigated fields, and no storehouses filled with abundance, nor did they find a population that lived up to the reputation of fierceness formerly attributed to the Ópata. Instead, they found a relatively small and poor population living in scattered rancherías, anxious for missionization.

The tendency has been to assume that the explorers had lied about their conquests or at best had exaggerated, in order to gain greater favor with their sovereign, and it was almost universally assumed that early Spanish documents were unreliable.

Although the great pueblos with 700 terraced buildings have not been found, nevertheless the general pattern of the archeological record does indicate that the character of the Serrana Culture corresponds to the descriptions of the conquistadors. The disparity between their accounts and what the Jesuit fathers found requires some other explanation.

A possible explanation is suggested by two lines of evidence. One consists of the inclusion of organic material as temper in the manufacture of pottery, a practice introduced by the Iberians (William Wasley, personal communication). The organic material was usually in the form of dried manure and obviously was accompanied by the introduction of livestock. The resulting sherds are unmistakably recognized by a jet-black core produced by the permeation of the paste by organic carbon when the vessels were fired and the presence of numerous tiny holes in the paste left behind when the fibrous material was burned out.

This San Miguel ware, in the form of San Miguel Red and San Miguel Brown, is found all over Sonora in very early historic times. The specific site distribution and its association, or lack thereof, with prehistoric material, are significant here. In southern Sonora the ware is frequently found in the same sites as late prehistoric pottery, suggesting a continuity of occupation. In contrast, San Miguel sherds are never found in association with late phase prehistoric types in the northern Serrana Culture. This suggests a marked disruption in village occupation before the arrival of the Jesuit fathers and subsequent introduction of San Miguel ware in the north.

However, aside from the fact that, in general, the late phase prehistoric patterns compare favorably with the explorers' accounts in all respects except the very largest towns, a second line of evidence indicates that the late phase sites were still occupied after Coronado's entrada. An excellent example of such evidence is a burial uncovered in a late phase Río Sonora site less than a kilometer immediately north of present-day Banámichi. This burial was found inside a structure and partially under an adobe wall, indicating that some construction had taken place after the internment. The burial was unusual in a number of respects. Data suggest that the body had been mutilated or that death had come violently, as the head appeared to have been severed before burial, one lower leg was missing, and the fingers of one hand had been removed and placed in the individual's mouth.

If we can assume that grave goods are an indication of status, this individual was certainly a special person. Associated with the grave were ten pristine triangular micropoints, one large bifacial knife, five shaft abraders, eleven shell beads, three turquoise beads, and most importantly, one badly corroded metal object, probably a knife blade, as well as three whole, and several fragments of, Venetian blue glass beads.

The burial was clearly interred in historic times, following the Coronado entrada at the earliest, and yet it is clearly not a Christian burial and therefore predates the mission period, particularly in view of its proximity to Banámichi, where one of the earliest missions was founded. Significantly, no other historic material has been found at the site, including no San Miguel ware. The site is purely late phase Serrana Culture.

Data such as these indicate that late phase prehistoric sites were those occupied when Díaz, Coronado, and Ibarra came through, which also further supports the conclusion that the inhabitants were Ópata. Reff (1991) has postulated that the disparity in population and settlement between the time of Coronado and that of the missions was due to depopulation resulting from introduced disease. Subsequent settlements established by the mission program concentrated the scattered population into a few mission towns, which explains the absence of San Miguel ware on the late Serrana sites. Thus, the impact of disease is apparent among the Mayo in southern Sonora after missionization began and among the Ópata prior to missionization. It is this difference that resolves the apparent contradiction between the accounts of the Coronado entrada and the conditions found by the missionaries and supports our confidence that what the conquistadors reported is what they saw.

CHAPTER 12

The 76 Ranch Ruin and the Location of Chichilticale[1]

WILLIAM A. DUFFEN AND WILLIAM K. HARTMANN

he 76 Ranch Ruin, in southeast Arizona, was suggested by Emil Haury and Herbert Bolton as the site of the famous Chichilticale stopover point on the prehistoric trading route from Sonora to Cíbola, described by the Coronado expedition in 1540. Little information has been available about this site. We describe the only professional excavations, made by Duffen in 1936. The site is similar to other late Salado sites in southeastern Arizona and southwestern New Mexico and probably dates from the 1300s. Chichilticale was probably this ruin or one of the other Salado pueblos in the broad region stretching from the Sulphur Springs Valley to Safford, Arizona. Natives in 1540 told Coronado's party that Chichilticale was built by people from the direction of Cíbola; modern investigation of Chichilticale candidate ruins supports this. This circumstance shows how the discovery of Coronado's exact route will allow use of Coronado-era records to clarify significant archeological problems.

Importance of Chichilticale

Reconnaissance by Marcos de Niza in 1539 and reports from the Coronado expedition in 1540 state that the final approach to Cíbola (Zuni, New Mexico) was across a twelve- to fifteen-day despoblado or wilderness, which apparently began near the Gila River. A ruin, widely known at that time, existed on the trail about a day south of the beginning of the despoblado, and served as a camp on the trade route to Zuni. This ruin itself and the surrounding area (within about a day's travel), were both called Chichilticale. Coronado himself stated that he and his advance guard camped there two days and wanted to stay longer, but their food was giving out.

The location of this important ruin has been a mystery for generations. Solving it would be a critical step in identifying the Coronado route to Cíbola, and hence a major prehistoric trade route. Scholars have placed it anywhere from Casas Grandes in Chihuahua to Casa Grande in Arizona. Writing on "The Search for Chichilticale," Emil Haury (1984) stated that in 1940 he and Herbert Bolton visited a large ruin on the 76 Ranch in the Sulphur Springs valley when Bolton was researching the Coronado route (see Map 9). Haury (1984: 18) stated that he returned several times and believed that "the most likely place where Chichilticale stood [is] within a half dozen miles of the 76 Ranch." Bolton himself (1949), in a few sentences, also proposed the 76 Ranch Ruin, noting that Carl Sauer had proposed the Haby Ranch Ruin, a few miles northwest in the same valley. The work of Haury and Bolton gives one of the most precise suggested identifications of Chichilticale by the generation of archeologists and historians that knew the southeastern Arizona ruins before they reached their present state, in most cases vandalized or destroyed by farming and urbanization. However, Haury's (1984) six-page article provided surprisingly little supporting evidence for his view, nor much data on the ruin.

In that article, Haury asserted that Juan Bautista de Anza visited the Chichilticale ruin in 1775 and quoted Anza as describing it as having adobe walls that were painted with red ochre. This statement is an error. The statement Haury quotes is Anza's well-known description of Casa Grande when his expedition to San Francisco stopped there in 1775; as far as is known Anza never visited the region of the 76 Ranch. We are unable to explain the origin of this error in Haury's article.

The 76 Ranch Ruin was not listed in the Arizona State Museum site files at the time we began this work, nor does the Amerind Foundation of Dragoon, Arizona, have materials or documents relating to the site in their files. Therefore, it is important to document the only known professional excavation conducted at the site, four years before the Haury/Bolton visit.

Background to This Work

After Duffen finished an M.A. in archeology in 1936 at the University of Arizona under Dean Bryan Cummings, Cummings helped arrange a job as a helper on the 76 Ranch, which was a dude ranch at that time. Duffen spent roughly July through September 1936 on the ranch. Upon arrival, he found that "dudes" had already been picking through three rooms of the ruin and he felt that a more professional

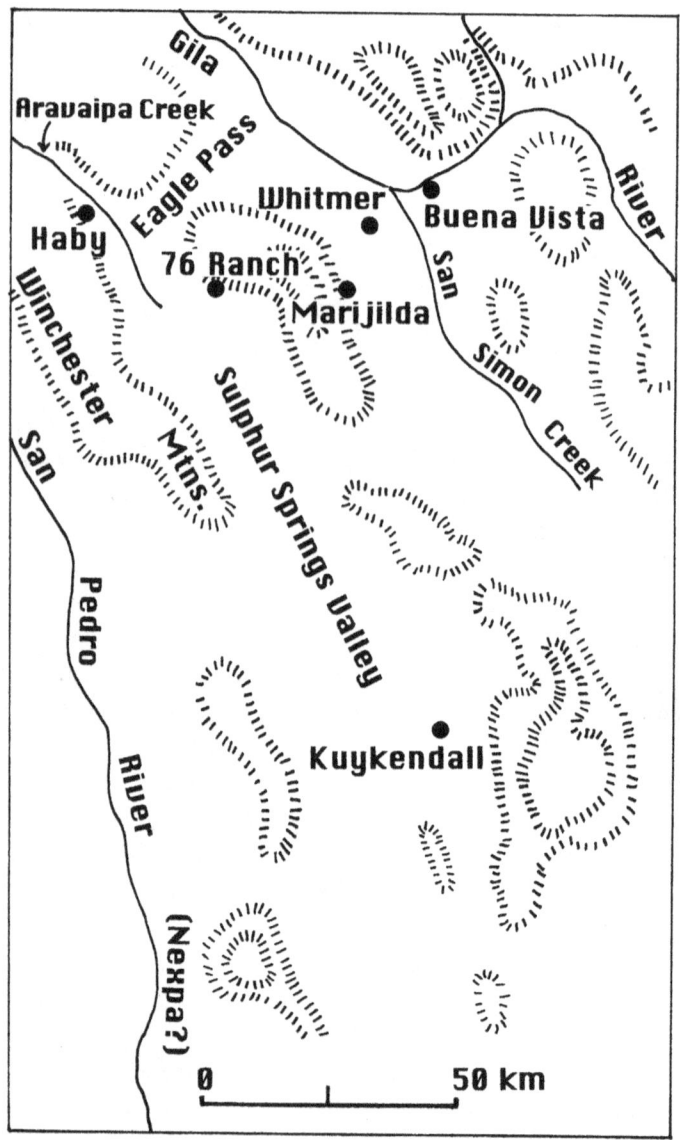

Map 9. Sulphur Springs Valley area, Arizona, with selected fourteenth-century Salado sites.

excavation was critical. The owners allowed him to begin excavation of several additional rooms between other jobs. The excavations were done as professionally as possible, but on a catch-as-catch-can basis, and often interrupted by other assignments (see Figure 12.1).

The 76 Ranch Ruin and the Location of Chichilticale

Figure 12.1. Excavation of 76 Ranch Ruin, 1936, view to north. Photo from William Duffen's collection.

After about three months, Duffen had an offer of a more secure job, and left the 76 Ranch with the intention of returning to do more excavation and/or publish a more complete report. He did publish a four-page report (Duffen 1937), but when he returned some months later he found that the entire collection of excavated artifacts had disappeared, apparently given to or carried off by "dude" guests. This made it difficult to pursue a larger professional publication on the excavation.

Duffen retained numerous photos of the 1936 excavation and because they were never published, we include some of them here to illustrate the magnitude of the ruin. The 1936 photos reproduced here are from Duffen's original negatives, as well as from prints given to him by visitors to the ranch. (A more complete set of notes and prints has been filed at the Arizona State Museum.)

The Early Report of the 76 Ranch Excavation—1937

Duffen's (1937) is the only published report on the excavation. The only photo in the report (not by Duffen) shows the ruins as they appeared before his excavation. Because the report is hard to obtain today, we list some highlights, along with some comments from the unpublished field notes. The site is described (Duffen 1937) as

> a surface pueblo of the compound type covering roughly some 15 acres, and composed of three main groups. Each group apparently surrounds three sides of a large patio, while the fourth side is composed of a wall.

During this time the writer, with the aid of two laborers, succeeded in uncovering nine rooms on the north side of the middle group. . . .

The rooms were all single-storied. With the exception of one large room, which had the features of a ceremonial room [Duffen now calls it a kiva], all of the rooms had their long axes east and west.

The walls had an average thickness of about sixteen inches, and were composed of adobe with very few stones incorporated. At the bottoms, however, slabs were set into the wall and plastered over, which was, without doubt, to prevent undercutting.

Typical room size was about 3.7 x 5.4 m.

Ceramics at the site were categorized by Duffen (1937) as plain, corrugated, and polychrome. The plain and corrugated wares were types common to the middle Gila region and varied from dark brown to red. The polychrome was almost all Gila Polychrome. Intrusive wares included Fourmile Polychrome and Chihuahua Polychrome and appeared only as a few sherds. The Fourmile Polychrome came from the trash mound and the Chihuahua Polychrome from the fill of an abandoned room.

At the time of the excavation, an important issue in Arizona archeology was the extent of northern influences into the south. (The 1937 article does not use the term "Salado.") Duffen (1937) noted several points bearing on the cultural affiliations of the occupants of the ruin. 1) He identified one room (VIII) as a kiva (see Figure 12.2). The unpublished field notes indicate that this room had a floor level about fifteen cm below that of other rooms. It was nearly twice as big as the other rooms, at about 4.9 x 7.8 m, with the long axis approximately north-south. The room had a slab-lined fire pit, a rectangular stone-lined pit symmetrically located on the other side of the room, traces of painted walls, and contained no utilitarian objects. The second pit was noted as "practically identical" to one found by Frank H. H. Roberts (1931: 98 Plate 8a) in a kiva at Kiatuthlanna, Arizona, *downstream on the Zuni River from Cíbola*, nearly 250 km north-northeast of the Sulphur Springs Valley. 2) Duffen found "mealing bins . . . composed of two metates set into bins at an angle with a divider stone between them. One stone was always coarse and the other was fine" (see Figure 12.3). Duffen noted that this style was not known at that time farther south than Canyon Creek, approximately 160 km to the north-northwest, near the Grasshopper Site (Bartlett 1933: 3). The one burial that Duffen found had an extended position with the head to the west; the skull had lambdoidal flattening—which may again suggest northern practices.

Duffen (1937) also described artifacts such as a steatite bird effigy, turquoise beads, obsidian drills and points, beads of olivella shell, rings of conus shell, a pair of ear pendants of pectin, and a small ear pendant or bracelet of glycymeris. A few

Figure 12.2. Room VIII, 76 Ranch Ruin, 1936, showing floor features. Photo by William Duffen.

years later, he heard anecdotal evidence of copper bells found in the site, but the size and shape are unknown.

Based on all these results, Duffen (1937) suggested a strong "northern influence [indicated by] wall niches, mealing-bins, full-grooved axes, and . . . a ceremonial room having a floor cache." He also concluded that the ruin "was occupied around the 1300s by a group of the Gila Polychrome people who were agricultural." These northern attributes are important in considering the relation of the site to Chichilticale, as discussed later. Duffen believes that his comments of that time may have influenced Haury and Bolton's suggestion that Chichilticale and the 76 Ranch Site were synonymous.

Description of the Ruins—1936–1995

Because of sheet wash sedimentation and the eroded and vandalized condition of some mounds and sherd scatters, it has been difficult to confirm the exact number of separate structures at the site or their relation to each other, from either the early records or our recent visits. In Duffen's 1936–1937 terms, each "mound" consisted of "groups" of room clusters; he excavated what he called Mound 1. Although the 1937 report clearly refers to the three groups bounding three sides of a plaza with a wall on the fourth side, the architecture of the plaza and wall at the site excavated remains unclear. Duffen's reports indicate that the excavated rooms on the north

Figure 12.3. Mealing bins, Room IV, 76 Ranch Ruin, 1936. Photo by William Duffen.

side were the middle group of rooms suggesting a wall across the south. The photos in the field notes and the measurements of wall heights show that the excavated rooms were most eroded on the south side; the "kiva" room extended farthest south of anything excavated, and although its wall height was about 1.2 m on the north in the midst of the mound, it was as low as 0.56 m along the south (see Figure 12.2). In 1994–1995, Duffen recalled that the area had several mounds. Most of the smoothly eroded mounds were still undisturbed and wall tops were eroded flush with the tops of the mounds; at least one post was exposed nearly flush with the surface at the top of one mound and at least one other post was found partially intact in rooms excavated (see Figure 12.4).

In 1994 Duffen referred several times to one of the mounds (not the one he excavated, but one toward the south) as being higher than the others, raising the possibility of one two-story complex.

Similar details come from Haury and Bolton. Haury (1984: 18) says that when he and Bolton visited the ranch in 1940, "we inspected several adobe ruins." Bolton (1949: 106) says, "on the 76 Ranch near the foot of Eagle Pass there are extensive pueblo ruins, one of which may well be the remains of the structure . . . called Chichilti-cale." Consistent with Haury's placement of the ruins within half a dozen miles of 76 Ranch, the features we describe in what follows are about three miles from the ranch house.

The 76 Ranch Ruin and the Location of Chichilticale   165

Figure 12.4. Room VI, 76 Ranch Ruin, 1936, showing floor features and juniper fragment. Photo by William Duffen.

In order to clarify the nature of the 76 Ranch Site, we made several visits to the site, on November 21, 1994 (Duffen and Hartmann); March 11, 1995 (Hartmann, Gayle Harrison Hartmann, Betty Lee, and Robert Lee, both of Thatcher, Arizona); March 13, 1995 (Hartmann and Gayle Hartmann); and April 23, 1995 (Duffen, Hartmann, Gayle Harrison Hartmann, Betty Lee, and Robert Lee). Features in an area about 2 km x .6 km, bordering the west side of Babcock Wash, include the following: On the north end were sherd scatters previously visited by Betty Lee in her surveys of sites in the Sulphur Springs Valley. We noted about a dozen plainware sherds and several check dams up to at least 38 m long extending roughly east-west across the many shallow drainage channels (.5 m to 1.5 m deep) that traverse the *bajada*. We interpreted this area as agricultural fields.

Extending south from that area are numerous scattered crude rock alignments, some probably marking room wall remnants, and several low mounds, up to about 1.8 m high and typically about 20 m in diameter, usually marked by sherd concentrations. There may now be half a dozen low mounds in the area fitting this description, although it is hard to be precise because of the erosion and sedimentation, caused by outwash from the nearby mountains. The observations were consistent with the early descriptions of several mounds scattered over fifteen acres, although we believe the site covers a larger area than that, if features such as check dams are included.

We attempted to locate the specific mound excavated in 1936. Triangulating landscape features shown in the 1936 photos, we concluded that the excavation was near the south end of the group of features mentioned. Approaching a position that gave the best triangulation, we came upon a large mound, about 1.8 m high and 22 m in diameter, with evidence of excavation, and exposed stone foundations of room walls. Examination showed room outlines not only in this mound but extending beyond it, flush with the ground. (A modern dirt road crosses several of the room walls). Numerous visible rooms, including rooms in the excavated mound, appeared to define a room block about 52 m long in a roughly northeast-southwest orientation. Old ranch fence posts, as well as triangulation, fitted the description given by Duffen and we believe this may be the site he excavated; alternatively, this may be the larger mound noted by Duffen near the one he excavated. It was not possible to determine the complete layout of this structure. At the west end, rooms appeared to extend south, indicating that this group of rooms may mark the north side of a larger structure surrounding a plaza, consistent with Duffen's description.

The totality of evidence, including our recent visits, indicates that in the 1930s, several distinct mounds, perhaps three main mounds, were dotted over at least fifteen acres, with additional smaller features nearby. Each main mound apparently represents a complex of rooms, at least some with plazas.

We tabulated sherd statistics from the entire 76 Ranch Site, to test the hypothesis that it was a late site that might have been standing during the Coronado period. Random counts including all the mounds and the "fields" to the north (we detected no local variations) gave a sample of 196 sherds. A breakdown includes 57 percent plainware (111 sherds), 35 percent corrugated (69 sherds), 7 percent Gila Polychrome (14 sherds), and .5 percent each of San Carlos Buff and St. Johns Black-on-red (1 sherd each).

By comparison, less detailed statistics on sherds were recorded in the 1936 field notes. The floor of room VI yielded an unspecified number of sherds tabulated as 19 percent plainware, 80 percent corrugated, and 1 percent "late Gila Polychrome." The floor of the "kiva," Room VIII yielded "a half dozen or so" plainware sherds. "Scattered through the *fill* above the floor in 'kiva' Room VIII were several hundred sherds," giving a lower ratio of plainware to corrugated: 8.5 percent plainware, 90 percent corrugated, and 1.5 percent Gila Polychrome. The 1936 field notes indicate that small numbers of plainware, corrugated, and Gila Polychrome sherds were found in other rooms. In all samples, corrugatedware was unusually strong compared to other sites in and near the Sulphur Springs Valley.

Sheet wash runoff appears to have affected the whole bajada by erosion and deposition. In support of this, we noted shallow rivulet beds lacing the area, and .5 m diameter boulders that had been undercut by water flow. The ranch manager, Phil Clifton, reported that heavy sheet runoff in 1978 and 1983 was especially devastating, the latter threatening damage to the store in the town of Bonita, Arizona. Similar sheet wash flooding is indicated in prehistoric times: the 1936 field notes indicate that fifteen cm of sandy sediment had infilled Room VII in prehistoric times; a few additional artifacts (a turquoise mosaic, two axes, two metates) atop the infill indicated later occupation or visitation.

Dating of the 76 Ranch Site

The best available dating of the site comes from the painted wares recorded in 1936 and in 1994–1995, which were overwhelmingly Gila Polychrome. Duffen also mentioned small amounts of intrusive Fourmile Polychrome (from a trash mound) and Chihuahua Polychrome (from room fill). In an inventory of painted sherds alone, we recorded twenty-six painted sherds of which twenty-four (92 percent) were Gila Polychrome, one (4 percent) was St. Johns Black-on-red, and one (4 percent) was Santa Cruz Red-on-buff. David Breternitz's (1966) summary of tree-ring data places Gila Polychrome primarily in the period A.D. 1250–1385; Fourmile Polychrome at A.D. 1300–1385; and St. Johns Black-on-Red, A.D. 1137–1385. Chihuahua Polychrome is believed to be contemporaneous with these. Of the total inventory of many dozens of painted sherds in the 1936 and current records, only one, the Santa Cruz Red-on-buff, gives a date outside that range, roughly A.D. 875–975 (Dean 1991). Based on the total sample, the most likely occupation of the 76 Ranch Site appears to have been A.D. 1300–1385. Duffen's field note evidence for prehistoric occupation both below and atop a fifteen cm sand fill in Room VII suggests possible lingering population in the area after primary abandonment of the site; this may be analogous to the Polveron Phase occupation described in the Phoenix area by Sires (1984). Such occupation may have lasted well past A.D. 1400. It would also be consistent with the description of Chichilticale as a site on the Cíbola trail, widely visited for more than a century after abandonment.

Relation to Other Salado Period Pueblo Ruins

Many similarities exist between the 76 Ranch Ruin and other Salado pueblo ruins in southeast Arizona, in terms of ceramic types and architecture. Two of these sites are shown in Map 9. Several are notable in the Sulphur Springs Valley. The Haby Ranch Ruin, favored by Sauer as Chichilticale, is on a low spurlike ridge above a spring on the west side of Aravaipa Valley; it is as much as 12 km or more beyond (northwest of) the older trails that cross the pass, which makes it less attractive as Chichilticale than the 76 Ranch area. In recent years it has been damaged by two bulldozer pits and construction of a house on the hillside. The Eureka Springs

Ranch marks a spring and campsite on the west side of the Aravaipa Valley (north end of the contiguous Sulphur Springs Valley), facing Eagle Pass; a ruin is said to have occupied the site before the present buildings. Another ruin, a few miles north on the same ranch, has abundant Gila Polychrome and is currently grossly vandalized. Thus, there are several candidate sites at the southern entrance to Eagle Pass. Betty Lee (private communications 1995–1996) has assembled field notes and sherd counts on most of the Sulphur Springs Valley sites.

J. L. Brown (1974) and Michael Woodson (1995) describe more Salado sites in the Safford area (long known as the Pueblo Viejo ruins), and also related Salado sites in southeastern Arizona, including three in the northern San Pedro Valley. Mills and Mills (1969) report on the Kuykendall pueblo (roughly 80 km southeast of the 76 Ranch in the south part of the Sulphur Springs Valley) and the Dinwiddie pueblo (roughly 110 km east-northeast of Safford).

Most of these bear distinct similarities to the 76 Ranch Ruin, in terms of dominance of Gila Polychrome among decorated wares and in terms of architecture (see Figure 12.5). Commonly found are rows of rectangular and slightly trapezoidal rooms, typically four to five meters on a side, mostly with roof entry, surrounding a plaza ten to fourteen meters wide. Based on sherd counts and architecture, the three Salado ruins most similar to the 76 Ranch Ruin are the Whitmer Ranch Site in the east foothills of the Pinaleno Mountains south of Safford, the Buena Vista House 1 Site east of Safford and Solomon, Arizona, and the Kuykendall Site. The Whitmer Site is relatively small with walls "constructed of adobe reinforced with vertically set cylindrical river cobbles" (Brown 1974: 21). This echoes Duffen's (1937: 13) report that "slabs [of stone] were set into the wall and plastered over," as well as our observations of foundations of double rows of stone at the 76 Ranch Site. Mills and Mills (1969) report two archeomagnetic dates of A.D. 1385 ± 23 years and A.D. 1375 ± 18 years for two fire pits at the Kuykendall Ruin, in accord with our ceramic dates at 76 Ranch. In view of their importance, it is striking that virtually none of the Salado pueblos in southeast Arizona has been fully excavated in a modern professional manner.

The Location of Chichilticale

Because Bolton and Haury specifically identified the 76 Ranch Ruin as the most likely site of Chichilticale, we deem it critical to review the current status of that possible identification. In assessing Chichilticale's location, records in addition to those of the expedition itself are useful and have been underutilized in the past. Marcos de Niza, reconnoitering the route in 1539, stopped at a village in the last populated valley he visited (San Pedro River valley?—see also Chapter 5). This was the last village he mentioned before Cíbola. Here, he was told that it was four days

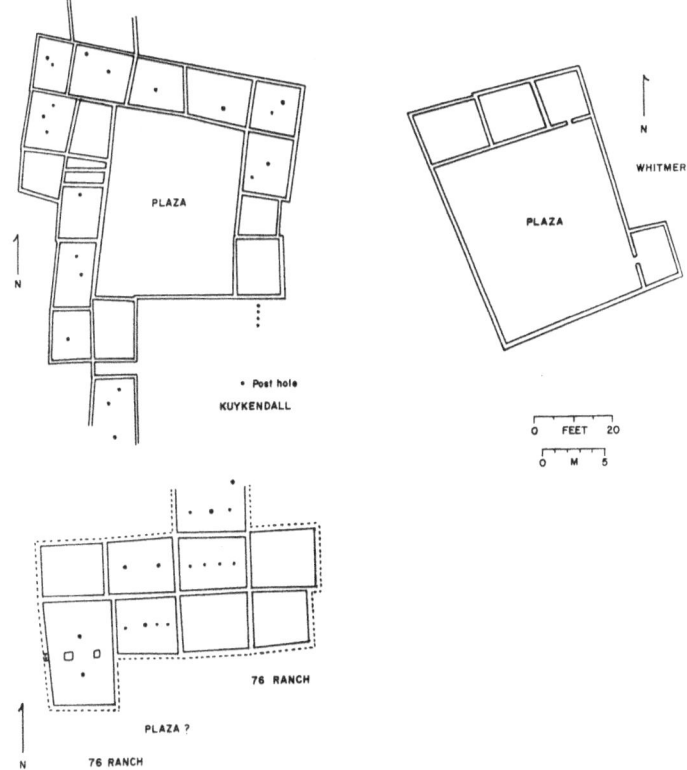

Figure 12.5. Site plans, late Salado sites, Sulphur Springs Valley area, Arizona.

to the beginning of the large despoblado. The villagers asked him to rest there while they organized a party to go with him. From this village, Marcos reports, many men had already gone ahead with Estevan. Many more assembled to go with Marcos, not only "to serve me" but also because they "expected to return rich men." Marcos chose "30 chiefs, very well dressed with their necklaces of turquoises, some of them having five or six loops." All this indicates a substantial village as the jumping-off point, from which Marcos proceeded toward the despoblado on a traditional route. Although Marcos himself does not mention the ruin or use the name Chichilticale, Pedro de Castañeda indicates that Marcos did observe the ruin (Winship 1896: 143).

Some months later, Coronado's scout, Melchior Díaz, and his exploratory party of fifteen horsemen interviewed people of this same village, or a nearby village, from which men had gone with Estevan to Cíbola. They confirmed Marcos's accounts of Cíbola, and that the death of Estevan had occurred as Marcos reported. Díaz then wintered in the Chichilticale area early in 1540. He says he declined to enter the despoblado "on account of heavy snows and the cold" (Winship 1896: 172), indicating that the despoblado began in and traversed higher country. Thus, the accounts of Marcos and Díaz, taken together, indicate that Estevan, Marcos, and Díaz himself all followed the same well-established trade route that was later followed by Coronado in this area.

Castañeda mentions that the people of the Chichilticale district (and beyond?) were different from those in the villages along the valleys; they were "the most barbarous" yet seen, were hunters, and "live in separate cabins, not in settlements" (Winship 1896: 143). Carr Tuthill (1947) and Michael Woodson (1995) describe a broad zone of contact that existed in the 1300s between the Salado compound builders and culturally distinct pithouse villagers; it ran from the Tres Alamos Site on the San Pedro (in the area of Marcos's final village) to the region of Safford. Even after the pueblos were abandoned, a crude political boundary between the San Pedro villages and the Chichilticale region to the east may have persisted. In any case, it seems that the Chichilticale region was a relatively unsettled desert lowland, one or two jornadas before entering the higher-elevation despoblado; it had been abandoned a few generations before by the "red house" builders, and was now occupied only by "barbarous" nomads. This explains the curious fact that the (San Pedro?) villagers spoke of having to cross a distinct four-day region after leaving their village, but before entering the great, mountainous, fifteen-day despoblado to Cíbola.

All of this is amplified in the Coronado expedition records. The route to Cíbola was said by Juan de Jaramillo (Winship 1896: 143) to proceed along a "Señora" valley through "Ispa" (also referred to as Arispa by Castañeda), then four days through deserted country north of Ispa to a "Nexpa" river. If we adopt the widely held view that Corazones was near Ures, that the Coronado expedition moved north up the well-populated Sonora Valley, and that the "Ispa" of Jaramillo and "Arispa" of Castañeda are modern Arizpe, it is hard to escape the conclusion that the company came out of the north end of the Sonora Valley, crossed the Cananea grasslands, and proceeded along the San Pedro, that is, the "Nexpa."

Jaramillo now says, "we went down this stream two days and then left the stream, going toward the right to the foot of the mountain chain in two days journey, when we heard news of what is called Chichilticale. Crossing the mountains, we came to a deep and reedy river [the Gila?]" (Hammond and Rey 1940: 297), which marked the beginning of the long despoblado to Cíbola. (Compare Map 9.) Several chroniclers of the Coronado expedition name Chichilticale, which they considered a famed stopping point. The name, generally attributed to Nahuatl for "red house," referred to the ruin. Being Nahuatl, even the name supports the idea that Chichilticale was on a significant trade route. Castañeda refered to the "fame of Chichilticale" (Hammond and Rey 1940: 207). Jaramillo also noted that "to this pass we gave the name of Chichilticale, because we learned this was what it was called, from some Indians whom we left behind" (Hammond and Rey 1940: 296). He also adds, "from this river back at Nexpa . . . it seems to me that the direction was nearly northeast" (Hammond and Rey 1940: 298).

All this agrees with Marcos's account of a four-day trip from his last village on the San Pedro to the beginning of the great despoblado on the Gila. Presumably, based on Castañeda's testimony, Marcos saw the Chichilticale ruin during these four days. Castañeda (Winship 1896: 143) also refers to "Chichilticalli [as] where the wilderness begins," where the mountains swing west, and where the "spiky vegetation ceases."

All the testimony fits (but does not prove) a route from the San Pedro a few days east and north through the Sulphur Springs Valley, across Eagle Pass, and then across the Gila River, somewhere near Safford. This is also the route proposed by Stewart Udall (1984) and Haury (1984).

The several-day right turn from the river to reach an unusual pueblo ruin not only supports the Salado ruins of the Sulphur Springs Valley and Safford areas as candidates for Chichilticale (see Map 9), but also seems fatal to theories that have Coronado east of the Sonora River Valley, and/or traveling directly north. In particular, they contradict the theory of Di Peso, Rinaldo, and Fenner (1974: 98) that Chichilticale was about fifty km south of the southeast corner of Arizona; Di Peso's favored route includes no two-day right turn to reach Chichilticale, nor does his location correspond to a notable change in mountain range axes toward the west; the mountains along his route run essentially north and south. His route appears also not to correspond to an end in the spiky vegetation. The comment on the spiky vegetation and the pass to the deep, reedy river also contradicts hypotheses that place Chichilticale much farther south than the Sulphur Springs Valley.

The region of Chichilticale was also described by Castañeda (Winship 1896: 143) as an area where mountain sheep with big horns began to be seen by the army. This also fits the Sulphur Springs Valley. A map of bighorn sheep distribution in 1860, compiled from museum records and early literature (Hook and Lee 1990), shows the sheep scattered throughout all ranges south of the Gila, *except for ranges in the southeast corner of the state.* The 1860 "contact line" marking the south end of the sheep range—probably approximating where Coronado's men would have first seen sheep—runs through the Huachuca Mountains near Benson, Arizona, up the Sulphur Springs Valley, approximately through Eagle Pass, past Safford, and then south down the San Simon Valley. Phil Clifton reported to us that, today, mountain sheep are sometimes seen around the northern Sulphur Springs Valley, or the contiguous southern Aravaipa Valley near Eagle Pass.

In view of the abundance of Salado pueblo ruins in southeast Arizona, the intense interest during 1539–1540 in the technology of Cíbola, and the native reports that Chichilticale was built by a splinter group from Cíbola, it is notable that the Coronado expedition apparently visited only one such pueblo, and that Díaz's report did not describe any others. Marcos cited his informants' description of the Cíbola buildings at great length in his *Relación*, but did not describe any Salado pueblo ruins in that document, although he apparently talked of having seen Chichilticale, judging from Castañeda. These circumstances suggest that Chichilticale was the only ruin on the main trail, and was not visited just as an attraction, but because it offered the only abundant water nearby. This supposition would fit sites near foothill springs in the Sulphur Springs Valley, because the main valley itself has no stream down its center like the San Pedro or the valleys traversed in Sonora.

In short, a Salado pueblo ruin near a water supply in the Sulphur Springs Valley, a few days northeast of a departure point on the San Pedro and about a day or two south of the Gila, matches many reported features of Chichilticale.

As for the specific Chichilticale ruin, Coronado wrote (Winship 1896: 178) that he and his vanguard party (about eighty horsemen, thirty foot soldiers, and a large number of native allies; Bolton 1949: 93) rested there two days. Castañeda, with the body of the expedition, says Coronado was disappointed when the famous building turned out to be "one tumbledown house without a roof, although it appears to have been a strong place at some former time when it was inhabited" (Winship 1896: 110). In another place Castañeda says "the house was large and appeared to have been a fortress" (Winship 1896: 143). These descriptions might have fit the largest remaining structure in any of the Salado pueblo groupings of the area, which would have been abandoned for about 150 years when the Spaniards saw them.

None of the 76 Ranch Ruin's rooms excavated in 1936 had outer doors; they were apparently entered by ladder. Some doorways between rooms had been blocked and filled in. A wall closed off one side of the plaza. Such architecture would have contributed to a Spanish impression of it as a fortress. Independent evidence that late Salado ruins impress visitors as being defensive (whether they were or not) comes from O. T. Tatman (Brown 1974), describing his excavations in House 1 of the Buena Vista Site. His words echo Castañeda 400 years earlier: "the entire structure, including connecting walls, that were evidently constructed for the purpose of defense, formed a square, with the usual court in the center" (Brown 1974: 6).

Apparently Chichilticale, or Red House, consisted of red earth or red-painted adobe. We cannot confirm that the 76 Ranch Ruin appeared red. However, Duffen did find red hematite samples in the rooms, which might have been used for pigments, and he found traces of painted walls in the "kiva" room, with red, green, and white pigment, according to his field notes. Haury's citation of Anza's comments on Casa Grande in 1775, misapplied by Haury to Chichilticale, suggests that Casa Grande was originally colored red with ochre, confirming that such a practice did occur in the region.

We cannot argue strongly that Chichilticale was specifically the 76 Ranch Ruin, but Chichilticale probably was one of the several Salado pueblo structures in the area of the Sulphur Springs Valley or the Safford area, abandoned shortly before or after 1400, and still standing in 1540.

A little noticed point of interest is that the archeological evidence at 76 Ranch (Duffen 1937) and other Salado sites confirms the report of the natives that Chichilticale had been built by people generally from the north. Castañeda (Winship 1896: 143) quotes them as saying that Chichilticale had been built by "people who separated from Cíbola"; in another place (1896: 110) he quotes them as saying that the builders were "a civilized and warlike race of strangers who had come from a distance." The comment about Cíbola need not be taken literally, but rather as an affirmation that the builders were known to the southern Arizona natives in 1540 as people who had come (not many generations before) from the northern pueblo communities. The great-grandparents of the villagers Coronado met could have traded with people living in the Chichilticale pueblo. By 1540, Cíbola was the closest large pueblo trading center.

Modern data, after years of controversy, dramatically support the native testimony. Brown (1974) stresses the "close cultural relationship" between the Salado ruins of the area and the Point of Pines Western Pueblo Complex to the north. Lindsay (1987) proposed a Tusayan Anasazi intrusion into the Point of Pines area and a Kayenta Anasazi intrusion into the San Pedro Valley. Woodson (1995) specifically investigates the Safford-area Salado sites in the context of Western Anasazi migrations. He concludes about the Goat Hill Salado Site (about nine miles west of Safford and east of Eagle Pass) that "an 'intact' Anasazi community (or communities) migrated to the Safford Valley during the late thirteenth century and occupied the site for about forty years."

The striking archeological confirmation of the 1540 native reports recorded by Coronado's chroniclers has not been adequately emphasized by earlier authors. Neither Brown nor Woodson, for example, even refers to the Coronado records in their discussion of the origins of the southeast Arizona pueblos. This illustrates how the Coronado-era chronicles have been underutilized as eyewitness accounts of conditions and traditions 150 years after the Hohokam collapse in the area, largely because of uncertainty over the expedition's route. Confident identification of Coronado sites will allow better use of the observations of Marcos, Castañeda, and others.

Making a specific identification of the 76 Ranch Ruin or other sites in the area as Chichilticale is more difficult. A positive point is Jaramillo's statement that the name Chichilticale was also given to a "pass" that was crossed after the stop at Chichilticale. This could be Eagle Pass, ten miles northwest of the 76 Ranch, which provides the only easy access north from the Sulphur Springs Valley into the Gila River Valley and which Haury (1984) and Udall (1984) have the expedition cross in order to reach the Gila (see Map 9). Artifacts from the pass show a long history of use as a route to the Gila (Betty Lee, personal communication 1995).

Future Work on Chichilticale

If diagnostic evidence of a Coronado-era campsite—for example, clusters of crossbow boltheads (Chapter 3; Rhodes 1992; Flint 1995)—were found in the Sulphur Springs Valley, would this affirm the expedition's route through that area? One must be cautious with this approach in southeast Arizona because such material might belong to Melchior Díaz and his fifteen horsemen who were sent north in late 1539 to confirm Marcos de Niza's findings. We do not know that they camped on the Coronado route of 1540. Furthermore, Spanish artifacts might have been moved around by native villagers, as with various chain mail pieces found in Indian mounds in Kansas. How do we distinguish a Díaz camp from a Coronado camp? Did Díaz's party roam widely in the southeast Arizona area during their winter stay? We might evaluate expected numbers of crossbow boltheads and other artifacts from each group by the total number of person-days that each group spent in the Chichilticale area:

Díaz Party:
    15 Spaniards x 30 to 50 days? = 450 to 750 person-days?
Coronado and Advance Guard:
    110 Spaniards x 2 days = 220 person-days
Coronado's Main Force:
    200 Spaniards x 1 to 2 days? = 200 to 400 person-days?

These numbers do not include the additional stop by the expedition during its return, which, two days north of Chichilticale, met a small northbound reinforcement party that had apparently also camped there. The figures do suggest that Díaz's party may have left as many Spanish artifacts and small camps in the area from roughly Sierra Vista to Safford as the full expedition did. The problem, therefore, is that if Díaz's party moved around in the area after they "decided not to go any farther until the winter was over" (Viceroy Mendoza's words) (Hammond and Rey 1940: 157), then discovery of an isolated camp with crossbow boltheads or other Coronado-era equipment might not establish the main expedition's route.

The best indicator of the Coronado expedition route would be evidence of a large camp of Spaniards and Mesoamerican allies, or, better yet, firm identification of the Chichilticale ruin itself by means of Spanish materials and native items of trade with Cíbola. Native items at Chichilticale might come from a considerable range of time and space, since the ruin was a major stopover on the trade route from Sonora to Cíbola, presumably for several centuries after the pueblos were abandoned around 1385–1400.

Interestingly, Díaz confirmed Marcos's remarks that the natives of the villages just south of the despoblado (that is, the San Pedro/Nexpa villages?) had turned against the Spanish because of the violent encounter with Estevan at Cíbola; Díaz recounts that messages from Cíbola had stirred up these villagers and wrote of "the coolness with which they received us, and the mean faces they have shown us" (Hammond and Rey 1940: 160). This supports that Díaz may have made his winter camp not close to the villages of the Nexpa (San Pedro?), but at the well-watered, and otherwise deserted, camp spot of Chichilticale itself, several days away, near the beginning of the despoblado. In this likely scenario, Díaz's main camp would be *on* the Coronado route.

Another line of evidence on Chichilticale's location could come from continued work with Spanish archives. Marcos refers briefly to his own second report containing names of villages and islands, but it has been lost. Coronado, in his August 3, 1540, letter to the viceroy, says he sent a map of his route, but it has never come to light. Riley (1973) describes evidence for a Coronado-era document paraphrased in the 1630 *memorial* of fray Alonso de Benavides; it cites a town name, possibly in the Sonora Valley, not mentioned in other Coronado accounts. Benavides may have had access to one of the above two missing documents of fray Marcos.

Although many Salado sites in the Sulphur Springs Valley are being mercilessly vandalized, several others, including the 76 Ranch Ruin, may be sufficiently well preserved to allow fruitful professional excavation in cooperation with private owners. This could possibly resolve an important issue in contact-era archeology. One of these sites is very likely to be the famed Chichilticale.

Note

1. This work was supported in part by a grant from the Arizona Archaeological and Historical Society.

PART IV

The Coronado Expedition, Cíbola to Río de Cicúye

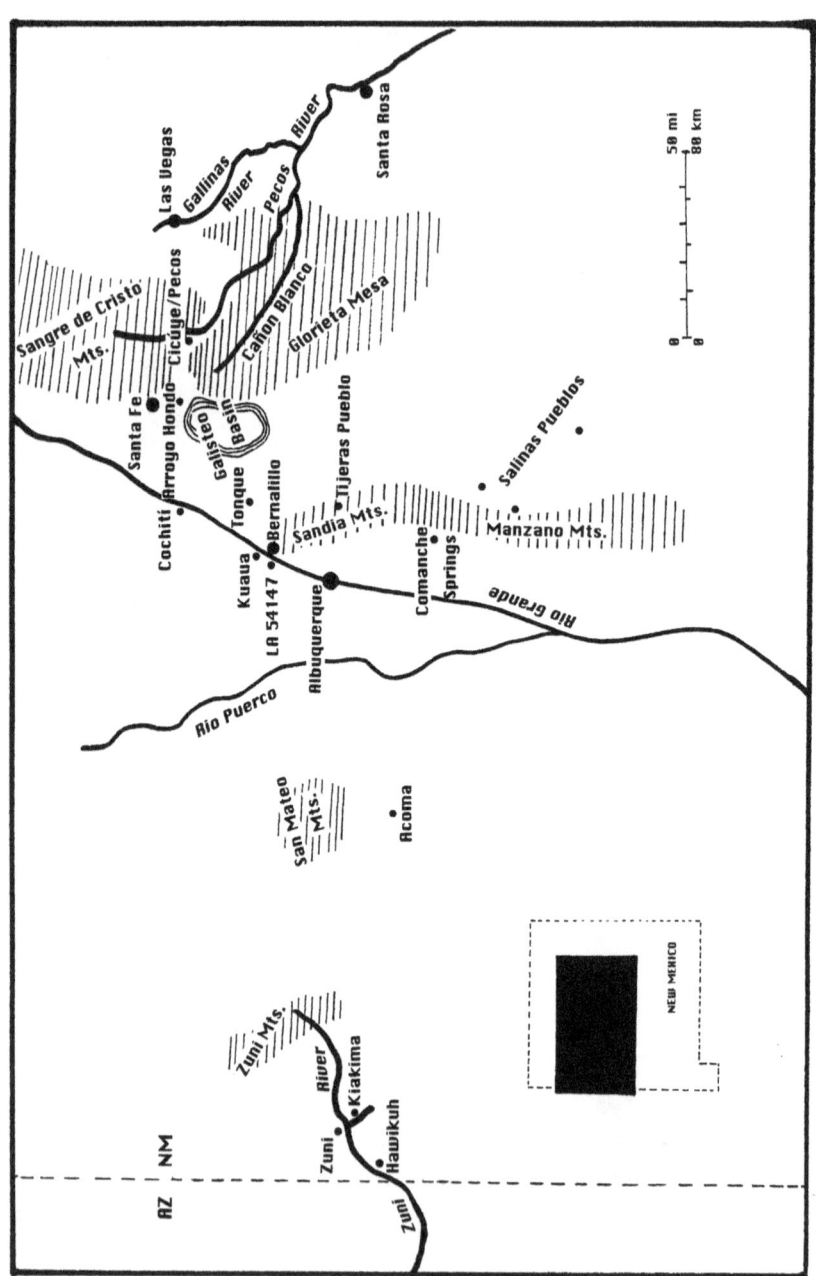

Map 10. Cíbola to the Río de Cicúye, New Mexico.

CHAPTER 13

A Historiography of the Route of the Expedition of Francisco Vázquez de Coronado
Cíbola to Río de Cicúye

JOSEPH P. SÁNCHEZ

Zuni to Tiguex on the Rio Grande

In late summer of 1540, Vázquez de Coronado ordered Hernando de Alvarado to go east and investigate what villages lay before them and to see the land where the *cíbolo* or buffalo roamed. With a small contingent of men and Indian guides, Alvarado set out. Of this leg of the expedition, he wrote:

> We set out from Granada [Zuni] toward Coco [Acoma] on Sunday, August 29, 1540. . . . After marching two leagues we reached an old building resembling a fortress; a league farther on we found another one, and a little farther on still another. Beyond them we came to an old city, quite large. . . . Half a league farther on, about a league from the latter, we found the ruins of another city. Its wall must have been very good, about an estado high, built of very large granite stones, and above this of very fine hewn blocks of stone.
> Two roads branch out here, one to Chiah [Zia], the other to Coco. We followed the latter, and reached the said place, which was one of the strongest ever seen, because the city is built on a very high rock (Hammond and Rey 1940: 184).

Alvarado's statement is the first view of the route from Zuni to Acoma to the Rio Grande. However, it also includes a number of perplexing details, especially those related to time and distance traveled as well as the descriptions of ruins along his route.

Riley and Manson marshalled all the archeological and documentary evidence at their disposal to establish a route from Zuni to the Rio Grande. Their hypothesis is that the expedition followed the best known route of the protohistoric period in the Upper Southwest: the complex trunk route that ran from Zuni to the Tiguex pueblos of the Rio Grande (Riley and Manson 1983: 351). Following this route, Alvarado was able to reach Acoma, via El Morro and the Malpaís. However, Riley and Manson questioned the distances mentioned by Alvarado. They wrote:

> If Alvarado left from Hawikuh (Granada), he reached the Chia or Zia road after four leagues plus "a little farther," a distance of about fifteen miles. If he went east from Hawikuh, perhaps working his way through the Plumasano Wash area, he would have reached no farther than about the line of modern New Mexico State Highway 32. There are ruins in this area, especially along the ridge that runs south of Ojo Caliente, but nothing as impressive as those described. If Alvarado marched north and east, toward the main Cíbolan settlements, fifteen miles would have brought him to the Halona area. Most likely the Alvarado party was measuring not from Hawikuh but from the Cíbolan towns around Dowa Yalanne. In such a case, the four to five leagues would put Alvarado in the Ramah area where, at a later time the trail forked, one route going to El Morro and onward to Agua Fria Spring and to Acoma, more or less following the line of New Mexico Highway 53. There are ruins in this general area, although Alvarado's descriptions seem exaggerated. The other route crossed the Zuni Mountains and Agua Fria Canyon and proceeded down Zuni Canyon to present-day Grants. The fork in the trail could have been as far west as Pescado or as far east as El Morro. Actually, these routes do not lead respectively to Zia and to Acoma, for they join a few miles east of Zuni Canyon where a break in the malpais occurs. Thus, it seems reasonable that Alvarado with his mounted Spaniards and perhaps a cart or two may have preferred the flatter and easier road past the mouths of Agua Fria and Bonito Canyons. The Indians, on the other hand, may normally have used the shorter trail down Zuni Canyon (Riley and Manson 1983: 355–356).

Meanwhile, Vázquez de Coronado departed Zuni, taking a different route than that of Alvarado. The documentary references are vague, however; Riley and Manson speculate that it is likely he veered to the southeast to visit Tutahaco, possibly near Socorro, although its location is also in dispute. By analogy with later expeditions, they suggest the possibility that Vázquez de Coronado may have swung south and east from El Morro to a point near Socorro by way of Techado Mesa and Pietown, or may have detoured toward present-day Datil (Riley and Manson 1983: 356). Riley holds to that route today (1995: 170).

A. Grove Day suggested that the expedition may have swung through Cebolleta Canyon and followed the San José River to reach Tutahaco, which he describes as a Tiwa province in the vicinity of Isleta on the Rio Grande (Day 1940: 353). From there the general consensus is that he traveled up the Rio Grande to rendezvous with the rest of the expedition, which had set up winter quarters near present-day Bernalillo.

Vázquez de Coronado's Tiguex: The Bernalillo Campsite

Identification of Vázquez de Coronado's winter campsite of 1540–1541 is part of the long list of unresolved locations of the expedition. The documentary sources state that the expedition occupied the pueblo of Coofer or Alcanfor (Hammond and Rey 1940: 326–347). The exact location of Coofer is unknown. Riley suggested that it was on the west bank of the Rio Grande (Riley 1981: 207). And Bradley J. Vierra throughout the summer of 1986 excavated a site (LA 54147) west of Santiago Pueblo in which sixteenth-century Spanish colonial artifacts were identified (Vierra 1989), leading to the speculation of a possible campsite related to the Vázquez de Coronado expedition. At that time, Vierra was careful to state that the site was clearly sixteenth-century Spanish colonial without specifying which expedition may be associated with it. But he states the case for the site's being associated with the Coronado expedition today (see Chapter 16).

The Tiguex Province sites have never been positively identified and much speculation surrounds their locations. Riley has suggested that the prehistoric pueblo of Arenal may be the archeological site LA 717 on the open, flat land near the east bank of the Rio Grande. He also proposed that Alcanfor or Coofer may be Santiago Pueblo (Bandelier's Puaray, LA 326), almost two and a half kilometers south of Kuaua on the west side of the river from present Bernalillo (Riley 1995: 170). Riley has previously speculated that Alameda lay between Alcanfor and Arenal (Hammond and Rey 1940: 335; Riley 1981: 206). Basing his conclusions on later expeditions, Charles Wilson Hackett suggested that Alameda was on the west bank (Hackett 1915: 391). (Compare Chapter 15.)

The events surrounding the expedition's stay along the Rio Grande are well known. Although mistrust of Spanish intentions among the Tiwa was evident because of events at Pecos and Zuni, the cold winter weather was a factor resulting in the Tiguex War of 1540–1541 (Sánchez 1988: 13). The ill feeling was aggravated by Vázquez de Coronado's desire to gather clothing to distribute among his men as cold weather with snow and wind occurred. For that purpose he requested that the Indians furnish "three hundred or more pieces of clothing," which the Spaniards needed to keep warm. The attacks on Moho, Arenal, and several other villages in the Tiguex Province by Vázquez de Coronado's men did not go unnoticed by

Spanish officials who investigated the matter after the expedition had returned to Mexico.

From Tiguex to Pecos and Beyond, Spring 1541

Although the Spaniards had traveled from the Rio Grande to Pecos several times, no clear route to it is mentioned. One may speculate that they traveled from Tiguex to the Galisteo Pueblos, which they had explored previously, then northeast to Pecos, or that the expedition marched north along the Rio Grande to Quirix, that is, the Keresan Pueblos south of present La Bajada, picking up supplies there before veering east around the Sangre de Cristo Mountains and then to Glorieta Pass to Pecos. In preparation for leaving Tiguex, Vázquez de Coronado sent men north along the Rio Grande to collect supplies and one detachment west as far as Zia Pueblo (Bolton 1949: 234–239).

The route from Tiguex to Galisteo was known. Castañeda described it thus: "between Cicuye [Pecos] and the province of Quirix [Keres] there is a small, strong pueblo, which the Spaniards named Ximena, and another pueblo, almost deserted, for only one of its sections is inhabited. This pueblo must have been large, to judge by its site, and it seemed to have been destroyed recently. This was called the town of Los Silos, because big maize silos were found in it" (Hammond and Rey 1940: 257). The Spaniards were aware of warfare between the various pueblos and their Plains enemies. As best as they could determine, the Spaniards learned that a large body of Teyas had besieged Cicúye sixteen years previously, but could not take the powerful pueblo. Just beyond Los Silos the Spaniards found another large pueblo completely destroyed. "The patios," wrote Castañeda, "were covered with numerous stone balls as large as jugs of one arroba. It looked as if the stones had been hurled from catapults or guns with which an enemy had destroyed the pueblo" (Hammond and Rey 1940: 258).

Bolton suggested that the first phase of the march was covered in four days between Tiguex and Pecos. They went, he wrote,

> north up the Rio Grande, around the end of Sandia Mountains, and eastward through Galisteo Valley, passing the famous turquoise mines. On the way they noted several towns similar to those of Tiguex, some of whose ruins are still to be seen today. The first pueblo, reached after one day's travel, had about thirty inhabited houses. Coronado stopped here in passing, embraced the chief, and instructed the people to tell their neighbors to remain quiet in their homes . . . the implication is that these people had joined in the Tiguex rebellion but were now forgiven (Bolton 1949: 239).

Next they passed through Los Silos, evidently picking up corn from its storage rooms, before proceeding north. Bolton suggested they went northeast "presumably through Lamy Canyon and Glorieta Pass, or perhaps more directly over the mountains, to Cicuique, or Pecos" (Bolton 1949: 240). Juan de Jaramillo corroborated the itinerary, writing, "after leaving this settlement and the river, we passed two other pueblos whose names I do not know, and in four days we came to Cicuique . . . this route was to the northeast" (Hammond and Rey 1940: 300).

That they went to Pecos and camped there is a given. Castañeda's description of the pueblo has become a classic statement. Of it he wrote:

> Cicuye is a pueblo containing about 500 warriors. It is feared throughout that land. It is square, perched on a rock in the center of a vast patio or plaza, with its estufas. The houses are all alike, four stories high. One can walk on the roofs over the whole pueblo, there being no streets to prevent this. The second terrace is all surrounded with lanes which enable one to circle the whole pueblo. These lanes are like balconies which project out, and under which one may find shelter. The houses have ladders to climb to the corridors on this terrace. There corridors are used as streets. The houses facing the open country are back to back with those on the patio, and in time of war they are entered through the interior ones. The pueblo is surrounded by a low stone wall. Inside there is a water spring, which can be diverted from them. The people of this town pride themselves because no one has been able to subjugate them, while they dominate the pueblos they wish. The inhabitants [of Cicúye] are of the same type and have the same customs as those in the other pueblos. The maidens here also go about naked until they take a husband. For they say that if they do anything wrong it will soon be noticed and so they will not do it. They need not feel ashamed, either, that they go about as they were born (Hammond and Rey 1940: 257).

Castañeda left some clues with reference to the geographic perspective regarding New Mexico's location and how far they had traveled to that point. Given his knowledge of the Sierra Madre Occidental and the Sierra Madre Oriental, he believed that the Sierra Madre Occidental curved westward following the configuration of the coast and that possibly the two ranges widened out to the north, and within them lay the Great Plains. Castañeda recorded his observations as follows:

> We have already told of the terraced settlements, which, it seems, were located in the center of the cordillera, in the most level and spacious portion of it, for it is 150 leagues across to the plains located between the two mountain ranges. I refer to the one along the North sea and the one on the South sea, which on this coast could be more properly called West sea. This cordillera is the one at the South sea. Thus to better understand how the settlements I am describing extend along the middle of the cordillera, I will state that from Chichilticale, which is the beginning of this stretch, to Cíbola, there is a distance of eighty leagues. From Cíbola, which is the first pueblo, to Cicuye, which is the last one on the way across, is seventy leagues; from Cicuye to the beginning of the plains it is thirty leagues.

Perhaps we did not cross them directly but at an angle so that the land seemed more extensive than if it had been crossed at the center. The latter route might have been more difficult and rough. One can not determine this very clearly because of the bend which the cordillera makes along the coast of the gulf of the Tizon [Colorado] river (Hammond and Rey 1940: 260–261).

Having departed Pecos led by Indian guides who hoped to lose the expedition in the wilderness before them, the Spaniards proceeded for several days until they reached a river "we Spaniards called Cicuique," wrote Jaramillo (Hammon and Rey 1940: 300). Castañeda reported that the Spaniards "traveled in the direction of the plains, which are on the other side of the mountain range. After four days' march, they came to a deep river carrying a large volume of water flowing from the direction of Cicuye. The general named it the Cicuye River" (Hammond and Rey 1940: 235). How the expedition reached the Pecos River is not known with certainty.

Bolton suggested that Vázquez de Coronado left Pecos Pueblo, "situated on an arroyo tributary to Pecos River" (Bolton 1949: 242), and followed a route paralleling the present-day highway to Las Vegas. Descending the valley, the expedition kept Glorieta Mesa to its right. On its left was the Pecos River. Passing present-day Rowe, speculated Bolton, the expedition proceeded to present-day San José before reaching the Pecos River where today's highway crosses it. From there, the expedition followed the river downstream, past present-day Ribera, San Miguel, El Pueblo, and Villanueva. They proceeded along this route until they reached Anton Chico, where Vázquez de Coronado ordered a bridge to be built across the Pecos River. Once across the river, the expedition began a new phase of their search for Quivira which, they supposed, was on the Buffalo Plains.

The Search for Coronado's Bridge

"If I remember correctly, it seems to me that to reach this river, at the point where we crossed it, we went somewhat more to the northeast. Upon crossing it we turned more to the left, which must be more to the northeast, and we began to enter the plains where the cattle roam," wrote Jaramillo (Hammond and Rey 1940: 300). Was Jaramillo mistaken about the direction of march? Could it have been a slip of memory or an error in transcription by the sixteenth-century copyist? Other accounts of the expedition such as the *Relación del Suceso* (see Hammond and Rey 1940: 289) clearly state that the line of march was southeast. The error, if indeed it is one, has confounded historians and searchers for Coronado's bridge for over a century.

Working with great dedication for more than a dozen years to determine the route from Pecos Pueblo to the Pecos River, Richard and Shirley Flint have proposed an alternative to the Bolton hypothesis. Thoroughly analyzing primary and secondary sources, the Flints have discounted many other hypotheses regarding the route to the Pecos River. With great methodological skill, they examined the hypotheses advanced by proponents of the following bridge sites: the Rio Grande, the Gallinas River, the Canadian and the Pecos Rivers (see Chapter 17). Their assessments of the various hypotheses are based on four critical elements: the location of Cicúye; the direction of the expedition's line of march from Cicúye; the distance of march to the Río de Cicúye's bridge site; and the identity of the Río de Cicúye.

In 1962 Albert Schroeder reconsidered the Bandelier and Winship hypotheses and determined that the bridge could have been constructed on the Canadian River near Conchas Dam, New Mexico. Based on the direction of march taken by the expedition and the great distance and terrain covered, the Flints felt that the Canadian River theory did not fit the distance criteria established by the expedition's chroniclers (Flint and Flint 1991).

The Pecos River hypothesis has the best possibilities, but the Flints are cautious because of the distance factor. For example, Frederick S. Dellenbaugh, in 1897, proposed a Pecos River crossing near Roswell, New Mexico. A more reasonable proposal was advanced by Frederick W. Hodge in 1899, namely, that Pecos Pueblo was the beginning point, with a line of march in a southeasterly direction and a distance of seventy-five to eighty miles. Hodge proposed that the crossing was made on the Pecos River at or a little south of Puerto de Luna, New Mexico. And Carl Sauer supported that claim, suggesting that the expedition descended the west bank of the Pecos River, made its crossing at Puerto de Luna, and turned east across the Llano Estacado (Sauer 1932: 142–144).

In 1944, William C. Holden took a middle-of-the-road approach in support of the expedition's southeastern direction from Pecos Pueblo, but concluded that the bridge was constructed north of Santa Rosa (Holden 1944: 7). In one part of his analysis, he wrote, "It is probable that the bridge was built at Anton Chico" (ibid.). Later in his study, he alluded to the expedition having passed "not very far north of Santa Rosa," and started across the plains to the east of there. "It is our opinion," continued Holden, "that Coronado stayed on the Llano Estacado from Santa Rosa to the Querecho village" (Holden 1944: 9). Thus, he proposed a route from Pecos Pueblo to the High Plains via the Pecos River by following a line along the west side of the Pecos River Valley to Anton Chico where the Spaniards built a bridge. Once across the river, Holden suggested that the expedition proceeded in an east-southeast direction paralleling the river on its east side until it reached the vicinity of Santa Rosa. Before it reached Santa Rosa, the expedition veered to the east and reached the High Plains at Frio Draw to the south of Tucumcari.

In 1937, Paul A. Jones supported the Pecos River crossing but made no determination as to its location other than suggesting that the bridge was constructed forty to fifty miles from Pecos Pueblo. He did, however, support a southeasterly line of march (Jones 1937: 46). Bolton (1949: 242–243) corroborated the Pecos River hypothesis and placed the crossing at forty-five to fifty miles near Anton Chico, New Mexico. Although Hodge, Jones, Holden, and Bolton appear correct in their conclusion that the direction of march was southeast, the Flints conclude that Hodge went too far; Jones is too vague; they express no opinion on Holden; and they surmise that Bolton had the expedition meeting the river too soon, though his is the most likely of the previous hypotheses.

In summary, they advance a new theory, as follows:

> Upon leaving Cicúye in the first week of May 1541, the Coronado expedition proceeded south to the area of modern Rowe, New Mexico. At that point they ascended a relatively gentle natural ramp onto Glorieta Mesa. Following the drainages of the mesa's gently tilted surface, they traveled south and slightly east to the vicinity of modern Leyba, New Mexico, and into Cañon Blanco. The canyon then served as a roadway all the way east to its junction with the Pecos River. The army then followed the river east and slightly south to its confluence with the Gallinas River. Not far downstream from there (roughly 65 miles southeast of Cicúye) a bridge was built across the Pecos River and the whole company of people and animals crossed over [see Chapter 17].

CHAPTER 14

Zuni on the Day the Men in Metal Arrived[1]

EDMUND J. LADD

He Zuni tradition is an oral tradition. We're the ones who the intruders wrote about. We are the intrudees who had no voice until a very short while back, until after the Second World War when there was some movement to get Indians like myself, Leigh Jenkins, Al Ortiz, Dave Warren, Bea Medicine, and a whole host of "scholars" involved in Native American studies and Native American programs. And now we're beginning to make a little headway.

In thinking about Zuni and European traditions about Coronado, I am reminded of a little story about two Indian individuals, one a Hopi and the other a Navajo. They were told by the *bahana* (white man) to take a ruler and go out and measure a flagpole in the yard to see how tall it was. So the two Indians went out there. And they were standing with their hands behind their backs and they said, "Gee, I wonder how we're gonna do this. How do we measure this thing?" And pretty soon the white man came along and said, "Why don't you take that pin out and lay the pole down and measure it?" And one of the Indians said, "What do you think, I'm dumb. I don't want to know how long it is. I want to know how tall it is."

So a lot of what we're talking about is measuring the same "pole" from different points of view. We're not trying to change the written history, but we are saying there is another side to the interpretation. We are in a position now to take a critical look at the history that has been written about our people by the outsiders who were visiting us for the first time with only a limited time of contact.

The first "white man" who visited us was a Moor, a house servant, Estevan de Dorantes from Azamora, Morocco. When he crossed from La Florida back to Mexico with Álvar Núñez Cabeza de Vaca and the other survivors of the Pánfilo Narváez expedition, he worked very well with the native people they met. Maybe because he was black or because he was more observant of some of the rituals they performed, he became a kind of "medicine man." On return of the Florida survivors to Mexico, they told of the wealthy cities to the north as told to them by the natives they came in contact with on their trail. And so Viceroy Antonio de Mendoza, back in Mexico City, commissioned fray Marcos de Niza to go up north to see where these fabulously wealthy towns were. Estevan was assigned to go with fray Marcos as a guide.

So, the priest and "slave" started northward in search of these cities. Sometime in April 1539, probably around Eastertime, Marcos decided he wanted to rest and reconnoiter awhile, so he made a camp. And he told Estevan, "Walk ahead of me. Go ahead one day and make a place for me. And if you hear any news that is very good, send back a cross with one of your bearers; send back a cross that is a palm (span) in length. And if the news is absolutely fabulous, out of this world, send back a cross that is as long as an arm (two spans)" (Hammond and Rey 1940: 66). So off went Estevanico ahead of fray Marcos. That was his first mistake. He got ahead of fray Marcos by a considerable distance.

About Easter Sunday here comes one of Estevan's bearers with a cross as big as himself on his back. And fray Marcos thought, "this must really be fabulous." And the bearers also had robes, probably buffalo robes, with them. If memory serves me right, that was the first time that the word *cíbola* was associated with the seven cities (Hammond and Rey 1940: 66). Actually, before that they were referred to only as the "Seven Cities." Probably the bearers were pointing to the robes and saying, "Cíbolo, cíbolo," because the word for buffalo in the Zuni language is *ciwolo*. From then on the Seven Cities of Cíbola were established as part of the historical documentary record.

Estevanico got ahead of the main party and went on into Zuni, to the village of Hawikuh. (The name of these ruins has been spelled several different ways; I prefer "Hawikuh.") I think it was Hawikuh; I don't think it was Kyaki:ma as proposed by others. Dr. Rodack (Chapter 6) quoting Cushing about Estevan states that "when the roofs were on Kyaki:ma a black man came with chile lips." Cushing calls him the "Black Mexican" or "Chile-Lips." This is one of those classic examples of poetic license taken by Frank Hamilton Cushing. The quote is inaccurate, I think, due to the fact that it comes from Cushing using English terms not in the Zuni vocabulary and is not from a Zuni point of view. If Estevan came to Kyaki:ma, he would have had to climb what is called Pointing Face, the south-facing cliffs or barranca that faces the St. Johns, Arizona, area. It would have been a very arduous climb. And the "rainbow" springs, the artesian hot (warm) springs, are in that area, but there is no description of the route he took.

Traveling traders came to Zuni who spoke strange languages, probably Nahuatl or some other southern language. They were long-distance traders and who talked about the land where they came from, the land of eternal summer. The reason that we believed them was that they carried the red, yellow, orange, and blue feathers of the macaw (*mu la*), which they brought to trade, and seashells, and so forth. They told of white men coming there and that they were very vicious, cruel. They had seen with their own eyes whole villages wiped out by big grey-white dogs that ate the people and by men on great animals using fire sticks that could blow a hole right through you. The story goes on that the native people whom the white men captured were strung like rabbits on a rabbit stick and herded away to the mines to live and die in work.

What the long-distance traders were bringing into the Zuni villages was not only material like macaw feathers, bells, seashells, and so forth, but also the news from farther south. That news was not very good because what they were describing were slave raids by Beltrán Nuño de Guzmán and others in the southern Sonora area. So the Zunis knew pretty well what was happening to the south of them. They were already aware of the strange, cruel, and greedy people in their land, but they had not actually seen them, had only heard stories and rumors from the infrequent contacts through their trade connections. But they were thankful that they didn't have any of the shiny yellow stone that the newcomers would go crazy about and kill for. They would say, "We're lucky. We're too far north and all we have is the *ihl/ aqua*, the turquoise from the east. We don't have any of the shiny yellow stone that we can be afraid of."

The oral traditions are not this detailed, but just imagine, a warm spring morning in April, everyone is busy getting ready for the spring planting and the arrival of summer. When all of a sudden there appears on the horizon a cloud of dust under which the Zunis see strange shapes and forms of a dozen people carrying bundles on their backs led by a tall figure (I imagine Estevan to be tall, taller than his traveling companions and dressed in flamboyant clothing). There are no accounts that I could locate that describe his size or stature. Here is a man, either ignored or avoided by history, who is a very important Southwestern historical personality. He was one of the first to see the Mississippi River, the first to contact the Pueblo people and the first to die at the hands of the native people—his place in history is as important as Viceroy Mendoza, Coronado, or Antonio de Espejo.

After the first sighting from the rooftops, the bow priest or war priest immediately called a council. He assembled the order of the bow priests outside the village on the plains to meet these strange people. The Zunis only spoke their own language, no Spanish. The visitors probably spoke Spanish and some other native language from the south. Here is most definitely a language barrier! By sign language and pantomime, they determined some limited understanding of purpose. There was, without doubt, misunderstanding, misinterpretation from both sides. The decision was to house the visitors in a large house outside the village.

Estevanico was ready to make another mistake. The following is suspicion, based not entirely on the Zuni oral tradition, but on other sources tempered by interpretations of Zuni spiritual and moral values, of what probably transpired during the following days after Estevan and his party arrived at Hawikuh.

The Zunis were friendly at the outset, it is their nature to be, until the purpose of the visitor became clear. I suspect that Estevan started to make demands and started to try and intimidate the Zunis by making demands for food, gifts, and I suppose women, as he had done with other people he came in contact with along the way. The Zunis were not intimidated. The demands did not work, so he started another ploy, another mistake. He apparently always had been successful with his "medicine gourd," so, he sent that into the council expressing his "medicine power," which the Zunis did not buy. The head war chief took the gourd and dashed it to the ground and said, "This is not from our people." At this point Estevan was probably summoned into the council. There he made his final mistake.

To impress the council he declared he was the leader of white men who were following and who were more powerful than himself. Therefore, he said, "I demand those things I have requested." I can imagine the reaction to those words "leader of white men." He is black; "more powerful," "white men following." Remember Guzmán's raids into Sinaloa; killing, slave raids? All of these elements were without doubt computed by the war priest. The only thing that came up was "*slave spy.*" So Estevan was killed, unfortunately for Estevan. He was killed not because he was black, not because of his demands, but because of his statement that he was "leading white men more powerful than himself."

Fray Marcos, in the meantime, got the man-sized cross, lifted up his skirts, and ran as fast as he could to catch up with Estevan. And he found, coming back from the Cíbola village, some of Estevan's bearers, running in the opposite direction. He tried to find out what had happened and they said that the Cíbolans had killed Estevan and they were running away. Marcos went farther and farther northeastward until he looked over the valley and saw a city, "a city as large as Mexico

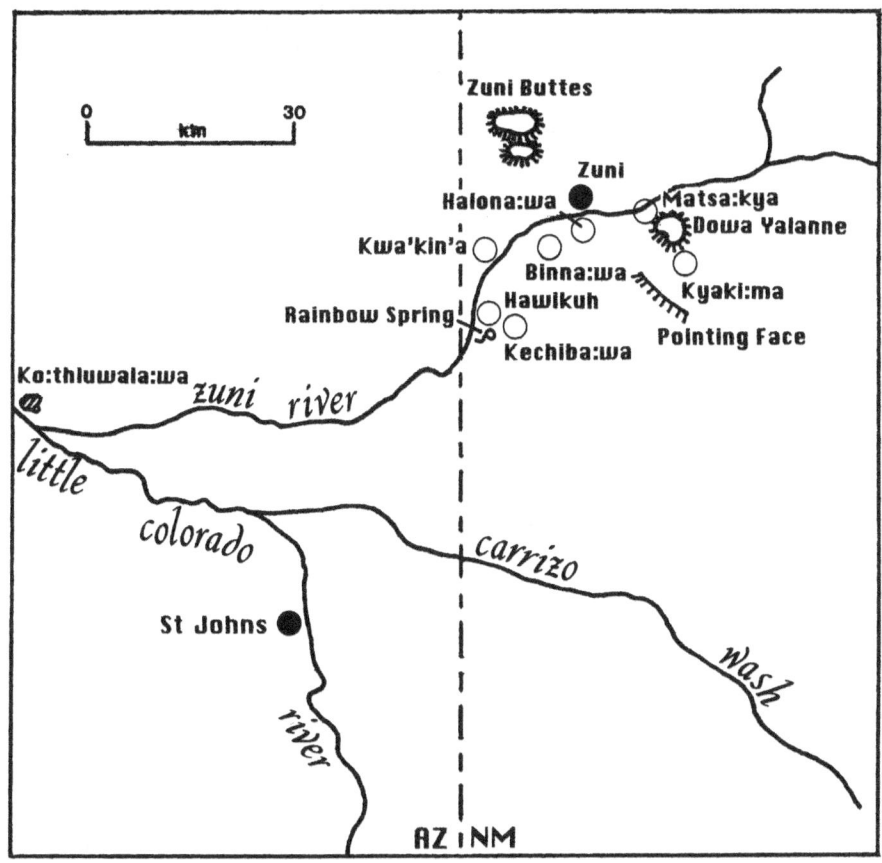

Map 11. Sixteenth-century Cíbola.

City," according to the record. He made a cairn of stones, erected a cross, and took possession of the "kingdom" in the name of the king of Spain. Then, he lifted up his skirts again and ran as fast as he could back to Mexico and conjured up a story about this fabulous place. I don't know why and I don't suppose history will ever know why fray Marcos made up such a story, if he did. This according to the record.

However, I hasten to add, I'm fairly certain that when fray Marcos reported a "city bigger than Mexico City," the story was blown all out of proportion as the story went from mouth to mouth, until the "Seven Cities" became the "Seven Cities of Gold," and became real. So, the floodgates were opened and the "rush" began. I sincerely believe Marcos never said "there is much gold." All he said was the city was as big as Mexico City.

Nevertheless "the fat was in the fire"; the whole of Mexico blew up in greed and avarice for the yellow shiny stone they were looking for. And as a result, an expedition assembled at Compostela in February 1540 and headed northward under the command of don Francisco Vázquez de Coronado.

Now, the arrival of Coronado at the village of Hawikuh is a very, very important time, a very important date. And the events leading up to that date are very important, too, because they bear heavily on the interpretation of where Coronado's route was and what was happening. The historical documents say that, as the Spaniards were approaching what is now the ruins of Hawikuh, Coronado sent out a small party of soldiers to reconnoiter a "bad passage" (Hammond and Rey 1940: 167). He sent an officer and some soldiers to this pass, where there might be an ambush. And that, I think, was on the trail that I describe later. The officer and the soldiers went and they camped at the pass. And during the night in the gap they were "attacked" by a small band of Indians. That is very significant. Also, as the expedition was going northeastward they could see "smoke signals" (Hammond and Rey 1940: 167) off to their right, to the south. That is a most significant thing that relates to this particular event. They were paralleling somebody who was moving along in the same direction, parallel to what we now call the Zuni River. The "barefoot trail" also parallels a spiritual lifeline between the sacred lake and the villages of Zuni.

And the men in metal were arriving at Hawikuh on July 7, 1540 (Hammond and Rey 1940: 179). That was during a very significant time of year, the time of year when the summer solstice was being celebrated. It is an eight-day ceremony during which pilgrims, elders, go to a place called *Ko:thluwala:wa,* which is at the junction of the Zuni and Little Colorado Rivers just below present-day St. Johns, Arizona. This is still a very, very important place for us, even in modern days. The pilgrims go there and return, and no one, but no one, is to cross the path of these pilgrims either coming or going. So, what was going on in the night at the gap was that the attackers of the little party of Spaniards were the bow priests and the people who were guarding the pilgrims' trail. What the bow priests were saying was, "Don't cross the trail." Here was a group of strangers who didn't know what was happening, so they attacked them and tried to scare them off. I don't think they tried to kill them. I think they just tried to scare them off.

The next day the whole of Coronado's group came to Hawikuh and the Zuni people were assembled there because, I think, Hawikuh was the place where the pilgrimage was being sponsored for that year. All the people were there. Coronado (Hammond and Rey 1940: 168) wrote to the viceroy later, saying that all the warriors had been out on the plains and Castañeda (Hammond and Rey 1940: 208) reported that "the people of the district had gathered there." But the people were at

Figure 14.1. Shu'la:witsi. Drawing by Richard Flint.

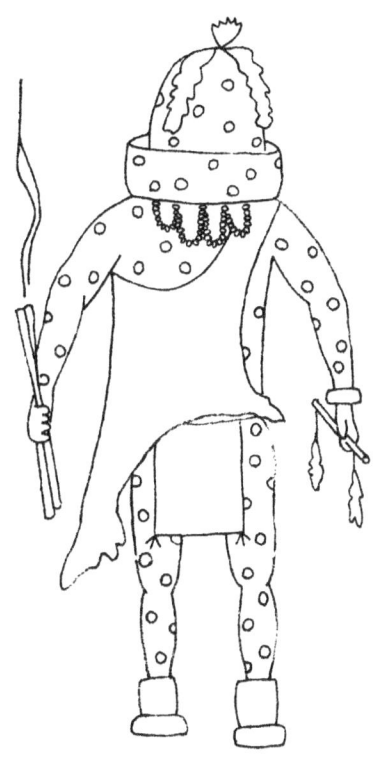

Hawikuh for another reason than the coming of Coronado and that was for the solstice ceremony. The people were assembled on the rooftops, looking to the west.

Here the smoke signals are very important because the smoke signals are a part of the ceremony performed by the little fire god, who is one of the pilgrims. The fire god, *Shu'la:witsi*, goes along the "barefoot trail" with his firebrand and he burns small trees and small shrubs as part of the ceremony. Those were smoke signals alright, but they had nothing to do with Coronado. They were smoke signals to the villagers back up on the rooftops at Hawikuh, looking toward the south and west and seeing where the pilgrims had gotten to. The smoke is also symbolic of making rain and bringing in the clouds, but it had absolutely nothing to do with Coronado.

So, all the people were on top of the roofs looking toward the west and here came a cloud of dust with all kinds of animals, waving flags, and shining armor. Coronado was stumbling onto the solstice ceremonies. He had no knowledge of what was going on. And so the bow priest went out in front of the village and met the column and said, "Do not enter, right now; we're having a ceremony." And as part of the request he drew a line of cornmeal across the path. When a cornmeal line is drawn it means, "Do not enter, now." It doesn't mean, "Do not enter, forever." But it says, "Do not enter, now, because we're having a ceremony that you should not disrupt."

Whoever was interpreting for Coronado misunderstood or didn't understand at all what was happening. I think Coronado took the gesture of the cornmeal line as a threat. As a result, the battle began. I sincerely think that if Coronado had arrived four or five days earlier or four or five days later, there would have been no battle. The Zunis probably would have greeted the strangers with welcoming and open arms.

However, the Zunis had killed Estevan the year before as a spy and now here came another group of people with the same kind of dogs, riding on strange animals, waving flags, and with hundreds of bearers (their "slaves") that were carrying their gifts and their belongings. There was no interpretation that the Zunis could make other than that this was a slave-raiding party. That may have been another cause for the battle.

But the main reason, I believe, is that Coronado and his people did not know that the ceremony was going on. And the reason that there were lots and lots of people at Hawikuh was that the people from *Kechiba:wa*, maybe as far away as *Kyaki:ma*, were at the village to observe the ceremony of the solstice. That's what I think happened and that's my interpretation (compare Huff 1951).

Fact one, Estevan came to Hawikuh. Fact two, fray Marcos de Niza, according to reports, painted a glowing picture of Cíbola that precipitated the Coronado expedition. Fact three, Coronado arrived at Hawikuh in early July disrupting a sacred ceremony. And fact four, early July was the time of solstice ceremonies at Zuni, involving pilgrimage to the sacred lake and the lighting of small fires along the way. The combination of these factors resulted in violence at Hawikuh, violence in which both parties misunderstood what the other was up to.

Note

1. This was given as a spontaneous "lecture" recorded on tape and transcribed. The author has tried to maintain the informal tempo of the original.

CHAPTER 15

The Geography of Middle Rio Grande Pueblos Revealed by Spanish Explorers, 1540-1598[1]

ELINORE M. BARRETT

hen Spanish explorers arrived in the American Southwest in the sixteenth century, the greatest concentration of settled farming villages was in the Rio Grande Region. Some ninety-three pueblos were located in an area that stretched south from Taos Pueblo 215 miles along the Rio Grande rift valley, in addition to outlying areas to the east and west. Within the Rio Grande Region the general settlement pattern in the 1540–1598 contact period consisted of loose groupings of linguistically related pueblos that occupied specific drainage areas.

Spanish explorers found the largest number of inhabited pueblos in the central part of the Rio Grande Region, the Albuquerque-Belen Basin (in this study called the Middle Rio Grande Subregion).[2] Within the basin, twenty-two pueblos were located along a sixty-mile stretch of the river between the Rio Puerco confluence on the south and the Jemez River junction to the north. Within this territory of the Southern Tiwa people, twelve to thirteen pueblos were clustered within a fifteen- to twenty-mile distance at its northern end, with the other eight or nine spaced irregularly over the southern two thirds. Map 12 and Table 15.1 show attempts to correlate pueblos reported by the explorers with known archeological sites. (The basic work of site identification has been

Table 15.1. Pueblos Reported by Sixteenth-Century Spanish Explorers

Pueblo Name	LA Number[a]	Coronado 1540–1542	Rodríguez/Chamuscado 1581–1582	Espejo 1582–1583	Castaño de Sosa 1590–1591	Oñate 1598	1602 Map
MIDDLE RIO GRANDE SUBREGION NORTH (TIGUEX)							
Kuaua	187	—	Medina de la Torre	Poguana	—	—	—
Santiago	326	Alcanfor	Palomares	Comise	—	—	Santiago
Watche	677	—	Campos	Achine	unnamed	—	—
Sandia	294	—	Cáceres	Guagua	unnamed	—	—
Corrales	288	—	La Palma	Gajose	—	—	—
Puaray	717	—	Malpaís	Simasse	unnamed	Puaray	—
Maigua	716	—	Nompe	Suyte	unnamed	—	—
?	—	—	Cempoala	Nocoche	—	—	—
Alameda	421	—	Villarasa	Hacala	unnamed	—	—
Chamisal	22765	—	Culiacán	Tiara	—	—	—
Calabacillas	289	—	Analco	Taycios	unnamed	—	—
Piedras Marcadas	290	—	San Pedro	Casa	—	—	—
?	—	—	Puaray	Puala de los Martires	—	—	—
Subtotal		13	[12]	13	13[b]	[15]	incomplete[c]	[12][d]

Pueblo Name	LA Number[a]	Coronado 1540–1542	Rodríguez/Chamuscado 1581–1582	Espejo 1582–1583	Castaño de Sosa 1590–1591	Oñate 1598	1602 Map
MIDDLE RIO GRANDE SUBREGION SOUTH (TUTAHACO)							
?	—	—	San Mateo	—	—	—	—
Pur-e Tu-ay	489	—	—	—	—	—	Mesilla
Isleta	724	—	Santa Catalina	Guajolotes	—	—	unnamed
Be-jui Tu-ay	81	—	Taxumulco	unnamed	—	—	unnamed
Valencia	953	—	Tomatlán	—	—	—	unnamed
?	—	—	—	despoblado	—	—	—
Ladera del Sur	50257[e]	—	Mexicalcingo	despoblado	—	—	unnamed
Casa Colorado	50249[f]	—	—	unnamed	—	San Juan Bautista	San Juan
?	—	—	Piquinaguatengo	—	—	—	—
Abó Confluence	50241	—	Caxtole	El Corvillo	—	—	unnamed
San Francisco	778	—	Pueblo Nuevo	unnamed	—	—	—
?	—	—	Ponsitlán	unnamed	—	—	—
Subtotal	12	[8]	9	8	no data	incomplete[c]	7

[a] New Mexico Laboratory of Anthropology site number.
[b] A list of thirteen names is given, but no locational information.
[c] Of this list of ten pueblo names in the Middle Rio Grande Subregion, only Puaray and San Juan Bautista can be matched to sites.
[d] Eleven pueblo symbols designated "Valle de Puara" are shown without regard to specific locations.
[e] Nearby Ladera Pueblo is LA50259.
[f] LA 50249 is the earlier and LA50261 the later component of the site.
[ ] Total number of pueblos reported.

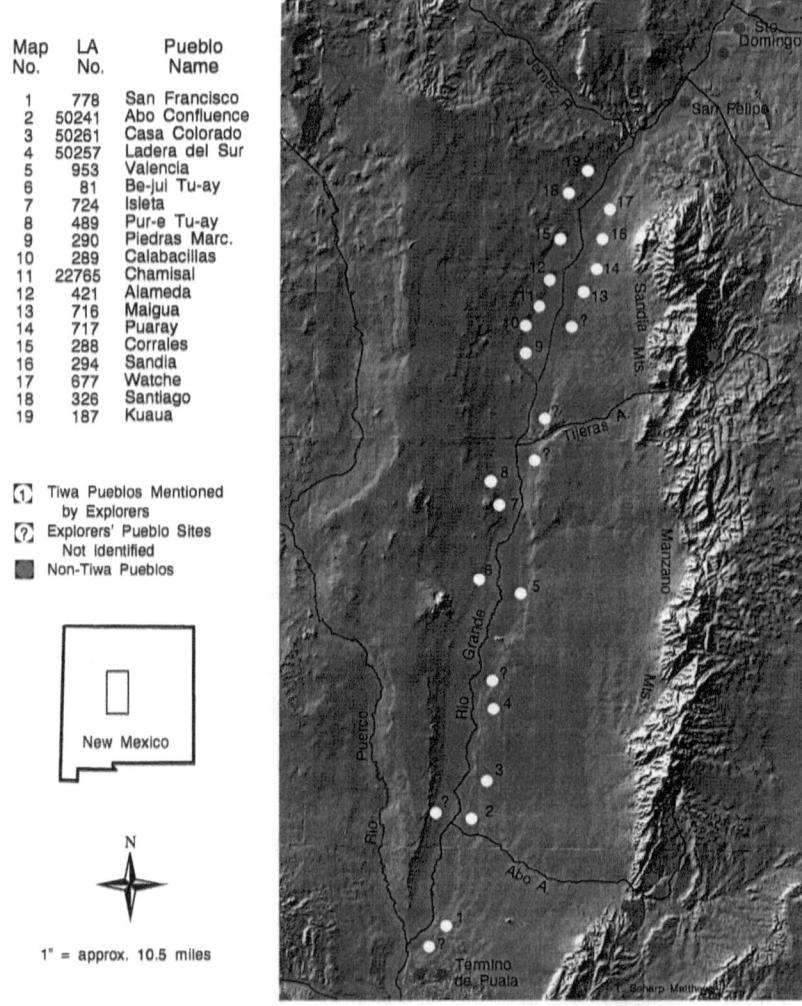

Map 12. Middle Rio Grande Pueblos, 1540–1598. By Tracy Scharp Matthews.

done by Bandelier [1892], Fisher [1931], Mera [1940], and Marshall and Walt [1985].)

These correlations have been made with varying degrees of certainty because neither the information provided by the explorers nor the dating of the sites is precise enough to make unqualified identifications in all cases.[3]

Coronado's people were the first Spaniards to enter the Middle Rio Grande Subregion and they differentiated between the two groupings of pueblos by giving them names as separate provinces: Tiguex on the north and Tutahaco on the south. They had arrived in Pueblo country at the Zuni pueblos (their Cíbola Province) about 125 miles west of the Rio Grande, and it was from there that Coronado sent out advance parties to explore the new lands. Captain Hernando de Alvarado was the first to travel east to the Rio Grande, which he called the Nuestra Señora (Winship 1896: 594; Hammond and Rey 1940: 183). His party traveled east five days to Acoma Pueblo and another three to the Rio Grande, arriving in Tiguex Province (Winship 1896: 430, 431, 490, 491; Hammond and Rey 1940: 218, 219).

Coronado himself later led a party to the Rio Grande, also in eight days, arriving in Tutahaco Province (Winship 1896: 432, 492–493; Hammond and Rey 1940: 220–221). Although he indicated that Tutahaco was south of Tiguex, his route to the Rio Grande is so vaguely described that the only clues as to how far south he went are the distance, which could not have been greatly different from that covered by Alvarado because the number of days is the same, and the likelihood that his Zuni guides would not have taken the party to a destination that was inconvenient for their own return. It is, therefore, probable that Tutahaco was located in the southern part of the Albuquerque-Belen Basin, and not farther south in the Socorro Basin as has been suggested (Riley 1995: 170). Coronado reported a total of twelve pueblos in Tiguex and eight in Tutahaco but mentioned few individual pueblos. Only one can be identified with any confidence, Santiago (LA 326), which the Spaniards took over as their headquarters and which they called Alcanfor or Coofer[4] (Winship 1896: 432, 451, 454, 492, 519–520, 525, 567, 569, 576, 594; Hammond and Rey 1940: 183, 220, 253, 259, 290, 309, 326, 347; Vivian 1932: 67; Snow 1976b: 166–167; Winter 1982: 185; Chapter 16).

The reports of the 1580s give a more complete picture of the Tiwa settlements in the Middle Rio Grande Subregion. Starting from the southern frontier, Hernán Gallegos, chronicler of the expedition led by Francisco Sánchez Chamuscado, mentions a total of twenty-two pueblos north to the northern border while Diego Pérez de Luxán of the Antonio de Espejo expedition notes at least twenty-one, both listing thirteen in the cluster at the north end of the subregion, a figure also mentioned by some of Coronado's men (Hammond and Rey 1966: 103–105, 116–117, 176–177, 203; Bancroft Library 1551). Although there is some similarity in the number and location of the pueblos they report in the southern part of the subregion, there is also considerable discordance, despite the lapse of only a year and a half between the visits of the Rodríguez/Chamuscado and Espejo expeditions.[5] At one time an extensive uninhabited frontier zone was thought to exist between the Southern Tiwa and the Piro people to the south, largely because there were no known sites in the area and because it was considered a buffer zone between two hostile peoples. But some sites have been identified in this area and, although statements by explorers indicate there was conflict, Espejo noted that only a half league (1.5 miles) separated the Piro and Tiwa Provinces[6] (Mera 1940: 17–18; Wilcox 1991: 132–133; Marshall and Walt 1985: maps; Riley 1995: 230; Hammond and Rey 1928: 290; Hammond and Rey 1966: 82, 221, 303). The listing of pueblos by Gallegos and Luxán further reinforces the likelihood that there was no significant no-man's-land at the Piro–Southern Tiwa frontier.

After Espejo returned from visiting the Estancia Basin to the east, the expedition decamped from Termino de Puala at the southern border of Piro territory, and traveled four leagues (twelve miles) along the Rio Grande (their Río del Norte) to a pueblo they named El Corvillo, passing some small pueblos and many deserted ones along the way. One of these small pueblos might have been at the San Francisco site (LA 778) located four miles north of Termino de Puala (Sevilleta site, LA 774) (Archeological Records Management Site files of the Laboratory of Anthropology, Museum of New Mexico, Santa Fe [ARMS]; Mera 1940: 8; Marshall and Walt 1984: 211, 345). LA 778 might also have been Gallegos's Ponsitlán or his Pueblo Nuevo, both of which were located along the Rio Grande (his Guadalquivir). A distance of four leagues would have put El Corvillo in the vicinity of Abó Arroyo where there was a small pueblo (LA 50241) that could possibly have been occupied at that time (ARMS; Marshall and Walt 1985: n.p.; Marshall and Marshall 1992: 75). This eastside pueblo could also have been Gallegos's very small Caxtole.

As Espejo's people continued north they observed that all of the pueblos were deserted, the inhabitants having fled the Spaniards' approach. It was known that the Tiwa people were responsible for the deaths of two priests from the Rodríguez/Chamuscado expedition who had insisted on staying behind when that expedition returned to New Spain. They called their next campsite, four leagues north of El Corvillo, Los Despoblados. It was between two pueblos, one very large, which, given the distance, would have been near the Ladera del Sur site (LA 50257). Ladera del Sur is not a large site but Ladera Pueblo (LA 50259), located 150 yards away, is (ARMS; Marshall and Walt 1985: n.p.; Marshall and Marshall 1992: 40). Archeological evidence does not indicate that the latter was occupied in the contact period but the site is badly damaged and such evidence could have been destroyed. It seems reasonable, if Luxán could observe that both pueblos were deserted, the two pueblos would have been in sight of each other. There are no other pueblos that fit the information Luxán gives. A pueblo they encountered along the way might have been at the Casa Colorado site (LA 50249 or 50261), which was also on the east side of the Rio Grande.

It is here that matching Luxán's and Gallegos's pueblos becomes especially difficult. Gallegos mentions a large westside pueblo he called Piquinaguatengo opposite Caxtole at Abó Arroyo. But there is no such site at that location and Luxán does not mention a comparable pueblo.[7] Gallegos's next pueblo, Mexicalcingo, was on the east side but whether it occupied the site at Casa Colorado or at Ladera del Sur cannot be known because he does not give the distance. Above Mexicalcingo was his Tomatlán and across the river opposite it on the west side was Taxumulco. These pueblos fit the sites of Valencia (LA 953) and Be-jui Tu-ay (LA 81) respectively and are not likely the same as the two pueblos near Luxán's Despoblados camp because the latter were presumably on the same side of the Rio Grande.[8]

From Los Despoblados, the Espejo expedition covered five leagues (fifteen miles) to a pueblo called Los Guajolotes. This distance would have brought them to the Isleta site (LA 724), which is located on the west side of the Rio Grande. Luxán noted another deserted pueblo along the way, one that could have been either Valencia or Be-jui Tu-ay. That he does not mention both, when it is very likely that these were the sites of Gallegos's Tomatlán and Taxumulco, further brings out just how speculative is the reconstruction of the settlement pattern in this area. Espejo had been traveling along the east side of the Rio Grande but at some point, perhaps at Valencia, his party must have crossed the river, although Luxán does not mention it, because they actually entered Los Guajolotes, noting its abundant provisions, including turkeys. Here, at the Isleta site, there again seems to be a correspondence with Gallegos, with his westside Santa Catalina Pueblo. Above Isleta lay the first pueblo of the northern cluster, called Puaray by Gallegos and Puala by Luxán. Luxán gives the distance as three leagues (nine miles) and mentions no pueblos along the way, whereas Gallegos notes one, San Mateo, placing both it and Puaray on the east side.

Both Gallegos and Luxán list twelve pueblos above Puaray/Puala (Table 15.1).[9] Unfortunately Luxán does not continue to mention each pueblo encountered as Espejo's expedition moved north through the northern cluster of Tiwa pueblos (Coronado's Tiguex Province), but later when he names the pueblos in this area, Puala is the thirteenth and last on his list, reinforcing its location as the southernmost of these pueblos (Hammond and Rey 1966: 203). It cannot be said that the other pueblos on his list are in any geographic order, but Gallegos does supply this order. Above Puaray he notes five pueblos on the east side of the Rio Grande: Cempoala, Nompe, Malpaís, Cáceres, and Campos. Above Cempoala, the sites to which they could correspond are respectively: Maigua (LA 716), Puaray (LA 717), Sandia (LA 294), and Watche (LA 677), although occupation of the latter during the contact period is questionable (ARMS; Mera 1940: 18–19; Winter 1982: 183–185; Scurlock 1982: 179–182). A bigger question surrounds Cempoala for which no site has been found. Two other contact period sites that today are on the east side of the Rio Grande, Alameda (LA 421) and Chamisal (LA 22765), were located on the west side of the river at that time.[10] Gallegos's westside pueblos were: San Pedro, Analco, Culiacán, Villarasa, La Palma, Palomares, and Medina de la Torre beyond which lay the pueblos of the Keres people. The westside sites to which they correspond are probably: Piedras Marcadas (LA 290), Calabacillas (LA 289), Chamisal (LA 22765), Alameda (LA 421), Corrales (LA 288), Santiago (LA 326), and Kuaua (LA 187).

The location of Puaray in the 1580s remains a puzzle. It was at this pueblo that members of the Rodríguez/Chamuscado expedition took leave of two priests who insisted on staying behind and there that the latter were probably later killed (Hammond and Rey 1966: 109). When the Espejo expedition, whose purpose it was to learn the fate of the priests, arrived, they named the pueblo Puala de los Martires (Hammond and Rey 1966: 177). Gallegos had established its location on the east side of the Rio Grande and Luxán put it three leagues (nine miles) north of Isleta. Luxán also mentioned that when they were camped near Puala they were visited by a delegation that had come from eight to ten leagues (twenty-four to thirty miles) upriver, making it likely they were Keres people from San Felipe Pueblo (Hammond and Rey 1966: 178). If the distance were ten leagues, it would have brought them to that site three leagues north of Isleta where Luxán located Puala. That site would have been two miles above the Rio Grande–Tijeras Arroyo junction (or just south of Albuquerque in the general vicinity of the Rio Bravo Boulevard and Highway 47 intersection), an area where there are no known pueblo sites. It would also have been about ten miles south of the other twelve closely spaced pueblos of the northern cluster.

A location somewhat farther north would seem more likely for Puaray and consensus among modern scholars does place Puaray in the midst of the pueblos on the east side at the LA 717 site (Fisher site #13), which is about seven leagues north of Isleta (Fisher 1931: n.p.; Vivian 1932: 59, 63; Snow 1975: 463–480; Riley 1981: 210; Scurlock 1982: 180). This location also accords with information provided by Gaspar Castaño de Sosa in 1591 and Juan de Oñate in 1598 (Hammond and Rey 1966: 293; Hammond and Rey 1953: 319). Castaño de Sosa gave the distance from the first Southern Tiwa pueblo he encountered to his main camp at Santo Domingo as five or six leagues. Six leagues, or twenty-four miles (at four miles to the league), would be roughly the distance from Santo Domingo to the LA 717 site, an indication that his first pueblo might have been Puaray or a pueblo close to it. Oñate also established the location of Puaray in the vicinity of LA 717, and not farther south, when he, too, stated that it was six leagues from Santo Domingo, a Keres pueblo to the north. While at Puaray, one of his men, Gaspar Pérez de Villagrá, claimed he saw on a wall inside one of the houses a mural depicting the death of the two priests, but the scene had been painted over with whitewash and it is doubtful its contents could have been clearly discerned (Villagrá 1933: 142). Oñate did not report it and scholars have tended to treat it as apocryphal (Snow 1975: 464; Riley 1987: 227). Even if it were true, it does not prove that the pueblo where the killings took place was LA 717. Residents of Luxán's Puala de los Martires could have painted the scene in a different pueblo.

A possible explanation of the discrepancy between the reports of Gallegos and Luxán and those of Castaño de Sosa and Oñate might be that there were two Puarays: the one of the 1580s and the one of the 1590s. After the Espejo expedition left Pueblo country, the people of Puaray/Puala, wishing to disassociate themselves from the place where the killings took place, might have destroyed their pueblo and moved to the one at LA 717, giving it the same name. Perhaps Gallegos's San Mateo and Cempoala, located respectively south and north of his Puaray, were destroyed at that time as well, leaving the area devoid of identifiable sites.

Which other pueblos of the northern cluster were still inhabited in the 1590s cannot be determined from either the Castaño de Sosa or Oñate reports. Castaño de Sosa visited pueblos on both sides of the river, which he called the Rio Grande, claiming there were a total of fifteen, but he did not name any of them (Hammond and Rey 1966: 292). Because he probably approached the area through Tijeras Canyon from the east side of the Sandias, the first pueblo he would have encountered was the most southerly on the east side[11] (Hammond and Rey 1966: 291–292; Snow 1988: 95–97). He found this pueblo deserted and was told that the people had fled because it was they who killed the priests, but inhabitants fled from the other pueblos as well, so it is difficult to know if that particular pueblo was Puaray. It probably was not because from that first pueblo Castaño de Sosa proceeded up the east side of the Rio Grande, visiting four other pueblos before crossing to the west side. Above Puaray (LA 717) the only sites are Sandia (LA 294) and Watche (LA 677), and there is some doubt about the latter's occupancy during the contact period.[12] Castaño de Sosa's first pueblo was probably Maigua (LA 716), which is less than a mile south of Puaray (LA 717). Identity of the fourth pueblo is still in question, but in this area of intense urban settlement it would not be surprising if this site has been lost.

On the west side Castaño de Sosa's pueblos are even more difficult to link to known sites, but it is possible that the pueblo across the river from the first one he encountered on the east side was Alameda (LA 241) and the other near it was Chamisal (LA 22765). The southernmost, which he describes as very large, might have been Piedras Marcadas (LA 290) (ARMS; Marshall 1988: 13). Oñate gives a list of Tigua (Tiwa) pueblos on the river he called the Río del Norte, but the only recognizable name is Puaray (Hammond and Rey 1953: 314, 346). The 1602 map shows twelve pueblos (Map 13). Unfortunately, eleven are placed without regard to location, designated together as "Pueblos del valle de Puará," but the twelfth, Santiago, is correctly placed at the north end of the west side. This latter location might well be the site of Coronado's headquarters (Alcanfor/Coofer), indicating that it continued to be occupied.

To return to the southern part of the Albuquerque Basin, the explorers who came after Rodríguez/Chamuscado and Espejo have little to add. Castaño de Sosa did not visit the area and Oñate moved through it quickly, mentioning only newly built San Juan Bautista four leagues (sixteen miles) above Sevilleta (LA 774), which would have put it at the Casa Colorado site (LA 50261)[13] (Hammond and Rey 1953: 319). The 1602 map, based on information from a member of Oñate's expedition, is more helpful. The arrangement of symbols indicates that the pueblo sites could have been Abó Confluence, Casa Colorado (named San Juan), Ladera del Sur, and Valencia on the east side of the Rio Grande, Be-jui Tu-ay and Pur-e Tu-ay on the west side, and Isleta on an island in the river (actually, a volcanic outcrop in the western floodplain). The northernmost pueblo on the west side was named Mesilla, a name that would fit the Pur-e Tu-ay site (LA 489), which is on a small butte. Although its late ceramics leave open the possibility that Pur-e Tu-ay was established after the end of the contact period, it does not preclude the possibility of occupation at the time of Oñate's arrival (ARMS; HPD; Marshall and Walt 1985: n.p.).

In combination, the reports of the sixteenth-century Spanish expeditions to New Mexico constitute a rich source of information about the geography of the Rio Grande pueblos. This study has drawn on the information they provide about the number and spatial distribution of pueblos in the Middle Rio Grande Subregion, integrating it with archeological data, to establish the overall pattern of settlement. This area seemed to experience a fair degree of settlement stability compared with other parts of the Rio Grande Region. Ceramic evidence indicates that twelve of the thirteen pueblos in the northern Albuquerque Basin were occupied in all phases of the Classic Period (1300–1600). The explorers are quite consistent in the number of pueblos they reported, both at the beginning and at the end of the contact period. However, they did contribute to disturbed conditions. Their need to requisition food and clothing from the pueblos, in addition to other matters, caused considerable friction, which led in some cases to Spanish attacks on pueblos, especially by members of the Coronado expedition, who destroyed a number of pueblos in the northern Albuquerque Basin. In the same area the people of Puaray Pueblo may have destroyed their pueblo and moved to another because they were linked to the killing of two Spanish priests from the Rodríguez/Chamuscado expedition. But reports from later explorers seem to indicate that damaged or destroyed pueblos were rebuilt and that the number of pueblos and their overall

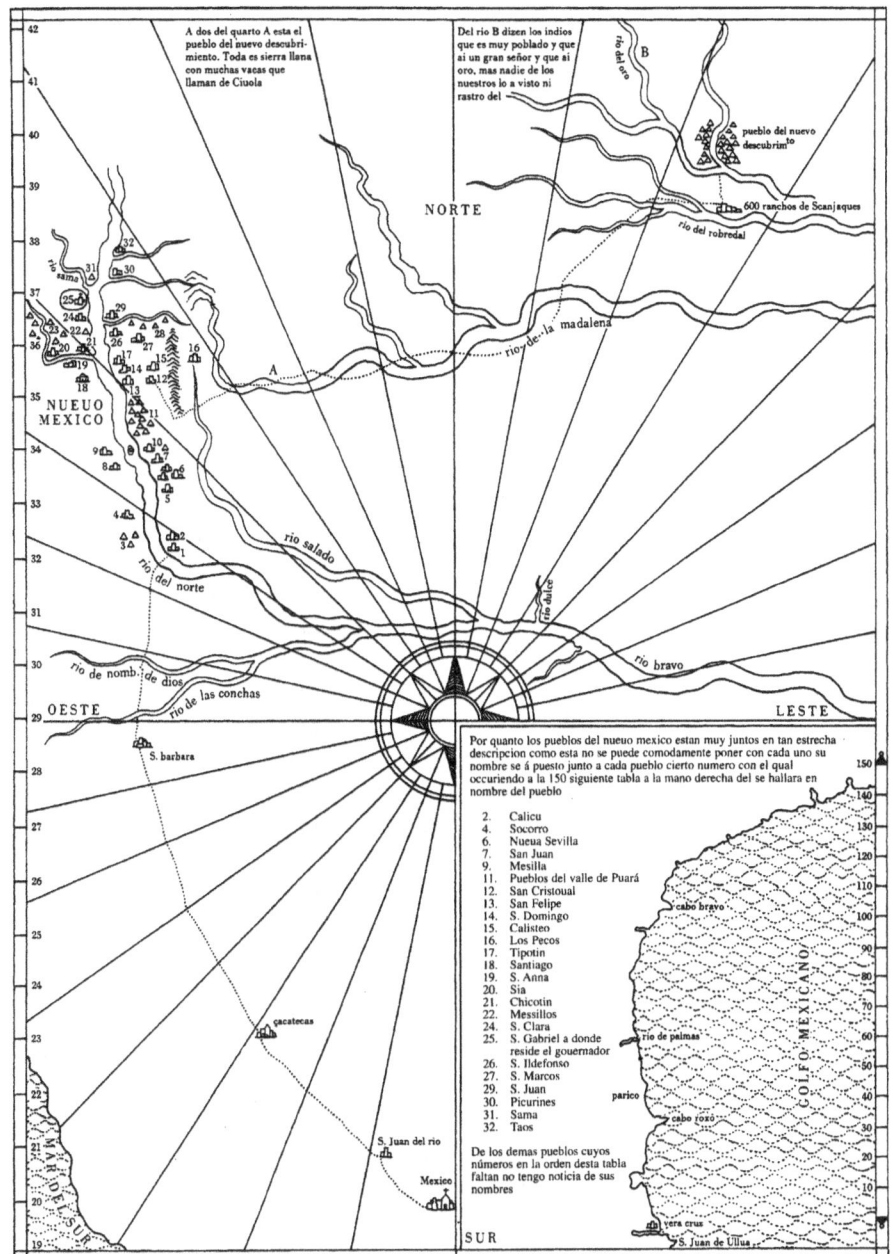

Map 13. Pueblos of New Mexico based on the Enrico Martínez Map of 1602. Reprinted by permission of the University of New Mexico Press.

location pattern did not change significantly as a result of Spanish intrusions during the 1540–1598 contact period. Thus, the reports of the Coronado, Rodríguez/Chamuscado, Espejo, Castaño de Sosa, and Oñate expeditions provide a geography of Pueblo settlement that most likely reflected the needs of those societies, but one that did change drastically once Spanish settlement replaced exploration.

Notes

1. This chapter is a specially prepared extract from *The Geography of Rio Grande Pueblos Revealed by Spanish Explorers, 1540–1598* (Barrett 1997).

2. Between 1540 and 1598 five Spanish expeditions to New Mexico left records of the Pueblo societies they encountered in the Rio Grande Region. These expeditions were led by Francisco Vázquez de Coronado (1540–1542), Francisco Sánchez Chamuscado (1581–1582), Antonio de Espejo (1582–1583), Gaspar Castaño de Sosa (1590–1591), and Juan de Oñate (1598). An additional document is a map drawn in 1602 by Enrico Martínez based on information provided by one of Oñate's men. (See Wheat 1957: 1: 29–33; Hammond and Rey 1966: 63 for discussions of this map.) (See Map 13.)

3. Although there is information about Pueblo settlements in all of the sixteenth-century Spanish chronicles of New Mexico, these accounts cannot be coordinated to give an entirely clear idea of pueblo numbers and location for a number of reasons: the explorers probably did not encounter the same occupied pueblos in all cases because some were abandoned and others reoccupied during the period; chroniclers did not report settlement location in an unambiguous manner and gave different names or no names to the pueblos; and they undoubtedly varied in their understanding of what they were told by local people.

Archeological identification of pueblo sites that were occupied during the 1540–1598 contact period is also burdened with many problems (Cordell and Gumerman 1989: 295). The dating of sites is based on the presence of certain ceramic types, the chronology of which is derived from such measures as tree-ring analysis from a few sites (Breternitz 1966: 105–107). Although there are questions about the regionwide applicability of these dates and the adequacy of surface collections (few sites have actually been excavated), it is the long duration of ceramic-type periods that creates the greatest problem for this study, which has a time frame of only fifty-eight years (Cordell 1984: 90–91). The diagnostic ceramic type for this period should be Glaze E—one of a series of glazed ceramic types that began with the introduction of Glaze A (1300–1475) and ended with Glaze F (1650–1700) (Warren 1979: 193; Chapter 21). Glaze E has been assigned dates between 1515 and 1650, making it possible that a site with this pottery could have been abandoned before 1540 or built after 1598. Evidence from some sites indicates that one type of Glaze F pottery might have been made as early as 1550, making it a possible indicator of pueblo occupation in the contact period (Sundt 1987: Table 2). In the same way, Glaze D may be an indicator because in some areas it continued to be made after 1515, possibly even into the seventeenth century (ibid.).

There is a further problem that bears on the identification of pueblo sites. Over time they have been subject to forces of destruction, natural and/or human. More so than in any other part of the Rio Grande Region, the disturbance of Tiwa sites in the Albuquerque-Belen Basin by intensive agricultural and urban development as well as by periodic flooding and channel shifting has made their identification and temporal placement especially difficult (Schaafsma 1987: 10).

4. In the documents related to the Coronado expedition are references to several Tiguex pueblos attacked by the Spaniards. Two referred to by name, Arenal and Moho, were scenes of major battles. Pueblo de la Cruz and Pueblo del Cerco were probably alternate names for Arenal and Moho respectively. Alameda was the name of a pueblo located between Arenal and Alcanfor. Although distances between these pueblos are given, they vary from one witness to another and there is no information to indicate whether they were north or south of Alcanfor or even if they were on the same side of the river. It seems likely they were all on the west side, but it has been suggested that Arenal may have been on the east side (Riley 1981: 206, 210; Riley 1995: 170). Despite voluminous testimony in the Coronado documents about the pueblos involved in attacks and the speculation of various scholars, there is not enough information to link them to known pueblo sites (Hammond and Rey 1940: 331–335, 347–349, 352–360; Bancroft Library 1551; Bancroft Library 1544; Bolton 1949: 206–208, 212, 216–219, 229; Tello 1891: 419–422, 425; Riley 1995: 177; Schroeder 1992a: 185–187; Scurlock 1982: 180; Chapter 16).

5. See Mecham (1926: map) for another interpretation of the pueblos encountered by the Rodríguez/Chamuscado expedition and Schroeder (1979: 243) for a comparison of the Southern Tiwa pueblos of the Rodríguez/Chamuscado and Espejo expeditions.

6. All distances are based on straight-line measurements taken from 1:250,000 maps prepared by the U.S. Defense Mapping Agency Topographic Center. These measurements are rounded and should be considered approximate as were the distances mentioned by the Spanish explorers, who gave them in leagues. The standard league measured 2.6 miles and the long league about 4.0 miles. The league used by Luxán of the Rodríguez/Chamuscado expedition quite consistently measured about 3.0 miles. Castaño de Sosa is only consistent in that his league measured either 2.6 or 4.0 miles and not some other value. Oñate used the long league of 4.0 miles. For a discussion of the Spanish land league as used in North America see Chardon 1980: 147–151.

7. There are two large west-side pueblo sites in the general area but neither is opposite the Abó Wash site: Abeytas (LA 780) five miles to the south and Los Trujillos (LA 50271) eight miles north; neither shows evidence of contact period occupation (ARMS).

8. The late ceramics (Glazes E and F) found at the LA 953 site cast some doubt about the occupation of this site in the contact period, but it has not been ruled out (ARMS; Mera 1940: 20; Marshall and Walt 1985: n.p.; New Mexico Historic Preservation Division [HPD]; Franklin 1994: 75, 88).

9. Another analysis of the Pueblo settlement pattern there is presented by Vivian (1932: 14–77). A listing of different interpretations by various scholars is found in Scurlock 1982: 180.

10. Alameda Pueblo (LA 421) was reported on the west side of the Rio Grande in Spanish chronicles and on maps as late as 1701 (Hackett 1915: 383–384; Mecham 1926: 277; Delisle 1701; and discussed in Wheat 1957: 1: 56–57). Subsequent reports, maps, and archeological investigations show its location on the east side. A shift in the river's channel has

been considered a possible explanation for this phenomenon. The river might have reoccupied, for a time, the more easterly channel it had established in an earlier era, but recent attempts to ascertain if this could have been the case have given inconclusive results (Staley 1981: 24; Martínez et al. 1985: 4.33–4.34, 4.6; Sargeant 1987: 38–39, 41–44; Kelley 1969: 15). A major flood in 1735 or 1736 might have caused the river to shift to the more westerly channel it still occupies (Martínez et al. 1985: 4.7). The Miera y Pacheco map of 1758 shows Alameda on the east side of the river (Kessell 1987: 510–511). If the river did alter its course, nearby Chamisal Pueblo (LA 22765), which was also located in the floodplain, was probably affected and it, too, is considered a west-side pueblo in the contact period.

11. For an alternate interpretation involving an approach from the north end of the Sandias see Schroeder and Matson 1965: 168–170.

12. The LA 677 site, also known as Nuestra Señora de Dolores, has been built over and much disturbed by a church and school complex that has prevented excavation adequate to determine precisely when it was occupied (Scurlock 1982: 179–182; ARMS; Mera 1940: 19; Winter 1982: 183–185; Marshall 1982: 2, 4).

13. The earlier site, LA 50249, might have been the one referred to by Espejo (Marshall and Marshall 1992: 58, 89).

CHAPTER 16

Let the Dust Settle
A Review of the Coronado Campsite in the Tiguex Province[1]

BRADLEY J. VIERRA AND STANLEY M. HORDES

Introduction

It was Francisco Vázquez de Coronado who led the first European expedition into the American Southwest in 1540. The expedition included at least 350 Spaniards, several hundred Indians, 559 horses, and 1,500 head of livestock (Hammond and Rey 1940). The expedition's route took the group through Cíbola (Zuni), Acoma, and then on to the Tiguex Province in the modern Albuquerque and Bernalillo area of New Mexico. It was here that they spent the winters of 1540–1542 in a pueblo called Alcanfor (Coofor) situated near the Rio Grande. Scholars have argued for years over which of the archeological sites in the Albuquerque-Bernalillo area might be the famous pueblo of Alcanfor. They wondered if something could have been left behind by the expedition that could help us identify the site; but what would a campsite of the Coronado expedition look like after 450 years? How would it be differentiated from the other sixteenth-century Indian campsites or sites associated with other Spanish entradas that passed through the area?

We were thrown into this debate after the discovery of a series of charcoal stains that had been exposed by road-grading activities along State Road 528 west of Bernalillo. What at first glance appeared to be a limited activity site associated with a nearby protohistoric pueblo (LA 326) eventually turned out to be something quite different. Excavations defined the presence of fifteen shallow trash-filled tent depressions, containing puebloan pottery, nails, a plate from a flexible armored vest, a Mexican obsidian blade fragment, and sheep bone. These latter objects were certainly not of a local Indian origin; but if we were not excavating a puebloan site, what was this?

Our multidisciplinary research led us to the conclusion that these simple tent depressions may be the remnants of a campsite associated with the Coronado expedition. Our findings have been presented in various professional forums and publications (Vierra 1989, 1992; Hordes 1989, 1992). In doing so, we have found that our colleagues are in general agreement with our arguments (for example, see Lees [1993]; Riley [1992]; Schroeder [1992]). Indeed, Schroeder states that we provide "excellent data for his [our] conclusions to identify the site as Spanish and to relate it to the Coronado entry of 1540–1542" (1992: 185). However, there are some disagreements on particular issues, and interpretations of the site data. This chapter provides a brief summary of our arguments, and then responds to some of the criticisms made concerning our research.

A Sixteenth-Century Spanish Campsite in the Tiguex Province
Site Description

Coronado would hardly recognize the rolling sand hills that compose Albuquerque's west mesa today. Urban development continues to level the dunes, and new housing projects are constructed on a daily basis. As a result of this development, road graders exposed a series of charcoal stains within the State Road 528 right-of-way west of Bernalillo, New Mexico. The road work was halted, and archeologists from the Museum of New Mexico were called in to excavate the exposed remains. Excavations revealed that the charcoal stains were trash-filled tent depressions. A total of fifteen shallow dugouts were excavated, and surface collections made of associated artifact scatters (Vierra 1989, 1992).

All but one of the dugouts were located within a 100 m area along the east side of the road. All together the site covered an area approximately 200 m long and 130 m wide within the right-of-way. A surface scatter of pottery did extend about 60 m to the east of the right-of-way, with the protohistoric pueblo of LA 326 being situated approximately 400 m farther to the east (see Vierra 1987a for a discussion of this pueblo). The dugouts ranged in size from 2 by 2 m to 4 by 5 m with a general depth of about 10 cm. The floors were unprepared, and had been stained by charcoal from interior hearths and calcium carbonate that had percolated down through the soil profile and onto the compacted surface. Several types of features were found on the floors of the dugouts, including hearths, burned areas, pits, and postholes. Only one dugout exhibited a consistent pattern of postholes, indicating the presence of some form of superstructure. This consisted of a line of four postholes along the back of the tent depression, one on either side, and three forming a triangle in the front (Figure 16.1). All the dugouts were filled with trash, consisting of a charcoal-stained soil mixed with bits of charcoal, burned corn kernels, and sherds, with lesser amounts of burned beans, debitage, ground stone, small bone fragments, bits of adobe, and metal artifacts. The fill appears to represent domestic trash that was deposited directly onto the floors of the structures soon after they were abandoned.

The majority of the artifacts recovered from the site consists of broken pieces of pottery. Approximately 7,000 sherds were collected, most of which were identified as Rio Grande Glaze E pottery made during the sixteenth century. Three hundred and six lithic artifacts were also found, consisting of 148 pieces of debitage, 4 cores, 4 hammerstones, 3 bifaces, a projectile point, 12 mano fragments, 6 metate fragments, and 36 comal fragments. A single obsidian blade fragment was identified as being made of Pachuca obsidian from the Valley of Mexico. Seventeen metal artifacts consisting of twelve nails, a jack plate, a clothes hook (of a hook and eye set), a clothes straight pin or sewing needle, a metal plate, and several metal fragments were also recovered (Figure 16.2). The nails may have been used in tool or weapons handles, boxes, or saddles. The jack plate is a single plate from a flexible armored vest. The macrobotanical remains primarily consist of burned corn kernels with some beans and cotton seed. The faunal remains consist of domestic sheep, pronghorn, mule deer, cottontail, and turkey.

Interpretation

The presence of the metal artifacts, sheep bone, and Mesoamerican blade fragments in what appeared to be a sixteenth-century context raised some important questions. When was the site occupied and by whom? Three corn samples were submitted for radiocarbon dating. The age of these samples are 380±70 B.P. (Beta-17471), 370±80 B.P. (Beta-17472), and 450±100 B.P. (Beta-19376). The calibrated date ranges for these samples at one standard deviation are A.D. 1436–1635, A.D. 1437–1640, and A.D. 1407–1609, respectively. The mean date for these ranges is A.D. 1527. The presence of the metal artifacts and sheep bone indicates that the site was occupied no earlier than A.D. 1540, as the earliest possible time that these items could have been introduced to the area would have been with the Coronado expedition (Hammond and Rey 1940; Hordes 1989). The absence of Rio Grande Glaze F, Tewa Polychrome, majolica, and European vessel forms (for example, soup plates) reflects a pre-Colonial occupation. Therefore, the site appears to have been occupied sometime between A.D. 1540 and the early 1600s.

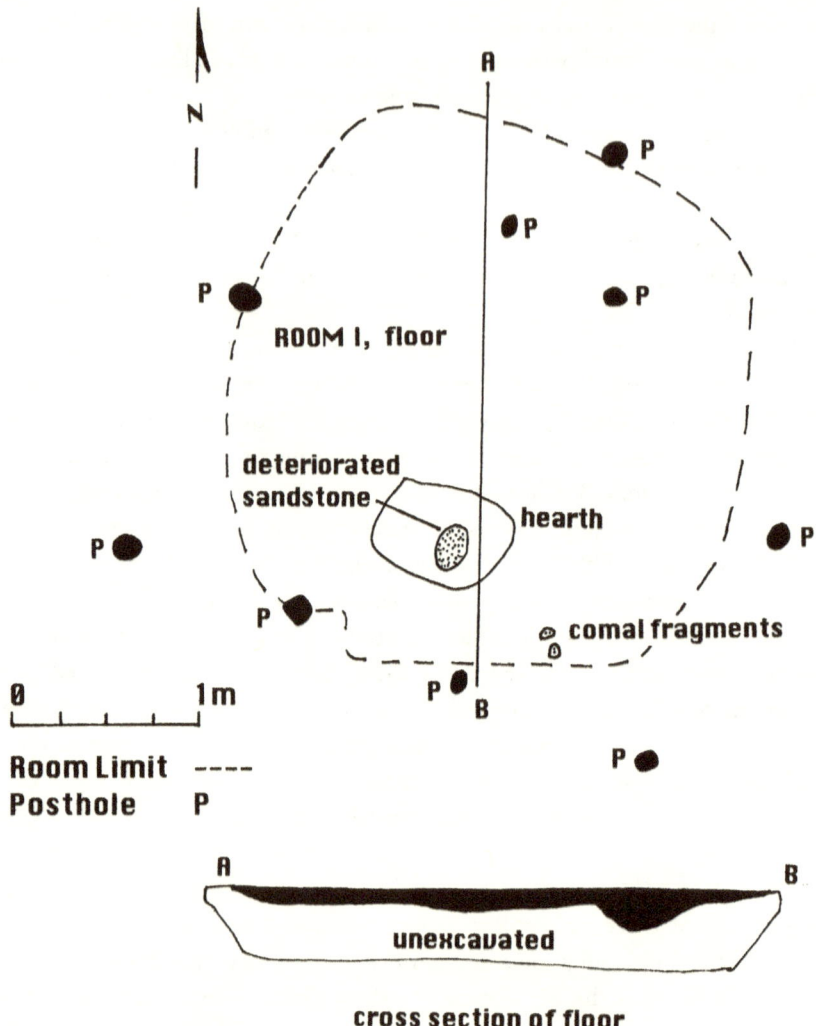

Figure 16.1. Plan view and cross section of a tent dugout from LA 54147. Adapted from illustration by Ann Noble and Ron Stauber.

Several groups could have camped in the area during the sixteenth century, including Puebloans, Apaches, and members of various Spanish entradas. A look at the data reveals that:

- The local Indian population did not have metal or sheep during the sixteenth century.

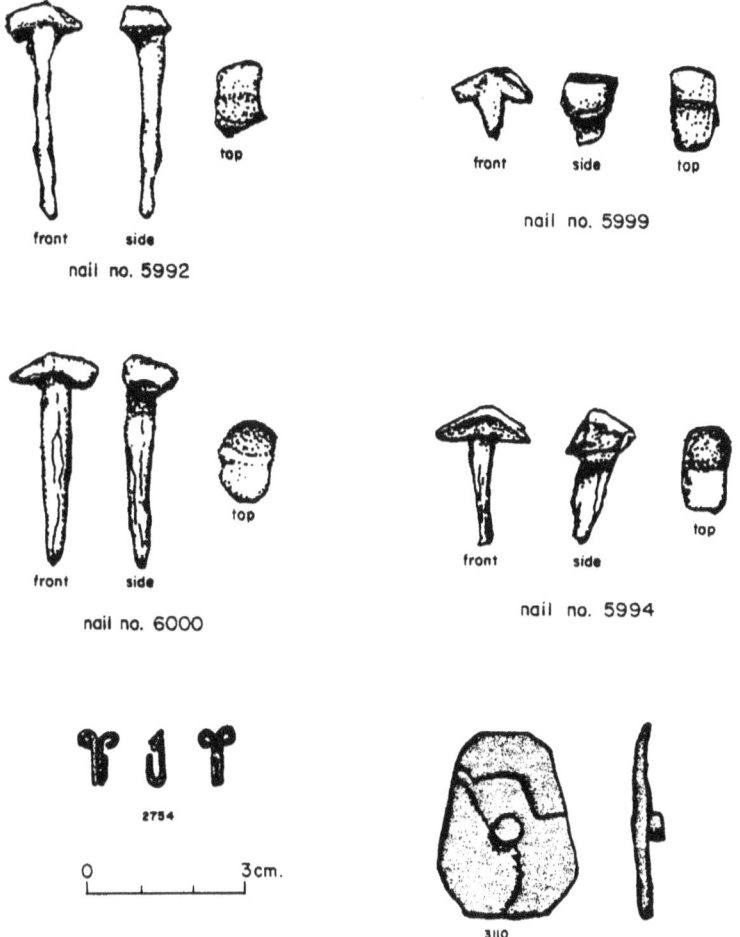

Figure 16.2. Nails, a clothing hook, and a jack plate from LA 54147. Illustration by Ann Noble and Ron Stauber.

- The metal items present include nails (one may be a horseshoe nail), clothing attachments, and a piece of armor; only the Spanish had all of these.

- The predominance of glazeware service vessels over utility vessels may indicate that metal pots were being used. That is, metal pots were used instead of puebloan utility vessels for cooking, and service vessels for eating.

- The general paucity of chipped stone artifacts seems to indicate that the site occupants were primarily using metal and not stone tools. One artifact was, however, identified as being made of a Mexican obsidian. The blade fragment was probably made in Mexico, and later brought to the site where it was used, broken, and discarded. A projectile point similar to those used in Mexico was also recovered.

- The presence of corn kernels and beans, in conjunction with many jar fragments, and the absence of wild plants indicate that the site occupants were probably consuming stored foods. Historical documents show that the members of the early Spanish expeditions commonly obtained foodstuffs and pottery from the local Indians (Hammond and Rey 1940, 1953, 1966; Hordes 1989). Together, this information seems to support a Spanish, rather than an Indian, occupation for LA 54147.

Given this interpretation, the next question was, which of the sixteenth-century Spanish entradas could have produced the campsite? Seven entradas passed through the area, including Coronado in 1540–1542; Agustín Rodríguez and Francisco Sánchez Chamuscado in 1581; Antonio de Espejo and fray Bernardino Beltrán in 1582–1583; Gaspar Castaño de Sosa, Juan Morlete, and Francisco Leyva de Bonilla and Antonio Gutiérrez de Humaña all during the 1590s; and Juan de Oñate in 1598. Coronado, Castaño de Sosa, and Oñate were the only larger expeditions that brought along domesticated animals, whereas the others were short-term excursions (Hammond and Rey 1940, 1953, 1966; Schroeder and Matson 1965; Hordes 1989). Therefore, the presence of sheep bone at LA 54147 would seem to indicate an occupation associated with either the Coronado, Castaño de Sosa, or Oñate expedition.

How then do we determine which of these entradas might have created the campsite? The goats associated with the Castaño de Sosa expedition were apparently consumed before the group arrived at Santo Domingo Pueblo. Otherwise, only a small contingent of men from that group were in the Tiguex area for a day or so, and they may have spent the night at a local pueblo. It appears that Oñate camped for a few days in the vicinity of Puaray Pueblo in late June 1598 before continuing north. Coronado's expedition, on the other hand, camped for a few months near a pueblo called Alcanfor. A portion of the expedition first arrived in September, and eventually the whole group moved into Alcanfor during the winter of 1540–1541 due to the cold weather. The pueblo was then reoccupied during the following winter of 1541–1542. The Coronado expedition also camped outside the besieged pueblos of Arenal and Moho for about fifty days sometime from February to April of 1541 (Hammond and Rey 1940, 1953; Schroeder and Matson 1965; Hordes 1989).

The dugouts at LA 54147 show at least some investment in their construction. They were excavated into the ground, had hearths situated both inside and outside the structures, and there was at least one outside activity area. Trash was discarded into the dugouts soon after they were abandoned, presumably by people camping nearby. The amount of trash present indicates that the site was used much longer than the few days Oñate would have stayed in the area. In addition, Coronado's camps were occupied during the fall and winter, unlike Oñate, who camped there in the summer. The fact that the dugouts were excavated into the soil (for greater insulation), and that the hearths were located inside the structures (for greater warmth), indicates that the site was probably occupied during the fall or winter cold season, and not the warm summer season. Finally, Puaray Pueblo (LA 717), where Oñate camped, is thought to be located about 8 km southeast of LA 54147 on the opposite side of the river, whereas Alcanfor and Moho were located on the west side of the river in the area of LA 326. This evidence seems to support an occupation by the Coronado and not the Castaño de Sosa or Oñate expedition.

A Response to the Reviews

Schroeder (1992) considers that LA 54147 does not represent a campsite associated with Coronado's winter encampment at the pueblo of Alcanfor, but rather the campsite used during the siege of Moho. He provides a detailed review of the documentary evidence concerning the correlation of pueblos referred to by the sixteenth-century chroniclers and the present-day archeological sites in the Albuquerque-Bernalillo area. The main points of Schroeder's article are that: a) LA 326 corresponds to the location of Moho and not Alcanfor pueblo, and b) the campsite of the contingent of the expedition under authority of García López de Cárdenas (Coronado's *maestre de campo*) was only occupied for a short duration (or not at all), before they moved into the pueblo of Alcanfor.

No consensus has ever developed among archeologists or historians with regard to the correlation between the pueblos described by the sixteenth-century chroniclers and the present-day archeological sites in the area (for example, see Scurlock [1982] for a review of this problem; compare Chapter 15). For example, various researchers have referred to LA 326 as Alcanfor (Coofor), Moho, Puaray, Culiacán, Santiago, and Kuaua Pueblos (Scurlock 1982: 55; Riley 1981: 205). We agree that LA 326 could be Moho. Nonetheless, our intention was to argue that the historic and archeological evidence best supported the fact that it was the Coronado expedition and not one of the other sixteenth-century entradas that resided at LA 326. This was based on the site being located to the west of the Rio Grande, the fact that it was occupied for several months, and that it was occupied during the winter. As Schroeder points out, the expedition was housed at the pueblo of Alcanfor from December to February of 1540–1541, and camped outside of the besieged pueblo of Moho from February to April of 1541 (Schroeder 1992: 185). However, differentiating between the pueblos of Alcanfor and Moho was not relevant to our argument since we simply wanted to distinguish between the Coronado group and the other sixteenth-century groups most likely to have produced the campsite (that is, Castaño de Sosa and Oñate).

It should be pointed out that López de Cárdenas's party represented the advance guard for the Coronado expedition into the Tiguex Province. It is unclear how much time they spent camped outside of Alcanfor before moving into the pueblo. The implications of Schroeder's argument are that the time was so limited that they could not have produced the amount of trash present at LA 54147. This contrasts with the roughly two-month period that a contingent was camped outside of Moho. We would like to suggest a third possibility. That is, LA 54147 may reflect an encampment of Mexican Indians who also resided at Alcanfor. This would explain the presence of the obsidian blade, projectile point, and small amount of lithic reduction debris in the trash fill. If so, then the campsite could have been used during the first and/or second winter occupations at the pueblo of Alcanfor.

David Snow (Chapter 21) presents an excellent discussion concerning the Rio Grande Glazeware chronology. We agree that the chronology is in need of critical reevaluation, and that the sequence is not a unilinear scheme, but one that reflects temporal overlap and contemporaneous usages. To make his point, Snow reviews a selected portion of Marshall's (1989) ceramic analysis of LA 54147. This assemblage is important because it represents a limited occupation span during the mid-sixteenth century. Marshall has identified the glazeware pottery at LA 54147 as being Glaze E, the prevalent pottery type present on sites in the area during this time period. Based on Marshall's illustration of a sample of rim sherds from LA 54147 (1989: 107 Figure 42), Snow argues that other glazeware rim forms are also present, and therefore questions the classification of Marshall's rim types as solely representing Glaze E.

Marshall's ceramic analysis was a detailed attribute analysis that was primarily oriented toward providing information on site function, rather than chronology. The site is characterized by a homogeneous ceramic assemblage that is presumably the result of a short-term occupation. Seven rim form variants were defined during the analysis (Marshall 1989: 107). The Group 1 forms are described by Snow as representing Glaze A, B, and C forms. We are reluctant to define any specific glazeware type based solely on rim cross sections. Nonetheless, the Group 1 sherds could be considered similar to a Glaze C rim form; however, the slip color and decorative treatment of the sherds are similar to the remainder of the assemblage. The Group 1 sherds only represent about 3 percent of the total ceramic assemblage, with the majority of the ceramics being typical of Glaze E wares. This analysis shows that there is some slight variation in rim form within a ceramic group that is otherwise characterized by similar exterior colors and designs. The Group 1 forms appear to be from shouldered bowls, reflecting some minor functional differences. We suggest that the homogeneous nature of the ceramic assemblage is due to the limited occupational span at the site, its unique depositional history (that is, a Spanish campsite), and not an implicit unilinear view of the Rio Grande Glazeware chronology.

Two other chapters in this volume follow in the footsteps of our original studies. Richard Flint's (1992; Chapter 4) study focuses on the identification of temporally sensitive artifacts that could be diagnostic indicators of the Coronado expedition. Based on his research he suggests that crossbows, copper or brass aglets, Nueva Cadiz glass beads, sheet brass Clarksdales bells, and obsidian-edged weapons might all be good indicators of the expedition. Of course we had already arrived at a similar conclusion in respect to crossbows. After reviewing the inventories of the sixteenth-century entradas we state that the "Coronado expedition appears to have been the last entrada to use crossbows as weapons" (Hordes 1989: 218; also see Vierra 1989: 141; Chapter 3).

Flint also stresses the importance of the Mexican Indian artifacts associated with the Indian contingent of the expedition (that is, obsidian blades/cores, projectile points, and comales). We too noted the importance of the obsidian blade found at LA 54147. It was both visually and chemically identified as being made of Pachuca obsidian from the Valley of Mexico (Vierra 1992: 170). The blade is characteristic of the material and reduction technique used during protohistoric times in the Valley of Mexico (Cressey 1974: 108; Spence 1967: 511). A side- and basally notched projectile point recovered from LA 54147 was reported as being similar to (although slightly smaller than) contemporaneous Texcoco points in Mexico (Cressey 1974: 107; Tolstoy 1971: 279–281). In contrast to the blade fragment, the point was of a local chert.

In 1992, Flint did, however, question the identification of the stone comal fragments from LA 54147 as being of Spanish rather than Puebloan origin. Thirty-six comal fragments were recovered from the various trash-filled tent depressions. In addition, possible comal rests were found adjacent to the hearths in Structures 11 and 12, as well as a comal fragment having been integrated into the wall of the hearth in Structure 9. This indicates that the comales were certainly being used by the occupants of the structures. Griddles or *piki* stones are present at contemporaneous pueblo sites in the region, including those recovered during Edgar L. Hewett's 1930s excavations at the nearby pueblo of LA 326. Marjorie Lambert was the laboratory director of that project. She stated to us that the griddles recovered from

LA 326 were different from the ones found at LA 54147 (Lambert, personal communication 1987). The pueblo griddles were rectangular, ground on both sides, and were often made of andesite. In contrast, the LA 54147 griddles were made of a thin tabular sandstone. No whole griddles were recovered, but the fragments were finely ground and polished on a single burned surface. The edges of the fragments were rounded onto the cooking surface, producing a cross section of roughly a 45-degree angle. This was done by pecking, grinding, and occasionally flaking the perimeter of the griddle. More importantly the griddles from LA 54147 were very similar to the comales recovered from the seventeenth-century *rancho* of Las Majadas near Cochiti Pueblo. These comales were also made of sandstone, being "flat, thin . . . smoothed on one side only; edges and corners are well-shaped and slightly rounded" (Snow 1973a: 26). The original collections from the site were studied at the Museum of New Mexico and the artifacts are indeed very similar to those recovered from LA 54147. It was based on this evidence that the LA 54147 griddles were classified as comales, and not piki stones. This classification was meant to imply a Spanish (or Mexican Indian), and not a Puebloan origin for the artifacts.

Diane Rhodes (Chapter 3) continues our initial research on crossbow boltheads. Our review of sixteenth- and seventeenth-century metal artifacts from the middle Rio Grande indicated that the boltheads were recovered from LA 326, Pecos, and possibly Kuaua (LA 187) pueblos (Vierra 1989: 137). Boltheads are also reported from the Mann-Zuris Site (LA 290) in Albuquerque (Sundt, personal communication 1986), and were apparently recovered during Hodge's excavations at Hawikuh in Zuni (Flint 1992). The documentary evidence is clear that the Coronado expedition visited Hawikuh and Pecos Pueblos, and had encounters with several pueblos in the Albuquerque area (Hammond and Rey 1940).

Epilogue

A great deal of attention has been focused on the discovery of this campsite along State Road 528 near Bernalillo, New Mexico. Most researchers seem to agree that these ephemeral trash-filled depressions are probably the remains of Coronado's tent camp; however, the debate has currently shifted to whether the nearby protohistoric pueblo at LA 326 might represent the sixteenth-century pueblo of Alcanfor or Moho.

We feel that the LA 54147 project was important for its multi-disciplinary research, the identification of the site as being a remnant of the Coronado entrada, and the attention that the excavation brought to a neglected portion of New Mexico's archeology. The result was the organization of a conference on the "Late Prehistoric and Early Historic Archeology of New Mexico" (Vierra 1992). Although the project did exemplify an event-oriented perspective, this was understandable given the salvage nature of the excavation and the unique character of the site. Nonetheless, we would like to emphasize the importance of problem-oriented research involving the Spanish colonial archeology of the northern Rio Grande (for example, see Snow 1992). The Coronado expedition did pave the way for the Spanish colonization of the northern Rio Grande Valley. Yet how the indigenous populations and Spanish settlers coped with the new uncertainties of living in the valley is an issue for future research to address.

Note

1. Funding for this project was provided by the New Mexico State Highway Department.

CHAPTER 17

The Coronado Expedition
Cicúye to the Río de Cicúye Bridge[1]

RICHARD FLINT AND SHIRLEY CUSHING FLINT

etween February 1540 and June 1542 an international cavalcade that numbered fifteen hundred people or more traveled, under the leadership of Francisco Vázquez de Coronado, on foot and horseback, trailed by a large herd of livestock, some four thousand miles from westcentral Mexico to the heart of the Great Plains of North America and back. They went to bring under the sway of the Spanish king a far-off land reputedly rich in material wealth and populated by "primitive" peoples ripe for assimilation into the Christian faith.

Members of the expedition tell of trudging over rugged highlands, immense plains, and treacherous rivers during their two years journeying to and from the north, and taking the measure of that land of fabulous possibilities, the terra incognita that is modern northern Mexico and the American Southwest.

Almost at the outset of the great march a delay of several days was necessary at a river deep in Mexico (now identified as the Río de Santiago near Centispác) to ferry the sheep in the stock train across one at a time, slung over the backs of horses. It was likely at this same Río de Santiago a little more than two years later, on the return trip, that while trying to ford the river a horse drowned and a soldier was attacked and killed by an alligator.

Over and over on the way north, swollen rivers rendered the necessary fords risky and toilsome. Then, late in the spring of 1540, Coronado, with a small vanguard, encountered a full-running river (now thought to be in either east-central Arizona or southwest New Mexico). Fording the river proved impossible, so the party built rafts upon which to float themselves and their animals across the river they named Río de las Balsas (rafts), to commemorate that crossing on makeshift flatboats.

As the season advanced and the expedition neared its immediate goal, the native cities of Cíbola, high rivers were no further problem. And still later in the year, chroniclers of the expedition record no difficulties in crossing and recrossing the great river on the banks of which winter quarters were established late in 1540 (almost assuredly the Rio Grande near present Bernalillo, New Mexico; see Chapter 16).

The spring of 1541 presented a new goal for the Spanish expeditionary force, the tantalizing wealth of distant Quivira. After leaving winter quarters the expedition marched for four days to the east of the Rio Grande; the first stop was the pueblo of Cicúye. Three or four days beyond that pueblo they encountered a deep river that they called Río de Cicúye. To get their baggage and large herds across, they resorted to building a bridge (although they apparently had not and did not again go to such effort to cross any other river on the expedition's course). The job took four days, after which they safely crossed the river and spent much of the remainder of the summer in a frustrating trek across the plains to the goldless grass huts of the actual Quivira.[2]

Sixteenth-century documentary evidence about the location of the bridge and the route from Cicúye to the bridge is vague and ambiguous. Direct references exist in two narratives written years after the expedition by members of the party Juan de Jaramillo and Pedro de Castañeda de Náçera.

JARAMILLO:
From here [Cicuique/Cicúye] we proceeded in three days to another river which we Spaniards called Cicuique. If I remember correctly, it seems to me that to reach this river, at the point where we crossed it, we went somewhat more to the northeast. Upon crossing it we turned more to the left, which must be more to the northeast, and we began to enter the plains where the cattle [bison] roam (Hammond and Rey 1940: 300).

CASTAÑEDA:
The army departed from Cicúye. . . . They traveled in the direction of the plains, which are on the other side of the mountain range. After four days' march they came to a deep river carrying a large volume of water flowing from the direction of Cicúye. The general [Coronado] named it the Cicúye River. They stopped

here in order to build a bridge [*puente*] for crossing it. . . . Ten days later they came to some rancherias of a nomadic people, called Querechos around there. Cattle [bison] had been sighted two days before (Hammond and Rey 1940: 235).

CASTAÑEDA:
On its return [from the buffalo plains] the army arrived at the Cicúye River more than thirty leagues below the town—I mean below the bridge [puente] which had been built on the way out. We marched upstream along its bank. . . . Thus, as I have said, the army went up the river until it reached the Pueblo of Cicúye (Hammond and Rey 1940: 243).

Before being confronted by the Cicúye River, the multitude of people and animals had repeatedly and successfully, if sometimes laboriously, swum, waded, and floated across rivers and streams. In the entire 4,000-plus-mile journey the Río de Cicúye bridge was the only such river crossing. Still later in the summer of 1541, when the expedition recrossed the same Cicúye River on its return from the wild goose chase in search of Quivira, evidently no bridge was needed.

The bridge over the Cicúye River was, thus, a unique product of the Coronado expedition. Reference to its construction and location stand out sharply in Castañeda's firsthand account of that earliest calculated incursion of Europeans into today's Arizona, New Mexico, Texas, Oklahoma, and Kansas.

The bridge's singularity makes it understandably a potential landmark for modern researchers seeking to track the long-ago route of Coronado. No eyewitness maps or charts of the route, however, have come to light, though some were drafted. In addition, of the place names assigned by the expedition, almost none are used today. And the narrative accounts of the explorers themselves are sketchy (those few that have survived) and are little concerned with pinpointing or minutely describing places and how they were reached. Lastly, the physical bridge itself may not have stood more than a few days or weeks. Certainly none of the subsequent Spanish expeditions reported even its remains.

The few extant details about the Río de Cicúye bridge and the expedition's route to its site have tantalized scholars for at least a hundred and fifty years. Numerous persons of historical bent have extrapolated from the fragmentary, sometimes contradictory, written evidence and have formulated equally numerous hypotheses about where the bridge was built and the route followed to the bridge site. The proposed (often pontifically proclaimed) locations of the bridge range over an area of central New Mexico measuring 160 miles (256 km) from north to south and 50 miles (80 km) from east to west, dot four different rivers, and represent widely separated places on those rivers (see Map 14). Previously hypothesized sites of Coronado's 1541 bridge and routes to the bridge are summarized in Table 17.1.

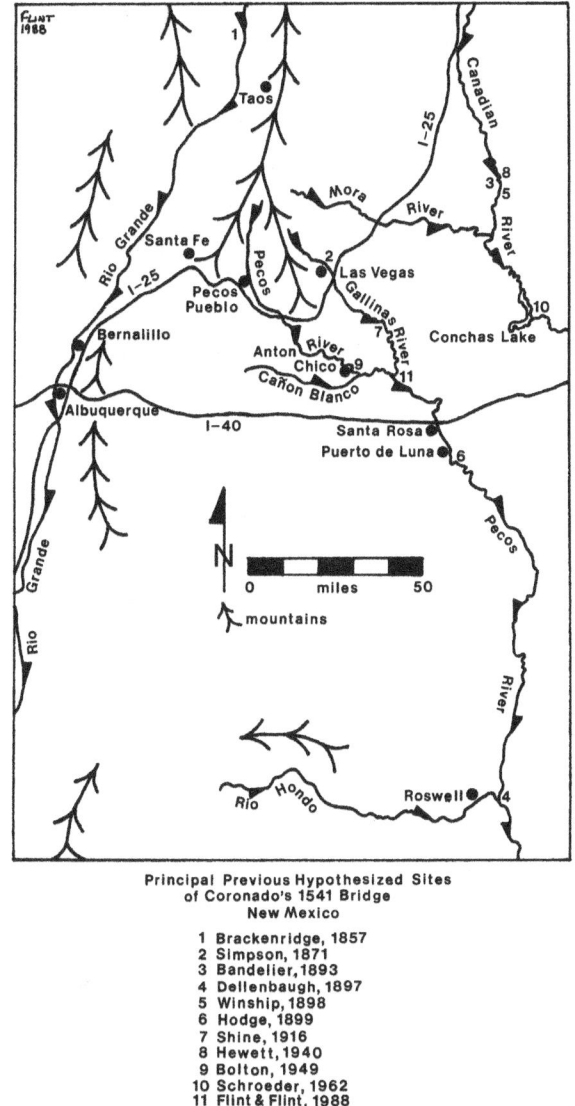

Map 14. *Principal previous hypothesized sites of Coronado's 1541 bridge, New Mexico.*

In nearly fifteen years of research we have assessed these hypotheses as to geographical/topographical plausibility, conformance with the sixteenth-century documents, and compatibility with current knowledge of the protohistoric Southwest. This assessment has revealed apparent flaws in each of the previous hypotheses.

Table 17.1. Cicúye to Río de Cicúye Bridge Route Hypotheses

Proponent	Location of Cicúye	Direction of March from Cicúye	Distance of March from Cicúye	River Bridged	Overall Assessment
H.M. Brackenridge 1857: 14[a]	Between Zuni and the Rio Grande. No precise location.	NE	Not specified	Rio Grande, probably above Taos	Mistaken location of Cicúye. Wrong direction of march. Wrong river.
James H. Simpson 1871: 336[b]	Pecos Pueblo	NE	"about 50 miles"	Gallinas River at or near Las Vegas, NM	Wrong direction of march. Wrong river.
Adolph F. Bandelier 1893: 223–224[c]	Pecos Pueblo	NE	Not specified (over 75 miles)	Probably the Canadian River	Wrong direction of march. Wrong river. Distance probably too great.
George P. Winship 1896: 232[d]	Pecos Pueblo	NE	Not specified (over 75 miles)	Canadian River "a little to the east of the present settlement and river of Mora"	Wrong direction of march. Wrong river. Distance probably too great.
Frederick Dellenbaugh 1897: 427[e]	Nogal (15 miles NW of Fort Stanton, NM)	E	Not specified (over 75 miles)	Pecos River near Roswell, NM	Mistaken location of Cicúye. Distance probably too great.
Frederick W. Hodge 1899: 2: 60–61[f]	Pecos Pueblo	SE	30 leagues (75–80 miles)	Pecos River at or a little south of Puerto de Luna, NM	Distance probably too great.
Michael Shine 1916: 7[g]	Pecos Pueblo	SE	Not specified (over 45 miles)	Gallinas River at or near Chaperito, NM	Wrong river.
Edgar L. Hewett 1940: 176[h]	Pecos Pueblo	NE	Not specified (over 65–75 miles)	Mora River or Canadian River northeast of Las Vegas, NM	Wrong direction of march. Wrong river.

continued on next page

Table 17.1—continued

Proponent	Location of Cicúye	Direction of March from Cicúye	Distance of March from Cicúye	River Bridged	Overall Assessment
Herbert E. Bolton 1949: 242–243[i]	Pecos Pueblo	SE	Not specified (approximately 45–50 miles)	Pecos River in the vicinity of Anton Chico, NM	The most likely of the previous hypotheses, but Bolton has the expedition meeting the river too soon.
Albert H. Schroeder 1962: 4[j]	Pecos Pueblo	ESE	Not specified (over 100 miles)	Canadian River near Conchas Dam, NM	Wrong river. Distance of march too great.
Richard and Shirley Flint 1988	Pecos Pueblo	SE	approximately 65 miles	Pecos River just below its junction with the Gallinas River	See narrative for sketch of rationale.

[a] "His {Coronado's} starting point was from Tiquex, between the Sierra Madre and the Rio Grande, which he crossed near its head, and probably above Taos."

[b] "Now all this, I think, can be reconciled by reference to the accompanying map, on which will be found laid down a route, the only one, I believe, existing at the present day between Pecos and Las Vegas on the Rio Gallinas.... The Gallinas is liable to be flooded ... this naturally would make necessary at such times a bridge to cross it."

[c] "On the fourth day he {Coronado} crossed a river that was so deep that they had to throw a bridge over it. This river was perhaps the Rio de Mora.... But it was more probably the Canadian River, into which the Mora empties."

[d] "The bridge, however, was doubtless built across the upper waters of the Canadian."

[e] "This was the Pecos River. They [the Coronado expedition] probably bore a course from Cicuye [Nogal location] about E.N.E., striking the river somewhere near the mouth of the Rio Hondo. They built a bridge here to cross on."

[f] "It would seem that the Pecos River was bridged at a point about where the buffalo plains begin, or somewhere between latitude 34 and 35.... This, it seems, would place the bridge crossing in the vicinity of Puerto de Luna—or more likely somewhat south of that point...."

[g] "The bridge, or crossing, was approximately about twenty-four miles north of the thirty-fifth parallel and about two miles east of the one hundred and fifth meridian."

[h] "The other [northern buffalo hunting trail] struck from Pecos Pueblo to the east, veered to the north near the present town of Las Vegas, to the Mora River, thence to the Canadian, then across to the Arkansas.... It would seem likely that he [Coronado] was guided over the northern trail."

[i] "At Villanueva ... the road ... swings eastward, and even northeastward, as Jaramillo says, to the river at Anton Chico. In this vicinity Coronado built a bridge and crossed the Cicuique River—that is, the Pecos."

[j] "In summary, 3 to 4 days east of Pecos Pueblo they [the Coronado expedition] reached the Canadian River and crossed it from the right to the left bank, somewhere near Conchas Reservoir."

Those hypotheses, as well as our assessment of them, hinge on determination of four critical elements: 1) the location of Cicúye, 2) the direction of the expedition's march from Cicúye, 3) the distance of march to the Río de Cicúye bridge site, and 4) the identity of the Río de Cicúye. A brief summary of the conclusions drawn by previous investigators regarding these elements is included in the table. Also included is our assessment of those conclusions.

Building on the scholarship of the past, we have formulated a new bridge site and route-to-the-bridge hypothesis. We have proposed that the route of the first four days of Coronado's march toward Quivira was this:

Upon leaving Cicúye in the first week of May 1541, the Coronado expedition proceeded south to the area of modern Rowe, New Mexico. At that point it ascended a relatively gentle natural ramp onto Glorieta Mesa. Following the drainages of the mesa's gently tilted surface, the expedition traveled south and slightly east to the vicinity of modern Leyba, New Mexico, and into Cañon Blanco. The canyon then served as a roadway all the way east to its junction with the Pecos River. The force then followed the river east and slightly south to its confluence with the Gallinas River. Not far downstream from there (roughly 65 miles [104 km] southeast of Cicúye) a bridge was built across the Pecos River and the whole company of people and animals crossed over.

We, like virtually all modern investigators, have concluded that Cicúye is the now long-abandoned Towa pueblo of Pecos (see Map 15). Castañeda's sixteenth-century descriptions of Cicúye match the archeological reconstruction of the Quadrangle (or north pueblo) at Pecos, and its modern physical setting is easily recognizable four and a half centuries later from Castañeda's words. In addition, archeological excavation has recovered crossbow boltheads (the tips of crossbow darts) at Pecos. These are items that were probably common only with the Coronado expedition among all the Spanish entradas (see Chapter 3).

Significantly, according to Edgar L. Hewett, "Sikuyé" was yet in modern times a southern Tiwa (Isleta) name applied to Pecos Pueblo (Hewett and Fisher 1943:145). Tiwa was doubtless the language spoken in the Tiguex Province of pueblos where the expedition wintered prior to leaving for Quivira. Hence Cicúye/Sikuyé may well have been the name for Pecos the Spanish found most familiar.

Furthermore, no other candidate pueblo with similar layout and site and with confirmed sixteenth-century occupancy is known. So to arrive at the bridge, we start from one of only a handful of well-established points along the whole of Coronado's route: Pecos Pueblo.

Our synthesis and interpretation of the sixteenth-century narratives result in tracking Coronado generally southeastward from Pecos Pueblo for sixty-plus miles (100+ km) to where the expedition encountered and bridged the "deep river." In

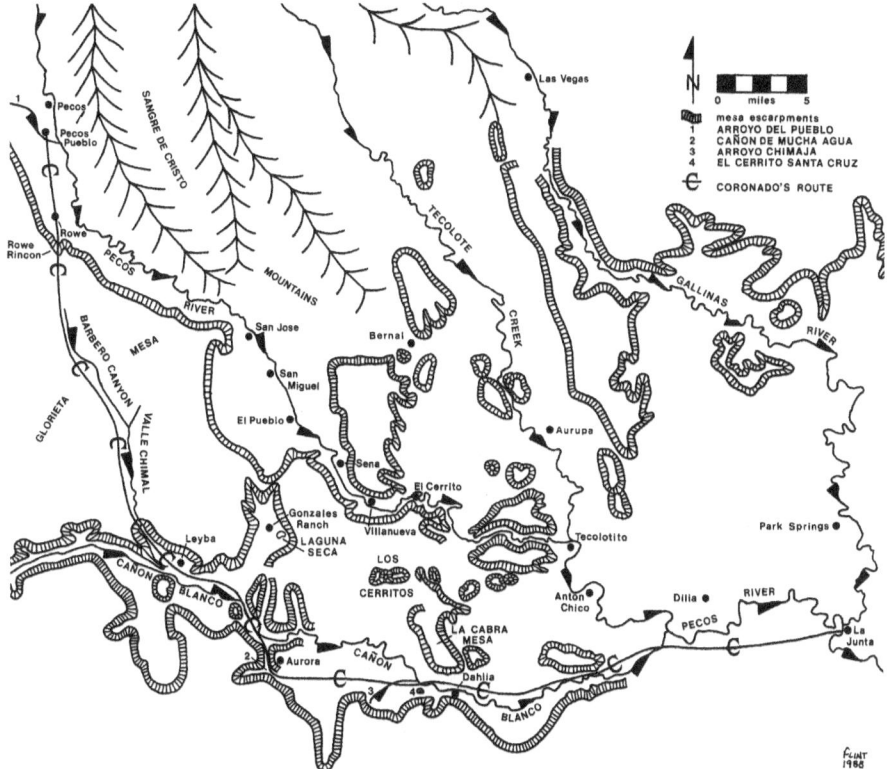

Map 15. Reconstruction of the Coronado expedition's route, Cicúye (Pecos Pueblo) to the Bridge (La Junta), New Mexico, May 1541.

support of this choice of direction, the *Relación del Suceso* (written probably in 1541 by an unidentified conquistador, possibly Hernando de Alvarado), in recapitulating the first month of march beyond Cicúye, reports that the army went "one hundred and fifty leagues, one hundred to the east and fifty to the south" (Hammond and Rey 1940: 291).[3] We view the statement as a summary of the *trend* of the march, that is, resolved into cardinal components. Thus, the overall trend of march was east-southeast. That is not to say that, necessarily, any specific segment of the route ran precisely in that direction. This interpretation seems particularly appropriate in light of the distance of march and the most likely identity of the Río de Cicúye.

Further corroboration is lent by statements of descendants of the residents of Pecos Pueblo who reported that to reach the buffalo plains (where Coronado spent most of the summer after leaving Pecos) the Pecoseños "never crossed the Pecos River at Cicúye . . . , but went far down the west bank before fording the stream"

(Jones 1937: 46). That would be southeastward. In this connection, note that throughout his exploration Coronado was not blazing trails, but was led by indigenous guides who followed already existing routes.

Our estimation of the distance the army traveled to the southeast to reach the bridge site is based on the contemporary documentary evidence. Juan de Jaramillo is the only member of the expedition known to have recorded time of the expedition's march between points now confidently identified along its route. He gives nine days of travel for a lightly encumbered reconnaissance party between a second town of Cíbola, by which was probably meant the Matsaki ruins just southeast of modern Zuni, New Mexico, and the Tiguex River, the modern Rio Grande in the vicinity of Albuquerque, a distance of approximately 160 miles (256 km) (Hammond and Rey 1940: 299). This yields an average daily travel of 17.8 miles (28.5 km). Jaramillo also reports that it took the entire company four days to march from Coofor, in the modern Bernalillo, New Mexico, area to Cicúye, a distance of at least 63 miles (101 km) (Hammond and Rey 1940: 300). For the whole expedition this converts to a pace of 15.8 miles (25.3 km) per day over this stretch.

Based on these figures, we project that the expedition was likely to have covered between 48 and 71 miles (77 and 114 km) in the course of the three or four days it marched from Cicúye to the bridge site. That this is a reasonable projection is further supported by the Hidalgo de Elvas's account of the Hernando de Soto expedition, a comparably sized and equipped force operating in the modern southeastern United States at the same time the Coronado expedition was in the Southwest. He reports that marches of the Soto expedition were ordinarily 13 to 15.6 miles (20.8 to 25 km) per day, occasionally increased by forced march to 18 to 21 miles (28.8 to 33.6 km) per day (Clayton et al. 1993: 1: 94).

From the documentary evidence it seems certain that it was the modern Pecos River that the expedition called Río de Cicúye and bridged en route to the buffalo plains. The expedition's practice elsewhere was to name rivers in the *immediate* vicinity of communities after those communities, for example, the Tiguex River, the Quivira River, and the Señora River. This habit strongly suggests that the Pecos River (within the valley of which Cicúye stands) is most likely to have been given the name of Cicúye. Amplifying the documentary evidence are Castañeda's statements that the Río de Cicúye flowed "from the direction of Cicúye" (Hammond and Rey 1940: 235) and that on its return from the buffalo plains the main body of Coronado's army "arrived at the Cicúye River more than thirty leagues below . . . the bridge . . ." and "went up the river until it reached the pueblo of Cicúye" (Hammond and Rey 1940: 243). Only the Pecos River leads to Pecos Pueblo (which stands above the Arroyo del Pueblo, also known as Glorieta Creek, a tributary of the Pecos, a mile and a half west of the main river).

Castañeda also reports Teyas Indians as relating the position of the Río de Cicúye in the regional drainage network this way: "this river joins the Tiguex . . . and . . . it flows to the east again" (Hammond and Rey 1940: 243). This faithfully records the junction of the Pecos River and Rio Grande along the modern Texas/Mexico border. Castañeda then makes the statement, "It is believed that it empties into the mighty Espíritu Santo (Mississippi) which don Hernando de Soto's men discovered . . ." (Hammond and Rey 1940: 243). By sixteenth-century standards, this geographical speculation on Castañeda's part is very understandable. Though it has long been known that the Rio Grande is not a tributary of the Mississippi, that was not the case in Coronado's time. More than two hundred years were to elapse before the Río de las Palmas and the Rio Grande were conclusively shown to be a single river emptying into the Gulf of Mexico (Horgan 1954:343).

We theorize that under the guidance of Indians from Pecos Pueblo the expedition marched south from Pecos to the vicinity of present-day Rowe, New Mexico. There they temporarily left the Pecos Valley, climbing to the top of vast Glorieta Mesa by way of a *rincón* (recess) now occupied for the same purpose by New Mexico Highway 34. Almost immediately upon reaching the mesa top they began dropping almost imperceptibly into Barbero Canyon and then into the Valle Chimal. Approximately twenty miles south and slightly east of the crest of the mesa they emerged into the broad expanse of Cañon Blanco.[4]

Our principal reasons for advancing this unprecedented route are these. It seems from the narratives that although Pecos Pueblo was only a mile and a half from the Pecos River, the expedition did not *reach* the river until three or four days later.[5] If the expedition had stayed in the narrowing Pecos Valley (as Herbert Bolton suggested), it would have been forced by topography to meet, and in fact, to cross the river repeatedly very shortly (certainly by the time it had reached the area of modern Sena, New Mexico, less than two days' march from Pecos Pueblo), rather than four days from Pecos, as was actually the case.

It is very likely that in 1541 the Pecos Indians had extensive acreage under cultivation in the Pecos Valley as far southeast as today's Villanueva, New Mexico. Shortly before the Coronado expedition set out for Quivira, the Pecoseños said they were in the midst of planting their fields. They would have been well aware of the damage done by Spanish livestock to crops in the Rio Grande Valley the previous fall. Certainly, they would not have wanted a throng of people and livestock trampling and churning up their newly planted fields. The people of Pecos would have had strong motive for prevailing upon or directing El Turco and Isopete (the two Plains Indian guides of the expedition, who had been living, perhaps in captivity, at Pecos) to lead the expedition as soon as possible up and out of the valley.

The Rowe rincón is the easiest egress from the valley and the only easy way out before cliffs close in enough to force traffic to the river.[6] This rincón has been a route of travel throughout historic times, and undoubtedly, prehistorically as well.

The wide and frequently level course of Cañon Blanco then led the expedition some 30 miles (48 km) east to its junction with the Pecos River just south of today's Upper Dilia, New Mexico. Three circumstances are particularly supportive of the thesis that Cañon Blanco served as a passageway for the Coronado expedition. There was, first, a need for plentiful drinking water for both people and animals. Glorieta Mesa is pocked with natural depressions that become seasonal ponds. And Cañon Blanco, Glorieta Mesa's principal southern and eastern drainage is, frequently in May, a succession of pools of snowmelt and even the residuum of rain from the previous autumn. This is particularly true after a wet, cold winter such as that of 1540–1541 apparently had been.[7]

Cañon Blanco served as a significant conduit for travel between the Pecos River (the edge of the buffalo plains) and the Tano pueblos of the Galisteo Basin for countless years before the arrival of the Europeans. The usage of this pathway is attested by the many campsites and scatters of tool-making debris found all along the canyon's length, underscored by a multipanel display of petroglyphs in the canyon near the now diminished settlement of Dahlia, New Mexico.

Very importantly, Cañon Blanco was certainly used as a route by two subsequent Spanish entradas: that of Gaspar Castaño de Sosa in 1591 (Schroeder and Matson 1965: 145–154) and that of Oñate in 1601 (Bolton 1916: 251–252). In addition, two other entradas (Rodríguez/Chamuscado, 1581 and Antonio de Espejo, 1583) may have used the Cañon Blanco route or part of it (Hammond and Rey 1966: 88–89; Kelley 1937: 11). The narratives of both the latter expeditions, while very vague, can be interpreted in that light. This use of Cañon Blanco by the Spanish would indicate that it was an active route throughout protohistoric times, including the spring of 1541.

Coronado's bridge crossing of the Pecos River could conceivably have been very near the mouth of Cañon Blanco, but we are convinced that it was below La Junta (the confluence of the Pecos and Gallinas Rivers). That point is approximately 10 miles (16 km) east-southeast of where Cañon Blanco joins the Pecos. Had Coronado crossed the Pecos above the Gallinas junction, he would have then had to cross the Gallinas as well (quite possibly also swollen in such a year). None of the expedition's chronicles mentions such a crossing. Little or nothing would have been gained by crossing above the Gallinas junction. And certainly the expedition leaders would have wanted to minimize the number of river crossings, since crossing of livestock, especially very poor swimmers such as sheep, was always perilous and time consuming.

During historic times there has been a ford at La Junta and two continue in use today. This suggests (together with significant quantities of aboriginal lithic debris on both sides of the river there) that these were likely also Indian trail crossings. This is especially likely since modern and historic routes (until the recent advent of massive earthmoving) have commonly followed ancient ones, being the paths of topographically least resistance.

Where are the scraps of metal, the broken ceramics, the remains of livestock slaughter, the names or symbols incised in rock, and the other tangible evidence of the passage of so large a party as the Coronado expedition that would convincingly settle speculation about the site of their 1541 bridge and the route by which the army reached it? Given that the expedition route was likely used (in its entirety) for only a single round-trip passage (and that now 450 years ago), can its detection at this late date be anything short of farfetched fantasy? Can the single transit of Coronado's 1,500 followers and their stock train of perhaps thousands of head be mapped except by means of scattered fortuitous finds of accidental debris?

Frustratingly little material evidence has been recovered or recognized along the expedition's suspected route all the way from its origin in Mexico to its terminus in Kansas during the last 450 years. However, heretofore, methodical, systematic field search of hypothesized Coronado routes has not been conducted. With regard to the Cicúye bridge segment, we hold that, before now, such search would have been misdirected. We have now proposed a very plausible route, consistent with the sixteenth-century documents; we have formulated a sizable catalog of probable material culture of the Coronado expedition (Chapter 4; Flint 1992a); and we have projected fourteen areas along the route most likely to yield evidence of the Coronado expedition. Preliminary survey of the route hypothesized in this article has shown that three of the fourteen target areas along the proposed route include possible route markers of the Coronado expedition (see Flint and Flint 1993). Thorough examination of all fourteen target areas is the object of our continuing work.

Notes

1. An earlier version of this article was published in 1992 in the *New Mexico Historical Review* 67(2): 123–138. Permission for republication has been granted by the editor of *NMHR*. In the interim the article has been revised and updated.

2. It has been suggested by several scholars that the Coronado expedition did not build a bridge over the Río de Cicúye, but rather improved a ford. (See, for example, Schroeder 1992: 115). Without physical evidence this possibility cannot be ruled out. Nevertheless, there are several good reasons to believe the expedition did build an above-water structure, a bridge of unknown design. (But see Flint 1992b.) First, Pedro de Castañeda, referring to the Río de Cicúye crossing, unambiguously uses the term "puente" three times. There is no

sixteenth-century evidence supporting any meaning other than an above-water structure. (See Covarrubias Orozco 1995: 839; Boyd-Bowman 1971: 755.) Second, bridge building was an often-used sixteenth-century expeditionary skill. For instance, in his 1599 expeditionary manuel Bernardo de Vargas Machuca devoted an entire chapter to methods of river crossing, including several bridge (puente) designs (1892: 1: 196–208). Chronicles of the Soto expedition record their building above-water bridge structures on numerous occasions (for example, see Clayton et al. 1993: 1: 66, 67, 70–71,114). Among many other sixteenth-century Spanish expeditions that built wooden bridges are the Hernán Cortés, Francisco Pizarro, and Juan de Oñate expeditions. Third, the expedition had previously crossed several rivers by fording, without remark, particularly without mentioning the term "puente."

3. Juan de Jaramillo writes, as quoted earlier, that he thinks the expedition went northeast to reach the river. We, along with nearly all other recent historians, presume that his memory failed him at this point. A northeasterly course from Cicúye would have carried the expedition into the rugged Cañon Largo country of the Canadian River breaks, which none of the chroniclers mentions, including Jaramillo. In explanation, it can be said that indeed the *net* direction of Coronado's movement that summer was to the northeast, but only because of a long stretch of northward marching when the Quivira journey was about half over.

4. As Bob Himmerich y Valencia has pointed out, travel would have been easier for the bulk of the expedition, including the large herds of livestock, if the expedition had divided in the Galisteo Basin. While Coronado and a small party went to Cicúye, most of the people and animals could have traveled directly to the head of Cañon Blanco by way of Arroyo de Jaspe. Thus, most of the expedition could have avoided the roundabout route by way of Pecos Pueblo. In this case, the two groups could have rejoined at the mouth of Valle Chimal in Cañon Blanco.

5. The manuscript of Castañeda's narrative, now preserved in the New York Public Library, reads, "a quatro dias andados de camino dieron en un Rio . . ." (Castañeda, 1596, 77v). "Dieron en" is the preterit of the idiomatic infinitive phrase "dar en," usually signifying "to hit, strike, or meet," certainly an unusual choice of words if the expedition had been marching on the bank of that same river for much of the four days as Bolton and others claim.

6. There are two *rincónes* south of Rowe, one on either side of the Punta de la Mesa. Either rincón could have provided access to the mesa top and both have been occupied by roads in modern times.

At the modern Lovato irrigation dam (just north of Sena) and again just below Sena, the river runs directly alongside its steep western bank. Then between Villanueva and El Cerrito, and in the long stretch of the Cañon de Pecos below El Cerrito, the Pecos Valley constricts so tightly as to necessitate that travelers leave the valley. Bolton, familiar with this latter gorgelike character of the valley, proposed that Coronado's route left the valley at Villanueva and ascended Glorieta Mesa as New Mexico Highway 3 does now. That proposal, however, ignores the other constrictions of the valley above Villanueva.

7. Castañeda speaks, for instance, of the Tiguex River (Rio Grande) having been "frozen for about four months, during which time it was possible to cross over the ice on horseback . . ." (Hammond and Rey 1940: 234).

PART V

The Coronado Expedition, Río de Cicúye to Quivira

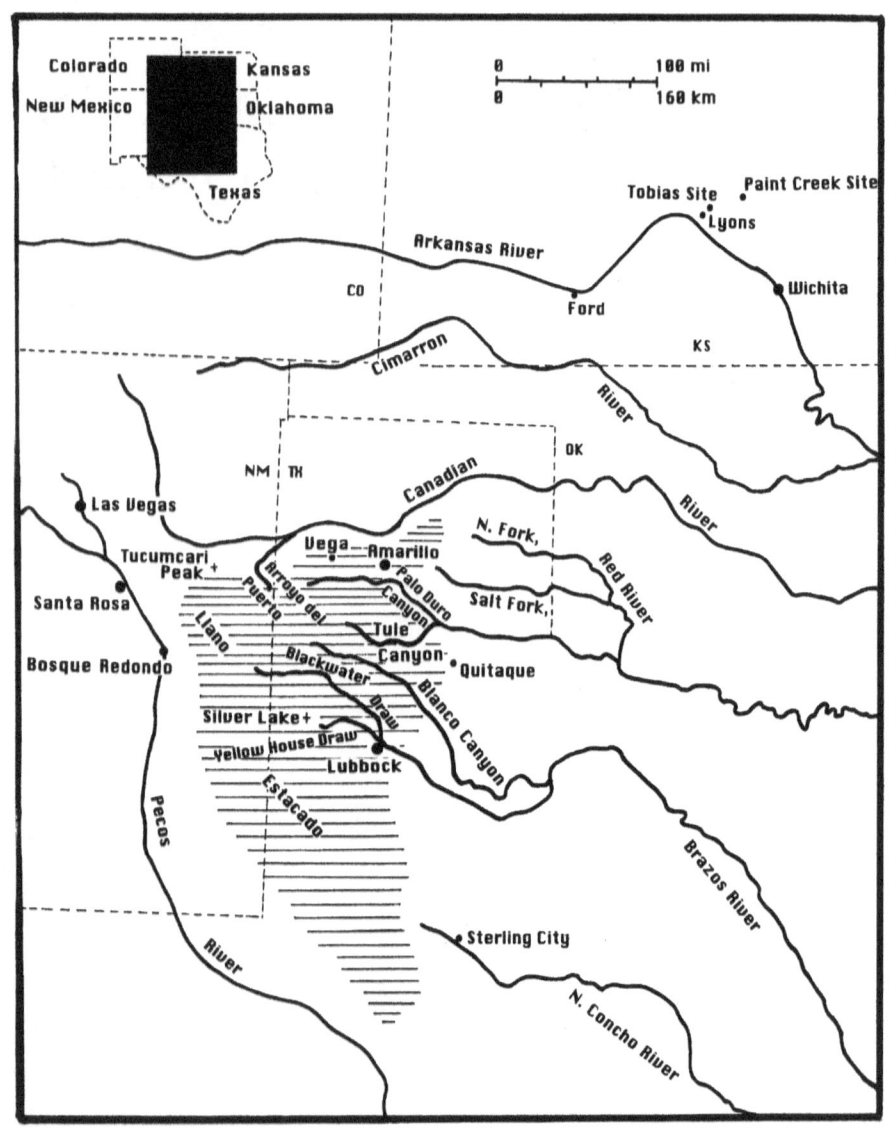

Map 16. Río de Cicúye to Quivira, New Mexico, Texas, Oklahoma, Kansas.

CHAPTER 18

A Historiography of the Route of the Expedition of Francisco Vázquez de Coronado
Río de Cicúye to Quivira

JOSEPH P. SÁNCHEZ

With the Main Army from the Bridge on the Río de Cicúye to the Llano Estacado and Back

aving crossed the bridge, which could have been anything from an actual wooden structure to a low water crossing, the expedition traveled four or five days to where they encountered large herds of buffalo. Bolton concluded they went "eastward across a wide plateau broken by boldly scarped mesas sprinkled with scrub juniper, cactus, and other desert plants" (1949: 243). Jones contended that "the route did turn to the northeast but the Turk, chief guide, kept bearing more to the east and finally turned to a southerly direction" (1937: 46). Bolton's route had the expedition moving northeasterly for a distance of a hundred miles or more along the southern drainage of the Canadian River until they reached the Texas Panhandle.

The Bolton route, after the expedition crossed the Pecos River, turned eastward following the Rock Island Railroad line and Highway 54/66. The expedition entered the Pajarito Creek Basin by way of Cuervo near Newkirk, New Mexico. Near there they could see the rampartlike cliffs for which the Llano Estacado or Palisaded Plain is named. "They were called Stockaded Plains," wrote Bolton, "from the rimrock which at a distance looks like a stone fortification. The usual explanation

235

about driving down stakes to avoid getting lost, is an engaging folk tale" (1949: 243). The expedition was within site of Tucumcari Peak.

The caprock and its canyonlands comprise the notable features of the Llano Estacado. Of the intriguing formation, Dan Flores wrote, "The old-time New Mexicans had a saying: 'Hay las sierras debajo de los llanos'—There are mountains below the plains. Modern travelers crossing the Southern Plains on the interstates from Oklahoma City to Albuquerque or San Antonio to Santa Fe might doubt it, but the New Mexicans were right. Below the level of the flat horizon, great canyons carve mesas and buttes, spires and badlands through the architecture of the Llanos of West Texas and New Mexico" (1990: ix).

Through Spanish colonial eyes, Castañeda wrote:

> Now we shall describe the plains, a vast level area of land more than 400 leagues wide in that part between the two cordilleras. The one was crossed by Francisco Vázquez de Coronado on his way to the South sea, the other by the men of Don Fernando de Soto when coming from Florida to the North sea. What we saw of these plains was all uninhabited. The opposite cordillera could not be seen, nor a hill or mountain as much as three estados high, although we traveled 250 leagues over them. Occasionally there were found some ponds, round like plates, a stone's throw wide, or larger. Some contained fresh water, others salt. In these ponds some tall grass grows. Away from them it is all very short, a span long and less. The land is the shape of a ball, for wherever a man stands he is surrounded by the sky at the distance of a crossbow shot. There are no trees except along the rivers which there are in some barrancas. These rivers are so concealed that one does not see them until he is at their edge. They are of dead earth [*son de tierra muerta*], with approaches made by the cattle in order to reach the water which flows quite deep (Hammond and Rey 1940: 261).

On the Llano Estacado the Spaniards noticed marks on the ground as if someone had dragged lances through the area. Curious, they followed the lines and came upon a ranchería or settlement of semi-sedentary Indians. The lines were made by the poles mounted on large dogs used in dragging their goods like a travois. The Querechos, Apachean people, were among the first tribes contacted on the Great Plains by the Spaniards. The expedition was, according to Bolton, approaching a point just west of the New Mexico–Texas line "where the trail to Quivira crossed the Canadian River" (1949: 249).

William C. Holden's study of the route in 1944 offers a historiographical review of earlier literature about Vázquez de Coronado's march through the Llano Estacado and beyond. In his critique, he discounted James H. Simpson's 1871 route. Simpson ran the route from Pecos Pueblo in a northeasterly direction crossing the Colorado–New Mexico line near Raton, thence east following a line south of the Arkansas River to present-day Kingman, Kansas. There, noted Simpson, Vázquez de Coronado, having been slowed by the large army, picked thirty men to go forward and turned the rest of them back to the Rio Grande. He then proceeded to the extreme northeastern part of Kansas. The body of the expedition, contended Simpson, returned through the northwestern corner of Oklahoma and marching in a southwestern direction crossed the Texas Panhandle by way of Hemphill, Roberts, Carson, Potter, Randall, and Deaf Smith Counties to the Pecos River near Fort Sumner, New Mexico. From there, wrote Simpson, the army went northwest to a point near Mora, and presumably crossed the mountains to the southwest to Pecos Pueblo (Holden 1944: 4; Simpson 1871: 336–337).

Holden also questioned the accuracy of George Winship's conclusions. Winship argued that the expedition left Pecos Pueblo in a southeasterly direction and crossed the Pecos River ten or fifteen miles south of Fort Sumner. From there, he claimed, the Spaniards crossed Bailey, Cochran, Terry, Lynn, Borden, Scurry, Mitchell, Coke, Runnels, and Coleman Counties in Texas. There the expedition divided, with the main force retracing its tracks and Vázquez de Coronado proceeding north into southern Kansas. Winship, as Holden saw it, concluded that "after making a big circle into north central Kansas, where Quivira was, he returned to Cicuye in a southwesterly direction, keeping the same route that later became the Santa Fe Trail" (Holden 1944: 4; Winship 1896: 400).

Seeking to support his hypothesis, Holden analyzed one more study. In 1929 David Donoghue suggested that the expedition had gone down the Pecos River on the west bank until reaching Santa Rosa where the bridge was constructed. From there the Spaniards went east onto the Llano Estacado. They passed through Quay County, New Mexico, across the southern portion of Deaf Smith and Randall Counties to Tule Canyon in the northeast corner of Swisher County, Texas. At Tule Canyon or Palo Duro Canyon is where the expedition divided, Donoghue claimed. Of the route taken by the returning main force, he proposed that it passed through northwestern Parmer County and Bailey County to Fort Sumner and followed the east bank of the Pecos River to the bridge north of Santa Rosa where it crossed to the west bank and continued to Pecos Pueblo.

Meanwhile, wrote Donoghue, Vázquez de Coronado went north from Palo Duro Canyon, traversing western Armstrong and Carson Counties into Hutchinson County where he crossed the Canadian River, which the Spaniards called the San Pedro y San Pablo. "Of this much I am certain," wrote Donoghue, "the expedition never left the Llano Estacado; Palo Duro Canyon and its tributaries are the only ravines that fit Castañeda's descriptions; the salt lakes are found only in the southern Llano Estacado; Quivira was on the Canadian, or some of its tributary creeks at the edge of the plains" (Holden 1944: 4–5; Donoghue 1929: 90).

Holden declared that Simpson and Winship were in error and that Donoghue had "come closer to the truth," but disagreed with him on the location of Quivira. Still Holden was concerned with the route of the expedition after it crossed the Pecos River. Curiously, he remarked, "the New Mexico highway markers indicate that the army crossed the Pecos at Puerto de Luna, eleven miles south of Santa Rosa, and went northeast, keeping just north of the caprock, going by Montoya, Tucumcari, and San Jon and climbing onto the Llano Estacado near Glenrio about the Texas–New Mexico line. This route would have been practically the same traversed by Highway 66, and New Mexico has placed markers along the highway indicating that such was Coronado's route. Recently we went over this route, checked the topography against the accounts and were unable to find any evidence to support the claims" (1944: 10). Although the expedition crossed through the general area, it would be inaccurate to claim that the route was the same as the present highway. By the same token, it would be inaccurate to deny that the expedition passed somewhere within a corridor in the area twenty miles wide on either side of the highway.

Once across the New Mexico–Texas line, the expedition crossed the Canadian River, the stream whose tributaries they had been following (Bolton 1949: 249; Holden 1944: 14). Holden states that "the Spaniards crossed streams like the Canadian without being impressed" (1944: 14). Castañeda explained that "from there the general sent don Rodrigo Maldonado ahead with his company; he traveled four days and came to a large barranca like those of Colima. At its bottom he found a large ranchería with people" (Hammond and Rey 1940: 237). However, traveling to this Teya ranchería, the expedition appears to have left the Canadian River route. Holden concluded that "with the possible exception of the bridge on the Cicuye river, the most pivotal landmark mentioned in all of the original accounts was the 'ravine like those of Colima'" (1944: 13).

Although most scholars agree that the expedition was following the southern branch of the Canadian River drainage, the question of the canyonlands presents another riddle concerning the line of march. The route across the Llano Estacado led to a series of canyons. Were these canyons along the Canadian River drainage as suggested by Albert Schroeder (1962: 3) or were they, as proposed by Bolton (1940: 237), part of the Red River system? Had the expedition entered the ravines near the Canadian Breaks? Or was the expedition in the Tule Canyon–Palo Duro Canyon system? If so, at which point did they leave the Canadian River and its tributaries?

The Tule Canyon–Palo Duro Canyon Hypothesis

Part of the Texas Panhandle is so flat it is possible to pass through the area and not see the great canyons of the Red River. There are no mountains and very little relief to betray their presence. The canyons lie below the horizon so that they do not come into view until the traveler is upon them. Members of the expedition who were separated from the main force had to find the canyons by looking for the upper and lower ends of the canyon where the camp was located. Castañeda relates an episode in which a scouting party under Captain Diego López, who had been reconnoitering an area to the east of the main expedition's camp just across the New Mexico–Texas line, approached a buffalo herd running in front of them. "As the animals were running away and jostling against one another," wrote Castañeda, "they came to a barranca, and so many cattle fell into it that it was filled and the other cattle crossed over them. The men on horseback who followed them fell on top of the cattle, not knowing what had happened. Three of the horses that fell, disappeared, with their saddle and bridles, among the cattle, and were never recovered" (Hammond and Rey 1940: 236).

In his book *Caprock Canyonlands*, Dan Flores (1990) described the labyrinthine formations of the Red River. He wrote:

> Palo Duro Canyon is the main canyon of the Red River, but there are several others. Immediately to the north along the escarpment is Mulberry Canyon and beyond it the sand-filled valley of the Salt Fork of the Red. Wind-drift sand softens and inundates the escarpment line beyond so that of the Red River drainages that come off the Llano here only McClellan Creek furrows deeply enough to create a rock-walled canyon. . . . Along the south wall of Palo Duro an eagle's-eye view would reveal three canyons so large and distinctive as to have identities separate from Palo Duro. North and South Cita canyons are two. Tule Canyon, a slit 700 feet deep, only a half mile across at the top . . . is the third. Along the remaining 140 miles of the Caprock Escarpment, four additional canyons carry the waters of the Brazos and the Colorado off the Llano Estacado . . . Blanco and Yellow House canyons . . . Double Mountain Fork Canyon of Garza County . . . Muchaque Valley (1990: 5).

Aside from the fifteen canyons in the area, Flores mentions Running Water Draw and Blackwater Draw as the two longest draws on the Llano originating in New Mexico.

The chief proponent of the Palo Duro Canyon route is Herbert Bolton, although Holden, Donoghue, and others assumed earlier that Palo Duro Canyon was the ravine Castañeda mentions. Holden was convinced that the Blanco Canyon site was where the expedition encountered the Teya ranchería. His conclusion was as follows:

> While the army rested in the ravine, Coronado and a party explored and "found another settlement four days from there." Four days would have been approximately sixty miles. We may speculate as to where the settlement was. Had he gone

east he would have soon been off the Caprock, and looking back would have seen what looked like a long, flat mountain. This we know they did not do, because nowhere did they see a "hill or hillock three times the height of a man." It is probable that Coronado did not explore to the west, for he had come from that general direction. This leaves the north and the south. In all likelihood the Indian settlement was along a water course. The Canadian River could have been reached within four days by going slightly northwest into Potter County, north of Amarillo. The Blanco could have been reached in the vicinity of Plainview within the time allowed by going south. In our opinion the settlements were on the Blanco for reasons we shall give later. . . . Assuming that the ravine in question was the Palo Duro, the return of the army from there to Cicuye can be traced with considerable accuracy. The landmarks, the distances, and the time element all fit in perfectly. The fact that this part of the route can be plotted so exactly lends to the evidence that the Palo Duro was the "ravine like that of Colima" (1944: 14–15).

After the return of Captain López to the main camp, the expedition followed the Querechos eastward for five days, probably in the Canadian River Valley (Bolton 1949: 253). Having ascended to the plains from the Canadian River drainage near old Highway 66 west of Vega, Vázquez de Coronado "swung southward, leaving the Canadian River at his back, whereupon Sopete again tried to make himself heard, protesting that the Turk was misleading them and had enlisted the collusion of the Querechos. Quivira was northeast and not south, he insisted" (Bolton 1949: 253). The expedition appeared to be headed south from the Canadian River drainage. Suddenly, Coronado was confronted with the first canyon, a giant slit on the flat terrain, and north of there was a second canyon. Bolton proposed that the first barranca (ravine), where they encountered a Teya settlement, was Tule Canyon, east of Tulia near the Swisher-Briscoe county line in Texas (1949: 263), and that the second, deeper one was Palo Duro Canyon.

At Tule Canyon the Turk was interrogated and the expedition changed its line of march. Within a day's travel in a northerly direction, the expedition came to another, even deeper canyon that Bolton declared to be Palo Duro Canyon. It was there, he wrote, that Vázquez de Coronado decided to proceed with a small band of thirty men, while the main expedition returned to the Rio Grande.

Bolton was convinced he had identified the canyons the expedition had passed through. "Clearly," he declared, "we must look for the two barrancas in the eastern edge of the Llano Estacado . . . the First Barranca . . . was Tule Canyon . . . [and] Palo Duro Canyon, now a State Park, was and is par excellence the 'Barranca of the Plains'" (1949: 267). Although Tule and Palo Duro canyons are impressive, not all scholars are as convinced as Bolton that they are the two barrancas seen by Vázquez de Coronado. Bolton, however, was more concerned with narration than with detail. In regard to the number of days Coronado had traveled between river drainages and ravines, he wrote, "the estimate of the eastward march was remarkably accurate, but for the southward distance it was a little too high, which should be no cause for surprise or censure. Our identification of the historic canyon rests upon topographical data, combined with the distances recorded, and upon contributory items as the story goes forward, that make the conclusion certain" (1949: 257).

Castañeda's mention of flora in the barrancas is one of the criteria used to question Bolton's hypothesis. Castañeda wrote, "Thus the army reached the last barranca, which extended a league from bank to bank. A small river flowed at the bottom, and there was a small valley covered with trees, and with plenty of grapes, mulberries, and rose bushes. This is a fruit found in France and which is used to make verjuice [sour grape juice]. In this barranca we found it ripe. There were nuts, and also chickens of the variety found in New Spain, and quantities of plums like those of Castile" (Hammond and Rey 1940: 239). However, based on different information, J. W. Williams proposed that Palo Duro and Tule Canyons were too far west to be the correct barrancas. Arguing that the flora of the area, inclusive of pecans, mulberries, and the date of ripening of wild grapes, had been almost totally ignored in prior studies, Williams wrote,

> One of the accounts of the [Hernando] De Soto Expedition told of a "walnut" found in the western part of the Southern States, but the words of explanation clearly described a pecan. Even if the historian of the Coronado trek could have referred to the dime-sized walnut, it should be pointed out that it does not grow in the canyon mentioned—Palo Duro and the others—or in the area that borders them on the east. The dime-sized walnut—except for a few trees on the creeks of Scurry County and a small mott [group] of three trees west of Quitaque—does not reach westward beyond the pecan country. Thus, whether the word means pecans or the small degenerate variety of the Western walnut, the conclusion must be the same—to have reached the area of native nut production, either walnut or pecans, Coronado must necessarily have gone some distance eastward of the Cap Rock of the High Plains (1959: 6).

The more he studied the native flora of the region, the more emphatic Williams became. He stated, "simply, it is this: Coronado reached the pecan country—the native pecans do not grow in Palo Duro Canyon, or Tule, or Quitaque, or in any of the canyons to the south or, with one minor exception, in any of the counties that border these canyons on the east. Coronado had to journey beyond the High Plains to reach the pecan country" (1959: 5). Using the abstract of the 1910 census and local informants, he examined the counties on the Llano Estacado to determine the number of pecan trees in the area and insisted that Coronado could not have reached the pecan country unless he traveled at least 200 miles east of the

New Mexico line (1959: 8). Williams's argument would have been stronger had he corroborated his information with paleobotanists who could have informed him of other plants, fruits, and nuts as well as climatic changes in the Texas Panhandle during the centuries since Vázquez de Coronado passed through the area.

In regard to Castañeda's observation that the expedition found a ripe fruit used to make verjuice, Williams concluded that the fruit was a wild grape. He surmised that because it was ripe, the expedition could not have been referring to its springtime march through the Texas Panhandle in April 1541, but to a time when fruit ripens—about August or September. Discovering that in the vicinity of the North Concho River, farther south than Palo Duro Canyon, wild grapes ripen as early as June, Williams proposed that the expedition had followed a southeasterly direction and reached the North Concho (1959: 11). Of the geographical perspective, he wrote, "the North Concho might well have been the last ravine, not only because it was the lone point within the pecan country near enough to the Rio Grande to satisfy the known arithmetic of Coronado's journey, but it was far enough south to have been the place where this party of Spaniards could have found ripe grapes" (1959: 13). He went on to discuss the distribution of mulberry trees in West Texas and again concluded that Vázquez de Coronado had reached the North Conchos River southeast of Sterling City, Texas (1959: 16). Williams found an ally in Robert M. Wagstaff who also identified the first barranca as the valley of the North Concho or one of its tributaries near Sterling City. Still, Williams's efforts, either for lack of popular visibility or for lack of persuasiveness, were not enough to overcome the Bolton hypothesis that Palo Duro and Tule Canyons were the ravines visited by Vázquez de Coronado.

Mysterious Cona: Place or Event?

Although Williams made use of Holden's route from Pecos to Frio Draw, both scholars found themselves at opposite ends of the pole when they discussed the Palo Duro Canyon dilemma. Contrary to Williams's hypothesis, Holden voted for Palo Duro and Tule Canyons, basing his proposal on two obvious themes found in the expedition's accounts: the ethnographical evidence and the expedition's consistent ability to find water in the area, presumably within the Texas Panhandle. He argued that both factors are related, in that Indian settlements contacted by the expedition were always near a water source (1944: 14). He noted that while the expedition rested in the ravine, a Spanish party explored the country and located an Indian settlement four days from there. That settlement, he maintained, was that of the Teyas, and Vázquez de Coronado passed through the Teya settlement he called Cona for three days (ibid.). It was from the people of Cona that the Spaniards learned that Quivira was far to the north. However, there are no absolutes in history and archeology. Although most professionals have assumed that Cona was a place, it may have been an event. Of the Teya country, Jane Holden Kelley wrote, "it is possible that the large camp that the Spanish noted was an annual gathering of tribes, rather than a constant concentration of population" (1964: 9).

Albert Schroeder (1962) disagreed with the Williams, Holden, and Bolton theories and presented an impressive argument against them with his proposal that the Canadian River drainage holds the secret to Vázquez de Coronado's route through the Texas Panhandle. Schroeder's route crosses into the Texas Panhandle a short distance north of the Canadian River. Accordingly, the expedition, moving northeasterly, encountered large buffalo herds as well as Querecho and Teya groups along the line of march. Schroeder noted that at a second Querecho village group, the expedition turned southeast until it reached the first barranca near the 101st meridian in the Canadian River Valley. One day's march from there, the Spaniards reached the last barranca, either on the north fork of the Canadian or the Cimarron River. Somewhere near the far northeastern corner of the Texas Panhandle, Schroeder believed, the expedition left Texas and crossed into Oklahoma on its way to Quivira.

In regard to the location of Teya sites, John Peterson, James Neely, Peter W. Nicholas, and S. Christian Caran (1988: 1–133 passim.) added credence to the Schroeder proposal in their study that centered on Palo Duro Creek (not to be confused with Palo Duro Canyon), which flows from the northwestern part of the Texas Panhandle and then north to its confluence with the Beaver River in Oklahoma. Although they suggested that the Teya encountered by the Vázquez de Coronado expedition were culturally similar to those at Palo Duro Creek, they did not argue conclusively that the Spaniards met them along the Canadian River drainage.

Schroeder disagreed with the proponents of the Palo Duro Canyon that the "southeasterly" direction of the expedition from the Canadian River drainage means that the Spaniards headed toward Palo Duro Canyon. Indeed, he maintained that the expedition traveled southeast along the Canadian River drainage, "since no change in direction is hinted in the documents and all suggest that the travel from the Querechos to the Teya rancherias was in the easterly or southeasterly direction, it is assumed that these Teya rancherias were four days travel down the Canadian River from the unnamed rancheria" (1962: 30).

All agreed that the expedition had visited the sedentary pueblos along the Rio Grande, the nomadic Querechos of the Southern Plains, and had progressed to the sedentary plains village settlements. But precisely where were the specific Indian sites visited by the expedition? Disagreement exists on the location of some of the Rio Grande pueblos visited by the Spaniards as well as the point at which the Querechos were seen by them for the first time. However, the critical location of the Teya villages is even more controversial among historians and archeologists.

Was it the North Conchos River, the Red River, or the Canadian River? The inability of modern man to prove which river drainage the expedition visited leaves the route through the Texas Panhandle in limbo.

The Body of the Expedition Returns to the Rio Grande

Once Vázquez de Coronado decided that the expedition on the Great Plains was too large to be supported logistically, he chose thirty men to proceed to Quivira under his command and sent the rest back to Tiguex under Tristán de Luna y Arellano. Arellano's route from Tule Canyon across the Llano Estacado, according to Bolton (1949: 273), was almost due west over the treeless plains and salt lakes in the Texas Panhandle. After reaching New Mexico, Bolton surmised, the main force followed the Santa Fe Railroad, which passes the salt lakes. Castañeda's account corroborates that by noting, "along this route they found many salt lakes, for salt abounds there" (Hammond and Rey 1940: 242). Indeed, he mentioned that some of the salt "was crystalline."

Tracing the distribution of waterholes or springs in the area, Bolton speculated on the availability of water found by the main expedition as it meandered its way back. In the South Tule Draw, Bolton claimed, Arellano found fresh water for twelve or fifteen miles westward beyond the present town of Tulia. More water was found at Running Water Draw, in the upper Blanco Canyon, and in the North Fork of Yellow House Canyon as far as Abernethy, Texas. He theorized that Arellano ascended the North Fork of the Yellow House and found water at Sodhouse Spring north of Littlefield and at Spring Lake north of Amherst, and in Blackwater Draw at Muleshoe, all in Texas. The main force proceeded, as Bolton hypothesized, to Portales, New Mexico, where it found a spring, and then found water again south of Melrose. Just before Arellano entered the valley of Taiban Creek, he descended the western escarpment of the Llano Estacado. Near the present town of Taiban, New Mexico, they found Taiban Spring, some fifteen miles from the Pecos River. Arellano crossed the Pecos River, Bolton asserted, seventy-five miles below the bridge at Anton Chico that had been built on the outward journey. Castañeda corroborated the point by writing, "on its return the army arrived at the Cicuye river more than thirty leagues below the town—I mean below the bridge which had been built on the trip out" (Hammond and Rey 1949: 243). At this point, Bolton remarked that he was accompanied by George Hammond and that he had consulted W. C. Holden, "who knows the country as well as he knows his own dooryard" (1949: 274).

Once on the Pecos River, Arellano marched along its bank and rejoined the outbound route at the bridge at Anton Chico (ibid.). Castañeda completed the narrative of the route by writing, "thus, as I have said, the army went up the river until it reached the pueblo of Cicuye. They found it unfriendly, for the inhabitants would not come out peacefully nor furnish any aid in the way of provisions" (Hammond and Rey 1940: 243). From there, the main body returned to the Rio Grande by way of Galisteo, retracing their line of march followed on the eastbound trip.

There is one perplexing afterthought. It concerns the escape of an Indian woman in the barranca country when the main portion of the expedition under Arellano was returning from its easternmost point. Of that event, Castañeda wrote, "during this trip a painted Indian woman ran away from Juan de Zaldívar. She fled down the barrancas when she recognized the land, for she was a slave at Tiguex where they had obtained her. This Indian woman had come into possession of some Spaniards from Florida, who had penetrated as far as that region in their explorations. I heard our men say when they returned to New Spain that the Indian woman told them that she had fled from the others nine days before, and that she named the captains" (Hammond and Rey 1940: 243). It happened that Luis de Moscoso, who had taken over the leadership of the expedition to Florida (1539–1543) after the death of Hernando de Soto, had attempted to find Vázquez de Coronado and had reached the eastern end of the Red River in Texas (Swanton 1985: 262–263, 275). Could it be that this reference corroborates the hypothesis that the barrancas mentioned are Palo Duro and Tule Canyons on the Red River?

North by the Needle Through Texas and Oklahoma

Because of great disagreements among scholars about where the main expedition separated from the chosen thirty, it is difficult to know where Vázquez de Coronado's starting point was when he departed for Quivira. Without that crucial and pivotal information, no one can determine the direction and distance traveled to Quivira. A wide arc on the map could place Quivira in central Kansas near Lyons as some have suggested or as far east as the vicinity of Tulsa, Oklahoma.

Vázquez de Coronado and his men reckoned distances and directions on the Great Plains by various methods. Often using the rising or setting sun as a guide, they traced their direction toward such points with a sea compass (Hammond and Rey 1940: 236). Sometimes they marked their trail with bones and cow dung so that they could follow each other when they got separated (Hammond and Rey 1940: 237). At one point they learned how Plains Indians determined their direction. "Their method of guiding was as follows," noted Castañeda: "early in the morning they watched where the sun rose, then, going in the direction they wanted to take they shot an arrow, and before coming to it they shot another over it, and in this manner they traveled the whole day until they reached some water where they were to stop for the night" (Hammond and Rey 1940: 242). About the expedition's way of determining distance, Castañeda wrote that "a man had been detailed to make the calculations and even to count the steps" (Hammond and Rey 1940: 240). It is the "sea compass" that Vázquez de Coronado possessed that has been the subject of much speculation about the leg of the route from the barrancas to Quivira.

A sample of opinions by scholars who have been obsessed with finding that route is enough to show the disparity of thought on the subject. Relying on Van Bemmelen's 1600 chart, Wagstaff suggested that the magnetic declination in 1541 was approximately zero; and if so, then Vázquez de Coronado went due north (1966: 151). He employed an interesting, yet convincing methodology. Basing his argument on a "reversal of calls from a known point," he backtracked from an identified point, the Great Bend of the Arkansas River, and concluded that the by-the-needle hypothesis was correct. Hodge reached a similar conclusion by drawing on his map a straight line from the North Conchos River to Quivira (1907: Map 3). A. Grove Day ran the route from the Texas border near the Canadian River, thence southward to the great ravines on one of the upper branches of the Brazos River in Texas. Leaving the main unit there, Day speculated that Vázquez de Coronado and the chosen thirty proceeded northward along the 100th meridian (1940: 247). In support of Hodge's proposal, Frank Hill (1936: 35–44) hypothesized that the expedition reached the Concho River before heading due north. Frank Bryan (1940: 21–37), like Donoghue, however, presumed that the expedition had gone north to Blanco Canyon where Arellano was sent back, then the chosen thirty went north to Quivira, which was someplace in northern Texas. John Peterson proposed that Vázquez de Coronado followed a northeasterly direction toward Kansas, based on a magnetic declination of ten to twelve degrees from true north, indicating that the Spaniards followed Wolf Creek between the Canadian River and Palo Duro Creek (1988: 30). W. H. Stephenson (1926: 64–84) believed that Vázquez de Coronado left the body of the expedition near the junction of Duck Creek and the Salt Fork in Kent County, Texas, and traveled due north, crossing the Canadian River near Amarillo, and then went north to the Great Bend of the Arkansas.

However, no one will ever know whether Vázquez de Coronado and his chosen thirty referred to magnetic north, true north as determined from their "sea compass," or a general "northerly" direction of march. As Bolton had done before her, Diane Rhodes examined the question of the magnetic declination, that is, the deviation between true north and magnetic north, and its non-uniform shifts through time as well as its irregular regional variations. For the early historical period, it is not a precise science. Rhodes, however, concluded that "it appears that the agonic linear line of zero declination in 1600 may have been close to Coronado's route. In general, the magnetic declination in the southwestern United States during the period between A.D. 1400 and A.D. 1600 ranged from about 2 degrees west to 2 degrees east, so an estimate of 0 degrees declination as proposed by Wagstaff is feasible albeit admittedly scientifically imprecise. Archeomagnetic data collected from areas in New Mexico, and dated independently to the 1500s, indicate an average declination of about 4 degrees (east) plus or minus a degree" (1990: 21). Ronald Ives agreed that the dearth of information regarding magnetic declination was a drawback. He wrote, "needed for this study is not only a 'state of the art' knowledge of magnetic surveying in Spanish times, but also some specific values of magnetic declination at known times and places during this period" (1975: 173).

Any conclusion on this segment of the route is, ironically, premature, given that interdisciplinary approaches and historical archeological data bases are, relatively speaking, only at the incipient stages in that region of the Greater Southwest. More work by linguists, paleontologists, geographers, and other workers in related fields is required before historians can rethink their hypotheses. However, the work of those who have gone before them will have played a key role in shaping their scholarly conclusions on the subject.

Quivira—at Last

"The general followed his guides until he reached Quivira. This journey required forty-eight days because of the great deviation toward Florida which they had made. Francisco Vázquez and his men were peacefully received" (Hammond and Rey 1940: 241). Before Bolton concluded that Quivira was in central Kansas, Hubert Howe Bancroft (1884), Adolf F. Bandelier (1892), George P. Winship (1896), Frederick W. Hodge (1895), and Jacob V. Brower (1899) had pointed out that Kansas was the most likely locale where Vázquez de Coronado had ended his quest for the Seven Cities of Gold. One early writer, Colonel Henry Inman, who was an assistant quartermaster in the United States Army in Kansas, ventured a guess that the St. Peter and St. Paul River mentioned in the chronicles of the expedition was the "Big and Little Arkansas" (1899: 5). Along more scholarly lines, however, Johan August Udden was one of the first to collect and study artifacts from the Paint Creek Site on the Smokey Hill River in south-central Kansas, between 1881 and 1889. By studying artifacts such as rusty chain mail found on the site, he was able to determine, at least, that the Paint Creek Site was populated during and after the arrival of Europeans in that region (1900: 66). Secondly, he was one of the first to show that the Spanish presence in Kansas was as old as the sixteenth century. By the same token, William B. Lees concluded that the few sites in Kansas that contain artifactual evidence of the Spanish colonial period are significant in contrast to those that do not because they represent a "relatively small number that have such evidence" (1990: 1).

Archeologist Waldo R. Wedel pondered the question of Vázquez de Coronado's Quivira for at least forty years. He concluded that the Quivira of the sixteenth-century Spanish documents and the central Kansas archeological sites were the habitat of the same native people; that Vázquez de Coronado in all likelihood reached Quivira situated in the locality of present-day Rice and McPherson Counties; and that the larger sites such as Malone, Saxman, Tobias, and Paint Creek were very likely among the grass house villages whose Wichita-speaking inhabitants were visited by the chosen thirty in 1541 (1990: 149). His conclusions were based on archeological fieldwork, ethnographical studies, historical research, and a touch of geographical intuition. In reviewing the literature associated with Quivira, Wedel wrote, "once these scholars had accepted that the Quivira River, which Coronado had named the River of Saints Peter and Paul, was the Arkansas River, they could not easily come to any other conclusion" (ibid.). To him the conclusion was obvious because sixteenth-century Spanish material cultural items such as chain mail found en bloc at the Saxman Site and chain mail fragments from the Paint Creek Site (1990: 147–148) are among the indisputable evidence of the Spanish presence in Kansas. Wedel was careful not to preclude other Spanish expeditions into Kansas later in the sixteenth century or the prospect that artifacts could be found in a site as a result of trade (1968: 369–385). Indeed, Lees pointed out that the presence of European goods at sites in Kansas "helps identify the contact period settlement pattern, differences in the occurrence of different types of European goods, and significantly identifies a prominent archaeological feature, the 'council circles,' [wide shallow ditches 30 to 60 yards in diameter indicative of trading activities] as a significant contact period feature" (1990: 6–7). In his book *Coronado and Quivira*, Paul Jones presented a curious footnote to the tale of chain mail in the Greater Southwest. He wrote, "in 1864 Colonel Kit Carson leading 400 cavalrymen and 75 Ute and Jicarilla guides, came into conflict with Kiowas in the Texas Panhandle country and killed a number of them. Among the slain was a young brave clad in a Spanish coat of mail" (1937: 150). Although trade or movement by the possessors of the chain mail into the area at a later time cannot be ruled out, neither can the high probability of coincidence that thirty men wearing chain mail very likely visited sites along and near the Great Bend of the Arkansas in the year 1541.

Juan de Jaramillo related that at the farthest point reached by the chosen thirty in Quivira they made some decisions. "This place, as I have said," he wrote, "was the last place reached by us. The Turk, realizing that he had lied to us, called on all these people to fall upon us some night and kill us. We found it out and took precautions. He was garroted that night, so he never saw the dawn" (Hammond and Rey 1940: 304). Domingo Martín, a member of the expedition, testified in 1544 that el Turco had been executed "in a pueblo called Tabas" (Archivo General de Indias 1544: Testimony 4). Fearing reprisals should the Quivirans discover the deed, the Spaniards decided to return to Tiguex by way of Cow Creek, which they had visited on their way to Quivira (Bolton 1949: 306).

Where was Tabas? Bolton reiterated that *el Turco* was killed at a place called Tabas, which he equated with *teucarea* and *taovaias*. He suspected that teucarea was a mistranscription of "taovaias" (1949: 293). Mildred Mott Wedel offered an explanation based on linguistics:

> Although Bolton equated both *tabas* and teucarea with the *taovayas*, i.e., Tawehash, today's linguists do not. David S. Rood (University of Colorado, pers. comm.) states that from a linguistic point of view, "I would unhesitatingly identify [teucarea] with the Wichita name for Towakoni, *tawa:khariw*." On the other hand, linguist Rood would accept Bolton's argument for tabas equating with Tawehash. Therefore, if Jaramillo can be trusted, it would seem that both of these Wichita bands were living just south of Smoky Hill River. The importance of teucarea may have resulted in part from their being considered, then and later, the foremost band of the Wichita. The concentration of population may have reflected the presence of the two subdivisions in the region and the fact that the Tawehash, at this time and later, composed the largest band. The Wichita who lived on Arkansas River tributaries in 1541 and 1601 are unidentified (1982: 121).

Possibly someday the site of el Turco's execution will be located and the starting point of the chosen thirty's return to Tiguex will be satisfactorily determined.

The Return of the Chosen Thirty

Jaramillo wrote, "we marched back—I do not know whether two or three days—to a place where we got provisions of shucked ears of green maize and dry maize for our return. At this place the general erected a cross, at the foot of which some letters were cut with a chisel, saying that Francisco Vázquez de Coronado, general of the army, had reached this place" (Hammond and Rey 1940: 305). Jaramillo's perplexing statement, perhaps a clue, could one day be an important source about the whereabouts of the chosen thirty after having reached the farthest point on their trek to Quivira. Of Jaramillo's statement, Bolton surmised that "presumably it [the cross] was made of wood, and was displayed in some conspicuous place along the trail. Since the carving was done with a chisel, and was at the foot of the cross, one infers that it was cut in rock on which the Christian symbol stood, although this is not certain" (1949: 305). He also concluded that "from all the known data it seems probable that the historic cross was erected at the village on Cow Creek near Lyons, Kansas, where Coronado had been welcomed by the Wichitas before he turned north from Arkansas River on his way to Tabas" (1949: 306).

It was probably mid-August 1541 when the chosen thirty reached the River of Saints Peter and Paul. Jaramillo related that after they left their trusted guide, Isopete, in Quivira where the cross had been erected, five or six Plains Indian guides led them back to the Cicúye River. "Here," he wrote, "they abandoned our previous route, and taking off to the right, they led us by watering places and among the cattle and over good road. Although there is no good road anywhere unless it be the paths of the cattle" (Hammond and Rey 1940: 305). Finally they arrived at an area they recognized, of which Jaramillo narrated, "finally we came to the region, and recognized it, as I said at the beginning, we found the rancheria where the Turk took us away from the route we should have followed. Thus omitting further details, we arrived in Tiguex where we found the rest of the army" (Hammond and Rey 1940: 306).

From these words, Bolton derived a hypothesis of the return route from Quivira to Tiguex. He concluded that Jaramillo's statement was the key to explaining the route from the crossing at the Arkansas (1949: 307). He also concluded that the ranchería mentioned by Jaramillo was the "second Querecho village seen by Coronado on his journey to Quivira, and was situated on the Canadian River near the Texas–New Mexico boundary" (ibid.). To Bolton, the statement solved a number of riddles: "it was the pivotal point in all three of the journeys east of Pecos River" (ibid.). He felt that the ranchería was the place where the Turk had urged Alvarado to turn northeasterly toward Quivira in late summer 1540; it was the place where the Turk turned the expedition away from a direct route to Quivira in spring 1541; and it was the place where the chosen thirty returned in their march from Quivira in late summer 1541. Confident in his conclusions, Bolton hypothesized that the route "approximated" the railroad line run by the Chicago, Rock Island, and El Paso Railway. To him, the information revealed the location of two ends of the return route: one at the Great Bend of the Arkansas River near Ford, Kansas; the other along the Canadian River near the New Mexico–Texas line (ibid.). He proceeded to outline the route as follows:

> Leaving the Arkansas River at Ford, in Kansas he passed through or near the sites of Bloom, Minneola, Fowler, Plains, Kismet and Liberal; in the Oklahoma Panhandle, Tyrone, Hooker, Optima, Guymon and Goodwell can claim him as their discoverer; in the Texas Panhandle he passed the sites of Texhoma, Stratford, Conlen, Dalhart, Middlewater and Romero. Crossing the line in New Mexico he brought into history the sites of Nara Visa, Obar, and Logan, on the north bank of Canadian River, opposite the place where the Turk first led him astray on his march to Quivira. For some distance after leaving the Arkansas River Coronado's return route was not far west of his northward line of march to the same stream (1949: 308).

Holden reviewed the same material as Bolton and concluded that the route from the Arkansas River to the site of the ranchería "would be extremely difficult to trace." He agreed that the chosen thirty crossed and "perhaps paralleled for some distance the Canadian River on one side or the other" (1944: 20). Regarding Jaramillo's comment about the "watering places," he remarked, "the water in the Canadian itself is brackish and unpalatable" (ibid.). He did resolve the issue of potable water by observing that many creeks flow into the Canadian River from either side. He concluded, as had Bolton, that from the ranchería, Vázquez de Coronado "traveled the same route he had come by way of the bridge at Anton Chico to Cicuye, and on to Tiguex" (ibid.). Castañeda was certain that the chosen thirty had traveled forty days from Quivira to Tiguex.

The Expedition Heads Home

Once the company was reunited at Tiguex, it was decided to return to Mexico. Although few details and commentary are referenced in the historical literature, it appears that the entire group, less those who elected to remain in the Tierra Nueva for missionary purposes, moved from Tiguex past Acoma westward over the Malpaís, to El Morro, and then on to Zuni, skirting Corn Mountain. From there they backtracked south of the Zuni River through the uninhabited mountainous terrain between there and Chichilticale. Two days beyond Chichilticale, the expedition met a supply caravan under Juan Gallego. Moving down the Sonora Valley, the retreating expedition reached Batuco. Because of Indian hostility in the area, the expedition hastened its return, crossing the Río Mayo, Río Fuerte, and the Río Sinaloa to Petatlán. Arrived at Culiacán, the expedition was officially dismissed. Some of the explorers remained at Culiacán with their families, others dispersed elsewhere. Francisco Vázquez de Coronado returned to Mexico City (Bolton 1949: 345–349).

CHAPTER 19

Which Barrancas?
Narrowing the Possibilities

DONALD J. BLAKESLEE

Introduction

For the past several years, I have been reviewing the Texas portion of Coronado's route. It is one of the two least understood segments of the route, the other being the segment from the Mexican border north to the Zuni pueblos. The reason for focusing on Texas is that, if we can resolve this most difficult section, we will have demonstrated the feasibility of tracing the whole.

My effort has involved review of the primary documents, old maps and aerial photos, and accounts of later expeditions across the same region. It also has involved two field expeditions. The first, including Waldo, Mildred, and Wally Wedel and Jack Hughes, was funded by the Don and Sybil Harrington–Amarillo Area Foundation, while the second was supported by Wichita State University.

The basic procedure I have tried to follow is to attempt to eliminate the wrong interpretations of the route and to see what is left at the end of the process. This is very different from trying to prove a single favored hypothesis and in the long run is far more effective. By reducing the number of reasonable alternatives, we can begin to look for concrete evidence for campsites and other evidence with reasonable hope for success.

There are two kinds of evidence to consider: textual and contextual. A good hypothesis must be consistent with the bulk of the primary texts. (None can be consistent with all of the documents, since they contradict one another in places.) Consistency with the records of other expeditions across the same region under similar circumstances is also important. A good hypothesis will also be consistent with other knowledge that is pertinent to the problem. This includes what is known of the physiography, geology, hydrology, botany, and archeology of the region.

Each kind of evidence, that from the texts and that relating to contexts, provides criteria by which any hypothesis can be evaluated. I review both sets of criteria in turn before evaluating three hypotheses about the route.

Consideration of the Routes

Criteria or considerations that apply to texts include questions of transcription, translation, interpretation, the identity and purpose of the author, the nature of the audience he is addressing, and consistency with other texts. I would like to focus attention here on two points: the differences between translation and interpretation and considerations of audience. Both are critical to the task at hand.

One problem of translation, among many, is Pedro de Castañeda's mention of "*uva morales y rosal*" in the last barranca visited by the expedition (Castañeda 1596: 84r). The surviving copy of Castañeda's account contains no punctuation, so it is not apparent whether he intended to indicate "uva," "morales and "rosal" or, alternatively, "uva morales" and "rosal." The former translates "grapes, mulberries, and roses"; the latter means "blackberries and roses." Since I have found no references to blackberries in the region, I tend to favor the former translation.

While the dividing line between direct translation and interpretation is a fuzzy one, translators sometimes go beyond what is obvious in the original to say something that fits their interpretation of the larger text. For instance, George Winship (1896: 237) translated the Spanish word, *nueces*, as "walnuts," rather than as "nuts." Both translations are technically correct, but which one did the author intend? Since the Coronado accounts include another reference to nueces in the vicinity of the United States–Mexico border, a spot where no walnuts grow, I prefer to interpret nueces as "nuts."

This issue is important to one of the hypotheses regarding the route discussed below. J. W. Williams (1959: 70) starts with Winship's interpretation of nueces as "walnuts" and then proceeds to argue that since there were no walnuts in the canyons of the eastern Llano Estacado, the reference must have been to pecans!

Turning to considerations of audience, it is important to keep in mind that the authors of all of the primary documents of the Coronado expedition were participants in the history-making journey writing for the benefit of their Spanish colleagues who did not participate. Unfortunately for us, none of the writers intended their reports to tell us how to follow the route they had taken.

I have noticed several passages where the author-audience relationship is important to our understanding. One is a passage in Castañeda's account that describes the vegetation in the last barranca that the expedition visited. In the Hammond and Rey translation (1940: 239), it reads, "grapes, mulberries and rose bushes. This is a kind of fruit found in France and which is used to make verjuice." The word Castañeda (1596: 84r) used was *agraz*, which is a sour sauce made from green grapes. In French, *verjus* is a sour sauce commonly made from green grapes, but that was sometimes made from other fruits.

Now consider the author-audience relationship. Castañeda was a Spaniard writing for a Spanish audience that was familiar with grapes, mulberries, roses, and agraz. If he had been referring to grapes in this passage, he would have been stating the obvious. Grapes had been common in Spain since at least Roman times and his intended audience did not need to be reminded what they were. Furthermore, to write for a Spanish audience that uvas are used to make agraz is like explaining to an American that apples are used to make applesauce. That is, it is an *explanation* in a context that requires none. Clearly, something is wrong with the translation or the interpretation.

Another problem is the reference to France. Since grapes were grown in Spain and were used there to make agraz and since most Spaniards would have known this, why did Castañeda say that this was something that was done in France? It turns out that there were fruits from which verjus was made in France but not in Spain in the sixteenth century. They are gooseberries and currants. Cultivated gooseberries originated in England and spread to Normandy after the Norman conquest of England. They did not spread to the rest of France until the sixteenth century, when Castañeda was writing.

Gooseberries are closely related to currants, and this is reflected in the French words for these fruits. Currants are *groseilles*, while gooseberries are *groseilles à maquereau*, or "mackerel currant." The Spanish terms are *grosella* or *uva espina* for the gooseberry. The former term is obviously a borrowing from the French; the latter is descriptive, as gooseberry plants can be distinguished from currants by the presence of thorns.

The plant genus that includes the wild American species of both currants and gooseberries is extremely diverse and widespread. Both currants and gooseberries are present in the region of Texas traversed by Coronado, where they ripen in May to early June, the time of year when Coronado came through. Since Castañeda specified that "we found some ripe" in the last barranca, I think it is likely that

Castañeda was referring to currants in the last barranca, not grapes, mulberries, blackberries, or roses.

There is also the possibility, raised by Jack Hughes (at the 1992 Las Vegas conference), that Castañeda dictated his account rather than writing it himself. If so, his immediate audience was a scribe who was expecting to hear a Spanish word when Castañeda said "groseilles" in reference to a kind of fruit used to make the equivalent of agraz in France. The Spanish word, "rosal," is close enough phonetically to groseilles to make this believable.

Clues to the Route in the Texts

In order to make the arguments that follow intelligible to readers who may not have pored over the Coronado documents recently, I excerpt here what I consider to be the critical passages and arrange them topically.

En Route

The route taken from Cicúye (Pecos Pueblo) was first across some high ground and then to the River of Cicúye, where the expedition built a bridge in order to cross the flooded stream. After a number of days of travel from there, it encountered two Querecho camps. From the second camp, Coronado sent forward two sequential scouting parties. Here, in chronological order of their occurrence in 1541, are some of the critical descriptions about this part of the trip.

Matías de la Mota y Padilla (a secondary source but one that includes some details that appear to derive from a now lost primary document) says (1920: 229) the expedition encountered four days of fog ("*andado cuatro jornadas por estos llanos, con grandes neblinas*") somewhere between Pecos and the Querechos. Noted anthropologist/archeologist Jack Hughes, a longtime resident of the Texas Panhandle, says that morning fogs are common enough in the spring for this to be believable, but that the fog usually burns off before noon. The fog may have slowed the rate of travel somewhat.

Isopete, a Wichita Indian, began complaining that the Indian they called the Turk was taking the expedition in the wrong direction as soon as they left the first Querecho camp (Hammond and Rey 1940: 237). Any route that took it toward the north or east would not have brought this response, since there was a series of trails in the region that led toward the Wichita settlements in central Kansas. From the northwestern edge of the Llano Estacado, one can go by Indian trails either north and then east or east and then north. Since the Spaniards would have been alerted to a problem if they started to go back west, the Turk must have led them either to the south or to the southeast.

The second Querecho camp the expedition encountered was on the High Plains, as one of the men became permanently lost in its vicinity because the ground was so level (Hammond and Rey 1940: 236). The plains in question could have been either north or south of the Canadian River Valley.

The Spaniards, and even their guides, became lost after leaving the second Querecho camp. Coronado (Hammond and Rey 1940: 186) says that this happened five days after reaching the Querechos, and this number seems to include two days of travel between the first and second Querecho camps and three days during which Diego López was separated from the main body on a scouting expedition. How lost were they and for how long? The failure of López to find a settlement called Haxa where the Turk and the Querechos said it would be may account for the statement that the Spaniards were lost. So too might the difficulty they had in following a second scouting party led by Rodrigo Maldonado.

Diego López (Hammond and Rey 1940: 237) reported that he saw nothing but cattle and sky in the twenty eastward leagues that his scouting party covered. This implies quite strongly that he never left the Llano Estacado; the eastern or northern escarpments would have been something worth reporting.

López (Hammond and Rey 1940: 236) stampeded some bison into a ravine (barranca) during this trip. This indicates that he crossed a drainage and the fact that Coronado looked for the tracks of the scouting party along a stream (ibid.) indicates the same. The drainage in question need not have flowed due north-south, but must have crossed the route of travel at some angle.

The First Barranca

Maldonado travelled four days and found Teyas in "a large barranca like those of Colima. At its bottom he found a large ranchería with people" (Hammond and Rey 1940: 237). Hence, the first barranca is larger than the minimum size needed for a Spaniard to call a gully or ravine a barranca (deep enough so that you can't see out when riding a donkey, according to one informant). The barranca was similar to some in Colima that were familiar to members of the intended audience, that is, to residents of New Spain who were not participants in the expedition.

According to the author of the *Relación del Suceso* (Hammond and Rey 1940: 291), the expedition traveled 100 leagues east and 50 leagues south before discovering that the guide was leading them away from where they thought they wanted to go. These directions, from a document contemporary with the expedition, contradict Juan de Jaramillo's recollection decades later that the expedition had moved first northeast and then more to the north from Pecos (Hammond and Rey 1940: 300).

"There are no trees except along the rivers which there are in some barrancas. These [barrancas, not rivers or trees as in Winship or Hammond and Rey] are so concealed that one does not see them until he is at their edge. They are of dead earth with approaches made by cattle in order to reach the water which flows quite deep" (Hammond and Rey 1940: 261).

The expedition was hit by a hailstorm in the first barranca and it broke all the pots in camp. The horses were driven to "places from which they were brought down with great difficulty" (Hammond and Rey 1940: 238). Hence, the first barranca should contain a site with large amounts of Rio Grande and perhaps some Mexican pottery. It should also contain talus slopes of considerable height.

"The general sent out exploring parties from there. After four days, they came to other rancherías resembling *alixares*. This was a densely populated country. It produced abundant *frijoles*, plums like those of Castile, and wild grapes. These pueblos of rancherías extended for three days' journey. It was called Cona" (Hammond and Rey 1940: 238–239). This seems to imply that the expedition remained in the first barranca for at least a week.

Second Barranca

"From here [the first barranca] the expedition went to a deep barranca" (Hammond and Rey 1940: 239). Hence, the second barranca was deeper (or does it just mean larger?) than the first.[1]

"We all marched together for a day to an arroyo flowing between some barrancas in which there were some good meadows" (Hammond and Rey 1940: 302). The second barranca was, thus, one day's travel from the last of the Teya camps and it contained good forage for the horses and other beasts that Coronado's expedition had with them.

"Thus the army reached the last barranca, which extended a league from bank to bank. A small river flowed at the bottom, and there was a small valley covered with trees, and with plenty of grapes, mulberries and rose bushes [but see above]. This is a fruit found in France and which is used to make verjuice. In this barranca we found it [some] ripe. There were nuts, and also chickens of the variety found in New Spain, and quantities of plums like those of Castile" (Hammond and Rey 1940: 239).

Many men got lost while hunting on the plains above the last barranca. Expedition members had to fire guns, blow horns, beat drums, and light great bonfires to guide them back to camp. This was because the ground was so level that inexperienced men became disoriented (Hammond and Rey 1940: 241). Hence, the second barranca was somewhere in the High Plains.

Return Route of the Expedition

The expedition returned to the Teyas from the last barranca to get guides (Hammond and Rey 1940: 242). Presumably, this was the last Teya camp, one day's travel from the barranca. The Teya guides used arrows to keep the direction of travel for part of the return trip to Tiguex (ibid.). Hence, the return route was not along a single draw or watercourse. The return route was so much more direct than the outward leg that it took only twenty-five days of travel rather than thirty-seven. The return route led by some very salty lakes. "One could see salt slabs on the water larger than tables and four or five fingers thick" (ibid.).

Distances

The scouting expedition of Diego López went eastward from the second Querecho camp for twenty leagues (in two days) without seeing anything but sky and bison. This implies that the second camp must be more than fifty miles west of the eastern edge of the caprock escarpment.

Maldonado took a similar group on a four-day scout before he found the first barranca. This scouting party set out after López had returned, and during the time that the first party was ahead, the expedition had moved forward, but at a slower rate. All of this implies that the first barranca lay three days of slow travel by the body of the expedition and four days of faster travel by the scouts from the Querecho camp. Thus, the camp had to lie somewhere toward the western side of the Llano Estacado, three days of slower travel from the stream course where Diego López returned, which in turn was four days of fast travel from the barranca of the Teyas.

According to the *Relación del Suceso*, the distance from Tiguex to the place where the Spaniards decided the Turk was lying was 100 leagues east and 50 leagues south. Coronado's letter to the king implies that the decision not to trust the Turk was made in the last barranca (Hammond and Rey 1940: 187). The first barranca could have been either north or south of the latter; no document specifies the direction of travel between them.

The distances cited above are obviously ballpark estimates, and an error of up to 15 percent seems likely. If the long league (3.46 miles) was intended, the spot indicated was east of the Llano Estacado and well to the south of the area where canyons or barrancas are found. Use of short leagues (2.63 miles) is therefore indicated.[2] The source does not specify precisely whether the measurements were from Tiguex or Cicúye. If the former was intended, the location specified is in the vicinity of Lubbock, Texas, and Yellow House Canyon. If the latter starting point was meant, then the directions take one to the vicinity of Blanco Canyon in Floyd and Crosby Counties, Texas.

If, in order to make the *Relación del Suceso* directions fit with Jaramillo's recollections, we assume that the directions and distances were 100 leagues east and 50 leagues north, then a location for the barranca in the northeastern corner of the Texas Panhandle is indicated.

Coronado left the expedition in the last barranca and traveled north for thirty days to intersect the Arkansas River in the vicinity of Ford, Kansas. While one source specifies that the daily legs of this journey were not very long, it is difficult to reconcile thirty days of travel with a location for the second barranca anywhere north of the Canadian River. Each day's travel would have been ridiculously low.

The expedition took thirty-seven days to make the outward trip, but Teya guides shortened the homeward leg by taking a more direct route.

Contexts

Any interpretation of the route should be consistent, not only with the texts, but also with knowledge of the physiography, geology, hydrology, botany, and archeology of the region. Most of the information summarized here I owe to Jack Hughes; any errors are, of course, my own.

Physiography

The High Plains of the Llano Estacado are cut by a series of draws that are fairly well watered but do not have vertical walls and, hence, are not candidates for either of the barrancas. Where they cut through the caliche caprock, however, the draws become barrancas with vertical cliffs and flat valley floors. Farther downstream, the waters cut through another resistant rock layer and the canyons become much deeper, with step-and-slope walls. In the largest canyons, this happens several times. Eventually the streams emerge beyond the escarpment into the broken hilly country to the east.

Geology

The caprock is a caliche formation within the Oglalla Formation that otherwise consists of unconsolidated gravels and sands. The next resistant layer is the Trujillo Formation, below which are more Triassic- and Permian-age beds. The alternation of porous and relatively impermeable layers determines the location of springs. Also important is the absence of Cretaceous-age salt beds from the region of the Llano north of the Blackwater Draw drainage. These deposits are the source of the salt in the playas of the southern Llano. Between Blackwater Draw and the Canadian River, salt playas are absent.

Hydrology

Springs issued from the margins of the major draws all the way west across the Llano Estacado. The draws used to be major river valleys that became choked with sediment when the Pecos River captured their tributaries in ancient times. When water tables were high prior to modern farming with its windmills and center-pivot irrigation, each major draw provided a relatively well-watered route across the plains.

The salt playas of the southern Llano also had fresh or fairly fresh water springs feeding into them. The majority of the salt dissolved from Cretaceous beds in the playa bottoms and the salt was concentrated, as water was lost to evaporation.

Springs also occur regularly where the draws flow over the caliche caprock. They come from the Oglalla and provide fresh water. More springs are found at the base of the caliche and they also are fresh water sources. Below the Trujillo Formation, the water sources become more saline and mineral-impregnated the farther downstream one goes. The water from the Triassic beds can be truly awful and will produce the same biological effects as Epsom salts. Accounts from later expeditions mention how bad the water was in these spots. East of the caprock escarpment good water was scarce except along the sides of some divides, where rainwater recharged freshwater seeps.

Botany

Local inhabitants prove to be better sources of information than books in regard to the distribution of tree species on the eastern edge of the Llano Estacado. The Coronado documents mention groves of trees, nuts, plums, "rosebushes," and various kinds of fruit. Two field trips that I have made thus far have documented the presence of native walnut trees in Palo Duro Canyon and pecan trees in Blanco Canyon. According to J. W. Williams's article, neither is recorded in official distribution reports, yet the trees are there. A native rosebush is present in the region, as are currants.

Archeology

In the region north of the Canadian River, one finds permanent archeological sites until perhaps a century or even half a century before Coronado's expedition. These include the Buried City Complex along Wolf Creek in the northern Texas Panhandle, but the people were definitely gone before the Spaniards came (David Hughes, personal communication).

South of the Canadian River are two archeological complexes, Tierra Blanca and Garza. These fall into the time frame of the Coronado expedition. Tierra Blanca sites occur along the northern part of the Llano Estacado at least as far west as Hereford and in the canyons of the eastern escarpment as far south as Blanco

Canyon. From Blanco Canyon south, one finds increasing numbers of Garza Complex sites, in the escarpment canyons, along streams east of the Llano, and along some of the draws running across the plains. Various people have suggested that the Tierra Blanca sites were left by the Querechos and the Garza sites by the Teyas. Correlating archeological complexes with particular tribes is notoriously difficult, however, and there is no clear proof of these assertions about Garza and Tierra Blanca.

Critiques

Bolton

Herbert Bolton's identification of the barrancas resulted in part from the route he proposed for the outward leg of travel from Cicúye and partly from what he saw during a brief trip to the Llano Estacado. He (1949: 253) traced Coronado's route along a trail south of the Canadian River to an access point to the Llano Estacado near Vega, Texas. The distances involved correlate pretty well with the days of travel mentioned in the Coronado documents and the route he proposes is along an old Indian trail that later became part of the Fort Smith–Santa Fe Trail. Since Coronado had Indian guides who would have led him along known trails, this has to be counted as a positive feature of his hypothesis.

The access point near Vega, however, does not fit well with the description of the scouting expedition by López. If he had gone eastward twenty leagues from any spot near Vega, he would have traveled off the escarpment and would have encountered a series of creeks that would have led him to the Canadian River. That is, he would have had far more to report than merely cattle and sky. Furthermore, Isopete would not have had any grounds for complaint if the Turk had been leading Coronado eastward from Vega. They had already passed Tucumcari Peak and one ford of the Canadian River. They would have been near another ford at the end of a trail along Punta del Agua Creek, but there were other trails and other fords farther east that were no less direct routes to what would become Kansas. The old trail that led from Ford, Kansas, to Adobe Walls, Texas, is one.

Bolton (1949: 266) identified the first barranca as Tule Canyon and the second as Palo Duro Canyon. When he accompanied local historians to a point overlooking the Palo Duro, he is reported to have become convinced that he was at the right spot. Indeed, both canyons fit the description "great barrancas" and both have "dead earth" or sides barren of vegetation. The Palo Duro is indeed a league wide at various points (and much wider in its lower reaches) and there are Indian trails leading down both sides that the Teyas might have used.

To make this identification, Bolton had to ignore the statement that described the second canyon as fifty leagues south of Tiguex (or Cicúye). Furthermore, and perhaps more importantly, the return route of the body of the expedition from this point could not have been significantly shorter than the outward leg, as various accounts state. I have measured Bolton's own map (1949: endpapers), and the difference in length of the outward and return routes that he draws is barely perceptible. It would account for no more than one day's difference in the length of the journey, not the twelve-day difference described in the documents.

In fact, there is no route from the Palo Duro to the Pecos at a point thirty leagues below the bridge that could be shorter than Bolton's proposed outward leg; it is just too direct. Furthermore, there are no salt lakes anywhere along the return route he proposes for the expedition. Finally, a camp in the deeper portion of Palo Duro Canyon would be a lousy choice. It is hot; the water is not as good as farther upstream; and the grazing is poor compared to what can be found in the upper canyons. To hunt bison on the uplands, the soldiers would have had to ride out every day up some very steep slopes. The major Tierra Blanca sites are found farther upstream in this and the other canyons, where the water and the pasturage are better and where access to the bison hunting ground is easier.

After leaving the main body, Coronado traveled with a select group of thirty horsemen for thirty days to reach the Arkansas River in southwestern Kansas. From the camp Bolton locates in the Palo Duro Canyon to Ford, Kansas, it is 170 miles north and 105 miles east. Both the direction and the distance seem to be off. Bolton (1949: 285) argues that a magnetic declination of about twelve degrees east of north caused Coronado's men to record this journey as having been to the north rather than the northeast, but the actual direction of travel would have been over thirty-one degrees east of north.

The direct line distance between the camp Bolton locates in Palo Duro Canyon and Ford, Kansas, is just under 200 miles. To take thirty days to travel this distance, the average day's travel would have been less than seven miles. While the legs of the journey are described as "not long," it is hard to reconcile the fact that Coronado picked the men with the best horses with the leisurely rate of travel that the distances imply. They could have done better on foot.

Schroeder

Albert H. Schroeder's proposed route pays attention to the directions that Castañeda gives from Cicúye to the bridge. He (1962: 4) proposes that the river the expedition spanned was the Canadian in the vicinity of Conchas Dam, New Mexico, and that the first Querecho village was near Dalhart, Texas (1962: 6). His first barranca is the Canadian River Valley or one of the canyons feeding into it, and the second barranca is the valley of the Cimarron River near the mouth of Horse Creek (Schroeder 1962: 9–10).

While this hypothesis has the advantage of fitting the most detailed description of the directions taken from Cicúye, it has many drawbacks. It leads to the High Plains, only north of the Canadian River rather than south of it. So far, I have been unable to find any evidence of an early trail that Coronado's guides might have used to take him in this direction.

What is clearly a drawback is the assertion that the Cimarron River was the second barranca. Neither it nor the Canadian is hidden from the view of an approaching traveler as described in the documents. Instead, both are surrounded by breaks that announce the presence of the rivers to travelers in their vicinity. Furthermore, the Cimarron Valley in the proposed location is low and wide, with gently sloping valley walls and sand banks. There is simply nothing about it that fits the concept of a barranca. Most dramatically, if Palo Duro is questionable as the second barranca because it is too far north, the Cimarron location proposed by Schroeder is even worse. It is only fifty miles from this spot to the Arkansas River at Ford, implying that Coronado and his selected horsemen averaged a regal two miles per day on their trip north.

Finally, there is in Schroeder's hypothesis an internal inconsistency in terms of the rates of travel that are implied. Coronado traveled from Tiguex to Cicúye in four days and the distance between them implies a rate of travel of 17.6 miles per day. From Cicúye to Schroeder's proposed bridge site, on the other hand, requires a rate of travel of 27.5 miles per day. From there his hypothesized route requires about 15 miles per day for the stretch between the bridge and the first Querecho camp, over 30 miles per day between the first and second camps, less than 2 miles per day from the second barranca to the Arkansas, and about 13 miles a day from there to Quivira. This is a most unlikely pattern.

Williams

J. W. Williams was an expert on early travel routes in Texas and he clearly invested a great deal of effort to produce a well-argued hypothesis regarding Coronado's route. His argument involves the location of known Indian trails and close consideration of the botanical context, including the distribution of pecan trees and the season of ripening of various species of grapes. He takes Coronado to a first barranca in the Tule Canyon–Quitaque Canyon region and to a second barranca on the North Concho River in the vicinity of Sterling City, Texas (Williams 1959: 92). The return of the bulk of the expedition is via the middle crossing of the Llano, roughly along Yellow House Draw (Williams 1959: 94).

This hypothesis has attractive features. The discussion of the trails used is reasonable; the distances traveled are consistent with the texts; and the direction of travel between the second barranca and Ford, Kansas, is close to a true north bearing. Williams has the Teyas living in the region where sites of the Garza Complex are found. Furthermore, the return route along Yellow House Draw needs to be modified only slightly to take it past Silver Lake and the large pile of bison bone on its south shore that fits a spot described by Castañeda.

The drawbacks to this route, however, are just as impressive. Like the Cimarron, the North Concho is not located in a barranca. Instead, it is in a wide, gently sloping valley with no vertical walls that I could find. The hills that border the valley are landmarks that would have made it difficult for the hunters from the camp in the second barranca to get lost in the fashion described in the documents. The spot simply does not correspond to the physical requirements established by the documentary descriptions of the second barranca.

One of the strongest points in Williams's argument appears to be his use of the botanical evidence, but all of his major points in this regard do not bear close scrutiny. First, he relied on the Winship translation and its interpretation of "nueces" as "walnuts." He then converted these to pecans because he was using only the English version of the document and was unaware that Winship could just as correctly have interpreted the Spanish as merely referring to nuts. Unaware also that there were some walnuts native to the area, he focused on the pecans that he believed were found only southeast of the Llano Estacado.

The actual facts are less clear-cut. In 1991 I obtained direct evidence that walnut trees are native to the middle portion of the Palo Duro Canyon, obviating all of Williams's arguments about walnuts and pecans. Later, local collector Jimmy Owens, who spends a great deal of time in Blanco Canyon, told me that there are some native pecans growing there. Neither of these isolated stands of nut trees was mentioned in the documents available to Williams, so he honestly believed that he had a solid argument.

He also argued that grapes would not have been ripe in late May or early June in the northerly locations proposed by other scholars. The passage in Castañeda's account that describes the fruit has already been discussed. The ripening fruit in question could have been grapes, mulberries, blackberries, gooseberries, or currants. Mulberries are not a likely candidate for the fruit in question, because Castañeda says it was used to make agraz, a sour condiment, and mulberries are not juicy until nearly ripe and insipid in flavor when they are ripe.

Blackberries, gooseberries, and currants are another matter. Since blackberries do not grow in the region, we do not need to consider them further. Anyone who has eaten gooseberry pie will realize the potential that gooseberries offer for a sour sauce, and the closely related currants are similarly sharply flavored and juicy prior to full ripeness. Both were used in France to make verjuice in the sixteenth century and both ripen at the right time of year for Castañeda to have picked some.

When Jack Hughes and I traveled across the Llano Estacado in 1991, we did so at the same season of the year that Coronado visited and there were currants ripening on a bush in Jack's front yard in Canyon, Texas.

All of this evidence removes Williams's arguments as to why Coronado must have journeyed far to the south. It leaves the main weakness of his argument: the fact that his second barranca is not one of the canyons of the Llano Estacado, a fact about which the Spanish descriptions of the landscape leave little doubt.

Conclusions

The intent of this chapter is to winnow the possible candidates for the barrancas visited by Coronado. To that end, I have examined three hypothetical routes in terms of both documentary and contextual evidence. Both Bolton's and Schroeder's proposed routes are northerly and both appear to fail for that reason. At the present time, I do not see how any route north of the Canadian River can be consistent with the bulk of the evidence. Bolton's route is barely acceptable in this regard, and both proposals fail to generate a return route for the body of the expedition that is significantly shorter than the outward segment of the journey.

As discussed in regard to the Bolton route, an entry onto the Llano Estacado at Vega is too far east to fit the documentary evidence. A point not previously discussed, that Coronado's party recognized the region in the vicinity of the first Querecho camp during their return to Cicúye from Quivira, on the other hand, suggests that the camp and the nearby entry point to the Llano must have been farther north than Pajarito Creek. A likely location for the camp is in the vicinity of Tucumcari Peak, a readily recognized landmark, and this suggests an entry point somewhere from Apache Canyon to Arroyo del Puerto.

Williams's arguments in favor of the Concho Valley being the second barranca are interesting, but that valley does not fit the physical descriptions we have, which are fuller for this spot than for any other part of the route. On the other hand, the distances traveled and the lengths of the various segments do make the canyons of the southeastern Llano Estacado possible candidates. All are in the region of the Garza Complex, which could be the remains of the Teyas. Garza points and Edwards Plateau chert, two of the diagnostic features of the Garza Complex, are found in campsites all along Williams's proposed return route to the Pecos, the Yellow House drainage.

Yellow House Canyon is not likely to have been the second barranca, however. If it were, the body of the expedition would only have had to follow its well-watered course all the way back to New Mexico. There would have been no need for the Teya guides to have used arrows to keep to a route across the unmarked Llano Estacado. The fact that they did so suggests that the guide led the expedition to the upper portion of the Yellow House drainage from some other canyon, perhaps in the vicinity of Blanco Canyon where a chain mail glove was found. This is one good candidate for either the second barranca or the starting point of the return trip. There may be others.

Notes

1. The original text reads, "a donde fue el campo a una barranca grande" (Castañeda 1596: 83v). Hence, the deepness of the last barranca is a product of Hammond and Rey's translation.

2. For a discussion of variation in Spanish leagues see Chardon 1980.

CHAPTER 20

The Teya Indians of the Southwestern Plains

CARROLL L. RILEY

rancisco Vázquez de Coronado marched eastward from the Rio Grande Valley in April 1541, to discover what he believed to be the wealthy civilization of Quivira. This supposed land of gold, actually the Wichita region of central Kansas, was described in glowing detail by his chief guide, a man called "Turk" by the Spaniards (Riley 1971: 304–306). Turk was probably a Pawnee Indian and his traveling companion, Isopete, was most likely a Wichita Indian (see Riley 1995: 169, 196). On this expedition, shortly after entering the Plains, the Spaniards encountered two major groups of Native Americans in what is now extreme eastern New Mexico and the Texas Panhandle. Both of these peoples were nomadic, hunting the bison and other animals. Both lived, at least part of the time, in tents and used the dog travois. The first of these major groups the Spaniards gave the name Querecho; the second, more easterly and southerly, they called the Teya. The Querecho lived in the drainage of the Canadian River and extended into the upper part of the Llano Estacado while the Teya were mainly in the central and southern regions of the Llano Estacado. If their later identification with the Jumano is correct, they also extended to the east and south in the valley of the Pecos River and in the Rio Grande drainage along Toyah Creek and at La Junta de los Rios, the junction of the Rio Grande and the Conchos Rivers

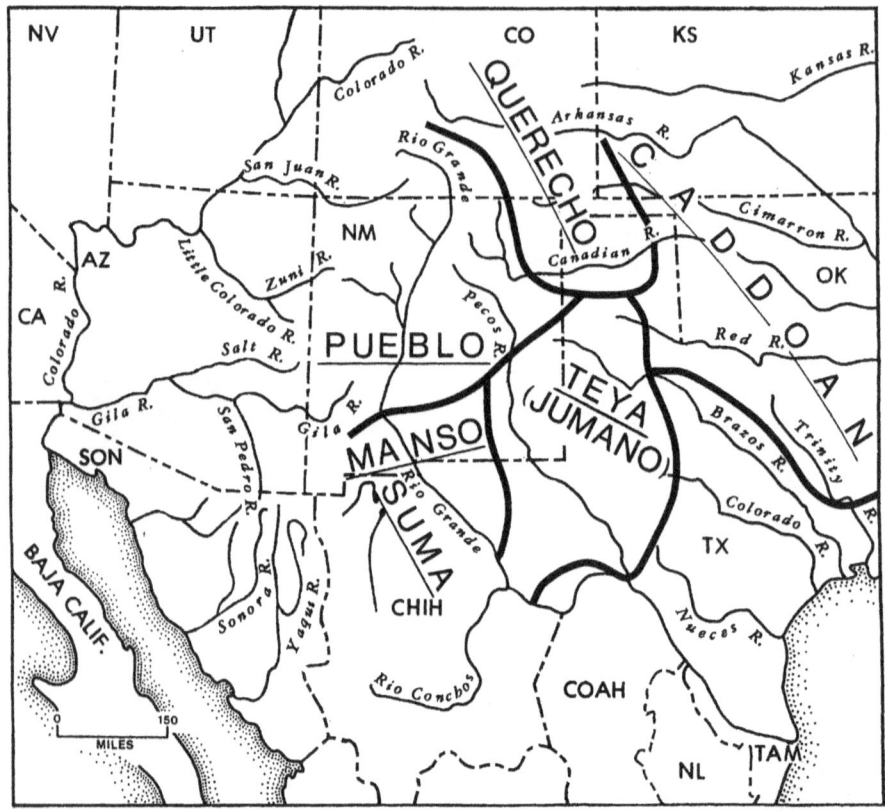

Map 17. Peoples of the Southwest and High Plains, 1540.

(Map 17). The identity of the Querecho has never been in any real doubt as the groups continued into later historical times. They were, clearly, Apachean speakers, ancestors of modern Apache and Navajo Indians. The name, itself, according to Frederick Hodge (Hodge, Hammond, and Rey 1945: 303), was from Tágukerésh, a Pecos Pueblo generic term for Apache. In 1582 an expedition led by Antonio de Espejo contacted these Indians, spelling their name "Cuerecho," as far west as the Hopi and Acoma areas of Arizona and New Mexico (Hammond and Rey 1966: 182, 189, 200–201). About a year earlier the expedition of Francisco Sánchez Chamuscado ran across Querechos in the Canadian River drainage of New Mexico and Texas (Hammond and Rey 1966: 89), roughly where Coronado had found them forty years before. Hernán Gallegos, chronicler for the Rodríguez/ Chamuscado expedition of 1581–1582, mentions nomadic settlements in this area without naming the group, but the account of Baltasar de Obregón, who interviewed one or more members of the Rodríguez/Chamuscado party, uses the term "vaqueros" (Cuevas 1924: 271).

The outlaw Leyva de Bonilla and Gutiérrez Humaña expedition, which began in 1593, was wiped out on the Plains with only one survivor, a servant of Humaña named Jusepe. The latter man was captured by the Vaquero Indians but escaped to the Pueblo area (Hammond and Rey 1966: 323). Juan de Oñate, colonizer of New Mexico, who interviewed Jusepe at San Juan Bautista (San Juan Pueblo) in February 1599, says that Jusepe had lived for a year as captive to the "Apache and Vaquero Indians" (Hammond and Rey 1953: I: 417). If these were actually Jusepe's words, it would seem that he first heard the term "Apache" several years before Oñate's arrival in New Mexico. Oñate, himself, had utilized the term a few months earlier—in September 1598 at San Juan Bautista (Hammond and Rey 1953: I: 345).

The origin of the term "Apache" is still much disputed. Morris Opler (1983a: 385) believes that it was from the Zuni word "apachu," the plural form of the Zuni word for Navajo. However, Albert H. Schroeder (1983: 163–164) suggested that "Apache" may have derived from one of the Rio Grande pueblos, since at the time Oñate first used the term he had not encountered any Zuni Indians. This situation would also be true of Jusepe whose travels in the mid-1590s had, as far as we know, not reached west of the Rio Grande Valley.

In 1598, Juan de Oñate used the word "Apache" for the area reaching "from the Sierra Nevada toward the north and east, and the province of Taos, with its neighboring pueblos and those that border upon it and those of that cordillera on the bank of the Rio del Norte" (Hammond and Rey 1953: I: 345). The Sierra Nevada refers to the Sangre de Cristo Mountains and the other cordillera mentioned is probably the Jemez range.

By the early seventeenth century, bands of Querechos had also moved into the Chama River Valley and they continued to spread south and west into New Mexico and Arizona. By the 1620s they were also found in the mountainous regions of southern New Mexico. Fray Alonso de Benavides, who worked in the New Mexico missions during that period, was able to identify various subgroups of the Apache. Benavides located the Apache de Perrillo (most likely the Mescalero) in the mountains of southeastern New Mexico; the Gila Apaches (Chiricahua and Western Apaches) in central and southwestern New Mexico; the Navajo Apache (Navajo) in northern New Mexico; and the "Quinia" and Vaquero Apache (Jicarilla) in extreme northeast New Mexico. (Forrestal and Lynch 1954: 41–44, 52–53; see also Basso 1983: 465; Gunnerson 1974: 79–81; Opler 1983b: 402; Opler 1983c: 420; Tiller 1983: 440–444.)

After leaving Querecho country Vázquez de Coronado and his men, in the spring of 1541, had a number of contacts with the Teya Indians. As already pointed out, these people appear as a nomadic group, living near to but somewhat to the south and east of the Querechos. We have several descriptions of the Teyas from various members of the Coronado party. Coronado, himself, in a letter to King Carlos dated October 20, 1541, says of the Teya:

> While we were hunting aimlessly over these plains [the Llano Estacado], some mounted men who went out hunting the cattle met some Indians who were also out hunting and who are enemies of [the Querechos] I met at the previous rancheria. They belong to another nation of people called the Teyas. They paint their bodies and faces and are large people of very fine appearance. They, too, eat raw meat like the Querechos. They live like them and follow the cattle (Hammond and Rey 1940: 186–87).

The chronicler Pedro de Castañeda mentioned how the Teyas "traveled with their packs of dogs, their women and children" (Hammond and Rey 1940: 239). In the barranca country (the eastern edge of the Llano Estacado) where the Teya Indians had their rancherías, Castañeda mentioned that

> we saw a Teya shoot an arrow through both shoulders of a bull. . . . These natives are intelligent people. The women are well treated, and through modesty they cover their whole body. They wear shoes and buskins of dressed skins. The women wear blankets over their short underskirts, all of skins, with sleeves tied at the shoulders. They wear a sort of short tunic over their underskirts, with small fringes reaching to the middle of the thighs (ibid.).

The anonymous *Relación del Suceso* from the Coronado expedition has some useful comments on the Teya:

> In these plains, among the cattle, two types of people are found; one group was called Querechos and the other Teyas. They are well built, and are painted; they are enemies of each other. They have no settlement or occupation other than to follow the cattle, of which they kill as many as they want. They tan the skins, with which they clothe themselves and build their tents. They eat the meat of the cattle, sometimes raw, and they also drink the blood when thirsty. Their tents are in the shape of pavilions. They set them up by means of poles which they carry for the purpose. After driving them in the ground they tie them together at the top. When they move from place to place they carry them by means of dogs, of which they have many. They load the dogs with their tents, poles, and other things. They make use of them, as I said, because the land is very level. The dogs drag the poles. What these people worship most is the sun. The hides of their tents are dressed on both sides, free from hair. The cattle and deer skins that they do not need, and the meat dried in the sun, they trade for maize and blankets to the natives at the river (Hammond and Rey 1940: 292–293).

Castañeda adds a little more information on dogs as beasts of burden (Hammond and Rey 1940: 262). "They go about like nomads with their tents and with packs of dogs harnessed with little pads, packsaddles, and girths. When the dogs' loads slip to the side they howl for some one to come and straighten them."

Another Coronado document, the *Relación Postrera de Cíbola*, perhaps written in Mexico after the expedition returned (conceivably by the famous Franciscan missionary, Motolinía), has an even more detailed account of the nomadic peoples of the region. This account does not use either the term "Querecho" or "Teya." Like the *Relación del Suceso* it is probably combining the descriptions of the two groups, though from the narrative it seems that primarily the Teya are being described. The *Relación Postrera* speaks of a large ranchería (200 houses) in which the Indians "sustain themselves entirely from the cattle, for they neither grow nor harvest maize"; (Hammond and Rey 1940: 310). The people lived mainly on bison products, making their houses from the skins, using the bladders for containers and the dung for fuel. Bison meat was eaten half roasted or raw and the blood was drunk "just as it comes out of the cattle. Sometimes they drink it later, raw and cold. They have no other food. . . . In addition to what they carry on their backs, they carry the poles for the tents, dragging them fastened to their saddles. The load may be from thirty-five to fifty pounds, depending on the dog" (Hammond and Rey 1940: 311).

There is also information on the groups between Pecos and Quivira in Francisco López de Gómara's *Historia general de las Indias*, published only a few years after Coronado's return. His account is very general and probably takes in both Querechos and Teya. According to López de Gómara (1922: II: 237–238) the nomadic Indians did not use bread, their diet being mostly meat which was often eaten raw because of lack of firewood. When cooked it had to be roasted since the Indians had no pottery. The blood was drunk warm or cold, mixed with water. The Indians used large dogs, fitted with packs, each animal being able to carry fifty pounds.

Although the information given by the Coronado party on dog transport concentrates on the pack arrangements, what we almost certainly have here is the ingenious travois, reported by later visitors to the plains. This consisted of two tent poles strapped to either side of a dog's body with transverse strips of wood fastened across the trailing poles. These formed a platform on which could be placed food or equipment, making the dog a beast of burden. The dog travois was eventually replaced by the more effective horse travois but continued to be occasionally used in the Plains as late as the nineteenth century.

Unlike the clearly Apachean Querecho, the linguistic affiliation of the Teya has been the focus of a great deal of argument. Perhaps the first scholar to consider the

Teya in detail was Adolph F. Bandelier, who undertook a combined archeological and historical survey of the Southwest for the Archaeological Institute of America, beginning in 1880. Bandelier (1890–1892: I: 179–180) quickly identified the Querechos as Apache but he was not clear as to the linguistic and ethnic origin of the Teya. He did consider them a distinct group, though he pointed out that nothing was really known about their language (Bandelier 1890–1892: I: 168). Bandelier (Bandelier 1890–1892: I: 167 n1) was perhaps the first scholar to suggest that the Teya might be identical with the Jumano, Indians who make their first appearance under that name in Spanish documents of the early 1580s. A survey of Jumano was made by the geographer Carl O. Sauer (1934: 65–76). Sauer believed the Jumano, to be related to the Suma, both groups probably belonging to the Uto-Aztecan family. France V. Scholes and Harry P. Mera (1940: 289) agreed with this evaluation at least for the southern Jumano though they suggested that Jumano may have been a general name for *rayados* (painted or tattooed) Indians (Scholes and Mera 1940: 275). In a later publication Scholes expressed his belief that Jumano of eastern New Mexico were Tompiro-speaking (Hodge, Hammond, and Rey 1945: 315). Neither Sauer nor Scholes and Mera dealt with the Teya as such.

An association of Teya with Apache came in 1940 when the linguist John P. Harrington stated that

> I must mention the Querecho Lipanans and the Teya Lipanans both because they are mentioned by Castañeda and because Teya has been wrongly thought to have something to do with the name of the State of Texas. The Coronado expedition encountered these two tribes on the plains east of the Rio Grande. Castañeda said ... "These people are called Querechos and Teyas." My discovery that Teya is the Pecos-Jemez word for eastern Apache, that is, Lipanan, proves that at least the Teya band mentioned by Castañeda was Lipanan and makes it probable the Querecho band was also Lipanan (1940: 512).

The word that Harrington identified with Teya was Togokyala, "eastern Navajo" or "eastern Athapascan," which sometimes was abbreviated to Togo or its plural form, Togosh (1916: 573; see also Gunnerson 1974: 19). The equation Teya=Togokyala or Togo(sh) seems a weak phonological fit and certainly a slim basis on which to rest a linguistic affiliation. A few scholars still tentatively accept the Harrington equation of Teya with Lipan Apache (see, for example, Gunnerson 1974: 20), but for the most part there is a tendency to see these people as non-Apachean.

A suggestion that the Teya were Caddoan-speaking came from George Hammond and Agapito Rey (1940: 239 n2). More recently, Albert H. Schroeder (n.d.; 1962: 8) has made the same identification. In fact, Schroeder (1983: 159) suggested that the term "Teya" was a Caddoan word meaning "allies." Timothy G. Baugh (1982:

206–208; see also 1984: 157, 162) not only equates the Teya with Caddoan but, following Sauer (1971: 145), suggests that the group had a marginal agriculture based on beans. In this chapter, I argue that Teya spoke a language related to Piro, the southernmost Puebloan language.

It might be a good idea to stop here and consider the three late prehistoric and early historic cultural complexes in this region that seem to be central to the problem of the Teya. The Tierra Blanca Complex was defined by Jack Hughes in the 1980s (Hughes 1991: 34–35) and is named after the Tierra Blanca Site in Deaf Smith County, Texas, in the western Panhandle, southwest of Amarillo (ibid.). It is a culture of hunter-gatherers, dating, perhaps, to the period 1400–1650 (Habicht-Mauche 1987: 176). The Tierra Blanca Complex certainly had some kind of relationship with both the Garza and the Wheeler Complexes, most likely something of the raid and/or trade variety. Tierra Blanca and Garza shared a type of ceramics generally known as Tierra Blanca Plain. This is a thin, dark, plain utility ware of coil construction and with mica inclusions that seems to be basically southwestern in origin and may represent a local copy of northern Rio Grande plainwares (Habicht-Mauche 1987: 183–188; Baugh and Eddy 1987: 797). Alternatively, it might be tradeware from the eastern edge of the Southwest. Pottery traded from the Rio Grande region begins with Glaze C, mid-fifteenth century in date, and continues well into historic times (Spielmann 1983: 264). The toolkit of Tierra Blanca peoples included, in Hughes's words (1991: 35), "triangular side-and-base-notched Harrell, side-notched Washita, and unnotched Fresno and Talco-like arrow points."

The Tierra Blanca people were bison hunters who traded with the eastern Pueblos (Habicht-Mauche 1987: 185; see also Spielmann 1982). They received relatively small amounts of turquoise and obsidian from the Pueblo area in what Katherine Spielmann (1983: 268) believed was a sort of gift exchange relationship. Ceramics, on the other hand, may have been part of a more commercialized trade relationship (ibid.) and this was perhaps also true of a trade in maize. In return, the Tierra Blanca people traded to the Pueblos bison products, freshwater shell, and Alibates dolomite (Spielmann 1983: 259, 261). In all probability the Tierra Blanca groups controlled the Alibates quarries north of modern Amarillo.

The Tierra Blanca groups seem to have lived part of the year in some sort of tipi as suggested by the Coronado expedition, but they also utilized jacal-like structures on stone foundations (Hughes 1991: 35). Whether they were agricultural is uncertain. Relations of Tierra Blanca with the Garza people and the Wheeler Complex people still need finer definition (Hofman 1989: 99). Hughes (1991: 35) has suggested that the Tierra Blanca peoples were the Querechos of Coronado and, indeed, there seems to be considerable agreement on this point. In other words they appear to be the archeological manifestation of the protohistoric eastern

Apaches. There are cautionary notes, however. A recent publication by Douglas K. Boyd and his associates (1993: 268) says of Tierra Blanca:

> It should be noted that some of the sites do exhibit a great deal of consistency in the material culture assemblage, but so few have been adequately investigated and reported that it is difficult to be certain of this. While it probably is a valid complex, many of the traits listed for Tierra Blanca . . . are so general as to be virtually indistinguishable from those of its southerly cousin, the Garza Complex. The Tierra Blanca Complex may prove to be an Apachean manifestation, but at present this interpretation can only be supported by circumstantial ethnographic evidence, and the archaeological evidence (including the ceramics) have not yet been proved to be technically distinctive.

The Wheeler Phase[1] represents a protohistoric occupation in the counties of southwestern Oklahoma. As described by Jack Hofman (1984) and Timothy Baugh (1986), sites include Edwards I in Beckham County, Taylor in Greer County, Goodwin Baker in Roger Mills County, Duncan in Washita County, and Little Deer in Custer County.

One might expect that one ancestor of the Wheeler Phase people was the agricultural and village-dwelling Antelope Creek people who were spread through the upper Canadian drainage in the Texas Panhandle, eventually disappearing sometime around A.D. 1500 (Lintz 1984: 340) about the inception time of the Wheeler Phase. However, relationships between the two groups are not particularly strong, mainly consisting of a shared emphasis on Alibates agatized dolomite as raw material for a variety of stone tools.

The Wheeler Phase people seem to have been seminomadic with little in the way of structures. Two wattle-and-daub structures were reported for the Goodwin-Baker Site (Baugh 1986: 173–174) and what may possibly be defensive earthworks (circular ditch enclosures) have been found at the Edwards I and Duncan Sites (Hofman 1984: 349). These people seem to have been bison hunters and traders. Trade with the Southwest included ceramic glazewares and Hopi Jeddito pottery, plus a considerable amount of Caddoan pottery from northeast Texas (Baugh 1986: 169). Tierra Blanca Plain sherds have been found in Wheeler Phase sites (Habicht-Mauche 1991: 66–67). There was also obsidian, probably from the Jemez region, and large amounts (about 70 percent of the total stonework) of Alibates and Tecovas chert from the Panhandle region of Texas (Hofman 1984: 356). There was also locally made gray pottery with sand temper sometimes with micaceous inclusions, the most common type being Edwards Plain (Hofman 1984: 352; 1989: 97; Baugh 1986: 171).

There is no clear evidence for agriculture in Wheeler Phase sites, though manos and a bison-scapula hoe were found at the Edwards I Site (Baugh, Baugh, and

Hofman 1982: 173, 177). The lithic assemblages include triangular Fresno points (70 percent of the total) but also include Washita and Harrell points. The triangular Garza point with its basal notch occurs in considerable numbers (Hofman 1984: 352; Baugh 1986: 172-173).

The ethnic identification of the Wheeler Phase people is still somewhat obscure. Baugh (1982: 209) suggests that the Wheeler Phase groups were Caddoan-speaking and a branch of the Teya-Jumano. Leaving out consideration of the Teya for the moment, Caddoan speech seems a logical possibility for the Wheeler Phase. At any rate, these people seem to be a bit out of the Querecho-Apache orbit, at least in the earlier period of their existence.

The Garza Complex was first defined by Hughes (Baugh 1986: 181; see also Hughes 1991). Garza materials seem to have first been noted by William C. Holden (1938), though not by that name. Beginning in the 1960s a number of Garza sites were investigated. These include the Country Club and Montgomery Sites in Floyd County (Word 1963, 1965; Northern 1979); the Bridwell, Grape Creek, and Pete Creek Sites in Crosby County (Parsons 1967; Parker 1982); the Garza Site in Garza County (Runkles 1964); the Lubbock Lake Site in Lubbock County (Johnson et al. 1977), all in Texas; and perhaps the Garnsey campsite in Chaves County, southeastern New Mexico (Parry and Speth 1984).

If I read him correctly, Baugh (1986: 181-182) cautiously relates the Wheeler Phase and Garza Culture. Judith Habicht-Mauche (1992: 256-257) is more specific. She associates the Teya with the Garza Culture and considers the Garza Culture to be a western extension of the Caddoan Wheeler Phase, while the related Tierra Blanca Complex, to the west and north, represented the Querechos. However, Plains archeologist Jack L. Hofman (1989: 99) warns that "the relationships [among] the Tierra Blanca complex, the Garza complex and the Edwards and Wheeler complexes have yet to be well defined."

The Garza people were primarily bison hunters, probably with a marginal agriculture, at least a bison-scapula hoe and bison-tibia digging stick tip were found at the Montgomery Site (Baugh 1986: 180). Metate and mano fragments have been recovered from the same site (Northern 1979: 50-51). There was a considerable trade in Pueblo pottery, especially Glaze-polychrome. Locally made pottery included Tierra Blanca Plain. From 1 percent to 7 percent of the lithics found on individual Garza sites are obsidian, presumably from the Jemez region. Occupation of Garza sites is generally from mid-fifteenth to early eighteenth century in date (Habicht-Mauche 1987: 177).

The basally notched Garza point is common on the sites but a number of other points including Fresno, Harrell, Lott, and Perdiz have been found (Northern 1979: 117). The latter type is interesting for it has a more southerly distribution and is indicative of the Cielo Complex (dated at about A.D. 1330–1690) in southern Texas and northern Chihuahua (Cloud et al. 1994: 126). The Garza Complex also contains turquoise and Pacific shell, traded in small quantities from the Pueblo area.

Generally speaking, the Garza Complex represents relatively sizable populations of bison hunters and probable agriculturalists living in the Blanco, Yellow House, and nearby canyons of the eastern Llano Estacado. The archeological descriptions dovetail convincingly with documentary information on the Teya of Coronado, and it seems reasonably clear that the archeological Garza and the historical Teya can be equated. Some archeologists remain skeptical (see, for example, Boyd et al. 1993: 270). However, the discovery of a Teya-associated Coronado expedition campsite in Blanco Canyon, the very heartland of the Garza Complex, is suggestive to say the least (see Chapter 23).

If the Teya are rooted in the Garza Complex, what happened to the group as the sixteenth century wore on? During the period 1581–1583, Spanish expeditions in the region where the Rio Conchos and Rio Grande join (La Junta de los Ríos) and along the Pecos River to the north began to describe nomadic Indians whom they called Jumano. We have already seen that Bandelier suggested the possibility that the Teya and Jumano were identical. Baugh (1982: 209) also believes that at least some of the Jumano were actually Teya. One of the hallmarks of the Jumano was the fact that they were tattooed or painted (rayados or *labrados*) and the Teya also practiced body painting (Hammond and Rey 1940: 186, 238).

As is the case with the Teya, a few scholars have suggested that the Jumano were Apachean-speaking. Jack Forbes (1959: 128–139, 144) makes this identification. In fact, Forbes (1957: 326–327, 333–334) considered the Suma, Janos, Jocome, Manso, and at least the Texas Jumano to be Apachean. J. Charles Kelley (1986: 143) considered the Jumano as Apachean-speaking. In addition, Kelley (1952: 277–278) tentatively associated Apacheans and the Jumano with the archeological Toyah Focus, an early historic West Texas manifestation. More recently, however, Kelley (1955: 982) has speculated that the Jumano merged with the Apache only in historic times.

I originally concurred in the Jumano/Apache equation (Riley 1987: 296) but have had second thoughts. For one thing, from the ethnohistorical evidence it seems likely that Jumano, Suma, and Manso spoke somewhat similar languages. Thomas Naylor (1981: 275–281) analyzed a group of Suma names of rebels executed at Casas Grandes in 1685 and argued cogently on the basis of those names that the Suma were Uto-Aztecan speakers. Because of similar lifestyle and overlapping territories, Naylor considered the Suma to be closely related linguistically to the Jumano and believed that both groups originated in the Bolsón de Mapimí region, spreading northward in late prehistoric times (1981: 278–279).

One reason why there has been the Jumano (and Suma, Manso, etc.) identification as Apacheans is that beginning in the late seventeenth century and continuing through the eighteenth, there was an "Athapaskanization" of these groups (Naylor 1981: 276: Griffen 1983: 330, 341; Kelley 1955: 982).

The linguist Nancy P. Hickerson (1994: 221) believes that the Jumano were part of the Tanoan family:

> I have argued that Jumanos spoke a Tanoan language and were probably affiliated with the Tiwa subfamily. Manso and Suma are, like Jumano, long extinct, and their languages are unrecorded; however, it now appears that they were part of the same grouping. With these inclusions, the Tanoan bloc inhabited much of New Mexico, the valley of the Rio del Norte [Rio Grande] at least as far south as La Junta, and the deserts of northern Chihuahua as far west as Casas Grandes. In addition, the territories occupied by the Jumano bloc extended east of the Rio del Norte and the Pecos to include the Llano Estacado and the upper valley of the Rio Colorado of Texas.

More specifically, Hickerson (1990: 12) considers that Jumano speech, along with Suma and Manso, was related to and perhaps identical with Piro. The Piro language was spoken along the Rio Grande from north of Socorro to the Elephant Butte region. Another cluster of speakers of a closely related dialect called Tompiro lived in the Salinas region across the Manzano Mountains to the east. Evidence for Piro/Tompiro is rather scanty. There are only a few sources for the Piro language, the largest being a vocabulary of 177 words collected by John Russell Bartlett in 1850 (see Bartlett 1909). In addition, there is a Piro version of the Lord's Prayer (origin unknown but perhaps dating from the seventeenth century) of sixty words. A scatter of other words, including place names, was collected by Bandelier in the 1880s and James Mooney in 1897.

John Harrington (1909) has compared Bartlett's word list with Southern Tiwa of Isleta del Sur in Texas and of Isleta Pueblo in New Mexico, the Northern Tiwa of Taos, the Towa of Jemez, and the Tewa of San Ildefonso. The accuracy of Bartlett's transcription has been questioned and, indeed, a few of the words on the list are transparently Spanish. The Amerind words fall into three categories. Some seem to relate more specifically to Tiwa than to the other Tanoan languages, or at least to the Tiwa of Isleta del Sur. A second group seems to be generically Tanoan, while a third group may be non-Tanoan. For reasons that are not overly clear, Harrington came to the conclusion that Piro was a dialect of Tiwa. He may have based this conclusion not on the purely linguistic evidence but on a statement by an Isleta del Sur informant that Piro and Tiwa were "pretty much the same language" (1909: 569).

Adolph Bandelier, who visited Isleta del Sur twenty-six years before Harrington's trip, was keenly interested in the Piro (Lange and Riley 1970: 156–166). Bandelier produced some anecdotal evidence suggesting that the Mansos and Piro had a common tongue (Lange and Riley 1970: 160), but not the Piro and Tiwa. Summarizing the various data in Volume II of his *Final Report* (Bandelier 1890–1892: II: 218–219), the Swiss American scholar reported that Piro was perhaps related to the Tanoan languages but that Piro and Tiwa were not mutually intelligible.

A student of Tiwa languages, William L. Leap (1971: 324), suggested that Piro may not be a Tanoan language at all, basing his argument in part on striking dissimilarities between the phonemic systems of Piro and Tanoan. In this case, Leap believes that the similarities between Piro and Tiwa could have been the result of extensive borrowing, perhaps in the post–Pueblo Revolt period (1971: 328–329).

Both George Trager (1967) and Irvine Davis (1979) have argued that Piro is a Tanoan language. Davis (1979: 403) believes that it is a separate Tanoan tongue, but most closely related to Tiwa. As seen earlier, Hickerson also takes this view (1988: 318–320).

As near as we can tell, the Spaniards considered Piro and Tiwa separate languages. The Spaniards, both missionaries and civil authorities, were in close contact with both groups during the latter sixteenth and much of the seventeenth centuries. The Spaniards noted the interesting fact that the spatially separated Pecos and the Jemez pueblos spoke the same language. Surely they would have mentioned the same for Tiwa and Piro if it were, indeed, true. (For a concurring opinion see Schroeder 1964.)

What I suggest is that Piro-Tompiro, Manso, Suma, and Jumano, at least in the mid-1500s, had very similar languages and were perhaps dialects of the same tongue. In this I agree with Hickerson. I do not think this language was Tiwa, though it does seem most likely that the languages or dialects were Tanoan and, quite possibly, closely related to Tiwa. I might stress that the important point in reconstructing the situation in the early historic southern Plains is that the Jumano, Piro-Tompiro, Manso, and Suma spoke cognate languages, and not the specific affiliation (whether or not Tanoan) of these languages. Not everybody agrees with this linguistic grouping. Patrick Beckett and Terry Corbett (1992: 36–37) believe that Suma and Manso spoke distinct languages and that the Manso tongue probably belongs to the Taracahitan language family.

If the Teya of 1541 became the Jumano of the 1580s and later decades, as numerous people have suggested (for example, Baugh 1982: 209; Habicht-Mauche 1992: 255; Hickerson 1990: 5; 1994: 228; Riley 1995: 191–193; Wilcox 1984: 141, among others), it follows that if the Jumano spoke a language similar to Piro, this was true of the Teya as well. In addition, if Teya and Jumano are identical, their territories as described by various Spanish parties would be much the same unless (as seems most unlikely) there was a drastic shift in Teya-Jumano territory between 1541 and 1582.

It would also be useful to clearly identify where the Teya were actually contacted by the Coronado expedition. This, in turn, involves the identification of Coronado's route to the Great Plains in 1541. Coronado's route has been the object of considerable controversy over the past century or so. In 1991 a survey of various suggested routes was made under direction of the National Park Service (Ivey, Rhodes, and Sánchez 1991). That range of routes shows Coronado in the Llano Estacado, to the north of it, and to the south of it.

For a number of years an identification made by the historian Herbert E. Bolton was widely accepted by the general public, if not necessarily by scholars. Bolton, who traced the Coronado route from central Mexico to the High Plains, believed that Coronado traveled from Pecos Pueblo in late April of 1541 (Julian calendar), down the Pecos River to about modern Santa Rosa, and then eastward to the northern Llano Estacado. Coronado reached a barranca, considered by Bolton to be Tule Canyon, which drains eastward to the Red River. Coronado then went north to what the chronicler Castañeda described as a "barranca grande" (large gorge) and this, Bolton believed, was Palo Duro Canyon, again in the headwaters of the Red River.

About June 1, 1541, Coronado decided to push on with a small party to Quivira. Taking about forty men, mostly mounted, Turk now a prisoner, the general moved off in a roughly northward direction toward Quivira.[2] The main party, after resting and collecting supplies, was to return to the Tiguex base on the Rio Grande. Bolton, plotting Coronado's trip to the central plains, made the ingenious suggestion that the little Spanish party went north "by the compass." Because of an east declination in this region of ten to twelve degrees, he was led to the Great Bend region of Kansas where lay Quivira (1949: 281, 285–287).

It is true that Coronado had what was described as a sea compass on the expedition (Hammond and Rey 1940: 236). The declination issue has its own problems; but in any case, I do not think that Coronado simply headed off into the unknown following the compass. Coronado's trips to and through the Southwest seem to have always involved guides. Certainly on the Quivira leg of his expedition he utilized Teya guides. In fact, his original group ran away after the first day or so of travel and the general sent back for additional guides. These were supplied by Teya at the great barranca, near whom the main army was encamped. According to Castañeda, the Indians supplied these guides voluntarily (Hammond and Rey 1940: 240). One would expect the guides to follow known trade routes, and I have previously argued that these routes would lead through the region of the Wheeler Phase sites in western Oklahoma (Riley 1992: 154). As discussed above, some scholars have pointed out the close relationship between the Garza and Wheeler Phase, and a very good case can be made for the equation Garza=Teya, so that Teya guides might be expected to follow trade routes that ran through Wheeler Phase sites.

Let me stress that the standard routing of Coronado up through the Texas Panhandle makes no sense. This was enemy, Querecho, country. The guides would be expected to avoid the Querechos, and in any case they would likely have very little knowledge of that particular stretch of country.

Since Bolton's time there has been considerable reevaluation of the Coronado route. Everyone agrees that the starting point was the Pueblo of Pecos, and most scholars believe that the river involved in the move into the Plains, and over which the party found it necessary to build a bridge, was the Pecos River.[3] Richard and Shirley Flint (Chapter 17) have made a persuasive argument that Coronado's route was southward from Pecos Pueblo onto Rowe Mesa somewhere near the modern town of Rowe. From there the large party reached the Cañon Blanco and followed it eastward to the Pecos. At some point, perhaps just below the junction of the Pecos and its main upper tributary, the Gallinas, Coronado and his party built a bridge.

Eastward from the Pecos River Coronado, with his large expedition comprising perhaps 1,700 or more human beings (Riley 1995: 183), and all the livestock brought from Mexico the previous year, worked their way onto the Llano Estacado. The distances given by various chroniclers suggest that they struck off somewhat farther south than allowed by Bolton. The barrancas under question may have been the Yellow House that runs near modern Lubbock, Texas, and/or the Blanco, the next major canyon to the north.

Another approach to the location of the great barranca is to consider the natural features. Castañeda described the first barranca as large "like those of Colima." The second great barranca was presumably even larger; in fact, according to Castañeda (Hammond and Rey 1940: 259), a league from bank to bank. It had a small river running through the bottom. Unfortunately, this description could fit either the Yellow House/Blanco barrancas or the Tule/Palo Duro barrancas.

At any rate, the region of Teya occupation between the barrancas was called Cona, with rancherías spread out over a three-day march. From Cona, the expedition entered the last barranca, a league wide, which contained (Castañeda 1596: 83v–84r, see also Winship 1896: 144) "*un pequeño rio en lo bajo y un llano lleno de arboleda con mucha uba morales y rrosales [Winship's transcription says rosales] que es fruta que la ay en frãçia y sirue de agraz en esta barranca la auiã madura abia nueses y galinas de la calidad de las de nueba españa y siruelas como las de castilla.*"

It is interesting to see what the two major translations of Castañeda make of this. Winship (1896: 237) says: "a little bit of a river at the bottom, and there were many groves of mulberry trees near it, and rosebushes with the same sort of fruit that they have in France. They made verjuice from the unripe grapes at this ravine, although there were ripe ones. There were walnuts and the same kind of fowl as in New Spain."

Hammond and Rey (1940: 239) have Castañeda reporting the following: "A small river flowed at the bottom, and there was a small valley covered with trees, and with plenty of grapes, mulberries, and rose bushes. This is a fruit found in France and which is used to make verjuice. In this barranca we found it ripe. There were nuts and also chickens of the variety found in New Spain and quantities of plums like those of Castile."

One point of interest is the "agraz" or verjuice. Hammond and Rey seem to be saying that rose hips were used in this product while Winship suggests grapes, interpolating the word "unripe," which does not appear in the original. Bolton (1949: 266) believed that it was mulberries that were used in making verjuice though it is hard to read this into Castañeda's statement. Donald Blakeslee (Chapter 19) has made the following very pertinent comments about this passage. On the grounds that Castañeda would hardly need to describe grapes to a Spanish audience, Blakeslee suggests that the "agraz" or verjuice of Castañeda was gooseberry, which was, in fact, used in sixteenth-century France for making a sour sauce. The plant may not have been present or common in Spain at that date. If this were the case, Castañeda intended to write "grosellas" (gooseberries) instead of "rosales" (rosebushes). According to Blakeslee there are, in fact, a number of wild gooseberries (*Ribes* sp.) in the area and they ripen in May to early June. The geographer John M. Morris (1997: 100), who has made a botanical study of this area, suggests that the rosales might have been *Ribes odoratum* or buffalo currant.

The word "nuts" (nueces) of the original Castañeda document was translated as "walnuts" by Winship. Blakeslee suggests that these could have been the wild walnut, pecan, or even acorns of the shinnery oak, all found in the general region.

The botanical information from the Coronado expedition fits well with the eastern edge of the Llano Estacado but, unfortunately, does not give us a very good north-south fix, although if the nueces of Castañeda were pecans, it might suggest the Blanco or Yellow House regions rather than Palo Duro.

There have been metallurgical finds, a number by a field researcher, Jimmy Owens, using a metal detector, in the upper part of the Blanco Canyon, including a number of copper crossbow boltheads (and one of iron), a chain mail gauntlet, horseshoes, and horseshoe and carpenter nails (see Chapter 23). These finds do tend to strengthen the case for a Spanish presence in Blanco Canyon in the mid-sixteenth century based on the increasing obsolescence of crossbows (Chapter 3). Flint (1994) thinks that Blanco Canyon may have been Coronado's first barranca and that the great barranca was farther north, Quitaque Canyon, Tule Canyon, or even Palo Duro Canyon.

The relation of the first and great barranca rests on the extent and location of the province of Cona. Because of the disputed meaning, I shall give the Castañeda text (1596: 83r–83v; also consult Winship 1896: 144):

> ... *desde alli embio el general a descubrir y dieron en otras rancherias a quatro jornadas a manera de alixares era tierra muy poblada adonde auia muchos frisoles y siruelas como las de castilla y parrales duraban estos pueblos de rancherías tres jornadas desiase cona desde aqui salieron con el campo algunas teyas porque asi se deçian aquellas gentes y caminaron con sus harrias de perros y mugeres y hijos hasta la prostera jornada de las otras donde dieron guias para pasar adelante a donde fue el canpo a una barranca grande.*

Translations of this statement, especially of the segment that deals with "alixares," differ considerably. Hammond and Rey (1940: 238–239) render it, "after four days they came to some other rancherias resembling *alixares*." Winship (1896: 237) simply says, "the general sent out to explore the country and they found another settlement four days from there," only referring to alixares in a footnote as perhaps meaning "threshing floors." Morris (1997: 85) thinks that the word "alixares" refers to the four-day journey not to the rancherías. In his opinion, *alijar* means something like barren ground or badlands, so that Castañeda was trying to say that the Spaniards traveled for four days over marginal country to the riches of Cona. Assuming that Morris's arguments for the meaning of alijar are valid, I tend to concur in this reading.

Admittedly, it is somewhat difficult to interpret Castañeda here. One possibility might be that the army, marching northward, took four days to reach the ranchería country and they marched through Cona for another three days. Then they went beyond that for an unspecified period to the great barranca. If Coronado was moving west of the caprock canyons, in a north-northwesterly direction, this length of travel would bring him back into Querecho country. If the expedition traveled slowly, and if the distance beyond Cona was perhaps a day or so, he might reach no farther than upper Palo Duro Canyon. But such a trip would still bring Coronado to Querecho territory if the archeological record of Tierra Blanca sites is any indication. If the barranca grande was in fact Palo Duro, it would place the Teya uncomfortably near their Querecho enemies.

A somewhat simpler explanation has been suggested by Morris, who believes that the Spaniards moved southeast from the Pecos and ascended into the middle section of the Llano Estacado. Then, they drifted in a general northeasterly direction toward modern Plainview. Becoming thoroughly lost in this featureless region,

Coronado sent Captain Diego López with ten men to scout ahead (Hammond and Rey 1940: 236), perhaps on a sunrise bearing, utilizing their sea compass. Following behind, Coronado reached a "small river" that Morris (1997: 59) identifies as Running Water Draw. Reunited with the scout party, the expedition moved on to the northeast. The barranca "like those of Colima" Morris (1997: 62–64) believes probably to be upper Tule Canyon (Morris, of course, had not seen the recent work of Michael Mathes, which increases the possibility that a southern canyon was the Colima-like one). By this time the expedition, eager for nonmeat provisions and for animal forage, turned south to Blanco Canyon where they found the settlement of Cona, an area especially rich in fruits and berries. The settlement of Cona, according to Morris (1997: 87), was in the second great barranca.

On the whole, I am inclined to Morris's interpretation. This would involve Coronado's party marching north to south from Tule or some nearby canyon to Blanco Canyon where lay Cona (which may be a district rather than a single settlement). It is true that the Castañeda text suggests that the canyon was beyond Cona and that the Spaniards came *back* to Teya country from the canyon. Perhaps, Coronado reached Blanco Canyon, where he discovered Cona, then went on, possibly, to Yellow House. Later, the main body of the expedition returned to the Blanco, the barranca grande, for the homeward trip. Or could the expedition simply have gone downstream in Blanco Canyon and retraced its steps?

There are a few suggestive points about the return journey of the main Coronado party after it parted with the smaller, Quivira-bound, group. For one thing, the soldiers saw a number of salt lakes, some supersaturated so that large slabs of salt formed around them (Hammond and Rey 1940: 242). This suggests the central or southern Llano Estacado. In addition, Castañeda (Hammond and Rey 1940: 279) mentions a great heap of cattle (bison) bones on the south side of a salt lake. The Spaniards thought that the bones may have been piled up by waves produced by high north winds and were astonished at their number.

It is not entirely clear if this bone bed was found by the main party on the way back to Tiguex, though the mention of a salt lake suggests it. In any case, only one site that could plausibly fit Castañeda's description has been reported. There is a bone bed on the south side of Silver Lake in the Yellow House drainage, some forty miles west-northwest of Lubbock. This lake extends for some .7 mile in an east-west direction and is .25 to .33 mile in width. When I visited Silver Lake several years ago, it was virtually dry. That particular season, however, was one of very little rainfall; when I visited again in 1996 after a week of heavy rains, there was a considerable extent of brackish water.

The bone bed stretches for some 180 yards and extends from the lakeshore along a steep slope to a terrace fifteen or twenty feet above the lake. Bones—

presumably bison, certainly large bovines—weather out of the soil at various points along the slope. It seems to represent the accumulation of many years, centuries, or even millennia of bone deposit (Kiser 1978: 333).

Assuming that Coronado's main force was retreating along the line of the Yellow House Draw, it would reach the Pecos River somewhere in the region of Hernandes Creek, between Bosque Grande to the south and Bosque Redondo to the north. According to Castañeda, this was thirty leagues south of the bridge over the Pecos. The Hernandes Creek area is, in fact, roughly thirty leagues (about seventy-five to eighty miles) below the bridge, assuming that the latter was built, as the Flints have argued, somewhere near and south of the Pecos-Gallinas junction.

If this is the case, Blakeslee (Chapter 19) points out that the Yellow House probably was not the great barranca because of a statement in Castañeda about the return trek (Hammond and Rey 1940: 238):

> ... they sought guides to take them over a more direct route. The [Teya] Indians furnished them willingly. ... Their method of guiding was as follows: early in the morning they watched where the sun rose, then, going in the direction they wanted to take they shot an arrow, and before coming to it they shot another over it, and in this manner they traveled the whole day until they reached some water where they were to stop for the night.

Blakeslee notes that this elaborate method of maintaining direction would hardly be necessary if the party was traveling along the Yellow House Canyon. If they wished to intersect the Yellow House from another canyon (perhaps the Blanco) it might be useful (see also Chapter 23).

Castañeda (Hammond and Rey 1940: 242) notes that the return party took twenty-five days, "hunting cattle on their way." Even if much of the evidence is equivocal, it does look as if a return march of the main group somewhere along the Yellow House drainage is far likelier than a more northerly route. For one thing, it stays pretty well within the region of the Garza Culture, which, as we have seen, was in all probability the archeological manifestation of the Teya. And it is the route that would naturally take the Spaniards to about where they claimed to be when they finally reached the Pecos River.

One telling argument comes from a comment of Castañeda (Hammond and Rey 1940: 243) when the main Spanish army was returning up the Pecos River: "the [Teya] guides said that this river joins the Tiguex [Rio Grande] more than twenty days' travel from there [the Fort Sumner area], and that it flows to the east again. It is believed that it empties into the mighty Espiritu Santo which Don Hernando de Soto's men discovered in Florida."

I have pointed out elsewhere (Riley 1995: 193) that:

The Teyas' information about the topography of the Rio Grande and Pecos valleys was strikingly correct, suggesting that they knew the entire Pecos River valley. Four decades later, Espejo, returning from the Rio Grande area to Chihuahua via the Pecos River, was guided by Jumanos. Seven years after Espejo, Castaño de Sosa, coming into the Southwest from northeast Mexico via the Pecos, also obtained information on the Jumanos. It is clear from the Espejo and Castaño accounts that the Jumanos occupied the Pecos throughout its middle and lower drainages, just as the Teyas must have done.

It seems very likely that the equation Garza=Teya=Jumano is the correct one, though that is hardly proven beyond all doubt. In any case, other questions remain. For example, was the Teya/Jumano language Tanoan as Hickerson and I believe; was it Caddoan; or did it belong to a third linguistic family? Were the specific relations of Garza/Teya and the Wheeler Phase peoples linguistic as well as that of trading partners? In addition, a greater refinement of Coronado's route is needed. Hopefully, future archeological work, especially work centered on the southern caprock canyons, will give more definitive answers to the question of Coronado's sojourn in the southern and central Plains. It may even shed light on the greater problems of ethnicity and relationships among the various Plains peoples.

Notes

1. Wheeler Phase, as used by Baugh (1986: 167–168), combines two archeological entities, the Wheeler Complex and the Edwards Complex. Jack Hofman (1984: 348–357; 1989: 99) argues that the two complexes are temporally separate, dating the Edwards Complex at A.D. 1500–1650 and the Wheeler Complex at 1650–1725. According to Hofman, Edwards Complex people utilized Alibates dolomite and traded for considerable amounts of obsidian as well as other southwestern trade goods, especially pottery. Wheeler Complex people primarily used Kay County chert with very little obsidian and Southwestern trade goods but with a certain amount of European trade goods (1984: 357). It is not entirely clear whether he considers the two complexes to represent disparate ethnic groups or simply two different time periods with disparate access to various raw materials.

On the other hand, Baugh (1986: 168) argues that the Wheeler Complex represented a geographical "hinterland" situation with the Wheeler sites farther upriver or on secondary streams while the Edwards Complex sites were on the major streams. Without entering into the terminological argument, what is called the Wheeler Phase in this chapter is identical to Hofman's Edwards Complex.

2. The Spanish party had decided that Turk was misleading them and switched their patronage to Ysopete, the second Plains Indian along. Once the party arrived in the Quivira-Harahey region, Turk was garroted. Jane M. Walsh (1993: 202) argues that the very name "Turk" was pejorative, because of the great enmity of the Spaniards and Turks in their struggle for Mediterranean hegemony. The expression "*el indio llamaron turco porque la pareçia en el aspecto*" used by Castañeda (1596: 51v) is normally translated "an Indian they called 'Turk'

because he looked like one." Walsh suggests that the word *aspecto* actually refers to Turk being an evil creature, as all Turks were evil. However, Turk, who may well have had Plains Indian physical features, tall and with a craggy nose, probably did look "Turkish" to the Spaniards. The initial attitude of the Spaniards to this individual does not seem to have been prejudicial. Walsh suggests that the appellation "Turk" was given him after his death. However, this leaves the question of what he was called before he lost favor with the Coronado group. There is no hint that Coronado's men used any other name than Turk.

Walsh (1993: 40, 202) points out that the term "Isopete" or "Ysopete" is an early modern Spanish rendition of Aesop, the Greek fable maker, and that the name had the connotation of a small ill-favored person who was also a trickster. However, Alexander Lesser and Gene Weltfish (1932: 15) say that Ysopete "seems to be a Wichita word." I wonder if the Spaniards may have heard a somewhat similar Wichita name and twisted it into "Isopete," perhaps because the individual *was* ill-favored. However, from the Spaniards' point of view he definitely was not a trickster.

3. A major exception is Albert H. Schroeder, who argued that the route of Coronado was basically northeastward and the river bridged by the expedition was the Canadian. (See Schroeder 1962, 1992, 1993.) Reasons why this is unlikely are given in Riley (1992: 153). (See also the critiques of Schroeder's paper in Wedel 1970 and Flint and Flint 1991; also the data on the probable Coronado campsite in Blanco Canyon in Chapter 23.)

CHAPTER 21

"Por alli no ay losa ni se hace"
Gilded Men and Glazed Pottery on the Southern Plains

DAVID H. SNOW

Introduction

Somewhere out there on the Llano Estacado lies what may be the mother of all pot breaks, the serendipitous result of a natural disaster, in late April or May of 1541, when a devastating hailstorm struck the Colima-like barranca, or ravine, in Teya country where Vázquez de Coronado's expedition was encamped, creating havoc on the ground. Pedro de Castañeda wrote later that, *"rrompio la piedra muchas tiendas . . . y quebro toda la losa del canpo y calabazos que no puso poca necesidad porque por alli no ay losa ni se hace ni calabazos"* (Castañeda 1596: 82v). In George Hammond and Agapito Rey's rendition this reads: "the hailstones rent many tents . . . and broke all the army's pottery and gourds, causing no little concern, because pottery is not made in that locality, nor are gourds found there" (1940: 238).[1] Discovery of that shattered debris should provide a definitive point of reference for more clearly deciphering the route of Coronado's expedition through the region. Equally important, from my own perspective, is the potential for illuminating some very critical issues involving the Rio Grande Glazeware chronology, and for providing insight into the kinds of ceramic vessels—that is, the forms and current typological classifications—carried by the Spaniards and their Native American allies as necessary equipment into uncharted territories.

In this chapter, I discuss the reliability (or lack thereof) of the Rio Grande Glazeware typology and sequence(s), and problems of using Rio Grande Glaze E as a temporal indicator. According to some, that pottery type figures prominently in efforts to determine the route of Coronado's expedition onto and across the Llano Estacado and the Texas Panhandle (Ivey, Rhodes, and Sánchez 1991). My focus here, then, is twofold, and can be rephrased as follows: what is the current chronological status of the Rio Grande Glazeware sequence prior to the appearance of Glaze F (Mera 1933, 1940; Kidder and Shepard 1936)? Second, what might the ceramic assemblages from early historical Southern Plains archeological sites, with Glaze E, tell us about Coronado's route, and those of subsequent expeditions (Vehik 1986)?

To anticipate, my response to the second question is, very little, for the present. With the exception of the so far unlocated pot break, I suspect that the currently known archeological occurrences of Rio Grande Glaze (and related) pottery types on the Southern Plains, more likely than not, indicate where the expedition was not. I am cautiously optimistic, nevertheless, that negative data also provide valuable insights.

As for the first question, the chronological estimates proffered by Harry Mera (1940) in support of the sequence from Glaze A through Glaze F have been augmented by new tree-ring dates and many of the original specimens have been recalibrated or discarded as undatable (Robinson, Hannah, and Harrill 1972; Robinson, Harrill, and Warren 1973). Consequently, an evaluation of the chronological significance of Glaze pottery types recovered from Southern Plains archeological contexts is in order. A case in point is the effort to date the Edwards Complex in extreme western Oklahoma. Jack Hofman (1984: 353) relies on the original estimates by Alfred Kidder and Anna Shepard (1936) for Glaze E (1600–1700) recovered from the Edwards I Site, which lacks European trade goods; while Timothy Baugh (1982: 187) extrapolates from Mera's estimates for glaze E to suggest a period between 1515 and 1650. The differences are significant for understanding the relationships—certainly, in terms of their chronological framework—between the protohistoric Edwards Complex (Baugh's Assemblage C, at Edwards I, especially) and the later Wheeler Complex.

The Glazeware Sequence

To the uninitiated, the Rio Grande Glazeware sequence, based as it is in the Southwestern tree-ring chronology, may seem a panacea—if you are wearing Plains-colored glasses. Formulated almost in tandem with the stratigraphically arranged sequence established by Kidder and Shepard (1936) from excavations at Pecos Pueblo, further efforts to refine (or redefine) Mera's 1933 broader geographical scheme were not undertaken for nearly thirty years. Shepard's (1942) recognition of the "Late Jornada Variant" in the Salinas and lower Rio Abajo is an exception. Not until the data resulting from Alvin Hayes's excavations at Las Humanas (Hayes, Young, and Warren 1981) and from salvage projects at Cochiti Dam (Honea 1968, 1973) did it seem necessary to rethink the Rio Grande Glazeware issue.

The result was what has come to be called the "8th 1/2" Southwestern Ceramic Conference, held in 1966, during which the primary focus was on typological lumping and splitting. A secondary concern was the chronology of the variations in rim forms throughout the nearly 400-year Glazeware sequence. The results were only slight adjustments of Mera's original efforts (Warren 1969; Warren and Snow 1976; Snow 1976a). Conceived originally as essentially a unilineal developmental sequence of rim modifications over time (Kidder and Shepard 1936: 82, for example), Mera's own work (1940) demonstrated regional differences already apparent in the early group.

The scarcity of Glaze B rims, for example, in the lower Rio Abajo (Mera's Eastern and Western Piro areas), led him to postulate a depopulation of those regions following Glaze A times (Mera 1940). The sequence there is from A to C (or D, followed by E–F). A much more reasonable explanation for Mera's observation of the lack of Glaze B is simply that it was not a significant component of the local tradition there (Hayes 1981; Baldwin 1983; Snow 1986).

Subsequent investigations have focused on rim variability, as well as on chronological problems (Shepard 1942; Hawley 1950; Hewett 1953; Lambert 1954; Voll 1961; Breternitz 1966; Dick 1965; Honea 1968, 1973; Warren 1969, 1979; Warren and Snow 1976; Hayes, Young, and Warren 1981; Snow 1982, 1986). Hayes, both initially and following later studies of rims from Abó Pass and Las Humanas (Baldwin 1984; Snow 1986), provided substantial evidence that the southern Rio Abajo sequence is distinct from that in the northern portions of the glaze-paint region. Unfortunately, in spite of advances in recognizing and describing variations within the Rio Grande Glazeware sequence, chronology remains the major gap in our understanding of its development, and the following represent my own best guesses for the early, middle, and late Glazeware groups.

EARLY GROUP: (GLAZE A RED, YELLOW, POLYCHROME; POTTERY MOUND POLYCHROME; LARGO GLAZE/RED, GLAZE/YELLOW, GLAZE-POLYCHROME)

Stuart Baldwin (1983) suggested that Glaze A Red may have lasted well beyond the estimated range of about 1350–1450 (see also Breternitz 1966); and Linda Cordell and Amy Earles (1984) reported that Glaze A types were recovered from archeomagnetically dated contexts at 1480 ± 22, and 1520 ± 50. Post-occupational fill in the burned room from which the samples were obtained yielded 20 percent A

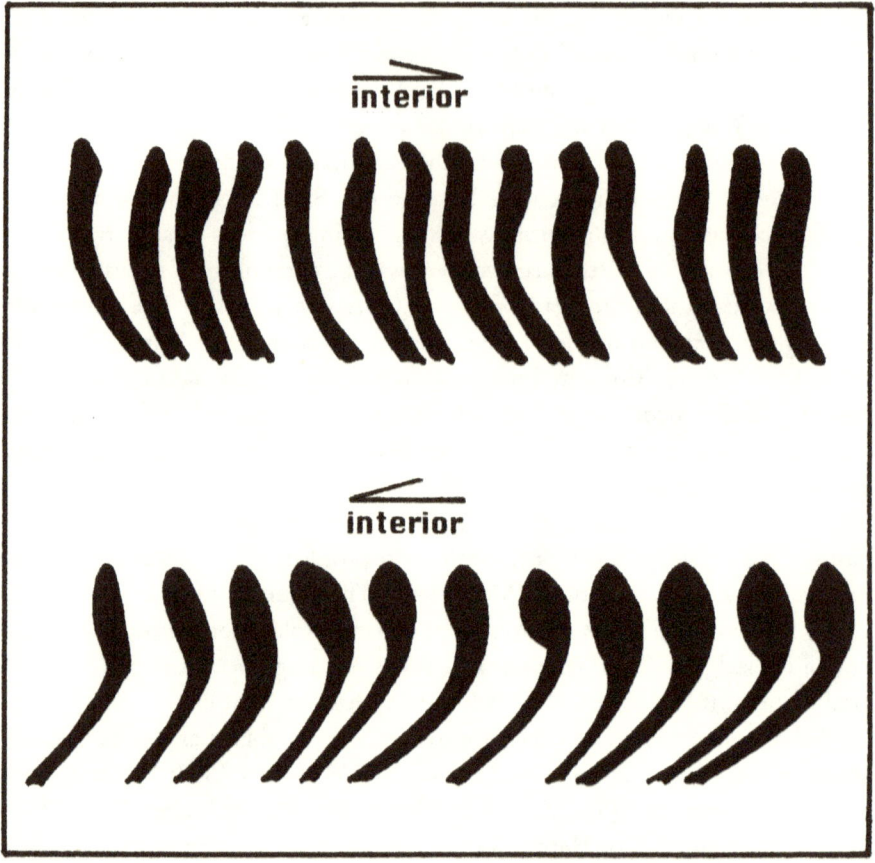

Figure 21.1. Bowl rim forms, Espinoso Glaze-polychrome (a Glaze C type) from LA 6455, top *(after Honea 1968); Pecos Glaze-polychrome (a Glaze E type)*, below *(after Honea 1967) (not to scale)*.

and B forms; the remainder were C and E–F forms. From a second room, beneath the wall of which they recovered a Glaze D rim, Glazes A–B represented 12 percent of those recovered. Unfortunately, the source of the fill in each of the rooms is not identified, but the circumstances in each suggest that Mera's estimated termination of Glazes A–B at about A.D. 1450 might be too early.

Michael Marshall (1987) and Hayes et al. (1981: 91–99) have also recognized the apparent persistence of Glaze A rim forms up to the contact Period (1540) in the Rio Abajo; and I have noted elsewhere the high frequency of Glaze A forms (20 percent) in association with Glaze F levels at Las Humanas (Snow 1986), suggesting its popularity well into the late sixteenth century.

Glaze B rims, predominately on white-slipped vessels, are nowhere found in quantity and are characteristic of the northern Rio Abajo (Galisteo Basin); minor production on red slips, however, occurred throughout the Rio Grande (Warren and Snow 1976; Snow 1986). The form appears to be nearly contemporaneous with Glaze A during the fourteenth and fifteenth centuries (Baldwin 1983) and overlaps considerably with the production and popularity of Glaze C and its varieties. Archeomagnetic samples in association with Glazes A through C provide a spread between A.D. 1350 and 1440 (Marshall 1982), clearly indicating the overlap among these forms. Glaze B, on yellow- and red-slipped vessels (forty-seven total rims), was the latest style recovered at Arroyo Hondo, where the latest tree-ring date is 1410; all other Glazeware sherds there were Glaze A (Habicht-Mauche 1993: 36).

Middle Group (Espinoso Glaze/red, Yellow, Polychrome)

Mera said of Glaze C style that it was "apparently comparatively short-lived," and that the varieties seem to have "run their allotted courses from about 1450 to 1490" (1940: 5). Glaze C rims did not occur at Arroyo Hondo Pueblo, whose latest cutting date is 1410 (Habicht-Mauche 1993; Lang and Harris [1984]. The above-cited archeomagnetic spread (1400 ± 12, 1400 ± 23, 1410 ± 60, and 1420 ± 20) suggests that Glaze C forms were well-established prior to A.D. 1440, but additional dates are needed to substantiate the approximate beginnings of this "transitional" style, as Mera called it. A similar association of Glazes A–C is from Kiva 54 at LA 6455, constructed by 1469, where Glaze C made up 32 percent of the floor fill (Honea 1968: 151, 165). As for the popularity, or life, of Glaze C forms, radiocarbon samples from floor features at LA 31746, containing 13 percent Glaze C, provided dates of 1570 ± 60 and 1610 ± 60 (Marshall 1987); and post-occupational fill from a room with archeomagnetic dates of 1480 ± 22 and 1520 ± 50, also contained Glaze C pottery (Cordell and Earls 1984). From these admittedly small samples, it can be argued that Glaze C forms were in use as late as the early decades of the sixteenth century, having been produced, perhaps, as early as about A.D. 1400±. Mera (1940: 3) argued that the rim style developed from Glaze A rims "with no intermediate forms"; they seem to be logical developments from the recently accepted Glaze A rim variant, Sanchez Glaze/red (with interior beveled rim, also on glaze/yellow and polychrome styles; Snow 1976a). Baldwin (1983) argues that for the Abó Pass area, and the Salinas region generally, Glaze C is simply a variant rim form of Glaze A, a position with which I concur.

Glaze C occurs in greater frequencies than does B, primarily outside of the Rio Abajo; and the type may or may not include the locally produced Pottery Mound glaze-polychrome in the Rio Abajo below Albuquerque (Voll 1961), as well as Mera's

Tiguex and Kuaua Glaze-polychromes (Mera 1933). Nevertheless, along with Glaze D, it is a minor component in any assemblage, in spite of its apparent persistence throughout the fifteenth century.

Glaze D, Kidder's imported Glaze IV at Pecos, was produced at and distributed from LA 240 (Tunque Pueblo) in the lower Santo Domingo Basin (Warren 1969); minor production elsewhere does not negate the fact that its manufacture was virtually the monopoly of that village (Dick 1965; Warren 1979). Its longevity is reasonably well defined from recent excavations and associated tree-ring dates (as well as from recalibrated dates on samples referenced by Mera in 1940). Mera assigned the brief span between 1490 and 1515 for the single Glaze D style rim, but it was clearly popular at LA 5, where it is the latest glaze style found, and where the latest tree-ring samples have been recalibrated to 1478 (Robinson, Harrill, and Warren 1973); Mera noted that Group C was "fully established" at LA 5; the peak of construction there is tree-ring dated between about 1457 and 1462.

Glaze D rims were present sometime shortly after 1469, on the floor and in fill deposits, in Kiva N at Las Humanas (Hayes, Young, and Warren 1981), as well as on the floor of Kiva 54, constructed in 1469, at LA 6455. Further confirmation of its pre-1490 occurrence comes from LA 70 (Snow 1976a). There it comprised 8 percent of floor sherds in Kiva 152, constructed by 1451. From Kiva 128, at LA 70, Glaze D comprised 14 percent of the floor sherds of the second period of use of that feature. Kiva 186, also at LA 70, was built between 1476 and 1486; there Glaze D reached a peak, representing 23 percent of the floor sherds. The type decreased to 14 percent again in the assemblage of floor sherds in Kiva 279, constructed between 1507 and 1520 (Snow 1976a). Marshall (1982) recovered two Glaze D rims from deposits dated by radiocarbon between 1570 and 1670.

These two middle-group types clearly overlap in time and are best dated to about A.D. 1425 and about 1550±. Glaze D vessels, relative to A–B or E–F, are nowhere found in quantity, but were popular items of trade throughout the northern Rio Grande, less so in the Rio Abajo. From Las Humanas, or Gran Quivira, the ratio of bowls to jars, during Glaze C–D production, decreased from 15:1 (A–B) to 5:1, and Glaze D (imported) jars from Pecos outnumber bowls by a ratio of 2:1 (Kidder and Shepard 1936; Snow 1986). Glaze C–D jars also dominate the glazes recovered from Southern Plains sites (Spielmann 1983). I propose, as a result, that Glazes C and D were made principally for specialized purposes (as Glaze D was so used at Pecos, with inhumations; see also Schaafsma 1968); and their absence at a particular site suggests that many local sequences run from A (or A–B) to E–F. This seems especially the case in the Rio Abajo, where 22 percent of the sixty Piro Division site assemblages examined by Mera (1940) contained only Glaze A and E–F, or Glaze A and D–E; as noted, Baldwin believes the local Piro sequence runs from Glaze A (in which he includes B and C rims) to D or E–F.

Marshall (1987) has indicated his belief that the late glazes (E–F), in the Rio Abajo, are post-Contact Period styles; if correct, it can be assumed that Glaze D was in use as late as 1540. I have argued elsewhere that it seems unreasonable to assume that the type disappeared a scant twenty years following the construction and use of the last kiva at LA 70, constructed by 1520 (Snow 1988). Both D and E rims occurred on the floor and upper fill, indicating only that the former continued into early Glaze E times. Glaze E at LA 70 is only 7 percent of the overall Glazeware assemblage, but it comprised 15 percent of the floor-fill ceramic assemblage of the last kiva (279) built at the site (Snow 1976a).

Extending Glaze D use beyond 1540 allows us to consider the existence of three Tiguex and Piro ruins as possibly historically documented villages in the mid to late sixteenth century: LA 50527, LA 50259 (Marshall and Walt 1984), and LA 719, Arenal Ruin (Mera 1940). Their inclusion in the historic pueblos of the Coronado and later expedition narratives appears to fill some of the gaps in correlating historical accounts and archeological sites in the area (Schroeder 1979; Snow 1988). The implications for the Southern Plains occurrences of the type are obvious.

LATE GROUP (PUARAY GLAZE-POLYCHROME; TIGUEX GLAZE-POLYCHROME; TRENEQUEL GLAZE-POLYCHROME; PECOS GLAZE V; KOTYITI GLAZE/RED, YELLOW, AND POLYCHROME AND RECENTLY ACCEPTED GLAZE F VARIANTS, INCLUDING THE "JORNADA LATE VARIANT")

Petrographic studies by Helene Warren (1981) and Anna Shepard (1942) suggest that the Salinas Pueblo group did not produce appreciable amounts of Glaze E, but did become significant manufacturers of Glaze F during the seventeenth century. As with Glaze D, Tunque Pueblo remained a major production center for Glaze E, although its manufacture is documented for the Picuris, Galisteo Basin, Zia, Cochiti, and Albuquerque areas as well.

Glaze E rims occur in significant numbers at a Spanish colonial site with construction dates of 1629 and 1631 (Snow and Stoller 1987), but better than about 70 percent of the Glazeware rims there are Glaze F variants. Mera supposed that the latter were confined to the period 1650–1700 (1940); Kidder and Shepard refer to an "early" (imported) and "late" (locally made) Glaze V style at Pecos, but assign both to the seventeenth century, relegating their Glaze VI to the latter half of the same century.

Baldwin (1980) has correlated Piro ruins with sixteenth- and seventeenth-century documentary accounts and concluded that Glazes E and F were contemporaneous on sites abandoned prior to 1580. As for a beginning date for Glaze E, the kiva floor deposits from LA 70 are informative. Post-1451 above-floor deposits in Kiva

152 contained 14 percent Glaze E; on the floor itself, Glaze D accounted for 8 percent of the assemblage (Glaze F did not occur on the site). The floor assemblage in Kiva 128 (constructed in 1469) contained nearly equal proportions of Glaze D and Glaze E—14 percent and 15 percent respectively; while Glaze D sherds from the floor of Kiva 186, constructed in 1486, amounted to 23 percent, but no Glaze E sherds were present in that assemblage. From the floor of Kiva 279, built in 1520–1521, the frequency of Glazes D and E were, again, nearly equal, amounting to 14 percent and 15 percent.

The absence of Glaze E from the floor fill in Kiva 186 at LA 70 suggests, nevertheless, that it was not yet in production (or, at least, not present in the Cochiti area) by the time it was abandoned sometime after 1486. On the basis of the floor fill from Kiva 279, however, it is reasonable to argue that Glaze E was fully established by 1520. Mera argued that it began about A.D. 1515, but Kiva assemblages from LA 70 suggest that it was being made sometime between about A.D. 1480± and 1500. The potential overlap in production/popularity of Glazes D and E, therefore, might have spanned the years from about 1486 to 1570±. If, as Baldwin concluded, Glazes E and F are contemporary on sites abandoned prior to about 1580, the potential overlap between these two types extends from the last decades of the sixteenth century until, perhaps the mid-seventeenth century.

Glaze F has long been suspected to have begun earlier than Mera's proposed date of 1650; and Baldwin's estimate of about 1550 seems reasonable, although perhaps only in the Rio Abajo. Its occurrence, along with Glaze E, in post-occupational fill in a room whose abandonment is dated by archeomagnetism at 1520 ± 50 years appears to strengthen that argument. Hayes et al. (1981) noted that Glaze F made up 32 percent of the floor and fill of the "late house" at Las Humanas, which was essentially completed by 1600. From subfloor deposits in the late house, Glaze F was only 3 percent of the assemblage there. Construction timbers from the late phase unit there range from the 1490s to the 1540s, with two at 1562 and a single 1582 cutting date (Hayes, Young, and Warren 1981: 27). Glaze F is the dominant type at LA 20000, a Spanish colonial *estancia* site, one of whose structures was built in the late 1620s and early 1630s, earlier than the 1650 date estimated by Mera and by Kidder and Shepard.

This brief review of the basis for a revised chronology for the Rio Grande Glazeware sequence, its types, and varieties might be a disappointment to those accustomed to relying on the seeming precision of Southwestern ceramic types. In spite of recalibration of older tree-ring specimens, to which the original sequence was pinned, and in spite of a significant number of new tree-ring dated samples from Glazeware contexts, we still lack firm control of the overall chronology. I believe, nevertheless, that the following estimates based on the review above will apply to the major groupings of early, middle, and late Glazewares in the Rio Grande:

EARLY: Glaze A variants from about A.D. 1275 to about A.D. 1525±;
Glaze B variants from about A.D. 1375 to about A.D. 1450±;
MIDDLE: Glaze C variants from about A.D. 1425± to about A.D. 1500+;
Glaze D variants from about A.D. 1450± to about A.D. 1550+;
LATE: Glaze E variants from about A.D. 1480± to about A.D. 1650;
Glaze F variants from about A.D. 1575± to about A.D. 1700.

With few notable exceptions, glaze sherds from Southern Plains sites are numerically a small component of the reported assemblages; but, aside from their sociocultural and historical connotations, their chronological importance is considerable to Southern Plains archeologists and ethnohistorians. The clusters of sites with glaze sherds belong to the Great Bend Aspect, on the Arkansas River in south-central Kansas; to the Edwards and subsequent Wheeler Complexes, principally in extreme western Oklahoma, bordering the Texas Panhandle, both on and below the Llano Estacado (Snow 1980; Baugh 1982; Spielmann 1983; Hofman 1984); and to the Tierra Blanca and nearby Garza Complexes, south of the Canadian River, along the headwaters of the Brazos and Red Rivers and their tributaries in the Texas Panhandle. Since the Great Bend Aspect sites are generally believed to have been the location of the sixteenth-century Quivira villages (Wedel 1942; Vehik 1986), they lie outside the focus of this paper.

Common to the other site-clusters, besides the occurrence of Rio Grande Glazeware is a more or less well-defined indigenous ceramic assemblage that seems to be a horizon marker for the period, about A.D. 1450–1650 (Baugh 1982). This consists of several apparently related varieties of utility pottery, remarkably similar to those that complement the glazes in the Rio Grande (Habicht-Mauche 1987, 1991; Kidder and Shepard 1936; Snow 1976a, 1982; Spielmann 1983). The locally produced utilityware occurs specifically at Tierra Blanca, Garza, and Wheeler Phase sites south of the Canadian, and generally south of Amarillo (Spielmann 1983; Baugh 1982). At such sites, Rio Grande Glazewares make up between 14 percent and 50 percent of the total assemblages, and consist, principally, of Glazes C–E, characteristically in jar form; but at Edwards I and the Wheeler Sites, only 2 percent or less of the assemblage consisted of Rio Grande Glazes (Hofman 1984: 353–354).

Judith Habicht-Mauche (1987, 1991) has correctly, I believe, correlated the Tierra Blanca and Garza Complexes with the Southern Plains groups encountered by Coronado and later entradas. In each case, sites of those complexes appear to represent primarily base-camp activities during hunting expeditions onto the Llano

Estacado. Again, it is important to note that, at each of these seasonally occupied camps of Tierra Blanca and Garza folks, a substantial locally produced utilityware ceramic assemblage is present. Castañeda mentions the use of pottery by both Querechos and Teyas in the preparation of pemmican (Winship 1896: 527).

The early glaze group, particularly Glaze A Red, is widespread on the Southern Plains, at permanent village sites, but nowhere in significant numbers. In contrast, the middle and late groups tend to be concentrated in sites on the Texas Panhandle (Spielmann 1983; Snow 1980) in contexts that Katherine Spielmann suggested were base-camp sites (and a single Glaze D jar from a cache near the Blackburn Site). The middle group glazes (C–D, the majority in each case) from these sites indicate a jar-to-bowl ratio of 3.4:1 (Tierra Blanca and Blackburn Sites; Spielmann 1983), which clearly is a reflection of the dramatic increase in C–D jar production reported from Las Humanas Pueblo (Snow 1986; Hayes et al. 1981).

Pots, Pans, and Losa d'jour

Recognition and correct identification of the fortuitous pot break involves consideration of three basic attributes of the ceramic assemblage: vessel form, ceramic typology, and source of supply. What kinds of vessels might be expected as necessary items for Coronado's "army," whose expedition members consisted of men and women of diverse cultural and ethnic backgrounds, ranging from *peninsulares* and *criollos* from New Spain, *mestizos, mulatos,* and *negros,* to the large contingent of Mexican Indians, the latter perhaps representing multiple Mesoamerican cultural traditions? Where such vessels were obtained and the rate of replacement of the requisite forms between Culiacán and the Texas Panhandle are critical issues, if we are to anticipate the formal and typological content of the historic sherd scatter.

Is it reasonable to expect that a sufficient quantity of indigenous Mesoamerican ceramic vessels (principally, it might be supposed, of west Mexican origin) survived the vicissitudes of the trip to the ravine? Can we expect that European and *indio* contingents with the army maintained social and/or cultural boundaries by the use of significantly distinct ceramic types and styles? Might we expect to encounter clusters of vessel forms (regardless, perhaps, of archeologically imposed stylistic typologies) that reflect significant differences in the storage, preparation, and consumption of foodstuffs?

Our ability to identify and recognize the site of the barranca encampment also depends on its size and the distribution (and organization) of the expedition's personnel. To what extent, if any, did the diverse cultural and ethnic members of the expedition select for discrete spatial distribution of campsites? Did, for example, the Mexican Indian contingent characteristically locate itself at a distance from the European components? How big an area sufficed to maintain order and control of the encamped expedition; and how, generally, might we expect individuals and family units to have organized their campsites? If the expedition characteristically slept and cooked in the tents (ripped by the hail) as Vierra's presumed Coronado campsite on the Rio Grande (LA 54147) suggests, why were all (or most) of the pots and pans out-of-doors?

These and other factors relevant to the identification of the barranca site require far more consideration than is possible in this brief essay, but it is worthwhile addressing in more detail here some specific observations. From the outset, the Spaniards extolled the Pueblos' ceramic craft, while providing only an occasional clue concerning vessel forms and function; it is, therefore, difficult to identify the specific forms referred to in the accounts of various sixteenth-century expeditions to the Rio Grande. By the same token, efforts to match the repertoire of the Rio Grande potter with the sixteenth-century Spanish terminology meet with little success.

Castañeda's reference to earthenware (losa) glazed with "*alcohol*" (in this case meaning simply a distillate, or essence, of metal), and well-made jars (*jarros*), is often repeated (Winship 1896: 452; Hammond and Rey 1940: 260), as is his mention of glazed earthenware at Yunqueyunque (opposite San Juan Pueblo), where they saw "*muchas ollas llenas de metal escogido rreluciente con que bedriaban la losa*" (Castañeda 1596: 91v), "many jars filled with selected shiny metal with which they glazed the pottery" (Hammond and Rey 1940: 244). Castañeda also referred to ground jerky prepared by both the Teyas and Querechos, in an olla filled with water (Hammond and Rey 1940: 426). Based, presumably, on eyewitness accounts by members of the expedition, Viceroy Mendoza wrote to the King that the Indians of Cíbola "eat out of flat bowls, like the Mexicans" (unfortunately, the original Spanish is not provided (Winship 1896: 550). Jars for storing water and for disposing of night soils are also mentioned by Coronado (Winship 1896: 563).

Folk classification of ceramic vessels, particularly in Mexico, has proven to be a slippery subject (for example, see Kempton 1981), in which form and function are key variables affected by any number of secondary attributes (presence of one or more handles, glazed surfaces, size of orifice). Moreover, geographically diverse terminology appears to have changed as a result of European contact and the impacts of modern technologies.

For example, in his study Willet Kempton found that, while the term "*jarro*" is distinguished (from "*jarra*" generally with a spout) by an increased ratio of height to width, the form is otherwise virtually the same as the "ollas" illustrated (1981: Figures 3.1–3.5). Generational and geographical differences among his informants clearly reflected inability to provide acceptable discrete definitions of either form. In terms of function, however, the latter seldom holds liquids, except during cooking, while the jarro is never used for cooking. Both consistently have one or two handles, as do a small number of Rio Grande Glazeware jar forms.

Words for presumably clay vessels that appear in later sixteenth-century accounts include "*chicubite*" (variation of *chiquihuite,* meaning "basket," from Nahuatl), and "*jicara,*" which has come to refer to any smaller hemispherical vessel with a wide mouth (from Nahuatl, the fruit of the tree of the same name), in addition to "olla," "*tinaja,*" "comal," and "*cajete.*" The latter most frequently refers to a deep *cazuela* (bowl) that lacks one or more glazed surfaces; the term was used by Gaspar Castaño de Sosa in the early 1590s in reference to vessels at Pecos (Hammond and Rey 1966). The "tinaja" is consistently used throughout Latin America, including the Southwest, to refer to a large water-storage container, either of clay or of pitch-coated basketry.

Clay comales have not been reported from archeological contexts in the Southwest; rather the familiar piki-stones in use at Hopi and formerly found in protohistoric and Spanish colonial sites up and down the Rio Grande (Snow 1990) are of sandstone or other lithic materials. Moreover, the traditional Spanish (and Mesoamerican) shape is round, rather than rectangular, as is the case in the Southwest; and those made in western Mexico, at least, are often shallow bowls in which corn and other materials are roasted. Their appearance (Pennington 1969, 1980) is quite like the familiar *puki,* or ceramic support, used by Rio Grande and other Southwestern potters in fashioning the base of larger vessels. Possibly the shallower Glaze V bowls at Pecos and from the Galisteo Basin centers, even though they have a distinct rim, might have been similar enough to the shallow bowls of the western Mexican indigenous tradition to warrant the analogy to comal by sixteenth-century Europeans.

Other terms occurring in the accounts of the Rodríguez/Chamuscado, Antonio de Espejo, and Castaño de Sosa expeditions are similarly difficult to identify. The word "comal" has been consistently translated by Hammond and Rey as "flat earthenware pan." They (1966: 84) translate "chicubites" ("chiquihuites") as a "pan for *baking* bread," although the original Spanish apparently reads, "in which they *prepare* their bread" (my emphasis), a potentially significant difference. Elsewhere, they equate "dishes" with "chicubites from which the natives eat" (Hammond and Rey 1966: 114). "Jicara," a spouted vessel equivalent to a pitcher (Kempton 1981), they translate as "very beautiful cups," or as "bowls" (Hammond and Rey 1966: 190, 278). The Rio Grande Glazeware "cup" or "mug" form is a rare one; the familiar Mesa Verde Black-on-white "mug" form seldom occurs in earlier Glazeware series (although see Kidder and Shepard 1936).

Other incidental references to pottery among the Pueblos between 1540 and 1592 specify dishes for eating and for carrying and storing water (lids "of the same material" were provided). Lids are not identified in the Glazeware series, but Beckett (1981) has suggested that stone discs, abundant at Salinas region sites, may have served that purpose for Chupadero and Tabira Black-on-white (B/w) jars (see also, Snow 1986). "Drinking vessels," "earthen bowls," "plates," "salt containers," and "basins" also occur in translation, but were not provided with the Spanish equivalents (Hammond and Rey 1966). Glazing was referred to in the Coronado accounts, as well as by Castaño de Sosa ("some of the pottery is glazed" at Pecos; Hammond and Rey 1966: 278); and most remarked the quality and decoration of Pueblo pottery ("all decorated and of better quality than the pottery of New Spain"; "richly painted"; "even surpass the pottery made in Portugal"; "which is like that of New Spain"; "red, figured"—that is, decorated—and "black," specifically at Pecos).

Assuming that some of the forms characteristic of Rio Grande Glazewares did accompany Coronado's expedition onto the Southern Plains, from where were they "purchased"? There is scant indication in the various sixteenth-century accounts that the Spaniards actually obtained pottery from the Pueblos visited. Coronado, however, did send the viceroy two wicker baskets and "some plates decorated" with turquoises (Hammond and Rey 1940: 176); and the Rodríguez/Chamuscado party presented "specimens of the dishes [chicubites] from which the natives eat and other crockery made in their settlement" to the viceroy (Hammond and Rey 1966: 114). Servants with the Espejo party reportedly entered a kiva at Hawikuh in order to "get earthen bowls" (Hammond and Rey 1966: 186). Viceroy Mendoza, referring to the flat bowls used among the Pueblos for eating, might well have had specimens at hand, returned with Coronado's expedition in 1542, but this is speculation. There is no evidence in the Coronado expedition documents concerning pottery that might have been among the original supplies carried, initially by horses and Indians and later on the backs of the gentlemen, but it must be supposed that replacement of any such crockery occurred with some frequency.

Within the Rio Grande region, Glazeware production, although widespread, was virtually limited to those areas south of Santa Fe. Picuris, and to some extent, Jemez, are minor exceptions; and Florence Hawley Ellis (see Snow 1976a) once proposed a type, San Juan Glaze-polychrome, as yet unrecognized in the overall series. Competing with the glazes were a number of traditional indigenous mattepaint black-on-white types produced, curiously enough, around the peripheries of the glaze-production centers in the Galisteo Basin and Rio Abajo pueblos.

Biscuit and Sankawi styles were produced exclusively among the Tewas (Kidder and Shepard 1936); Vadito B/w in the Picuris (and presumably Taos) area (Dick 1965: 131–132); Jemez B/w, restricted to that area in production as well as movement; and Tabira B/w and Polychrome, among the Salinas villages, also infrequently traded. Since most or all of those regions were visited by Coronado's people, might we not expect one or more such types also to be present at the pot break? With the exception of possible seventeenth-century Tewa red and polychrome vessels in Great Bend Aspect and Wheeler Phase sites, none of those traditional Rio Grande black-on-white tradition sherds appear in Southern Plains contexts with the glazes.

The expedition, almost from the beginning, constantly searched for and plundered (when not offered) food from the various groups with whom they came into contact. At one point, says Coronado, the maize secured from Cicúye having been exhausted, they had eaten nothing but meat for "some days" as they traversed the plains (Hammond and Rey 1940: 187). Meat must be boiled (as in a stew) or roasted, the latter requiring no other equipment than a spit and a knife. With little or nothing with which to add to such a stew, might it not be expected that soldiers lugging their own equipment gradually lessened their loads of purloined pueblo pots as unnecessary baggage? What functions, consequently, might pueblo (and other Native American) vessels have served the individuals and families of the expedition; and what forms might we expect to see as a result?

Pueblo jars are seldom fitted out with lids and carrying lugs (although see Beckett 1981), and glaze bowls do not characteristically nest (an inverted Glaze C bowl was found fitted and caulked with lime plaster over a Glaze D bowl, which contained feathers and cotton string [Steen 1980]). The presence of glaze jars on Southern Plains protohistoric sites, in spite of their occasional high frequency at some, is seemingly redundant (Lintz 1986), but indicates container-specific requirements best fulfilled by such vessels. While it is possible that Spaniards might have had the same requirements (for carrying water, perhaps), sufficient stored water could only have been carried on horseback in jars, unless the Spaniards temporarily adopted the tump-line!

We are basically ignorant of the customs and practices of sixteenth-century Spanish field food preparation and consumption: was there a special mess unit that carried all of the vessels required? I suspect that, for the most part, the common camp (iron) kettle served for cooking, to be dipped into by individuals with their hands, tortillas, or gourds. One or a very few utility vessels might well have served the family or the individual soldier unfortunate not to have possessed an iron (or copper) kettle. Transportation of the fragile and awkward Rio Grande Glaze vessels, I imagine, precludes the presence of large numbers with the expedition's baggage.

European-style (or manufactured) earthenware vessels, similarly, are fragile (majolica, for example) as well as bulky. Listed among the items delivered as gifts at Zuni, nevertheless, were some "small glass dishes." More sturdy vessels, such as the familiar "olive-jar," might have arrived at Tiguex, carrying luxury foodstuffs; but it seems unlikely that such bulky and heavy jars were toted onto the Plains. No mention is made of metal vessels in any of the sixteenth-century expedition documents, nor have fragments been identified from suspected sixteenth-century sites on the Plains.

Prior to having eaten their corn supplies, some distance beyond Pecos Pueblo, we might expect to encounter fragments of Rio Grande ceramics, not just glazes, both jars and bowls; as well, perhaps, as olive-jars, metal comales, and kettles. Less well-known vessel forms might be expected to mark the trail of the expedition, particularly indigenous canteens. These are fitted with loop handles for transport, and are characteristic of both Chupadero and Tabira B/w types, but are less frequently recognized (or manufactured) in the glaze tradition. Similarly, the duck- or shoe-pot utilityware vessel (and occasionally, in the Glaze series) might also be diagnostic. These are reminiscent of a peculiar form, the *pinolero*, or *patojo*, for cooking beans, or in which corn is parched for making *pinol*, as among the Tarahumaras and other groups. The Espejo expedition (1581–1582) referred to Indians at Hopi traveling with a "bag and bowl [jicara] of pinole" (Hammond and Rey 1966: 190), but the pinolero and patojo are, in modern folk classification, designated ollas. One such vessel, in utility style, was associated with Glaze D at LA 70 (Snow 1976a).

Finally, two remaining observations before I turn to the reliability of Glaze E as a diagnostic type for determining Coronado's route across the Panhandle. First, and by analogy to his presumed campsite on the Rio Grande (Vierra 1989 and Chapter 16), if all the pots were, in fact, kept inside the tents for cooking and eating, that mother of all pot breaks locality should produce evidence of very shallow, subterranean pit structures, over which tents were erected. Second, if all the pots and pans and dishes were broken by the hail in the ravine, what was left to carry on to Quivira, some thirty days' travel northward (Wedel 1942)? The occurrence of Glaze E sherds in Great Bend Focus sites, along with other suitable artifacts of Pueblo and European manufacture, is implied as evidence that this was the Quivira of Coronado. Perhaps, in fact, "toda la loza" referred to very few ceramic vessels in the expedition's possession by the time the ravine was reached. Mother of all pot breaks or simply a pot drop?

Glaze E: Losa d'jour?

The "reliability" of Glaze E as a diagnostic time marker for the second half of the sixteenth century on the Southern Plains and, therefore, as a possible contemporary of Coronado's expedition there in 1541 must stand on associated tree-ring and archeomagnetic dates. These are few and far between. Moreover, it seems entirely plausible to think that, as it does in the Rio Grande, Glaze E (and variants) might occur in the same contexts as Glaze D (and possibly, Glaze C) at Southern Plains sites. Glaze F, apparently, appears too late in the sequence, probably not until the last decades of the sixteenth century; and neither Glaze A nor B seems to be particularly diagnostic from a temporal perspective.

Marshall's (1989) identification of all glazes recovered from the suspected Coronado campsite on the Rio Grande near Bernalillo as Glaze E forms may be behind the issue of the "reliability" of that type as diagnostic of the expedition's sojourn in the Texas Panhandle. If Marshall is correct in his assertion, LA 54147 is the *only* site with glazewares so far investigated in the Rio Grande (surface or excavation) to yield one, and only one, single style within the series! Marshall claims that the 6,597 sherds recovered from that site must represent "long-term" occupation, but admitted that this is a relative concept. Does "long-term," from his perspective, refer to the occupation at Alcanfor during the winter and spring of 1540–1541, or to a siege camp during the two-month assault on Moho or nearby Pueblos?

Evidence for the considerable overlap in production and occurrences of Glazes C through E, and particularly of D and F rim forms in the Rio Grande, indicates that Marshall's identifications warrant closer scrutiny. Although I have not personally examined the rims illustrated by Marshall in Vierra's monograph, the small sample depicted suggests strongly that all rim forms from A through E are represented in the assemblage (see, especially, his Groups 01, 03, and 06, wherein are clearly illustrated several Glaze C rims, together with one Glaze D, and one Glaze F rim; several may, in fact, be Glaze A rims).

Marshall's explanation for the dramatic decrease in the ratio of pueblo utility to decorated wares, reflecting, he says, the use by the Spaniards of metal camp kettles, does not explain why 45 percent of the assemblage is made up of standard Pueblo utilityware sherds. The decorated ware assemblage is about evenly divided between bowls (53 percent) and jars. I suspect that these figures reflect differences in the functions of decorated vessels; and a similar ratio of decorated to utility sherds occurs at a roughly 1625–1631 Spanish estancia (Snow and Stoller 1987; see also Snow 1973b), where the same observation is made with respect to seventeenth-century Spanish colonial estancia assemblages. Interestingly, Marshall identified sixteen "intrusive" indigenous pottery types, indicative of late sixteenth-century manufacture, including Acoma, Zuni, Hopi, and Tewa styles, all of which have also been recovered from the 1631 colonial estancia referred to above (and five Hopi yellowware sherds are reported from the protohistoric assemblage at Edwards I; Baugh 1982: 188).

Three acceptable dates from fifteen excavated shallow features at LA 54147 provide a range between 1386 and 1650 for its occupation. The mean dates are 1559 ± 70, 1486 ± 100, and 1570 ± 80. The two sixteenth-century dates are clearly post-Coronado, even though the overall range would include the time of Coronado's sojourn in Tiguex. More importantly, that range also includes the periods of popularity of each of the glaze types, from Glaze A through F, as the rims illustrated by Marshall seem to indicate. Marshall's illustration of rims recovered does include a number of standard Glaze E rims, nevertheless, and the range of dates provided offers additional support for the best-guess temporal bracketing of that type suggested earlier. Even if Coronado did occupy LA 54147, Glaze E is not the only (although perhaps the most typical) indicator of the period 1540–1541. Bearing in mind their overlapping production, however, Glaze C possibly, and Glaze D probably, can also be considered diagnostic temporal markers for the period of initial contact between Europeans and Native American groups on the Southern Plains.

Conclusions

Castañeda's observation that there is no pottery there, nor do they make it (indeed, not even gourds were available) makes it clear that the expedition and, one assumes, the Teyas as well were bereft of receptacles from that point on. If Castañeda's memory was correct in this regard, it seems to me that the expedition might not have been encamped in Tierra Blanca– or in Garza-land, where contemporary archeological manifestations, indicating base-camp sites, contain distinctive locally produced utilityware assemblages and varying amounts of Rio Grande ceramics, *but, as yet, little or no firm indications of Coronado's encampment.* If, for the sake of argument, this is a reasonable one, the conclusion ought to be that the ravine and the encamped Teyas may be located where they have not traditionally been sought (Bolton 1949; Ivey, Rhodes, and Sánchez 1991). The problem of just where some hapless archeologist might encounter that historical pot break, I leave to the experts.

Note

1. In Castañeda's original manuscript the word *calabazo* clearly appears, meaning "gourd jug," rather than *calabaza* (gourd) as Hammond and Rey, and Winship as well, read it.

CHAPTER 22

A Large Canyon Like Those of Colima

W. MICHAEL MATHES

n the "Relación de la Jornada de Cíbola," its author Pedro de Castañeda (1596: 80v–81r), a former resident of Culiacán and member of the expedition of Francisco Vázquez de Coronado of 1540–1542, stated that after four days' march across the plains, Rodrigo Maldonado reached "*una barranca grande como las de colima,*" where the entire expedition subsequently camped for an unspecified time. While the eastern escarpment of the Llano Estacado Caprock is broken by several large canyons and Castañeda had had ample experience observing the great barrancas of the Pacific slope of the Sierra Madre Occidental in his travel from Culiacán and the march northward, this particular canyon of the Llano Estacado was, to him, specifically and notably different from those others, in that it was "like those of Colima" (Mora 1992: 101). The question therefore arises relative to Castañeda's need for such a precise topographic description of the campsite barranca.

In the sixteenth century the *alcaldía mayor* of Colima, centered on the *villa* of Colima, incorporated a far greater territory than the modern state of the same name. The jurisdiction was bounded on the south by the Pacific Ocean, on the east by the Río Coahuayana, on the west by the Ríos Purificación and Apamila, and on the north by a line extending eastward from a point somewhat south of Autlán,

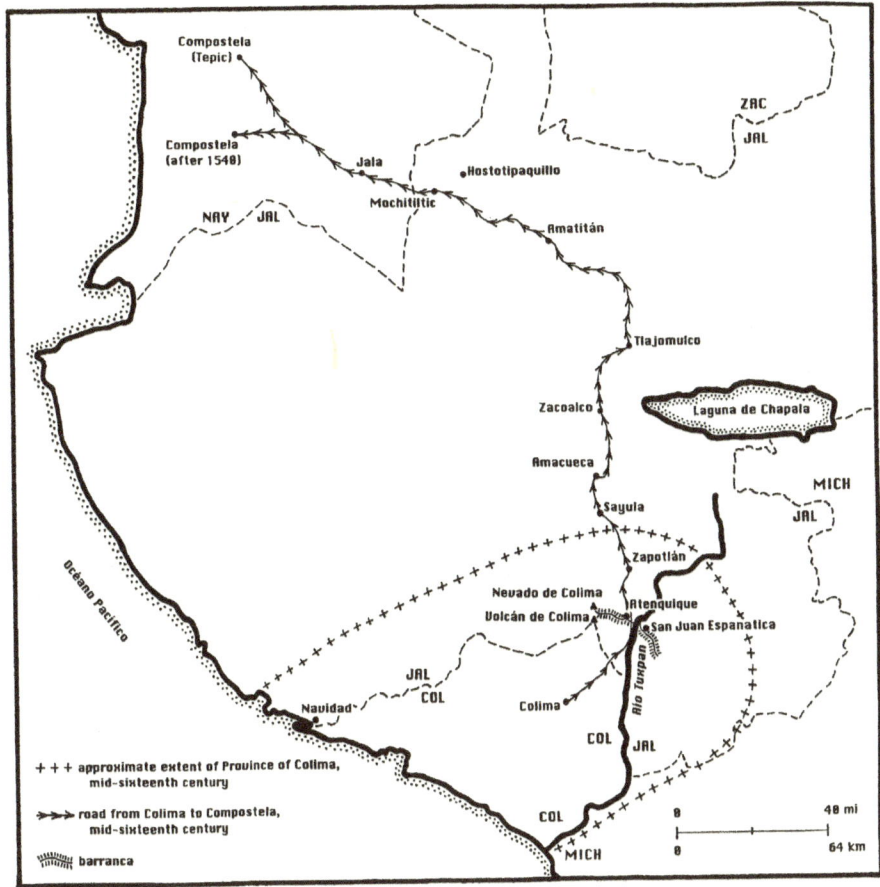

Map 18. Road from Colima to Compostela, mid-sixteenth century.

continuing south of Tapalpa and Sayula, and thence southeasterly to Jilotlán. This administrative district incorporated the numerous barrancas to the east of the Nevado de Colima and Volcán de Colima formed by the Río El Naranjo and the Río Tuxpán.

The valley between the volcanoes and the Cerro de Tuxpán formed by these rivers was the principal route from the coast and villa of Colima to the crossroads at the commercial center of Sayula in the third decade of the sixteenth century and remains so today as the route followed by México 110 from Manzanillo to Guadalajara. During the sixteenth and seventeenth centuries, numerous mule caravans passed over this route to Sayula, from whence they continued northward to Guadalajara or eastward to Pátzcuaro and the Ciudad de México. Virtually anyone

Figure 22.1. La Barranca Atenquique, Jalisco. Photo by W. Michael Mathis.

traveling between the villa de Colima and the interior of the viceroyalty would be familiar with the canyons between that city and Zapotlán (Ciudad Guzmán) (Gerhard 1993: 178–182).

Although a part of the neovolcanic axis of the region, the subregion of valleys of escarpmented slopes formed by the rivers El Naranjo and Tuxpán is composed of yellow and white sedimentary soils with extensive diatomaceous, gypsum, and similar calcium deposits. These deposits are particularly evident between Quesería, Colima, and Atenquique, Jalisco. The canyons formed by these rivers are relatively shallow and wide, rarely exceeding 120 meters in depth, and frequently reaching a width of 2 kilometers. The alluvial soils in the bottoms and on the walls of the canyons allow extensive vegetation, particularly during the rainy season from June to November. Because of the width of the canyons, the bottoms are generally farmed or used as pasture. An individual traveling from Colima to Nochistlán would easily distinguish between these canyons and the deeper, narrow canyons cut by the heavily flowing and rapidly descending rivers of the Sierra Madre and the interior highlands of modern Jalisco and Nayarit (Secretaria de Programación y Presupuesto 1987). These northern barrancas frequently reach depths of over 350 meters and rarely exceed more than a few hundred meters in width at the bottom. Thus, the

Figure 22.2. Barranca near San Juan Espanatica, Jalisco. Photo by W. Michael Mathis.

canyons of Colima are specifically distinctive in size and nature from those found elsewhere on the northern Pacific watershed of New Spain.

A visual survey of the topography and composition of canyons of the eastern escarpment of the Llano Estacado Caprock shows clearly that red and orange color of soil/rock strata, lack of vegetation on the walls, and relatively greater depth distinguish Palo Duro, Tule, Caprock Canyons, and Quitaque from the barrancas of Colima. Similarly, its great width and isolated, outstanding mesas distinguish Yellow House Canyon from the Colima locations. On the other hand, Blanco Canyon fulfills all of the requisites of the latter in depth, width, vegetation, and soil color. Visual comparison of Blanco Canyon with the barrancas of Atenquique and Tonila, Jalisco, reveals extraordinary similarities (Flores 1990: 10, 18–19, 44–45). (Compare Figures 22.1, 22.2, and 23.1.)

As yet it has not been determined if Pedro de Castañeda de Náçera was familiar with the canyons of Colima prior to his joining the Vázquez de Coronado expedition or whether he became so following his return to Nueva Galicia. However, the sequence of these events is not relevant to his use of this highly specific means of describing and distinguishing the site on the margin of the Llano Estacado where the expedition camped in early summer 1541. Because Blanco Canyon is like no other of the large canyons of the region and is strikingly similar to the canyons of Colima, while the other Caprock canyons are not, there can be little doubt that Castañeda was describing Blanco Canyon with his comparison to the barrancas of Colima.

CHAPTER 23

Una Barranca Grande
Recent Archeological Evidence and a Discussion of Its Place in the Coronado Route

Donald J. Blakeslee, Richard Flint, and Jack T. Hughes

uring late spring and early summer 1541 the Coronado expedition pursued a course toward Quivira, a presumed wealthy land on the bison plains of North America. The expedition set out from the Tiwa pueblo of Coofor, in the Bernalillo, New Mexico, area, stopped briefly at Cicuique/ Cicúye or Pecos Pueblo, built a bridge to cross the Río Pecos just below its junction with the Gallinas River, and traveled on eastward, encountering at least two encampments of nomadic bison hunters, known to the Spaniards as Querechos. These were Apachean hunters possibly of the archeologically defined Tierra Blanca Complex.

Then the Spaniards ascended, without remark, the great Llano Estacado of eastern New Mexico and the Texas Panhandle. After more than thirty days of travel, summarized by the anonymous author of the *Relación del Suceso* (Hammond and Rey 1940: 291; Pacheco y Cárdenas 1870: 325) as covering 100 leagues to the east and 50 leagues to the south or southeast, the expedition reached the eastern edge of the Llano, at a large canyon (barranca grande), resembling the canyons of the province of Colima, in which were encamped more bison hunters. The habits of these Teya hunters were very similar to those of the Querechos; however, the peoples were of different stocks. The Teya may correspond to the archeologically defined Garza Complex.

309

Historians and archeologists have long assumed that this first barranca, summer home of Teya hunters, was one of the Caprock canyons that characterize roughly a hundred miles of the eastern scarp of the Llano from Palo Duro Canyon, not far from Amarillo, south to Yellow House Canyon near Lubbock.

Near-legendary authority on the Coronado expedition Herbert E. Bolton (1949: 266–267) insisted that this first barranca was Tule Canyon, southern companion of the Palo Duro. Both before and since Bolton's pronouncement nearly fifty years ago, others have pointed out that Tule Canyon does not fit the documentary evidence very well, as being the first barranca the expedition encountered. For starters, Tule Canyon is too far north (Chapter 19). Rough estimation of the first barranca's location, according to the *Relación del Suceso* measurement and assuming a starting point in the Bernalillo, New Mexico, area, puts the barranca in the Texas South Plains, in the general area of Lubbock, that is, about 260 miles (416 km) east of Bernalillo (which puts one approximately at the 102d meridian near Cliffside in Potter County, Texas) and 130 miles (208 km) south/southeast of there (or just a few miles south of Lubbock). Alternately, using Cicúye/Pecos as the starting point yields an area not far east of Crosbyton as the terminus. Actual walking distances and adjustment for magnetic declination would undoubtedly move either location somewhat farther north, though still well south of the Palo Duro and Tule Canyons.

Secondly, the transition from Querecho to Teya hunting territory noted by members of the Coronado expedition is consistent with the protohistoric territorial extent of the Tierra Blanca and Garza Complexes, as pointed out by Judith Habicht-Mauche (1992) and others. The Teya being representatives of the Garza Complex places the first barranca at the edge of the South Plains. The major concentration of Garza Complex sites is along Blanco Canyon south of Floydada, Texas, about thirty-five miles (fifty-six km) northeast of Lubbock.

As it happens, in the 1950s and 1960s, two pieces of chain mail were stumbled upon by ranchers in and immediately adjacent to Blanco Canyon. One object is a three-fingered glove or gauntlet. The other piece, which has since disappeared, was thought to be part of a vest or cuirass (Marble 1991 and 1995). None of the pieces has been confidently dated, but the gauntlet is not unlike sixteenth-century chain mail used by the Coronado expedition (Drake 1995).

Since 1993, a local collector, Jimmy Owens, has located a series of other objects in the same area. Most significant are three dozen copper projectile points and one of forged iron. All are ferruled to accept a shaft end roughly one cm in diameter. Let us deal first with the copper points. They are of a material and construction very similar, if not identical, to crossbow boltheads (dart points) recovered archeologically at Hawikuh, Santiago Pueblo, and Pecos Pueblo, all places

Figure 23.1. Blanco Canyon, Texas, view to southwest. Photo by William K. Hartmann.

visited by the Coronado expedition (Chapter 3) (see Figures 23.2 and 23.3). Such copper boltheads were likely to have accompanied only the Coronado expedition into the Southwest. The iron point (very different from the sheet metal comanchero points so common in the Panhandle), while of a different morphology than the copper points, probably derives from the same sixteenth-century Spanish crossbow tradition. Also identified, as a result of September 1995 survey work, are a number of whole and partial Spanish-style horseshoes, as well as horseshoe nails, and over 100 distinctive "caret-head" carpenter's nails similar to those recovered at the Soto encampment in Tallahassee, at the Bernalillo area campsite in New Mexico, and at sixteenth-century Caribbean sites. (See Figure 16.2 and the leftmost nail in Figure 7.2). Less temporally specific European objects have been found at the same levels in Blanco Canyon in the same scatter as boltheads and "caret-head" nails: a knife blade, a scabbard tip, and several pieces of harness hardware.

In addition to these items of European derivation, aboriginal material of types likely to have accompanied the Coronado expedition has been recovered archeologically in the vicinity. For instance, Rio Grande Glazeware sherds (particularly Glaze E) are found in relative abundance at the nearby Floydada Country

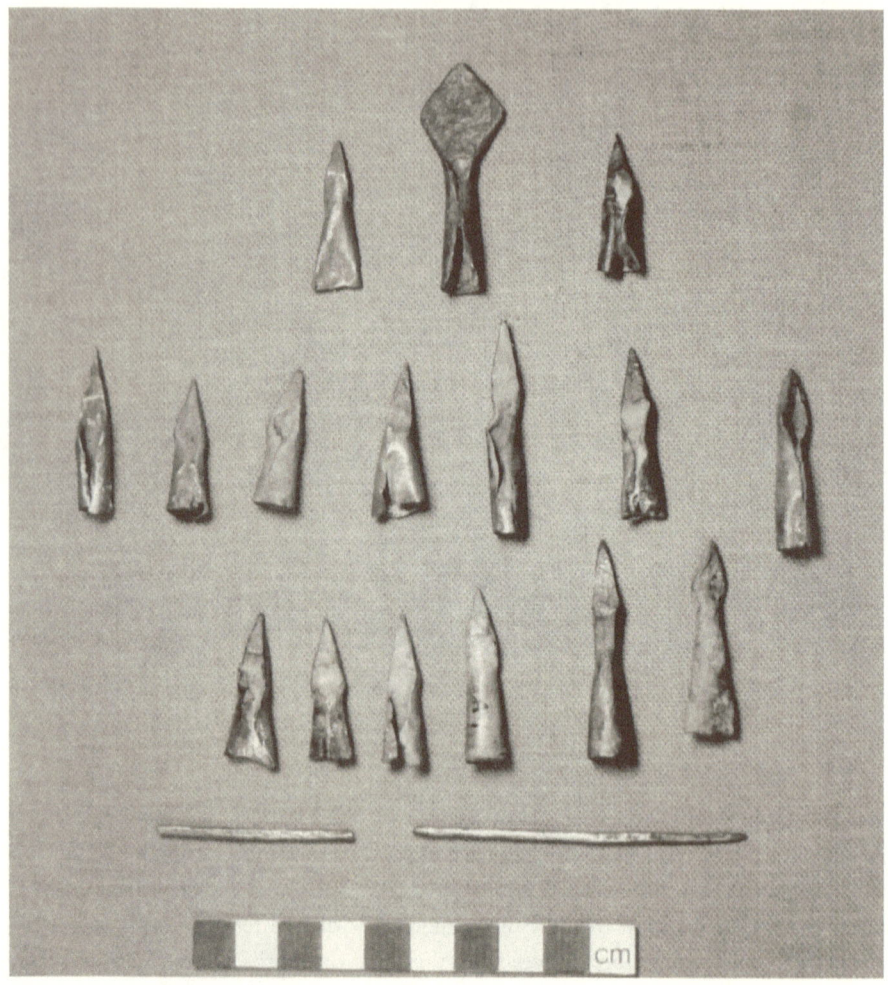

Figure 23.2. Crossbow boltheads, Jimmy Owens Site, Floyd County, Texas. Photo by Richard Flint.

Club, Montgomery, and Bridwell sites (all with substantial Garza Complex components). Furthermore, during a brief surface reconnaissance in August 1994, we located sherds from a single Glazeware pot, now identified by David Snow as a Glaze E jar, of Pecos Glaze Polychrome, dating from before 1600, perhaps as early as the beginning decades of the 1500s (Snow, personal communication), immediately across the intermittent watercourse of the White River in Blanco Canyon from the location where the iron projectile point was found.

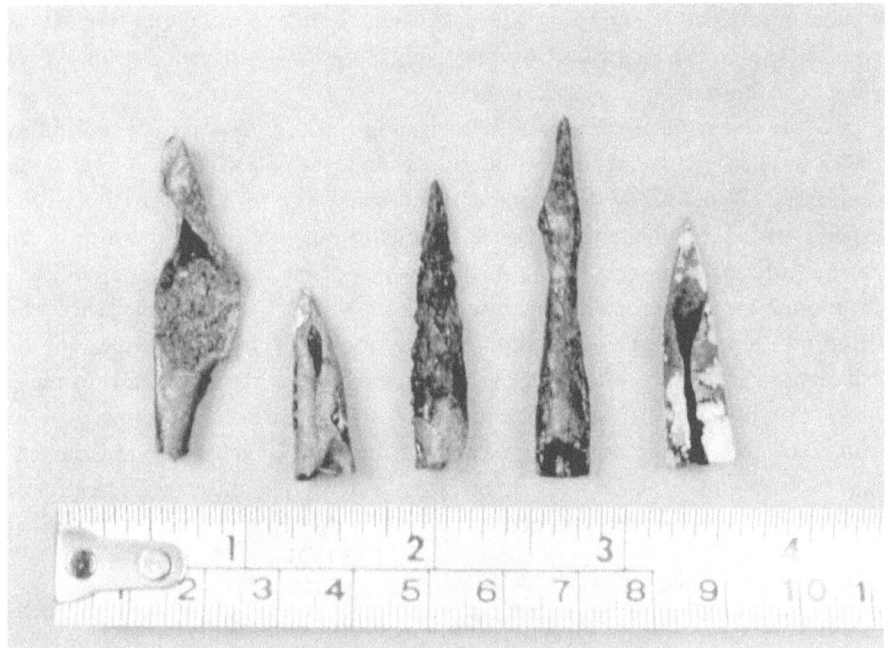

Figure 23.3. Crossbow Boltheads, Hawikuh, New Mexico. Photo by Pamela Dewey. Courtesy of the National Museum of the American Indian, Smithsonian Institution.

In addition, found near the iron point was what, from its description by the local collector who found it, may be a Mesoamerican obsidian blade fragment. Such blades formed the edges of macanas (swords), probably carried by many of the members of the Coronado expedition. Unfortunately, the fragment itself has now been lost.

Also, from the nearby Floydada Country Club Site, two red-painted, grog-tempered sherds have been recovered, tentatively identified by Reggie Wiseman and Stu Peckham of the Museum of New Mexico as possibly originating from Mexico. There is little doubt that ceramics from Mexico (the central plateau, the west coast, and the northwest) were present with the Coronado expedition.

This association of objects of material culture is fully consistent with what has previously been identified as characteristic of the pattern of Coronado expedition material culture (see Flint 1992a). Especially with the volume of copper crossbow boltheads in Blanco Canyon (more than from all other suspected Coronado expedition sites combined), it appears more and more likely that Blanco Canyon was visited by the Coronado expedition in 1541 and probably is one of the barrancas grandes mentioned in the Coronado documents. Furthermore, the nearby Montgomery Site or the Floydada Country Club Site may be the remains of a Teya village encountered by the expedition.

While systematic archeological investigation of the Jimmy Owens Site[1] (now under way) may confirm beyond doubt the presence of a Coronado expedition campsite in Blanco Canyon, a number of questions relevant to delineation of the expedition's route will remain. For determination of the expedition's route, the most significant of those is the question of which of the two barrancas specifically mentioned in the Coronado documents Blanco Canyon may be: one where the expedition appropriated a supply of bison hides at a Teya village and then was hit by a hailstorm or another where Coronado left the body of the expedition to travel north to Quivira with a small detachment. To put that issue in perspective, we outline two contrasting possibilities, both of which can be argued from documentary evidence, first that Blanco Canyon is the barranca like those of Colima (*como las de colima*) that was the first one encountered by the expedition and, second, that it is the last barranca (*barranca postrera*) described as being a league wide.

Blanco Canyon as the First Barranca

The native guide El Turco seems to have led the expedition from the bridge built across the Pecos River (Chapter 17) along the same route known to have been a favorite of New Mexican comancheros two centuries later:

1) eastward to the great landmark of Tucumcari Peak, where the first Querecho camp was likely encountered and where Isopete (a second Plains Indian guide) began insisting that the trail to Quivira branched off to the northeast (like the modern U.S. Highway 54);

2) eastward again to the Arroyo del Puerto on the present New Mexico–Texas line, where that broad, gentle draw provides the easiest possible access to the formidable northern rim of the Llano Estacado; and

3) thence southeastward into the middle reaches of the Llano.

At this point, both expedition and guides were lost and Coronado sent out scouting parties, one of which encountered "a large canyon like those of Colima" (Hammond and Rey 1940: 237).

The argument is made here that the measurements of 100 leagues east and fifty leagues south reported by the *Relación del Suceso* refer to the distance from the Bernalillo camp to the *first* barranca. This seems particularly likely since the author of the *Relación* (Hammond and Rey 1940: 291) writes that the measured point was reached two days after García López de Cárdenas broke his arm. By Castañeda

(Hammond and Rey 1940: 236) we are told that García López broke his arm far out on the Llano, several days before the expedition reached the *first* barranca.

Although the few documentary data recorded about this canyon or barranca would apply to many of the canyons along the eastern Caprock escarpment of the Llano, they seem to fit Blanco Canyon especially well (see, for instance, Chapter 22). In this first barranca was a Teya camp. At least three important Garza Complex locations are in Blanco Canyon: the Floydada Country Club Site, near the head of the canyon; the Montgomery Site, a few miles downstream; and the Bridwell Site yet farther downstream. All have been partially excavated (see Word 1991, 1965; Parker 1982). The Garza Complex appears to be geographically, chronologically, and culturally identifiable with the Teya. Components of the Garza Complex, however, have also been reported from several other Caprock canyons, both north and south of Blanco Canyon.

As the result of an intense hailstorm that struck the expedition in the first barranca, all of the expedition's ceramic and gourd vessels were broken (Hammond and Rey 1940: 238). Therefore, the area where the expedition was camped in the first barranca should be marked by a thin but extensive scatter of sherd clusters, many representing single vessels. If we are to take literally Castañeda's statement that the hailstorm in the first barranca broke *all* of the expedition's pottery, then direct association of ceramics with the Spanish camp should occur only in the first barranca and not at subsequent stops. Fragments of at least two utilityware pots have been recovered archeologically in close proximity and at the same level as "caret-head" nails at the Jimmy Owens Site in Blanco Canyon, making it quite likely the first barranca.

What the documents do not say about the first barranca may be significant. Though Pedro de Castañeda remarks specifically about the extreme width of the last barranca (one league), he is silent in this respect about the first barranca (Hammond and Rey 1940: 239). This would have been appropriate for Blanco Canyon, which is the least remarkable of the Caprock canyons when compared with those to its north.

Coronado evidently learned from the Teya in the first barranca that he was heading in the wrong direction, that Quivira was far to the north (Hammond and Rey 1940: 239). It seems most unlikely, therefore, that Coronado would have had any reason to take the expedition in any direction but north upon leaving the first barranca. It seems fairly clear that the entire expedition left the first barranca with a group of Teya and traveled (presumably northward) for three days among a series of Teya camps numerous enough to merit designation as the province of Cona. And thereafter, the Spaniards and their allies advanced one more day's journey to another barranca grande, where most of the expedition camped for at least a fortnight.[2]

Eighty-plus airline miles (more than 128 km) north from Blanco Canyon to Palo Duro Canyon could have been traversed by the expedition in the four days recorded, at a rate of 20-plus miles (32-plus km) per day. This would be somewhat faster than the 15 to 18 miles (24–29 km) per day the expedition is said to have averaged elsewhere (Chapter 17), but certainly within the realm of possibility (considering the level ground over the route, except for an easy crossing of Tule Canyon). Such a route would have led northward from Blanco Canyon a day's travel by way of the head of Quitaque Canyon, then northward again a second day's travel to the head of Los Lingos Canyon, then slightly northwestward for a third day's travel to an easy crossing of Tule Canyon at the old Rex Rodgers (now Adams) Ranch headquarters above MacKenzie Reservoir. A known Garza Complex site in Quitaque Canyon may represent one of the Teya camps in the province of Cona. Although Los Lingos Canyon has not been explored archeologically, there is very likely another Garza/Teya camp there. Another known Garza site near the ranch headquarters in Tule Canyon may represent the final Teya camp.

A fourth day's travel would have taken the expedition directly to the well-known "Indian trail" that leads down into the deepest and widest part of Palo Duro Canyon at the mouth of Cita Canyon. This ancient bison and Indian trail provides the easiest access from the south into this part of Palo Duro Canyon. This stretch of Palo Duro Canyon answers the documentary description of the last barranca, regarding width, better than any other canyon in the region. The expedition proceeded beyond Teya/Garza territory to reach the last barranca. On the floor of Palo Duro Canyon a Tierra Blanca Complex/Querecho site has been located, but no Garza site, despite considerable archeological investigation of the area. Thus, Palo Duro was probably outside of Garza/Teya territory.

When this barranca grande (Palo Duro) is approached along the trail from the south, the canyon is invisible until one reaches the very rim. Viewed from this rim, the gorge presents an impressive panorama fully as wide as the league estimated by Castañeda. The various kinds of vegetation mentioned in the documents (Chapter 19) all are present in Palo Duro Canyon. Thus, here the expedition would have had the much-needed wild-plant-food resources all to themselves (and much to the relief of the Teya).

If Palo Duro Canyon is the last barranca, where the expedition camped for two weeks while hunting bison, the broad uplands to the south, southeast, and southwest of the "Indian trail" ingress/egress would have made such hunting possible. Furthermore, the hidden character of the canyon might well have necessitated the lighting of fires and discharging of firearms to guide the return of hunters, as Castañeda (Hammond and Rey 1940: 241) recounts. Interestingly, a single fragment of chain mail and a sixteenth-century Spanish spur have been found in the area of Happy Canyon, just a few miles southeast of the "Indian trail."

Blanco Canyon as the Last Barranca

The arguments that can be made in support of the Jimmy Owens Site being in the last barranca, the one where Coronado left the body of the expedition, are varied. The simplest has to do with the directions and distances traveled to the point where the Spaniards concluded that El Turco was lying to them and that they should follow the advice of his rival, Isopete, and head north. This decision appears to have been made in the last barranca, but may also have been made before that point (Hammond and Rey 1940: 240). The *Relación del Suceso* implies that it was 100 leagues east and 50 leagues south from the expedition's starting point (the Bernalillo area) to this point of decision (Hammond and Rey 1940: 291). The *Relación* states that the measurements of 100 leagues east and 50 leagues south apply to the place where the decision was made to split up the expedition, with Coronado going on to Quivira. Castañeda (Hammond and Rey 1940: 240) states clearly that this decision was made in the *last* barranca. These distances from the *Relación*, as mentioned earlier (using 2.63 miles/4.21 km to the league; see Chardon 1980), place the camp in the South Plains, where Blanco Canyon is.

A more complex argument starts with Mildred Wedel's (1982) argument that the Spaniards misinterpreted El Turco's intentions, that he was leading the expedition not to Kansas, but to the lower Mississippi River Valley. Besides the documentary argument she made for such an interpretation, there are others. For instance, the idea developed by Coronado's men that El Turco had plotted with the leaders from Pecos, Bigotes and Cacique, to lead the Spaniards out onto the plains to starve to death (Hammond and Rey 1940: 301) suffers from several contradictions. One is that it was the testimony of El Turco that Bigotes had a gold bracelet that led the Spaniards to imprison Bigotes and even to set a dog on him. After this had happened, what are the chances that Bigotes would then trust El Turco to lead the Coronado expedition astray?

The other contradiction is even more damning. It is the idea that by leading the expedition onto the Llano Estacado, El Turco would cause its destruction from lack of food and water. This may have seemed a possibility from the Spanish point of view, but El Turco was a Plains Indian who would have had an entirely different perspective. He led the expedition into an area that, from his point of view, was filled with food. Eight days after crossing the Pecos River, the expedition entered the bison range and it was never out of sight of these animals until its return to that river. The Spanish accounts complain not about a total lack of food, but of a lack of maize. To a Plains Indian, bison meat was food enough.

Similarly, El Turco led Coronado's men onto the Llano during the season of peak moisture availability. The only document that makes any statement about lack of water is Coronado's October 1541 letter to the king, in which he mentions the necessity of going without water (Hammond and Rey 1940: 187). This, however, was in the context of his trip north from the last barranca to Quivira, not of the route over which he was guided by El Turco. Interestingly, Coronado's account of the northward trip is flatly contradicted by Juan de Jaramillo, who asserts that they never suffered from lack of water (Hammond and Rey 1940: 302–303). It is possible, in light of the ultimate failure of the expedition to locate wealth, that Coronado was trying to impress the king with exaggerated hardships he had endured.

What does all this have to do with the location of the first barranca? Simply that on the assumption that El Turco was leading the expedition toward the lower Mississippi Valley, he headed across the Llano to the appropriate exit point on the far side before he got lost. A good candidate for this exit is Quitaque Canyon (about thirty-five miles/fifty-six km north of Blanco Canyon) because of the availability of abundant good water there. For the same reason, Quitaque was later a rendezvous for Comanche and Kiowa cattle raiders and traders from New Mexico. If El Turco was leading Coronado toward the lower Mississippi River Valley, he realized that a good water supply was necessary for such a large group and would, therefore, have headed toward Quitaque Canyon. After El Turco became lost, Coronado sent a detachment ahead in the direction of the sunrise (to the east or northeast). Therefore, assuming the expedition had been more or less on a line to Quitaque, the Teya encountered by the detachment four days later were likely to be well to the north of Blanco Canyon.

One final argument in favor of Blanco Canyon being the last barranca has to do with the return trip that the body of the expedition made to the Pecos River. Castañeda (Hammond and Rey 1940: 241–242) writes that the expedition proceeded to the last barranca from the last of the Teya camps and that when it began the return trip to Tiguex, it first went back to the Teya for guides ("*el campo salio de la barranca la vuelta de los teyas,*" Castañeda 1596: 88r). These men then guided the expedition across featureless plains by observing the sunrise to orient themselves, then turning and firing an arrow in the direction of travel. As they approached the first arrow, they would fire another one in the same line over it, repeating this process to maintain a straight line of travel. Additionally, Castañeda (Hammond and Rey 1940: 242) describes salt lakes along their return route.

Starting with the last clue, it is possible to eliminate many of the canyons of the eastern Llano Estacado as their starting point. The salt lakes of the Llano are found from Yellow House Draw southward. Thus, the expedition must have crossed the Llano in such a way that it intersected Yellow House Draw.[3] They did not get to the salt lakes by traveling up Yellow House Draw, because if they did, there would have been no need to use arrows to guide them; they could simply have followed the valley. A similar argument applies to a route from either Palo Duro Canyon or Tule Canyon. The most direct route from there back to the Pecos River (and Castañeda writes that they took a very direct route) would have been by way of Tierra Blanca Draw, away from salt lakes and without need for using arrows for guidance.

Blanco Canyon, on the other hand, fits the description of the return route quite well. If Blanco were the last barranca, the expedition would have traveled to the nearest Teya ranchería, probably in Quitaque Canyon, from which it could have traveled west. In the first leg of their journey, there would have been no landmarks and the guides would have had recourse to shooting successive arrows, as described by Castañeda. Eventually, the expedition would have intersected Yellow House Draw with its salt lakes, and the draw would have led them nearly to the Pecos River in the vicinity of Bosque Redondo.

Conclusion

We should mention that a third possibility has recently been argued by John Morris (1997), who suggests that the need for plant foods and a conjectured significantly earlier ripening of plants to the south would have led Coronado to direct the expedition southward from the first barranca. That, in Morris's reconstruction, could have been Quitaque Canyon, while the last barranca was Blanco Canyon (but in its lower reaches, about twenty miles southeast of the Jimmy Owens Site).

Clearly, the known Coronado expedition documents and their existing translations do not provide evidence that is detailed and unequivocal enough to resolve the question of which camp has been found in Blanco Canyon. In particular, they provide no clear indications of distance or direction of travel between the barrancas. Fully annotated transcriptions and translations of the historical documents may make the case for identification of the barrancas stronger (as called for by Polzer in Chapter 2). But, ultimately, such a resolution may come only through further archeological investigation. At this point we can make some predictions as to how the remains of the camps in the two barrancas should differ. In the first barranca should be the debris caused by the hailstorm, and this should include a significant amount of pottery from the Rio Grande pueblos and perhaps some from Mexico as well. The same barranca should hold the remains of a Teya camp. In contrast, the campsite in the last barranca should be virtually without ceramics, but should contain a great deal of bison bone, the result of two weeks of heavy hunting. Since sixteenth-century Native American campsites occur in all of the canyons of the eastern Llano Estacado and all of them contain both Rio Grande ceramics and bison bone, it will take very careful work to determine which Coronado expedition campsite has recently been located in Blanco Canyon.

Notes

1. The site is named after the local amateur archeologist and metal detector who located the first boltheads and nails and had been instrumental in survey throughout the canyon.

2. "*Desde aqui salieron con el campo algunos teyas porque asi decian aquellas gentes y caminaron con sus arrias de perros y mugeres y hijos hasta la prostera [postrera] jornada de las otras donde dieron guias para pasar adelante a donde fue el campo a una barranca grande*" (Castañeda 1596: 83r–83v). Hammond and Rey translated this as "from this place [presumably the first barranca] a few Teya . . . accompanied the army. They traveled with their packs [packtrains] of dogs, their women [wives] and children, to the last of the rancherias [clearly, the manuscript does not mention rancherías here; rather it says something like "as far as the last day's journey," evidently referring to the three days' journey over which Cona extended]. From here [the end of Cona] the army went to a deep barranca" (Hammond and Rey 1940: 239). Bracketed notes are those of the present authors.

3. A more southerly route is not possible, given the location of one of the two camps in Blanco Canyon.

Concluding Remarks

ronouncements in the popular and scholarly press notwithstanding, *The Coronado Expedition to Tierra Nueva* makes it clear that it is all but impossible to say with certainty that any particular event recorded in the sixteenth-century Coronado documents occurred at any specific place locatable on the ground on a modern map. But the book not only reveals our lingering ignorance as to precisely where Corazones, Chichilticale, the first town of Cíbola, Coofer, the bridge across the Río de Cicúye, the Querecho villages, Cona, and even Quivira were; it also demonstrates that an active group of scholars is working with determination to yield increasing certainty about the route the Coronado expedition followed.

Indeed, in Sonora, Arizona, New Mexico, and Texas, archeological and historical research seems to be bringing us closer to testable hypotheses: to look for Corazones beneath Baviácora; to look for Chichilticale in the Sulphur Springs Valley; to look for Coofer (or Moho, or Arenal) at Santiago Pueblo; to look for the bridge below the junction of the Pecos and Gallinas Rivers; to look for Cona adjacent to Texas's South Plains. That means that much work remains to be done, after a strong, if slow beginning. The prodigious work of Herbert Bolton regarding the Coronado expedition route has so dominated the field that it has taken the better part of fifty years for scholars to look with fresh eyes at the sixteenth-century Greater Southwest. But that reexamination is under way and gathering momentum. The ranks of scholars with interest in unraveling the uncertainties of the Coronado expedition are growing.

Cal Riley once asked, "Do we need to put more resources behind documentary research or behind archeology?" The best answer is probably still, "We need both equally." In study of the historic period, insights from one discipline (history, ethnohistory, archeology, ethnology, ethnobotany, geology, or geography) stimulate shifts in perspective in the others. Knowledge of the mid-summer pilgrimage from Zuni to Ko:thluwala:wa or of the identity of *uva moral* or of the whiteness of the barrancas of Colima can decisively redirect research.

To what extent were the Mexican Indians of the Coronado expedition integrated under European command; to what extent were they independent; was el Turco involved in a plot or monumentally misunderstood; was the Tiwa world permanently disrupted by the expedition's stay; did relations between Zuni and Sonora suffer because of the events of 1539–1542?

Almost all the locations along the Coronado route remain to be examined archeologically or need to be reexamined. New documents need to be located and elucidated and all the known ones need to be made available in annotated original-language editions and translations that make clear their modern assumptions. The next several decades promise exciting times for Coronado expedition scholars and increasing popular awareness of the complexity and pertinence of the early history of the Southwest.

References Cited

Aiton, Arthur S., and Agapito Rey
    1937   Coronado's Testimony in the Viceroy Mendoza Residencia. *New Mexico Historical Review* 12(3): 288–329.

Alegre, Francisco Javier, S. J.
    1956–
    1960   *Historia de la Provincia de la Compañia de Jesus de Nueva España*. 4 vols. New edition annotated by Ernest J. Burrus and Felix Zubillaga. Bibliotheca Instituti Historici S. J., Rome. Originally published 1780.

Amsden, Monroe
    1928   *Archaeological Reconnaissance in Sonora*. Southwest Museum Papers No. 1. Southwest Museum, Los Angeles.

Anderson, Arthur J. O., Frances Berdan, and James Lockhart
    1976   *Beyond the Codices*. University of Berkeley Press, Berkeley and Los Angeles.

Anderson, Ruth Matilda
    1979   *Hispanic Costume, 1480–1530*. Hispanic Society of America, New York.

Archeological Records Management Site Files (ARMS), Santa Fe Laboratory of Anthropology, Museum of New Mexico, Santa Fe.

Archivo General de Indias (AGI), Sevilla
    1553   Proceso de pleyto . . . por parte de Francisco Vázquez de Coronado, Testimony of Juan Vermejo [Bermejo], question 10. Justicia 336.
    1544   Información contra Francisco Vázquez de Coronado, Justicia 1021, document 4.
    1539   Relación de fray Marcos de Niza. Patronato 20.

Archivo General de la Nacion (AGN), Mexico City
    1647   Carta de Marcos del Rio al Padre Visitador Pedro Pantoja. . . , Guasabus, 4 de Abril 1647. Misiones 25.
    1639   Puntos de Anua de la nueba mision de San Francisco Jabier, año de 1639. Misiones 25.
    1625   Carta annua de la Provincia de la Compañia de Jesus de Nueva España, Juan Lorencio. Misiones 25.

Arnold, J. Barto, III, and Robert Weddle
    1978   *The Nautical Archeology of Padre Island, the Spanish Shipwrecks of 1554*. Texas Antiquities Publication No. 7. Academic Press, New York.

Baldwin, Stuart J.
    1983   A Tentative Occupation Sequence for Abó Pass, Central New Mexico. *COAS* 1(2): 12–28.
    1980   Piro-Tompiro Archaeology and Ethnohistory Project. Ms. on file, Department of Archaeology, University of Calgary, Alberta, Canada.

Bancroft, Hubert Howe
    1886–
    1889   *History of the North Mexican States and Texas*. 2 vols. The History Company, San Francisco.
    1888   *Arizona and New Mexico, 1530–1888*. The History Company, San Francisco.

Bancroft Library, Berkeley
    1551   Relación sacada de la provanza . . . que trata con dn. Garcia Ramirez de Cardenas, AGI, Justicia 1021, document 3, transcribed by Agapito Rey. In Research Materials of Herbert Eugene Bolton.

1544   Información contra Francisco Vázquez de Coronado, AGI, Justicia 1021, document 4, transcribed by Agapito Rey. In Research Materials of Herbert Eugene Bolton.

Bandelier, Adolph F.
1981   *The Discovery of New Mexico*, edited and translated by Madeleine Turrell Rodack. University of Arizona Press, Tucson.
1893   *The Gilded Man*. D. Appleton and Co., New York.
1892   An Outline of the Documentary History of the Zuni Tribe. *Journal of American Ethnology and Archaeology* 3(4): 1–115.
1890–   Final Report of Investigations Among the Indians of the Southwestern United States,
1892   Carried on Mainly in the Years 1880 to 1885. *Papers of the Archaeological Institute of America, American Series* 3: 1–319. Boston.
1881   Historical Introduction to Studies Among the Sedentary Indians of New Mexico. *Papers of the Archaeological Institute of America, American Series* 1(1): 1–33. Boston.

Bandelier, Adolph F., and Fanny R. Bandelier (translators)
1923–   *Historical Documents Relating to New Mexico, Nueva Vizcaya, and Approaches Thereto,*
1937   *to 1773*, edited and annotated by Charles W. Hackett. 3 vols. Carnegie Institution of Washington Publication No. 330. Washington, D.C.

Barrett, Elinore M.
1997   *The Geography of Rio Grande Pueblos Revealed by Spanish Explorers, 1540–1598*. Latin American Research Paper No. 30. University of New Mexico, Albuquerque.

Bartlett, John Russell
1909   The Language of the Piro. *American Anthropologist* N.S. 11: 426–433.

Bartlett, Katherine
1933   Pueblo Milling Stones of the Flagstaff Region and Their Relation to Others of the Southwest. *Museum of Northern Arizona* 3: 26. Flagstaff.

Basso, Keith H.
1983   Western Apache. In *Southwest*, edited by Alfonso Ortiz, pp. 462–488. Handbook of North American Indians, vol. 10, William G. Sturtevant, general editor. Smithsonian Institution, Washington, D.C.

Baugh, Timothy G.
1986   Cultural History and Protohistoric Societies in the South Plains. In *Current Trends in Southern Plains Archeology*, edited by Timothy G. Baugh, pp. 167–187. Plains Anthropologist 31(114, pt. 2), Memoir 21.
1984   Southern Plains Societies and Eastern Frontier Pueblo Exchange During the Protohistoric Period. *Papers of the Archaeological Society of New Mexico* 9: 157–167.

Baugh, Timothy G. (editor)
1982   *Edwards I (34BK2): Southern Plains Adaptations in the Protohistoric Period*. Archaeological Society Survey, Studies in Oklahoma's Past No. 8. University of Oklahoma Press, Norman.

Baugh, Timothy G., Susan Thomas Baugh, and Jack L. Hofman
1982   The Stone, Bone, Antler, and Shell Artifacts from Edwards I. In *Edwards I (34BK2) Southern Plains Adaptations in the Protohistoric Period*, edited by Timothy G. Baugh, pp. 109–178. Archaeologcal Society Survey, Studies in Oklahoma's Past No. 8. University of Oklahoma Press, Norman.

Baugh, Timothy G., and Frank W. Eddy
1987   Rethinking Apachean Ceramics: The 1985 Southern Athapaskan Ceramics Conference. *American Antiquity* 54: 793–799.

Beals, Ralph L.
1932   Comparative Ethnology of Northern Mexico Before 1750. *Ibero-Americana* 2: 93–225. University of California Press, Berkeley.

Beckett, Patrick H.
    1981   An Alternate Hypothesis to the Mystery Disks of the Tompiro. *The Artifact* 19(3–4): 199–203.

Beckett, Patrick H., and Terry L. Corbett
    1992   *The Manso Indians*. COAS Publishing and Research, Las Cruces, New Mexico.

Bell, Robert E.
    1959   Obsidian Core Found in Western Oklahoma. *El Palacio* 66(2): 72.

Berdan, Frances F., and Patricia Rieff Anawalt (editors)
    1992   *Codex Mendoza*. 4 vols. University of California Press, Berkeley and Los Angeles.

Bloom, Lansing B.
    1941   Was Fray Marcos a Liar? *New Mexico Historical Review* 16(2): 244–246.
    1940   Who Discovered New Mexico? *New Mexico Historical Review* 15(2): 101–102.

Bolton, Herbert E.
    1949   *Coronado, Knight of Pueblos and Plains*. University of New Mexico Press and Whittlesey House, Albuquerque and New York.
    1916   *Spanish Exploration in the Southwest, 1542–1706*. Charles Scribner's Sons, New York.

Boyd, Douglas K., Jay Peck, Steve A. Tomka, and Karl W. Kibler
    1993   *Data Recovery at Justiceburg Reservoir (Lake Alan Henry), Garza and Kent Counties, Texas: Phase III, Season 2*. Report of Investigations, No. 88. Prewitt and Associates, Inc., Consulting Archeologists, Austin, Texas.

Boyd-Bowman, Peter
    1971   *Lexico Hispanoamericano del Siglo XVI*. Támesis Books Limited, London.

Brackenridge, Henry M.
    1857   *Early Discoveries of Spaniards in New Mexico, Containing an Account of the Castles of Cibola*. H. Miner and Co., Pittsburgh.

Brand, Donald D.
    1978   Erroneous Locations of Two Sixteenth-Century Spanish Settlements in Western Nueva España. In *Across the Chichimec Sea: Papers in Honor of J. Charles Kelley*, edited by Carroll L. Riley and Basil C. Hedrick, pp. 193–201. Southern Illinois University Press, Carbondale.

Braniff Cornejo, Beatriz
    1978   Preliminary Interpretations Regarding the Role of the San Miguel River, Sonora, Mexico. In *Across the Chichimec Sea: Papers in Honor of J. Charles Kelley*, edited by Carroll L. Riley and Basil C. Hedrick, pp. 67–82. Southern Illinois University Press, Carbondale.

Breternitz, David A.
    1966   *An Appraisal of Tree-Ring Dated Pottery in the Southwest*. Anthropological Papers of the University of Arizona No. 10. University of Arizona Press, Tucson.

Brower, Jacob V.
    1899   *Harahey, Memoirs of Explorations in the Basin of the Mississippi*, vol. 2. St. Paul, Minnesota.

Brown, Jeffrey L.
    1974   The Pueblo Viejo Salado Sites and Their Relationship to Western Pueblo Culture. *The Artifact* 12(2): 1–53.

Bryan, Frank
    1940   The Llano Estacado: The Geographical Background of the Coronado Expedition. *Panhandle-Plains Historical Review* 13: 21–37.

Burnett, Barbara, and Katherine Murray
    1993   Death, Drought, and De Soto: The Bioarcheology of Depopulation. In *The Expedition of Hernando de Soto West of the Mississippi, 1541–1543*, edited by Gloria Young and Michael P. Hoffman, pp. 227–236. University of Arkansas, Fayetteville.

Cabeza de Vaca, Álvar Núñez
    1944   Naufragios de Álvar Núñez Cabeza de Vaca. In *Paginas para la Historia de Sinaloa y Sonora*, vol. 1, pp. 7–74. Editorial Layac, Mexico.

Castañeda (de Naçera), Pedro de
    1596   Relación de la Jornada de Cíbola. . . . Ms. on file, Rich Collection (no. 63), Rare Books and Manuscripts Division, The New York Public Library, Astor, Lenox, and Tilden Foundations.

Castillo, Bernal Díaz del
    1956   *The Discovery and Conquest of Mexico, 1517–1521*. Translated with an introduction and notes by A. P. Maudslay. Farrar, Straus, and Cudahy, New York.
    1927   *The True History of the Conquest of Mexico, Written in the Year 1568*. Translated by Maurice Keatinge, with an introduction by Arthur D. Howden Smith. National Travel Club, New York.

Chadwick, Robert
    1971   Postclassic Pottery of the Central Valleys. In *Archaeology of Northern Mesoamerica*, edited by Gordon F. Ekholm and Ignacio Bernal, pp. 228–257. Handbook of Middle American Indians, vol. 10, Robert Wauchope, general editor. University of Texas Press, Austin.

Chardon, Roland
    1980   The Linear League in North America. *Annals of the Association of American Geographers* 70(2): 129–153.

Chavez, Fray Angelico, O.F.M.
    1968   *Coronado's Friars*. Academy of American Franciscan History, Washington, D.C.

Clavigero, Abbe' D. Francesco Saverio
    1807   *The History of Mexico*. Translated from the original Italian by Charles Cullen. 2 vols. 2nd ed. J. Johnson, London.

Clayton, Lawrence A., Vernon J. Knight, Jr., and Edward C. Moore (editors)
    1993   *The De Soto Chronicles*, vol. 2. University of Alabama Press, Tuscaloosa.

Clifford, James
    1988   *The Predicament of Culture*. Harvard University Press, Cambridge.

Cloud, William A., Robert J. Mallouf, Patricia A. Mercado Allinger, Cathryn A. Hoyt, Nancy A. Kenmotsu, Joseph M. Sánchez, and Enrique R. Madrid
    1994   *Archeological Testing at the Polvo Site*. Office of the State Archeologist, Report 39. Texas Historical Commission and USDA Soil Conservation Service, Austin.

Cordell, Linda S.
    1984   *Prehistory of the Southwest*. Academic Press, New York.

Cordell, Linda S., and Amy C. Earls
    1984   *The Rio Grande Glaze "Sequence" and the Mogollon. Recent Research in Mogollon Archaeology*. Occasional Papers No. 10. The University Museum, New Mexico State University, Las Cruces.

Cordell, Linda S., and George J. Gumerman
    1989   Northern and Central Rio Grande. In *Dynamics of Southwest Prehistory*, edited by Linda S. Cordell and George J. Gumerman, pp. 293–335. Smithsonian Institution Press, Washington, D.C.

Covarrubias Orozco, Sebastián de
    1995   *Tesoro de la Lengua Castellana o Española*. Edited by Felipe C. R. Maldonaldo and Manuel Camarero. Editorial Castalia, S.A., Madrid. Originally published 1611.

Cressey, Pamela
    1975   *Post-Conquest Developments in the Teotihuacan Valley, Mexico, Obsidian Industry*. Occasional Publications in Mesoamerican Anthropology No. 8. Museum of Anthropology, University of Northern Colorado, Greeley, Colorado.

1974 *The Early Colonial Obsidian Industry.* Research Report 1(4). Mesoamerican Research Colloquium, Department of Anthropology, University of Iowa, Iowa City.

Cuevas, Mariano
1924 *Historia de los descubrimientos antiguos y modernos de la Nueva España, escrita por el conquistador Baltasar de Obregón, año de 1584.* Departamento Editorial de la Sría. de Educación Pública, México.

Cushing, Frank Hamilton
1979 *Zuñi: Selected Writings of Frank Hamilton Cushing,* edited by Jesse Green. University of Nebraska Press, Lincoln.

Davis, Irvine
1979 Kiowa-Tanoan, Keresan, and Zuni. In *The Languages of Native America,* edited by Lyle Campbell and Marianne Mithun, pp. 390–443. The University of Texas Press, Austin.

Day, A. Grove
1940 *Coronado's Quest: The Discovery of the Southwestern States.* University of California Press, Berkeley and Los Angeles.

Dean, Jeffrey S.
1991 Thoughts on Hohokam Chronology. In *Exploring the Hohokam,* edited by George J. Gumerman, pp. 61–149. University of New Mexico Press, Albuquerque.

De l'Isle, Guillaume
1701 Carte des Environs du Missisipi par G. de l'Isle Geogr. donne par Mr d'Iberville en 1701. Copy on file, New Mexico State Historical Library, Santa Fe.

Dellenbaugh, Frederick
1897 The True Route of Coronado's March. *Bulletin of the American Geographical Society* 29: 398–431.

DePratter, Chester
1994 The Kingdom of Cofitachequi. In *The Forgotten Centuries,* edited by Charles Hudson and Carmen Chavez Tessar, pp. 197–226. University of Georgia Press, Athens.

Dick, Herbert W.
1965 Picuris Pueblo Excavation. Ms. on file, National Park Service, Southwest Region, Santa Fe.

Di Peso, Charles C., John B. Rinaldo, and Gloria J. Fenner
1974 *Architecture and Dating Methods. Casas Grandes: A Fallen Trading Center of the Gran Chichimeca,* vol. 4. The Amerind Foundation, Inc., Dragoon, Arizona.

Dobyns, Henry F.
1983 *Their Numbers Become Thinned, Native American Population Dynamics in Eastern North America.* University of Tennessee Press, Knoxville.

Documentos Para La Historia de Mexico.
1857 Estado de la provincia de Sonora,...segun se halla por el mes de Julio de este año de 1730, escrito por un padre misionero de la provincia de Jesus de Nueva España. Cuarta serie, tomo III. Vicente García Torres, Mexico.

Donoghue, David
1929 The Route of the Coronado Expedition in Texas. *New Mexico Historical Review* 4(1): 77–90.

Doolittle, William E.
1988 *Pre-Hispanic Occupance in the Valley of Sonora, Mexico.* Anthropological Papers No. 48. University of Arizona, Tucson.
1979 *Pre-Hispanic Occupance in the Middle Rio Sonora Valley: From an Ecological to a Socioeconomic Focus.* Unpublished Ph.D. dissertation, Department of Geography, University of Oklahoma, Norman.

Drake, Jerry
    1995   Letter to Nancy Marble, n.d. On file in the Floyd County Historical Museum, Floydada, Texas.

Duffen, William A.
    1937   Some Notes on a Summer's Work Near Bonita, Arizona. *Kiva* 2(4): 13–16.

Dunbier, Roger
    1968   *The Sonoran Desert*. University of Arizona Press, Tucson.

Ekholm, Gordon
    1947   Recent Archaeological Work in Sonora and Northern Sinaloa. *International Congress of Americanists, 27th Proceedings*, pp. 69–73. Mexico City.
    1942   *Excavations at Guadave, Sinaloa, Mexico*. Anthropological Papers No. 38(2). American Museum of Natural History, New York.
    1940   The Archaeology of Northern and Western Mexico. In *The Maya and Their Neighbors*, edited by Clarence L. Hay, pp. 320–330. D. Appleton-Century, New York.
    1939   Results of an Archaeological Survey of Sonora and Northern Sinaloa. *Revista Mexicana de Estudios Antropologicos* 3(1): 7–11.

Ellis, Bruce T.
    1957   Crossbow Boltheads from Historic Pueblo Sites. *El Palacio* 64(7&8): 209–214.

Ewen, Charles R.
    1989a   Anhaica: Discovery of Hernando de Soto's 1539–1540 Winter Camp. In *First Encounters, Spanish Explorations in the Caribbean and the United States, 1492–1570*, edited by Jerald T. Milanich and Susan Milbrath, pp. 110–118. Ripley P. Bullen Monographs in Anthropology and History No. 9. University of Florida Press and Florida Museum of Natural History, Gainesville.
    1989b   The De Soto–Apalachee Project: The Martin Site and Beyond. *The Florida Anthropologist* 42(4): 361–368.

Feldman, Lawrence H.
    1978   Of the Stone Called Iztli. In *Archaeological Studies in Mesoamerican Obsidian*, edited by Thomas B. Hester, p. 29. Ballena Press, Socorro, New Mexico.

Fisher, Reginald G.
    1931   *Second Report of the Archeological Survey of the Pueblo Plateau: Santa Fe Sub-Quadrangle A*. Bulletin No. 1. University of New Mexico, Albuquerque.

Flint, Richard
    1995   The Unique Pattern of Coronado Expedition Material Culture. *Transactions of the 30th Regional Archeological Symposium for Southeastern New Mexico and Western Texas*, pp. 73–81. Midland Archeological Society, Midland, Texas.
    1994   Identification of One of the Barrancas Visited by Coronado. Paper presented at the Twenty-third Gran Quivira Conference, Mountainair, New Mexico.
    1992a   *The Pattern of Coronado Expedition Material Culture*. Unpublished master's thesis, Department of Behavorial Sciences, New Mexico Highlands University, Las Vegas, New Mexico.
    1992b   Who Designed Coronado's Bridge Across the Pecos River? *Kiva* 57(4): 331–342.
    1992c   *Armas de la Tierra:* The Mexican Indian Component of Coronado Expedition Material Culture. Paper presented at the conference "Where Did the *Encuentro* Happen in the Southwest?" Las Vegas, New Mexico.
    1991   Impact of Native Cultures and Geography on the Coronado and de Soto Expeditions. Part II of The Coronado and de Soto Expeditions: A Contrast in Attitudes or Differences in External Circumstances? Ms. in possession of author.

Flint, Richard, and Shirley Cushing Flint
    1993   Coronado's Crosses: Route Markers Used by the Coronado Expedition. *Journal of the Southwest* 35(2): 207–216.

1992   The Coronado Expedition: Cicúye to the Río de Cicúye Bridge. *New Mexico Historical Review* 67(2): 123–138.

1991   The Location of Coronado's 1541 Bridge: A Critical Appraisal of Albert Schroeder's 1962 Hypothesis. *Plains Anthropologist* 36(135): 171–176.

1989   Identifying the Coronado Expedition's Route: Cicúye to the Río de Cicúye Bridge. Proposal for an Historical and Archaeological Project, San Miguel and Guadalupe Counties, New Mexico, submitted to the National Endowment for the Humanities. Ms. in possession of authors.

Flores, Dan
1990   *Caprock Canyonlands: Journeys into the Heart of the Southern Plains.* University of Texas Press, Austin.

Forbes, Jack D.
1959   Unknown Athapaskans: The Identification of the Jano, Jocome, Jumano, Manso, Suma, and Other Indians Tribes in the Southwest. *Ethnohistory* 6(2): 97–159.
1957   The Janos, Jacomes, Mansos and Sumas Indians. *New Mexico Historical Review* 32(2): 319–334.

Forrestal, Peter P., and Cyprian J. Lynch (editors and translators)
1954   *Benavides' Memorial of 1630.* Documentary Series 2. Academy of American Franciscan History, Washington, D.C.

Franklin, Hayward H.
1994   Valencia Pueblo Ceramics. Ms. on file, Office of Contract Archeology, University of New Mexico, Albuquerque.

Gerhard, Peter
1993   *A Guide to the Historical Geography of New Spain.* Rev. ed. University of Oklahoma Press, Norman.
1982   *The North Frontier of New Spain.* Princeton University Press, Princeton.

Gibson, Charles
1964   *The Aztecs Under Spanish Rule.* Stanford University Press, Stanford.

Gómara, Francisco López de
1964   *Cortés, the Life of the Conqueror by his Secretary,* edited and translated by Leslie Byrd Simpson. University of California Press, Berkeley.

González, Luis
1977   *Etnología y misión en la Pimería Alta, 1745–1740.* Universidad Nacional Autónoma de México, México.

Griffen, William B.
1983   Southern Periphery: East. In *Southwest,* edited by Alfonso Ortiz, pp. 329–342. Handbook of North American Indians, vol. 10, William G. Sturtevant, general editor. Smithsonian Institution, Washington, D.C.

Gunnerson, Dolores A.
1974   *The Jicarilla Apaches.* Northern Illinois University Press, Dekalb.

Habicht-Mauche, Judith A.
1993   *The Pottery from Arroyo Hondo Pueblo, New Mexico: Tribalization and Trade in the Northern Rio Grande.* School of American Research, Santa Fe.
1992   Coronado's Querechos and Teyas in the Archaeological Record of the Texas Panhandle. *Plains Anthropologist* 37(140): 247–257.
1991   Evidence for the Manufacture of Southwestern-Style Culinary Ceramics on the Southern Plains. In *Farmers, Hunters, and Colonists,* edited by Katherine A. Spielmann, pp. 51–69. University of Arizona Press, Tucson.
1987   Southwestern-Style Culinary Ceramics on the Southern Plains: A Case Study of Technological Innovation and Cross-Cultural Interaction. *Plains Anthropologist* 32(116): 175–191.

Hackett, Charles Wilson
    1915   The Location of the Tigua Pueblos of Alameda, Puaray, and Sandia in 1680–1681. *Old Santa Fe: A Magazine of History, Archaeology, Genealogy and Biography* 2(4): 381–391.

Hallenbeck, Cleve
    1950   *Land of the Conquistadores*. The Caxton Printers, Caldwell, Idaho.
    1949   *The Journey of Fray Marcos de Niza*. Southern Methodist University Press, Dallas.

Hammond, George P., and Agapito Rey (editors and translators)
    1966   *The Rediscovery of New Mexico, 1580–1594: The Explorations of Chamuscado, Espejo, Castaño de Sosa, Morlete and Leyva de Bonilla and Humaña*. University of New Mexico Press, Albuquerque.
    1953   *Don Juan Oñate, Colonizer of New Mexico, 1595–1628*. 2 vols. University of New Mexico Press, Albuquerque.
    1940   *Narratives of the Coronado Expedition, 1540–1542*. University of New Mexico, Albuquerque.
    1928   *Obregon's History of 16th Century Exploration in Western America*. Wetzel Publishing Company, Los Angeles.

Hanke, Lewis (editor)
    1976   *Los Virreyes Españoles en América durante el gobierno de la Casa de Austria, I*. Biblioteca de Autores Españoles, vol. 273. Ediciones Atlas, Madrid.

Hann, John H.
    1989   Summary Guide to Spanish Florida Missions and Visitas with Churches in the Sixteenth and Seventeenth Centuries. Ms. on file, Bureau of Archaeological Research, Tallahassee.
    1988a   Translation of the Florida Section of the Álvar Núñez Cabeza de Vaca Accounts of the 1528 Trek from South Florida to Apalachee Led by Pánfilo de Narváez. Ms. on file, Bureau of Archaeological Research, Tallahassee.
    1988b   Translation of the Apalachee Section of the Narrative about the de Soto Expedition Written by Gonzalo Fernández de Oviedo and Based on the Diary of Rodrigo Ranjel, de Soto's Private Secretary. Ms. on file, Bureau of Archaeological Research, Tallahassee.
    1988c   Transcription and Translation of the Apalachee Section of Fidalgo Elvas's *True Relation of the Labors That the Governor Don Fernando De Soto and Certain Portuguese Gentlemen Experienced in the Exploration of the Province of Florida. Now Newly Made by a Gentleman of Elvas*. Prepared for the Bureau of Archaeological Research, De Soto Project, Tallahassee.

Harrington, John P.
    1940   Southern Peripheral Athapascan Origins, Divisions and Migrations. *Smithsonian Miscellaneous Collections* 100: 503–532. Smithsonian Institution, Washington, D.C.
    1916   The Ethnogeography of the Tewa Indians. *Annual Report of the Bureau of American Ethnology for the Years 1907–1908* 29: 29–36. Washington, D.C.
    1909   Notes on the Piro Language. *American Anthropologist* N.S. 11(4): 563–594.

Hartmann, William K.
    1989   *Desert Heart*. Fisher Books, Tucson.

Hartmann, William K., and Gayle H. Hartmann
    1972   Juan de la Asuncion, 1538: First Spanish Explorer of Arizona? *Kiva* 37: 93–101.

Haury, Emil
    1984   The Search for Chichilticale. *Arizona Highways* 60(4): 14–19.
    1936   *Some Southwestern Pottery Types, Series IV*. Medallion Papers No. 19. Gila Pueblo, Globe, Arizona.

Hawley, Florence
    1950   *Field Manual of Southwestern Pottery Types*. Rev. ed. Bulletin, Anthropological Series Bulletin No. 1(4). University of New Mexico, Albuquerque.

Hayes, Alden C., J. Nathan Young, and A. Helene Warren
    1981   *Excavation of Mound 7*. Gran Quivira National Monument Publication No. 16. U.S. National Park Service. Government Printing Office, Washington, D.C.

Hedrick, Basil C.
1978   The Location of Corazones. In *Across the Chichimec Sea: Papers in Honor of J. Charles Kelley*, edited by Carroll L. Riley and Basil C. Hedrick, pp. 228–232. Southern Illinois University Press, Carbondale.

Hemingway, Ernest
1985   *On Writing*, edited by L. W. Phillips. Grafton Books, London.

Hewett, Edgar L.
1953   *Pajarito Plateau and Its Ancient People*. Revised by Bertha P. Dutton. University of New Mexico Press and School of American Research, Albuquerque and Santa Fe.
1940   Coronado Monument and Museum. *El Palacio* 47: 172–181.

Hewett, Edgar L., and Reginald G. Fisher
1943   *Mission Monuments of New Mexico*. University of New Mexico Press, Albuquerque.

Hickerson, Nancy P.
1994   *The Jumano: Hunters and Traders of the South Plains*. University of Texas Press, Austin.
1990   Jumano: The Missing Link in South Plains Prehistory. *Journal of the West* 29(4): 5–12.
1988   The Linguistic Position of Jumano. *Journal of Anthropological Research* 33(3): 311–326.

Hill, Frank P.
1936   The South Plains and Our Indian History. *West Texas Historical Association Year Book* 12: 35–44.

Hodge, Frederick W.
1918   Excavations at Hawikuh, New Mexico. In Explorations and Field Work of the Smithsonian Institution in 1917. *Smithsonian Miscellaneous Collections, 1917–1918* 68(12): 61–72.
1899   Coronado's March to Quivira. In *Harahey, Memoirs of Explorations in the Basin of the Mississippi*, vol. 2, edited by Jacob V. Brower, pp. 29–73. N.p., St. Paul, Minnesota.

Hodge, Frederick W. (editor)
1907   The Narrative of the Expedition of Coronado by Pedro de Castañeda. In *Spanish Explorers in the Southern United States 1528–1543*, edited by Frederick W. Hodge and Theodore H. Lewis, pp. 3–126. Charles Scribner's Sons, New York.

Hodge, Frederick W., George P. Hammond, and Agapito Rey (editors and translators)
1945   *Fray Alonso de Benavides' Revised Memorial of 1634*. University of New Mexico Press, Albuquerque.

Hofman, Jack L.
1989   Protohistoric Culture History on the Southern Great Plains. In *From Clovis to Comanchero: Archeological Overview of the Southern Great Plains*, edited by Jack L. Hofman, Robert L. Brooks, Joe S. Hays, Douglas W. Owsley, Richard L. Jantz, Murray K. Marks, Mary H. Manheim, pp. 91–100. Arkansas Archeological Survey Research Series, No. 35. Fayetteville.
1984   The Western Protohistoric: A Summary of the Edwards and Wheeler Complexes. In *Prehistory of Oklahoma*, edited by Robert E. Bell, pp. 347–362. Academic Press, New York.

Holden, William C.
1944   Coronado's Route Across the Staked Plains. *The West Texas Historical Association Year Book* 20: 3–20.
1938   Blue Mountain Rock Shelter. *Bulletin of the Texas Archeological and Paleontological Society* 10: 208–221.

Honea, Kenneth H.
1973   The Technology of Eastern Puebloan Pottery on the Llano Estacado. *Plains Anthropologist* 18(59): 73–88.
1968   Material Culture: Ceramics. In *The Cochiti Dam Archaeological Salvage Project, Part I: Report on the 1963 Season*, assembled by Charles H. Lange, pp. 111–169. Research Records No. 6. Museum of New Mexico, Santa Fe.

1967 *Revised Sequence of Rio Grande Glaze Pottery.* Archeological Survey Bulletin No. 1. Texas Tech University, Lubbock.

Hook, Bill, and Raymon Lee
1990 *Borrego: The Fall and Rise of Desert Bighorn Sheep in Arizona.* Arizona Desert Bighorn Sheep Society, Phoenix.

Hordes, Stanley M.
1992 A Sixteenth-Century Spanish Campsite in the Tiguex Province: An Historian's Perspective. In *Current Research in the Late Prehistory and Early History of New Mexico*, edited by Bradley Vierra, pp. 155–165. Special Publication 1. New Mexico Archeological Council, Albuquerque.
1989 The Historical Context of LA 54147. In *A Sixteenth-Century Spanish Campsite in the Tiguex Province*, edited by Bradley Vierra, pp. 207–222. Laboratory of Anthropology Note No. 475. Museum of New Mexico, Santa Fe.

Horgan, Paul
1954 *Great River: The Rio Grande in North American History.* Holt, Rinehart & Winston, New York.

Hudson, Charles, Chester DePratter, and Marvin Smith
1984 The Hernando de Soto Expedition: From Apalachee to Chiaha. *Southeastern Archaeology* 3: 66–77.

Huff, J. Wesley
1951 A Coronado Episode. *New Mexico Historical Review* 26(2): 119–127.

Hughes, Jack T.
1991 Prehistoric Cultural Developments on the Texas High Plains. *Bulletin of the Texas Archaeological Society* 60: 1–55.

Inman, Henry
1899 *The Old Santa Fe Trail: The Story of a Great Highway.* Crane & Co., Topeka.

Ives, Ronald L.
1975 The "High" Latitudes of Early Spanish Maps. *The Kiva* 41(2): 161–183.

Ivey, James E., Diane Lee Rhodes, and Joseph P. Sánchez
1991 *The Coronado Expedition of 1540–1542.* A Special History Report Prepared for the Coronado Trail Study. U.S. Department of Interior, National Park Service, Denver.

Johnson, Byron
1988 *Arms and Armor of the Spanish Conquest: A Brief Description.* The Albuquerque Museum, Albuquerque.

Johnson, Eileen, V. T. Holliday, M. J. Kaczor, and Robert Stuckenrath
1977 The Garza Occupation at the Lubbock Lake Site. *Bulletin of the Texas Archeological Society* 48: 83–109.

Johnson, Jean
1950 *The Ópata: An Inland Tribe of Sonora.* Publications in Anthropology No. 6. University of New Mexico, Albuquerque.

Jones, B. Calvin, and Gary Shapiro
1987 Nine Mission Sites in Apalachee. Paper presented at the Society for Historical Archaeology, Savannah.

Jones, Paul A.
1937 *Coronado and Quivira.* Lyons Publishing Co., Lyons, Kansas.

Kelley, J. Charles
1986 *Jumano and Patarabueye: Relations at La Junta de los Rios.* Anthropological Papers No. 77. Museum of Anthropology, University of Michigan, Ann Arbor.
1955 Juan Sabeata and Diffusion in Aboriginal Texas. *American Anthropologist* 57(5): 981–995.

1952   Factors Involved in the Abandonment of Certain Peripheral Southwestern Settlements. *American Anthropologist* 54(3): 356–387.
1937   The Route of Antonio de Espejo Down the Pecos River and Across the Texas Trans-Pecos Region in 1583, Its Relation to West Texas Archeology. *West Texas Historical and Scientific Society* 7: 7–25. Reprinted. Originally published in *Sul Ross State Teachers College Bulletin* 18(4).

Kelley, Jane Holden
1964   Comments on the Archaeology of the Llano Estacado. *Texas Archaeological Society Bulletin* 35: 1–17.

Kelley, Vincent C.
1969   *Albuquerque: Its Mountains, Valley, Water, and Volcanoes.* Scenic Trips to the Geologic Past No. 9. New Mexico Bureau of Mines and Mineral Resources, Socorro.

Kempton, Willett
1981   *The Folk Classification of Ceramics: A Study of Cognitive Prototypes.* Academic Press, New York.

Kessell, John L.
1987   *Kiva, Cross, and Crown: The Pecos Indians and New Mexico, 1540–1840.* University of New Mexico Press, Albuquerque.

Kidder, Alfred V.
1936   *The Pottery of Pecos, Vol II: The Glaze Paint, Culinary, and Other Wares.* Papers of the Phillips Academy, Southwest Expedition No. 7. Yale University Press, New Haven.
1932   *The Artifacts of Pecos.* Papers of the Southwestern Expedition, No. 6. Yale University Press, New Haven.

Kiser, Edwin L.
1978   The Re-examination of Pedro de Castañeda's Bone Bed by Geological Investigations. *Bulletin of the Texas Archeological Society* 49: 332–339.

Lambert, Marjorie F.
1954   *Paa-ko: Archaeological Chronicle of an Indian Village in North Central New Mexico, Parts I–V.* Monographs of the School of American Research No. 19. University of New Mexico Press, Albuquerque.

Lang, Richard W., and Arthur H. Harris
1984   *The Faunal Remains from Arroyo Hondo Pueblo, New Mexico: A Study in Short-Term Subsistence Change.* Arroyo Hondo Archaeological Series, Vol. 5. School of American Research Press, Santa Fe.

Lange, Charles H., and Carroll L. Riley (editors)
1970   *The Southwestern Journals of Adolph F. Bandelier, 1883–1884.* The Southwestern Journals of Adolph F. Bandelier, vol. 2. The University of New Mexico Press, Albuquerque.

Las Casas, Bartolomé de
1992   *The Devastation of the Indies: A Brief Account.* Johns Hopkins University Press, Baltimore. Originally published 1552.

Lavendar, David S.
1992   *De Soto, Coronado, Cabrillo: Explorers of the Northern Mystery.* Department of the Interior Handbook 144. Government Printing Office, Washington, D.C.

Leap, William L.
1971   Who Were the Piro? *Anthropological Linguistics* 13(7): 321–330.

Lees, William B.
1993   Review of *A Sixteenth-Century Spanish Campsite in the Tiguex Province,* edited by Bradley J. Vierra. *Historical Archeology* 27(1): 123–125.
1990   Evidence for Early European Contact with the Wichita in Kansas. Paper presented at the Conference on Historical and Underwater Archaeology, Society for Historical Archaeology, Tucson.

Lesser, Alexander, and Gene Weltfish
  1932   Composition of the Caddoan Linguistic Stock. *Smithsonian Miscellaneous Collection* 87(6). Smithsonian Institution, Washington, D.C.
Lindsay, Alexander J., Jr.
  1987   Explaining an Anasazi Migration to East Central Arizona. *American Archaeology* 6(3): 190–198.
Lintz, Christopher Ray
  1986   *Architecture and Community Variability Within the Antelope Creek Phase of the Texas Panhandle.* Archeological Society Survey, Studies in Oklahoma's Past No. 14. University of Oklahoma Press, Norman.
  1984   The Plains Villagers: Antelope Creek. In *Prehistory of Oklahoma*, edited by Robert E. Bell, pp. 325–346. Academic Press, New York.
López de Gómara, Francisco
  1922   *Historia general de las Indias.* 2 vols. Calpe, Madrid. Originally published 1554.
Lumholtz, Karl
  1902   *Unknown Mexico.* 2 vols. Charles Scribner's Sons, New York.
Marble, Nancy
  1995   Notes of Telephone Interviews with Mrs. J. S. (Kay) Hale and Thurmon Richards, September 5 and 6. On file in the Floyd County Historical Museum, Floydada, Texas.
  1991   Notes of Field Trip to Blanco Canyon, October 16. On file in the Floyd County Historical Museum, Floydada, Texas.
Marshall, Michael P.
  1989   The Ceramic Assemblage. In *A Sixteenth-Century Spanish Campsite in the Tiguex Province*, edited by Bradley J. Vierra, pp. 75–116. Laboratory of Anthropology Note No. 475. Museum of New Mexico, Santa Fe.
  1988   *An Archeological Survey of the Mann-Zuris Pueblo Complex.* Report to the New Mexico Historic Commission and the Miller-Brown Land Co., Phase II, Santa Fe and Albuquerque.
  1987   *Archeological Investigations in a 16th–Early 17th Century Piro Pueblo in the Village of San Antonio, New Mexico.* Office of Contract Archeology, University of New Mexico, Albuquerque.
  1982   *Excavations at Nuestra Señora de Dolores Pueblo (LA 6777), A Prehistoric Settlement in the Tiguex Province.* Office of Contract Archeology, University of New Mexico, Albuquerque.
Marshall, Michael P., and Cristina L. Marshall
  1992   *Investigations in the Middle Rio Grande Conservancy District: A Cultural Resource Survey of Irrigation and Drainage Canals in the Isleta-South to La Joya Area, Phase II Survey.* Bureau of Reclamation, U.S. Department of the Interior, Albuquerque.
Marshall, Michael P., and Henry J. Walt
  1985   *Archeological Investigations of Colonial and Mexican Period Cultural Properties in the Rio Medio Province of New Mexico.* 2 vols. Ms. on file, New Mexico Historic Preservation Division, Santa Fe.
  1984   *Rio Abajo: Prehistory and History of a Rio Grande Province.* New Mexico Historic Preservation Division, Santa Fe.
Martínez, Gregory, Mary Davis, and Kathryn Sargeant
  1985   Paleochannel Analysis in the North Valley of Albuquerque. In An Archeological and Historical Survey of the Village of Los Ranchos, edited by Kathryn Sargeant and Mary Davis. Ms. on file, New Mexico Historic Preservation Division, Santa Fe.
McGuire, Randall H., and Maria E. Villalpando
  1991   Prehistory and the Making of History in Sonora. In *Spanish Borderlands in Pan American Perspective*, edited by David H. Thomas, pp. 159–178. Columbian Consequences, vol. 3. Smithsonian Institution Press, Washington, D.C.

Mecham, John Lloyd
    1927   *Francisco de Ibarra and Nueva Vizcaya*. Duke University Press, Durham, North Carolina.
    1926   The Second Spanish Expedition to New Mexico. *New Mexico Historical Review* 1(3): 265–291.

Mera, Harry P.
    1940   *Population Changes in the Rio Grande Glaze Paint Area*. Technical Series Bulletin No. 9. Laboratory of Anthropology, Museum of New Mexico, Santa Fe.
    1933   *A Proposed Revision of the Rio Grande Glaze Paint Sequence*. Technical Series Bulletin No. 5. Laboratory of Anthropology, Museum of New Mexico, Santa Fe.

Mills, Jack P., and Vera M. Mills
    1969   *The Kuykendall Site: A Prehistoric Salado Village in Southeastern Arizona*. El Paso Archaeological Society Special Report for 1967, No. 6. El Paso, Texas.

Monjarás-Ruiz, Jesús, Elena Limón, and María de la Cruz Paillés H. (editors)
    1989   *Tlatelolco: Fuentes e Historia*. Obras de Robert H. Barlow, vol. 2. Instituto Nacional de Antropología e Historia, México.

Mora, Carmen de (editor)
    1992   *Las Siete Ciudades de Cíbola*. Ediciones Alfar, Sevilla.

Morris, John M.
    1997   *El Llano Estacado: Exploration and Imagination on the High Plains of Texas and New Mexico, 1536–1860*. Texas State Historical Association Publications, Austin.

Mota y Padilla, Matías de la
    1920   *Historia de la conquista del reino de la Nueva Galicia*. Edited by José Ireneo Gutiérrez. Talleres Gráficos de Gallardo y Alvarez del Castillo, Guadalajara. Originally published 1742.

Nader, Helen
    1990   *Liberty in Absolutist Spain: The Hapsburg Sale of Towns, 1516–1700*. Johns Hopkins University Press, Baltimore.

Naylor, Thomas N.
    1981   Apaches They Weren't: The Suma Rebels Executed at Casas Grandes in 1685. In *The Protohistoric Period in the North American Southwest: 1450–1700*, edited by David R. Wilcox and W. Bruce Masse, pp. 275–281. Anthropological Research Paper No. 24. Arizona State University Press, Tempe.

New Mexico Historic Preservation Division (HPD), Santa Fe
    Reports prepared for nomination to the National Register of Historic Places, National Park Service, U.S. Department of the Interior.

Northern, James M.
    1979   *Archaeological Investigations of the Montgomery Site, Floyd County, Texas*. Unpublished master's thesis, Department of Anthropology, Texas Tech University, Lubbock, Texas.

Oblasser, Bonaventure, O.F.M.
    1939   *Marco da Nizza, His Own Personal Narrative of Arizona Discovered*. Topowa, Arizona.

Opler, Morris E.
    1983a   The Apachean Culture Pattern and Its Origins. In *Southwest*, edited by Alfonso Ortiz, pp. 368–392. Handbook of North American Indians, vol. 10, William G. Sturtevant, general editor. Smithsonian Institution, Washington, D.C.
    1983b   Chiricahua Apache. In *Southwest*, edited by Alfonso Ortiz, pp. 401–418. Handbook of North American Indians, vol. 10, William G. Sturtevant, general editor. Smithsonian Institution, Washington, D.C.
    1983c   Mescalero Apache. In *Southwest*, edited by Alfonso Ortiz, pp. 419–439. Handbook of North American Indians, vol. 10, William G. Sturtevant, general editor. Smithsonian Institution, Washington, D.C.

Pacheco, Joaquín F., and Francisco de Cárdenas (editors)
    1870   Relacion del Suceso de la Jornada que Francisco Vazquez hizo en el Descubrimiento de Cibola. In *Colección de documentos inéditos relativos al descubrimiento, conquista, y organización de las antiguas posesiones españoles en América y Oceanía*, vol. 14, pp. 318–329. Transcription of AGI, Patronato, 20. Madrid.

Pagden, Anthony
    1982   *The Fall of Natural Man*. Cambridge University Press, Cambridge.

Pailes, Richard A.
    1984   Agricultural Development and Trade in the Rio Sonora Valley. In *Prehistoric Agricultural Strategies in the Southwest*, edited by Suzanne K. Fish and Paul R. Fish, pp. 309–325. Anthropological Research Papers No. 33. Arizona State University Press, Tucson.
    1980   The Upper Rio Sonora Valley in Prehistoric Trade. In *New Frontiers in the Archaeology and Ethnohistory of the Greater Southwest*, edited by Carroll L. Riley and Basil C. Hedrick, pp. 20–39. Transactions of the Illinois State Academy of Science 72. Springfield.
    1978   The Rio Sonora Culture in Prehistoric Trade Systems. In *Across the Chichimec Sea: Papers in Honor of J. Charles Kelley*, edited by Carroll L. Riley and Basil C. Hedrick, pp. 134–143. Southern Illinois University Press, Carbondale.
    1976a   Recientes investigaciones arqueologicas en el sur de Sonora. In *Sonora: antropología del desierto; primera reunion de antropología e historia del noroeste*, edited by Beatriz Braniff C. and Richard Felger, pp. 137–155. Colección Cientifica No. 27. Centro Regional del Noroeste, INAH, México.
    1976b   Relaciones culturales prehistoricas en el noroeste de Sonora. In *Sonora: antropología del desierto; primera reunion de antropología e historia del noroeste*, edited by Beatriz Braniff C. and Richard Felger, pp. 213–228. Colección Cientifica No. 27. Centro Regional del Noroeste, INAH, México.
    1973   *An Archaeological Reconnaissance of Southern Sonora and Reconsideration of the Rio Sonora Culture*. Ph.D. dissertation, Southern Illinois University, Carbondale. University Microfilms, Ann Arbor.

Parker, Wayne
    1982   *Archaeology at the Bridwell Site*. Crosby County Pioneer Memorial Museum, Crosbyton, Texas.

Parry, William J., and John D. Speth
    1984   *The Garnsey Spring Campsite: Late Prehistoric Occupation in Southeastern New Mexico*. Technical Report 15. Museum of Anthropology, University of Michigan, Ann Arbor.

Parsons, Mark L.
    1967   *Archeological Investigations in Crosby and Dickens Counties During the Winter, 1966–1967*. Archeological Program, Report 7: 1–108. State Building Commission, Austin.

Payne-Gallwey, Sir Ralph
    1903   *The Crossbow*. The Holland Press, London.

Peixotto, Ernest
    1916   *Our Hispanic Southwest*. Charles Scribner's Sons, New York.

Pennington, Campbell W.
    1980   *The Material Culture: The Pima Bajo of Central Sonora, Mexico*, vol. I. University of Utah Press, Salt Lake City.
    1969   *The Tepehuan of Chihuahua: Their Material Culture*. University of Utah Press, Salt Lake City.

Pérez de Ribas, Andrés
    1944   *Historia de los triunfos de Nuestra Santa Fe entre gentes las mas barbaras y fieras del Nueve Orbe*. 3 vols. Editorial Layac, México. Originally published 1645.

Peterson, Harold Leslie
    1956   *Arms and Armor in Colonial America, 1526–1783*. The Stackpole Company, Harrisburg, Pennsylvania.

Peterson, John, James A. Neely, Peter W. Nicholas, and S. Christopher Caran
    1988   *Prairie Hinterland: The Archaeology of Palo Duro Creek; A Cultural Resources Inventory; Palo Duro Reservoir, Hansford County, Texas.* Submitted to Freese and Nichols, Inc. on behalf of the Palo Duro River Authority. Texas Antiquities Committee Permit #605.

Phillips, David A., Jr.
    1989   Prehistory of Chihuahua and Sonora, Mexico. *Journal of World Prehistory* 3(4): 373–401.

Pupo-Walker, Enrique (editor)
    1993   *Castaways: The Narrative of Álvar Núñez Cabeza de Vaca.* University of California Press, Berkeley.

Ramenofsky, Ann F.
    1987   *Vectors of Death, The Archaeology of European Contact.* University of New Mexico Press, Albuquerque.

Reff, Daniel T.
    1991   *Disease, Depopulation, and Culture Change in Northwestern New Spain, 1518–1764.* University of Utah Press, Salt Lake City.
    1981   The Location of Corazones and Senora: Archaeological Evidence from the Rio Sonora Valley, Mexico. In *Protohistoric Period in the American Southwest, A.D. 1450–1700,* edited by David R. Wilcox and W. Bruce Masse, pp. 94–112. Anthropological Research Papers 24. Arizona State University Press, Tempe.

Rhodes, Diane Lee
    1992   Coronado's American Legacy: An Overview of Possible Entrada Artifacts and Site Types and a Discussion of Texas Sites. *Bulletin of the Texas Archeological Society* 63: 27–51. Austin.

Rhodes, Diane, Joseph P. Sánchez, James Ivey, and John C. Paige
    1990   Draft Report of the Coronado Trail Study. Ms. on file, National Park Service, Denver Service Center, Denver.

Riley, Carroll L.
    1995   *Rio del Norte: Peoples of the Upper Rio Grande from Earliest Times to the Pueblo Revolt.* University of Utah Press, Salt Lake City.
    1992   Coronado in the Southwest. In *Archaeology, Art, and Anthropology: Papers in Honor of J. J. Brody,* edited by Meliha S. Duran and David T. Kirkpatrick, pp. 147–156. Anthropological Papers 18. The Archaeological Society of New Mexico, Albuquerque.
    1987   *The Frontier People: The Greater Southwest in the Protohistoric Period.* University of New Mexico Press, Albuquerque.
    1985   The Location of Chichilticale. In *Southwestern Culture History: Collected Papers in Honor of Albert H. Schroeder,* edited by Charles H. Lange, pp. 153–161. Anthropological Papers 10. The Archaeological Society of New Mexico, Albuquerque.
    1981   Puaray and Coronado's Tiguex. In *Collected Papers in Honor of Erik Kellerman Reed,* edited by Albert H. Schroeder and David A. Breternitz, pp. 197–212. Anthropological Papers 6. The Archaeological Society of New Mexico, Albuquerque.
    1979   Casas Grandes and the Sonoran Statelets. Paper presented to the Chicago Anthropological Society.
    1975   The Road to Hawikuh: Trade and Trade Routes to Cibola-Zuni During Late Prehistoric and Early Historic Times. *Kiva* 41: 137–159.
    1974   Mesoamerican Indians in the Early Southwest. *Ethnohistory* 21(1): 25–36.
    1973   Las Casas and the Benavides Memorial of 1630. *New Mexico Historical Review* 48: 209–222.
    1971   Early Spanish-Indian Communication in the Greater Southwest. *New Mexico Historical Review* 46(4): 285–314.
    1969   The Southern Tepehuan and Tepecano. In *Ethnology,* edited by Evon Z. Vogt, pp. 814–821. Handbook of Middle American Indians, vol. 8, Robert Wauchope, general editor. University of Texas Press, Austin.

Riley, Carroll L., and Joni L. Manson
- 1983 The Cibola-Tiguex Route: Continuity and Change in the Southwest. *New Mexico Historical Review* 58(4): 347–367.

Roberts, Frank H. H., Jr.
- 1931 *The Ruins at Kiatuthlanna Eastern Arizona*. Bureau of American Ethnology, Bulletin 100. Washington, D.C.

Robinson, William J., John W. Hannah, and Bruce G. Harrill
- 1972 *Tree-Ring Dates from New Mexico I, O, U: Central Rio Grande Area*. Laboratory of Tree-Ring Research, University of Arizona, Tucson.

Robinson, William J., Bruce G. Harrill, and Richard L. Warren
- 1973 *Tree-Ring Dates from New Mexico J–K, P, V: Santa Fe–Pecos–Lincoln Area*. Laboratory of Tree-Ring Research, University of Arizona, Tucson.

Runkles, Frank A.
- 1964 The Garza Site: A Neo-American Campsite Near Post, Texas. *Bulletin of the Texas Archeological Society* 35: 101–125.

Sahagún, fray Bernardino de
- 1961 *The People. Florentine Codex, General History of the Things of New Spain, Book 10*, edited and translated by Charles E. Dibble and Arthur J. O. Anderson. School of American Research and Museum of New Mexico, Santa Fe.

Sánchez, Joseph P.
- 1988 *The Rio Abajo Frontier, 1540–1692: A History of Early Colonial New Mexico*. History Monograph Series. Albuquerque Museum, Albuquerque.

Sargeant, Kathryn
- 1987 Coping with the River: Settlements in Albuquerque's North Valley. In *Secrets of a City: Papers on Albuquerque Area Archeology in Honor of Richard A. Bice*, edited by Anne V. Poore and John L. Montgomery, pp. 31–47. Anthropological Papers No. 13. The Archeological Society of New Mexico, Albuquerque.

Sauer, Carl O.
- 1971 *Sixteenth Century North America*. University of California Press, Berkeley.
- 1941 The Credibility of the Fray Marcos Account. *New Mexico Historical Review* 16(2): 233–246.
- 1937 The Discovery of New Mexico Reconsidered. *New Mexico Historical Review* 12(3): 270–287.
- 1934 The Distribution of Aboriginal Tribes and Languages in Northwestern Mexico. *Ibero-Americana* 5. University of California Press, Berkeley.
- 1932 The Road to Cibola. *Ibero-Americana* 3. University of California Press, Berkeley.

Sauer, Carl O., and Donald D. Brand
- 1932 Aztatlán, a Prehistoric Mexican Frontier on the Pacific Coast. *Ibero-Americana* 1: 1–92. University of California Press, Berkeley.
- 1931 Prehistoric Settlements of Sonora with Special Reference to Cerro de Trincheras. *Publications in Geography* 5: 67–148. University of California Press, Berkeley.

Scarry, John
- 1994 The Apalachee Chiefdom: A Mississippian Society on the Fringe of the Mississippian World. In *The Forgotten Centuries*, edited by Charles Hudson and Carmen Chavez Tessar, pp. 156–178. University of Georgia Press, Athens.

Schaafsma, Curtis F.
- 1987 Tiguez Province Revisited. In *Secrets of a City: Papers on Albuquerque Area Archeology in Honor of Richard A. Bice*, edited by Anne V. Poore and John L. Montgomery, pp. 6–13. Anthropological Papers No. 13. The Archeological Society of New Mexico, Albuquerque.
- 1968 Funeral Bowls from a Spanish-Contact Camposanto. *El Palacio* 75(2): 40–43.

Scholes, France V., and Harry P. Mera
  1940 *Some Aspects of the Jumano Problem*. Contributions to American Anthropology and History Publication 523. Carnegie Institution of Washington, Washington, D.C.

Schroeder, Albert H.
  1993 The Locale of Coronado's Bridge and Other Pertinent Matters. In *Why Museums Collect: Papers in Honor of Joe Ben Wheat*, edited by Meliha S. Duran and David T. Kirkpatrick, pp. 195–202. Anthropological Papers 19. The Archaeological Society of New Mexico, Albuquerque.
  1992a Vásquez de Coronado and the Southern Tiwa Pueblos. In *Archaeology, Art and Anthropology, Papers in Honor of J. J. Brody*, edited by Meliha S. Duran and David T. Kirkpatrick, pp. 185–191. Anthropological Papers 18. The Archeological Society of New Mexico, Albuquerque.
  1992b The Locale of Coronado's Bridge. *New Mexico Historical Review* 67(2): 115–122.
  1983 Querechos, Vaqueros, Cocoyes, and Apaches. *Anthropological Papers* 8: 159–166. The Archaeological Society of New Mexico, Albuquerque.
  1979 Pueblos Abandoned in Historic Times. In *Southwest*, edited by Alfonso Ortiz, pp. 236–254. Handbook of North American Indians, vol. 9, William G. Sturtevant, general editor. Smithsonian Institution, Washington, D.C.
  1964 The Language of the Saline Pueblos: Piro or Tiwa? *New Mexico Historical Review* 39(3): 235–249.
  1962 A Re-Analysis of the Routes of Coronado and Oñate into the Plains in 1541 and 1601. *Plains Anthropologist* 7(15): 2–23.
  1956 Fray Marcos de Niza, Coronado and the Yavapai. *New Mexico Historical Review* 31(1): 24–37.
  1955 Fray Marcos de Niza, Coronado and the Yavapai. *New Mexico Historical Review* 30(4): 265–296.
  n.d. A Study of the Apache Indians, Part 1, The Apaches and Their Neighbors. Ms. on file, Laboratory of Anthropology, Museum of New Mexico, Santa Fe.

Schroeder, Albert H., and Don S. Matson (editors and translators)
  1965 *A Colony on the Move: Gaspar Castaño de Sosa's Journal, 1590–1591*. School of American Research, Santa Fe.

Scurlock, Dan S.
  1982 An Historical Overview of Bernalillo, New Mexico. In *Excavations at Nuestra Señora de Dolores Pueblo (LA 677): A Prehistoric Settlement in the Tiguex Province*, edited by Michael Marshall, pp. 176–182. Office of Contract Archeology, University of New Mexico, Albuquerque.

Secretaría de Programación y Presupuesto
  1987 *Síntesis Geográfico de Colima*. Secretaría de Programación y Presupuesto, México.

Shapiro, Gary
  1988 Trailing the Apalachee. *Archaeology* 41(2): 58–59.

Shepard, Anna O.
  1942 *Rio Grande Glaze Paint Ware: A Study Illustrating the Place of Ceramic Technological Analysis in Archaeological Research*. Contributions to American Anthropology and History No. 39, Publication 528. Carnegie Institution of Washington, Washington, D.C.

Shine, Michael
  1916 The Lost Province of Quivira. *The Catholic Historical Review* 2(1): 3–18.

Simmons, Marc
  1979 History of Pueblo-Spanish Relations to 1821. In *Southwest*, edited by Alfonso Ortiz, pp. 178–193. Handbook of North American Indians, vol. 9, William G. Sturtevant, general editor. Smithsonian Institution, Washington, D.C.

Simmons, Marc, and Frank Turley
    1980   *Southwestern Colonial Ironwork*. Museum of New Mexico Press, Santa Fe.

Simpson, James H.
    1871   Coronado's March in Search of the "Seven Cities of Cibola" and Discussion of Their Probable Location. In *Annual Report of the Board of Regents of the Smithsonian Institution for 1869*, pp. 309–340. Smithsonian Institution, Washington, D.C.

Sires, Earl W., Jr.
    1984   Excavations at El Poveron. In *Hohokam Archaeology Along the Salt-Gila Aqueduct, Central Arizona Project, IV, (2), Prehistoric Occupation of the Queen Creek Delta*, edited by Lynn Teague and Patricia Crown, pp. 221–326. Arizona State Museum Archaeological Series 150. Tucson.

Smith, Marvin T.
    1987   *Archaeology of Aboriginal Culture Change in the Interior Southeast: Depopulation During the Early Historic Period*. University Press of Florida, Gainesville.

Smith, Watson, Richard B. Woodbury, and Nathalie F. S. Woodbury
    1966   *The Excavation of Hawikuh by Frederick Webb Hodge, Report of the the Hendricks-Hodge Expedition, 1917–1923*. Heye Foundation, Museum of the American Indian, New York.

Snow, David H.
    1992   A Review of Spanish Colonial Archeology in Northern New Mexico: "Where We're at, as They Say." In *Current Research in the Late Prehistory and Early History of New Mexico*, edited by Bradley Vierra, pp. 185–194. Special Publication 1. New Mexico Archeological Council, Albuquerque.
    1990   Tener Comal y Metate: Protohistoric Rio Grande Maize Use and Diet. In *Perspectives on Southwestern Prehistory*, edited by Paul E. Minnis and Charles L. Redman, pp. 289–300. Westview Press, Boulder.
    1988   Initial Entradas and Explorations. In *The North Central Regional Overview: Strategies for the Comprehensive Survey of the Architectural and Historic Archaeological Resources of North Central New Mexico*, assembled by Boyd C. Pratt and David H. Snow, pp. 70–128. New Mexico Historic Preservation Division. Santa Fe.
    1986   A Preliminary Ceramic Analysis, LA 120, Gran Quivira (1985): The Glazes and Black-on-White Wares. Ms. on file, Katherine A. Spielmann, University of Iowa, Iowa City.
    1982   The Rio Grande Glaze, Matte-Paint and Plainware Tradition. In *Southwestern Ceramics, A Comparative Review*, edited by Albert H. Schroeder, pp. 235–278. The Arizona Archaeologist No. 15. Arizona Archaeological Society, Tucson.
    1980   Rio Grande Ceramics from the Ozier Site. Ms. in possession of author.
    1976a   *Archeological Excavations at Pueblo del Encierro, LA 70, Cochiti Dam Salvage Project, Cochiti, New Mexico: Final Report, 1964–1965 Field Seasons*. Laboratory of Anthropology Note No. 78. Museum of New Mexico, Santa Fe.
    1976b   Santiago to Guache: Notes for a Tale of Two (or More) Bernalillos. In *Collected Papers in Honor of Marjorie Ferguson Lambert*, edited by Albert H. Schroeder, pp. 161–181. Anthropological Papers No. 3. The Archeological Society of New Mexico, Albuquerque.
    1975   The Identification of Puaray Pueblo. In *Collected Papers in Honor of Florence Hawley Ellis*, edited by Theodore R. Frisbie, pp. 463–480. Anthropological Papers No. 2. The Archeological Society of New Mexico, Albuquerque.
    1973a   *Cochiti Dam Salvage Project: Archeological Excavation of the Las Majadas Site LA 591, Cochiti Dam, New Mexico*. Laboratory of Anthropology Note No. 75. Museum of New Mexico, Santa Fe.
    1973b   Some Economic Considerations of Historic Rio Grande Pueblo Pottery. In *The Changing Ways of Southwestern Indians: A Historic Perspective*, edited by Albert H. Schroeder, pp. 55–72. Rio Grande Press, Glorieta, New Mexico.

Snow, David H., and Marianne L. Stoller
　　1987　　Outside Santa Fe in the Seventeenth Century. Paper presented at the Ethnic Relations in the Southwest Symposium, American Society for Ethnohistory, Berkeley.

South, Stanley, Russell K. Skowronek, and Richard E. Johnson
　　1988　　*Spanish Artifacts from Santa Elena.* Occasional Papers of the South Carolina Institute of Archaeology and Anthropology, Anthropological Studies No. 7. The University of South Carolina, Columbia.

Spence, Michael W.
　　1967　　The Obsidian Industry of Teotihuacan. *American Antiquity* 32(4): 507–514.

Spicer, Edward H.
　　1962　　*Cycles of Conquest: The Impact of Spain, Mexico, and the United States on the Indians of the Southwest, 1533–1960.* University of Arizona Press, Tucson.

Spielmann, Katherine A.
　　1983　　Late Prehistoric Exchange Between the Southwest and Southern Plains. *Plains Anthropologist* 28(102, part 1): 257–272.
　　1982　　*Inter-Societal Food Acquisition Among Egalitarian Societies: An Ecological Analysis of Plains/Pueblo Interaction in the American Southwest.* Unpublished Ph.D. dissertation, Department of Anthropology, University of Michigan, Ann Arbor.

Staley, David P.
　　1981　　Changes in the Morphology of the Rio Grande from Bernalillo to Isleta, New Mexico. Ms. on file, Office of Contract Archeology, University of New Mexico, Albuquerque.

Steen, Charlie R.
　　1980　　The White Rock Sealed Pots. *Pottery Southwest* 7(1): 2–4.
　　1939　　*The First European Explorers of the Southwest.* Article VI, United States Department of the Interior Memorandum for the Press. On file, Coronado National Memorial, Arizona.

Stephenson, Wendell H.
　　1926　　Spanish Explorations and Settlement of West Texas Before the Eighteenth Century. *West Texas Historical Association Year Book* 11: 64–84.

Strout, Clevy Lloyd
　　1958　　*A Linguistic Study of the Journals of the Coronado Expedition.* Unpublished Ph.D. dissertation, Department of Modern Languages and Literature, University of Colorado, Boulder.

Sundt, William M.
　　1987　　Pottery of Central New Mexico and Its Role as a Key to Both Time and Space. In *Secrets of a City: Papers on Albuquerque Area Archeology in Honor of Richard A. Bice*, edited by Anne V. Poore and John L. Montgomery, pp. 116–147. Anthropological Papers No. 13. The Archeological Society of New Mexico, Albuquerque.

Swadesh, Morris
　　1967　　Lexicostatistical Classification. In *Linguistics*, edited by Norman A. McQuown, pp. 79–115. Handbook of Middle American Indians, vol. 5, Robert Wauchope, general editor. University of Texas Press, Austin.

Swanton, John R.
　　1985　　*Final Report of the United States De Soto Expedition Commission.* 76th Congress, 1st Session, House Document No. 71. Smithsonian Institution Press, Washington, D.C. Originally published 1939.

Tello, Antonio
　　1891　　*Libro segundo de la cronica miscelanea, en que se trata de la conquista espiritual y temporal de la Santa provincia de Xalisco.* Guadalajara.

Tesar, Louis
    1980   *The Leon County Bicentennial Survey Report: An Archaeological Survey of Selected Portions of Leon County, Florida*. Miscellaneous Project Report Series No. 49. Bureau of Historic Sites and Properties, Florida Department of State, Tallahassee.

Thomas, David Hurst (editor)
    1989   *Archaeological and Historical Perspectives on the Spanish Borderlands West*. Columbian Consequences, vol. 1. Smithsonian Institution Press, Washington, D.C.

Tiller, Veronica E.
    1983   Jicarilla Apache. In *Southwest*, edited by Alfonso Ortiz, pp. 440–461. Handbook of North American Indians, vol. 10, William G. Sturtevant, general editor. Smithsonian Institution, Washington, D.C.

Tolstoy, Paul
    1971   Utilitarian Artifacts of Central Mexico. In *Archaeology of Northern Mesoamerica*, edited by Gordon F. Ekholm and Ignacio Bernal, pp. 270–296. Handbook of Middle American Indians, vol. 10, Robert Wauchope, general editor. University of Texas Press, Austin.

Trager, George L.
    1967   The Tanoan Settlement of the Rio Grande Area: A Possible Chronology. In *Studies in Southwestern Ethnolinguistics*, edited by D. Hymes and W. Bittle, pp. 333–350. Mouton & Co., The Hague and Paris.

Turner, Ellen Sue, and Thomas R. Hester
    1985   *A Field Guide to Stone Artifacts of Texas Indians*. Texas Monthly Field Guide Series. Lone Star Books, Texas.

Tuthill, Carr
    1947   *The Tres Alamos Site on the San Pedro River, Southeastern Arizona*. Amerind Foundation Publication No. 4. Dragoon, Arizona.

Udall, Stewart
    1984   In Coronado's Footsteps. *Arizona Highways* 60(4).

Udden, Johan August
    1900   *An Old Indian Village*. Lutheran Augustana Book Concern, Rock Island, Illinois.

Undreiner, George J.
    1947   Fray Marcos de Niza and His Journey to Cibola. *The Americas* 3(4): 415–486.

Upham, Steadman
    1982   *Politics and Power: An Economic and Political History of the Western Pueblo*. Academic Press, New York.

Vargas Machuca, Bernardo de
    1892   *Milicia y descripción de las indias*. 2 vols. Librería de Victoriano Suárez, Madrid. Originally published 1599.

Varner, John Greer, and Jeanette Johnson Varner (editors and translators)
    1980   *The Florida of the Inca by Garcilaso de la Vega*. University of Texas Press, Austin.

Vázquez, Pedro
    1866   Relación de la jornada que hizo Francisco de Sandoval Acazitli, cacique y señor natural que fue del pueblo de Tlalmanalco . . . cuando fue a la conquista y pacificación de los indios chichimecas de Xuchipila." In *Coleccion de documentos para la historia de México*, edited by Joaquín García Icazbalceta, vol. 2, pp. 307–332. Antigua Librería, México.

Vehik, Susan C.
    1986   Oñate's Expedition to the Southern Plains: Routes, Destinations, and Implications for Late Prehistoric Cultural Adaptations. *Plains Anthropologist* 31(111): 13–34.

Vierra, Bradley J.
    1992   A Sixteenth-Century Spanish Campsite in the Tiguex Province: An Archeologist's Perspective. In *Current Research in the Late Prehistory and Early History of New Mexico*, edited by

Bradley Vierra, pp. 165–174. Special Publication No. 1. New Mexico Archeological Council, Albuquerque.

1987a A Sixteenth-Century Spanish Campsite in the Tiguex Province: An Archeologist's Perspective. Paper presented at the 65th Annual Meeting of the Southwestern Social Science Association, Dallas.

1987b The Tiguex Province: A Tale of Two Cities. In *Secrets of a City: Papers on Albuquerque Area Archeology in Honor of Richard A. Bice*, edited by Anne Poore and John Montgomery, pp. 70–86. Anthropological Papers No. 13. The Archeological Society of New Mexico, Albuquerque.

Vierra, Bradley J. (editor)

1989 *A Sixteenth-Century Spanish Campsite in the Tiguex Province*. Laboratory of Anthropology Note No. 475. Museum of New Mexico, Santa Fe.

Villagrá, Gaspar Pérez de

1933 *History of New Mexico by Gaspar Pérez de Villagrá*. Translated by Gilberto Espinosa. Publication No. 4. Quivira Society, Los Angeles. Originally published 1610.

Vivian, Gordon

1932 *Restudy of the Province of Tiguex*. Unpublished master's thesis, Department of Anthropology, University of New Mexico, Albuquerque.

Voll, Charles R.

1961 Pottery Mound Polychrome. Ms. on file, Department of Anthropology, University of New Mexico, Albuquerque.

Wagner, Henry R.

1934 Fray Marcos de Niza. *New Mexico Historical Review* 9(2): 184–227.

Wagstaff, Robert M.

1966 Coronado's Route to Quivira: The Greater Weight of the Credible Evidence. *West Texas Historical Association Year Book* 42: 137–166. Abilene, Texas.

Walsh, Jane Maclaren

1993 *Myth and Imagination in the American Story: The Coronado Expedition, 1540–1542*. Ph.D. dissertation, Catholic University of America. University Microfilms, Ann Arbor.

Warren, A. Helene

1979 The Glaze Paint Wares of the Upper Middle Rio Grande. In *Adaptive Change in the Northern Rio Grande Valley*, edited by Jan V. Biella and Richard C. Chapman, pp. 187–216. Archaeological Investigations in Cochiti Reservoir, New Mexico, vol. 4. Office of Contract Archeology, University of New Mexico, Albuquerque.

1969 Tonque: One Pueblo's Glaze Pottery Industry Dominated Middle Rio Grande Commerce. *El Palacio* 76(2): 36–42.

Warren, A. Helene, and David H. Snow

1976 Formal Descriptions of Rio Grande Glazes from LA 70. In *Archeological Excavation at Pueblo del Encierro*, assembled by David H. Snow, pp. C1–C34. Laboratory of Anthropology Note No. 78. Museum of New Mexico, Santa Fe.

Wedel, Mildred Mott

1982a The Indian They Called Turco. In *Pathways to Plains Prehistory: Anthropological Perspectives of Plains Natives and Their Pasts: Papers in Honor of Robert E. Bell*, edited by Don Wyckoff and Jack Hofman, pp. 153–162. Oklahoma Anthropological Society Memoir 3. The Cross Timbers Press, Duncan, Oklahoma.

1982b The Wichita Indians in the Arkansas River Basin. In *Plains Indian Studies: A Collection of Essays in Honor of John C. Ewers and Waldo R. Wedel*, edited by Douglas H. Ubelaker and Herman J. Viola, pp. 118–134. Smithsonian Institution Press, Washington, D.C.

Wedel, Waldo R.

1990 Coronado, Quivira, and Kansas: An Archaeologist View. *Great Plains Quarterly* 10(3): 139–151.

    1970   Coronado's Route to Quivira 1541. *Plains Anthropologist* 15(49): 161–167.
    1968   After Coronado in Quivira. *The Kansas Historical Quarterly* 34(4): 369–385.
    1942   Archaeological Remains in Central Kansas and Their Possible Bearing on the Location of Quivira. *Smithsonian Miscellaneous Collections* 301(7).

Wheat, Carl I.
    1957   *Mapping the Transmississippi West, 1540–1861*, vol. 1. Institute of Historical Cartography, San Francisco.

Wilcox, David R.
    1991   Changing Contexts of Pueblo Adaptations, A.D. 1250–1600. In *Farmers, Hunters, and Colonists: Interaction Between the Southwest and the Southern Plains*, edited by Katherine A. Spielmann, pp. 128–154. University of Arizona Press, Tucson.
    1984   Multi-Ethnic Division of Labor in the Protohistoric Southwest. *Anthropological Papers* 9: 141–155. The Archaeological Society of New Mexico, Albuquerque.

Williams, Jesse W.
    1959   Coronado: From the Rio Grande to the Concho. *Southwestern Historical Quarterly* 68(8): 1–31.

Winship, George Parker
    1990   *The Journey of Coronado*. Fulcrum Publishing, Golden, Colorado. Originally published 1904.
    1896   The Coronado Expedition, 1540–1542. In *Fourteenth Annual Report of the U.S. Bureau of American Ethnology, 1892–1893*, Part I. U.S. Government Printing Office, Washington, D.C.

Winter, Joseph C.
    1982   Life in Old Bernalillo in the 15th Century. In *Excavations at Nuestra Señora de Dolores Pueblo (LA 6777), a Prehistoric Settlement in the Tiguex Province*, pp. 183–199. Office of Contract Archeology, University of New Mexico, Albuquerque.

Woodson, Michael K.
    1995   *The Goat Hill Site: A Western Anasazi Pueblo in the Safford Valley of Southeastern Arizona*. University of Texas at Austin Press, Austin.

Word, James H.
    1991   The 1975 Field School of the Texas Archeological Society. *Bulletin of the Texas Archeological Society* 60: 57–106.
    1965   The Montgomery Site in Floyd County, Texas. *Bulletin of the South Plains Archeological Society* 2: 55–102. Floydada, Texas.
    1963   Floydada Country Club Site 41-FL-1. *Bulletin of the South Plains Archeological Society* 1: 37–63. Floydada, Texas.

Contributors

Elinore M. Barrett is a professor emeritus in the Department of Geography at the University of New Mexico. Her special interest is the historical geography of Latin America and the American Southwest. In 2002 her volume *Conquest and Catastrophe: Changing Rio Grande Pueblo Settlement Patterns in the Sixteenth and Seventeenth Centuries* was published by University of New Mexico Press.

Donald J. Blakeslee, associate professor of anthropology at Wichita State University, is an archeologist and ethnohistorian who studies Plains Indians and their history. His *Along Ancient Trails: The Mallet Expedition of 1739* was published by the University Press of Colorado in 1995. Since that same year, Blakeslee has been directing archeological investigations at the Jimmy Owens Site, a Coronado expedition campsite in the South Plains of Texas.

William A. Duffen conducted the only professional excavation at the 76 Ranch Ruin, Arizona, a candidate to be the Chichilticale of the Coronado documents. He also worked at Tuzigoot National Monument and Tonto National Monument. He headed the WPA excavations at the Morhiss Mound Site, Victoria, Texas. He taught high school history in Tucson until his retirement.

Charles R. Ewen is associate professor of anthropology and associate director of the Institute for Historical and Cultural Research at East Carolina University. He was co-director of the excavations conducted at the Martin Site, the location of Hernando de Soto's encampment at Anhaica Apalache within modern Tallahassee, Florida. In 1998 he published, with John H. Hann, *Hernando de Soto Among the Apalachee: The Archaeology of the First Winter Encampment*, released by the University Press of Florida.

Richard Flint is currently director of the Center for the Study of Northern New Mexico and the Greater Southwest at New Mexico Highlands University. With his wife Shirley Cushing Flint, he directed the 1992 conference "Where Did the *Encuentro* Happen in the Southwest? Questions of the Coronado Expedition's Route in the Southwest, 1540–1542" from which this book derives. In 2002 his *Great Cruelties Have Been Reported: The 1544 Investigation of the Coronado Expedition* was published by Southern Methodist University Press. And in 2003 the University of New Mexico Press published *The Coronado Expedition from the Distance of 460 Years*, edited by both Flints.

Shirley Cushing Flint is an independent historian. She is completing a book manuscript entitled *The Estrada Women: The Power of Family Structure in Sixteenth-Century New Spain*. She and her husband, Richard Flint, have recently completed an annotated, dual-language edition of 34 documents deriving from the Coronado expedition that will be published by Southern Methodist University Press. It is titled *They Were Not Familiar With His Majesty, Nor*

Did They Wish to Be His Subjects: Documents of the Coronado Expedition. Together they also organized and directed a four-day conference in 2000, "Contemporary Vantage on the Coronado Expedition Through Documents and Artifacts," held at New Mexico Highlands University and in Floyd County, Texas.

Jerry Gurulé is a historian and linguist in the National Park Service's Spanish Colonial Research Center located at the University of New Mexico. He is involved in many projects, including one currently focused on Hispanic contractors and employees at Fort Union, New Mexico. He is also on the staff of the *Colonial Latin American Historical Review*.

William K. Hartmann is a Tucson planetary scientist, writer, and painter with an abiding interest in Southwest history. His research has involved planetary origin and evolution. He was co-investigator in NASA's Mariner 9 mapping of Mars and is jointly the author of the leading theory of lunar origin. In 2002 he published a work of historical fiction dealing with fray Marcos de Niza's 1539 trek titled *Cities of Gold: A Novel of the Ancient and Modern Southwest*, published by Forge Books.

Stanley M. Hordes served for a number of years as the New Mexico state historian. Since 1985 he has operated a historical consulting firm, HMS Associates, Inc., specializing in litigation support, research, and expert witness testimony in land and water rights cases. He is currently researching "The Sephardic Legacy in New Mexico: A History of the Crypto-Jews," a project sponsored by the Latin American Institute of the University of New Mexico, where he is an adjunct research professor.

Jack T. Hughes was, until his death in 2001, considered the dean of Texas Panhandle archeology. He was professor emeritus of anthropology at West Texas A&M University. His numerous publications include *Prehistory of the Caddoan-Speaking Tribes*. He was instrumental in defining the Garza and Tierra Blanca Complexes of the Texas Panhandle.

Edmund J. Ladd, a Zuni anthropologist, was curator of ethnology at the Laboratory of Anthropology of the Museum of Indian Arts and Culture in Santa Fe, New Mexico, until his death in 1998. He was involved with repatriation of human and cultural remains with Southwestern Indian communities. In 1994 his article "Cushing Among the Zuñi: A Zuñi Perspective" was published in the *Gilcrease Journal*.

W. Michael Mathes is a professor emeritus of the University of San Francisco, where he taught Iberoamerican history for thirty years. He is currently library director in El Colegio de Jalisco, Guadalajara. He is a specialist in Spanish exploration on the Pacific coast of America in the sixteenth to eighteenth centuries. On this subject he has published numerous books and articles in English and Spanish, among them the nine-volume series *Californiana*, Madrid, 1965–1985.

Richard A. Pailes, associate professor, University of Oklahoma, Norman, researches the Greater Southwest, arid lands, and inter-regional relations. His field research has focused on northwest Mexico, particularly Sonora, where he has directed major archaeological work. Trade and peripheral frontier cultures are special interests.

CONTRIBUTORS   347

Charles W. Polzer, S.J., was, until his death in 2003, retired editor-in-chief of the Documentary Relations of the Southwest at the Arizona State Museum, which has published documentary works on a variety of topics, including the evolution of the presidial system in northern New Spain. His books include *Presidio and Militia in Northern New Spain; Northern New Spain, A Research Guide; Pedro de Rivera's Inspection of the Northern Frontier; Kino's Biography of F. X. Saeta;* and *A Kino Legacy.* In 1987 he was made a Knight of the Order of Isabel La Católica by King Juan Carlos of Spain for his work on Spain in the Americas.

Daniel T. Reff is an associate professor in the Division of Comparative Studies at Ohio State University. His publications include *Disease, Depopulation, and Culture Change in Northwestern New Spain, 1518–1764,* published by the University of Utah Press in 1991. With Maureen Ahern and Richard Danford, he has published a critical, English-language edition of Andrés Pérez de Ribas's monumental history of the Jesuit missions of northern Nueva España titled *History of the Triumphs of the Holy Faith Among the Most Fierce and Barbarous People of the New World.* The book was released by the University of Arizona Press in 1999.

Diane Lee Rhodes is an archeologist with Parsons Engineering. Before her retirement from the National Park Service she served as a member of the study team that produced the 1992 *Coronado Expedition, National Trail Study/Environmental Assessment,* and she coauthored "The Coronado Expedition of 1540–1542, A Special History Report Prepared for the Coronado Trail Study." In 1992 she published "Coronado's American Legacy: An Overview of Possible Entrada Artifacts and a Discussion of Texas Sites" in the *Bulletin of the Texas Archeological Society.*

Carroll L. Riley, an archeologist and ethnohistorian working on the protohistoric Southwest, is a distinguished professor emeritus from Southern Illinois University, Carbondale. His recent publications include *The Frontier People: The Greater Southwest in the Protohistoric Period,* revised and expanded edition (University of New Mexico Press, 1987); *Rio del Norte: People of the Upper Rio Grande From Earliest Times to the Pueblo Revolt* (University of Utah Press, 1995); and *The Kachina and the Cross: Indians and Spaniards in the Early Southwest* (University of Utah Press, 1999).

Madeleine Turrell Rodack is a retired ethnohistorian with the Arizona State Museum. She has translated Adolph Bandelier's *History of the Colonization and Missions of Sonora, Chihuahua, New Mexico and Arizona to the Year 1700.* And she translated and edited *Adolph Bandelier's Discovery of New Mexico by the Franciscan Monk Fray Marcos de Niza in 1539,* which was published by the University of Arizona Press in 1981.

Joseph P. Sánchez is director of the Spanish Colonial Research Center, a joint project of the National Park Service and the University of New Mexico. He is author of numerous studies dealing with Spanish colonial history, including *Spanish Bluecoats: The Catalonian Volunteers in Northwestern New Spain, 1767–1815* (1990) and *Explorers, Traders, and Slavers: Forging the Old Spanish Trail, 1678–1850* (1997). He is also editor and founder of the *Colonial Latin American Historical Review (CLAHR).*

David H. Snow, an anthropologist and historical archeologist, is retired from the Museum of New Mexico. In 1998 the Hispanic Genealogical Research Center of New Mexico published his compilation *New Mexico's First Colonists: The 1597–1600 Enlistments for New Mexico Under Juan de Oñate, Adelantado & Gobernador*. His primary professional interests are directed toward the impact of European cultures and societies on the indigenous New World cultures.

Bradley Vierra is archeologist for Los Alamos National Laboratory. For the Museum of New Mexico he directed excavation of LA 54147, a probable Coronado expedition campsite near Bernalillo, New Mexico. His report on that excavation was published by the Museum of New Mexico in 1989 under the title *A Sixteenth-Century Spanish Campsite in the Tiguex Province*.

Index

Page numbers in italics indicate illustrations.

Abeytas (pueblo, New Mexico), 207
Abó Arroyo/Wash (New Mexico), 200, 201, 204, 207
Abra (Sonora), 125, 126
Acoma, Coco (New Mexico), 28, *178,* 179, 180
Aconchi (Sonora), *142, 149,* 156
Aglets (lace tips), peculiar to Coronado expedition in Upper Southwest, 49, 217
Agraz. *See* Verjuice
Agua (Sonora), 144
Ahacus. *See* Hawikuh
Alameda (LA 421, New Mexico), 201, 202, 207
Alamos (Sonora), 150
Alarcón (Alarçón), Hernando de , 36; leader of sea-going resupply of Coronado expedition, 4, 68; reached Gila-Colorado River junction, 4; cancellation of second voyage, 4; carried soldiers' personal baggage, 68
Albuquerque (New Mexico), 28 , 48, *178*
Albuquerque Basin (New Mexico), 204
Alcanfor. *See* Coofer
Alcaráz, Diego de, 6, 7
Alibates Quarry (Texas), 273
Altar-Magdalena drainage (Sonora), 3
Alvarado, Hernando de: advised Vázquez de Coronado to winter in Río Grande Valley, 5; led expedition from Zuni to Tiguex, 179–81; led expedition to Buffalo Plains with fray Juan de Padilla, 4; reached Río Grande, 199
Amacueca (Jalisco), *305*
Amatitlán (Jalisco), *305*
Amsden, Monroe: defined Río Sonora Culture, 150
Analco (pueblo, New Mexico), identified as Calabacillas (LA 289), 202
Anhaica Apalache (Florida), 98, 99, *102, 105;* abandonment by native population, 98–99; arrival of De Soto expedition, 99; description by Garcilaso de la Vega, 99; De Soto's winter quarters, 96; hypothesized to be Martin Site, 103; mission founded, 100; mission relocated, 100; principal Apalachee village, 107;

reoccupied by native population, 100; suggested as being in the Tallahassee area, 100
Animas Valley (New Mexico), 117
Antelope Creek people (Texas), 274
Antelope Pass (New Mexico), 117, 122, 140
Antilia, Seven Cities of, 63
Anton Chico (New Mexico), *223;* location of bridge over Río de Cicúye, 184, 185
Anza, Juan Bautista de, 159, 173
Apache Indians: identified by Alonso de Benavides, 269; identity of, 269, 271–72, 277; origin of name, Morris Opler, 269; origin of name, Schroeder, 269
Apalachee (province, Florida), 98, 99, 107; settlement pattern, 100, 105
Aravaipa Creek/Valley (Arizona), 118, 119, 122, *160,* 167, 168, 172
Arenal (pueblo, New Mexico), 47, 48; attack on, 207; Coronado campsite, 214; location of, 181
Arizpa (Sonora): identified as Arispe, 170
Arizpe/Arispe (Sonora), *112, 113,* 132, 134, 144, 154, 156, 170
Arkansas River (Kansas), 6, *234*
Arquebus (arquebuz), 39
Arroyo Cuchujaqui (Sinaloa, Sonora), 150
Arroyo de los Cedros (Sinaloa or Sonora), 116, 127, 130
Arroyo del Puerto (New Mexico), *234,* 265, 314
Arroyo Hondo (pueblo, New Mexico), *178*
Atenquique (Jalisco), *305,* 306, 307
Aucilla River (Florida), 98, 100
Autlán (Jalisco), 304
Aztecs. *See* Mexica

Bacadehuachi (Sonora), 120
Bacanuchi (Sonora), 132
Bacapa (Sonora), 132
Bacoachi (Bacuache, Bacuachi, Sonora), 127, 132, 136, 140
Baicatcan (Sonora), 118
Baldwin, Stuart: on ceramic chronology, 289, 291, 292, 293–94

Banámichi (Sonora), 125, 133, *142*, 143, *149*, 153, 157
Bancroft, Hubert Howe, on location of Quivira, 247
Bandelier, Adolph F., 137; on location of bridge over Río de Cicúye, 224; on location of Quivira, 247; on Querechos, 272; opinion of Marcos de Niza, 66; suggested Kiakima as first city of Cíbola, 86
Barbero Canyon (New Mexico), *227,* 229
Barrancas (Colima), *305*
Barrancas (Texas), 6; discussion of identity, 18–20; first barranca, 17, 240; identified with Caprock canyons, 6; second barranca, 17, 257, 262
Batuco (Sonora), 129, 133–34; on return route of Coronado expedition, 251
Baugh, Timothy G., 274–75, on ceramic chronology, 288; on Teyas, 272–73
Baviácora/Babiácora (Sonora), 132, 140, *142*, 143, *149*, 156
Bavispe (Sonora), 120
Beads (faceted amber), 106; Beads (glass): blue Venetian, 157; faceted chevron, 106; Nueva Cadiz, 49, 106, 217; peculiar to Coronado expedition in Upper Southwest, 49, 217
Beckett, Patrick H., on stone discs, 299
Be-jui Tu-ay (LA 81, New Mexico), 197, 201, 204
Bells, Clarksdale: peculiar to Coronado expedition in Upper Southwest, 49
Benavides, fray Alonso de, 175, 269
Benjamin Hill (Sonora), 80
Benson (Arizona), 122, 171
Bernalillo (New Mexico), 16, 28, 43, 53, *178*, 181, 209, 210, 218, 221
Bigotes (Indian from Pecos), 5, 317; accused of stealing gold bracelet, 5; member of trading party to Cíbola, 5; said to have conspired to lead Spaniards astray, 5
Binna:wa (New Mexico), *191*. See also Zuni
Bison, 6, 65, 221, 256, 262
Black River (Arizona), 123
Blackwater Draw (Texas), *234*, 239, 244, 259
Blakeslee, Donald J., on vegetation of the barrancas, 281
Blanco Canyon (Texas), *234*, 239, 258, 276, 280, 281, 310, 314; as first barranca, 281, 314–16; as last barranca, 317–19; compared with barrancas of Colima, 307, 308; crossbow boltheads found in, 40; material culture of, 311; one of the barrancas grandes, 313–14;

possibly the Great Barranca, 6; Teya ranchería, 239–40; Tierra Blanca sites in, 260–61. *See also* Jimmy Owens Site
Blue River (Arizona), 122
Bolsón de Mapimí (Chihuahua), 276
Bolton, Herbert E., 30, 31, 137; critique of route hypothesis, 261–62; on barrancas, 240–41, 310; on erection of cross, 249; on location of bridge over Río de Cicúye, 186, 225; on location of Chichilticale, 159, 168; on location of Quivira, 247; on location of Tabas, 249; on return to Tiguex, 244, 250; proposed route of Coronado expedition, 27–28, 115, 121–23, 182, 184, 232n6, 235–36
Bonito Creek (Arizona), 122
Bosque Grande (New Mexico), 284
Bosque Redondo (New Mexico), *234*, 284, 319
Boyd, Douglas K., on the Tierra Blanca Complex, 274
Brackenridge, Henry M., on location of bridge over Río de Cicúye, 224
Brain, Jeffrey, 101
Bridwell Site (Texas), 312, 315
Brower, Jacob V. on location of Quivira, 247
Bryan, Frank, on route to Quivira, 246
Buena Vista House 1 Site (ruin, Arizona), *160*, 168, 172
Buffalo Plains, 28, 38; reached by Hernando de Alvarado and Juan de Padilla, 4; reached by the Coronado expedition, 5
Buried City Complex (Texas), 260
Bylas (Arizona), 122

Cabeza de Vaca, Álvar Núñez, 2, 62, 68, 77, 79, 84, 85, 116, 141, 188; given deer hearts at Corazones, 78; named Corazones, 4, 133, 147; presumed to have been in Sonora River Valley, 4; received word of town-dwelling Indians to north, 72; rejected request to join Soto, 98
Caborca (Sonora), 81, 82, 85, *112*
Cáceres (pueblo, New Mexico), 201; identified as Sandia (LA 294), 201
Cacique (Indian from Pecos), 5; accused of stealing gold bracelet, 4–5; said to have conspired to lead Spaniards astray, 317
Caddoan language, 272, 275, 285
Cale (Florida), 98
Calendars: Gregorian, 14; Julian, 21n1, 66, 83, 279
Campos (pueblo, New Mexico), 201; identified as Watche (LA 677), 201, 203

Cañada Ancha (Sonora), 127
Canadian River (New Mexico, Texas), 17, 185, 224, 225, *234,* 236, 238, 240, 243,m 246, 259, 262, 267; known as Río de la Madalena, *205*
Cananea (Sonora), 4, 85, *112, 113,* 128, 129,
Cananea Plain (Sonora), 127, 133
Cañas, Cristóbal de, 144, 146n5
Cañon Blanco (New Mexico), 6, 16, *178,* 186, *223, 227,* 230; as location of important Indian trail, 230
Canyon Creek (Arizona), 162
Caprock Canyons (Texas), 307, 308, 310, 315
Carpenter's nails (caret-head), 311, 315
Carrizo Wash (New Mexico, Arizona), 4, 122, 123, *191*
Casa Colorado (LA 50249 or LA 50261, New Mexico), 197, 200, 204, 208n13
Castañeda de Náçera, Pedro de: description of barrancas, 239, 304, 308; description of bison bed, 283; description of Cicúye, 183, 226; description of Plains, 236; description of salt beds, 244; description of Señora Valley, 143–44; on Chichilticale, 171; on Cona, 282; on expedition route, 183–84; on last barranca, vegetation of, 241, 254–55; on location of bridge over Río de Cicúye, 221–22; on location of Río de Cicúye, 184, 228–29; on method of determining direction, 245–46; on pottery break, 287; on pottery usage, 296, 297; on return from the barrancas, 284; on return to Nueva Galicia, 307; on route from Tiguex to Galisteo, 182
Castaño de Sosa, Gaspar, 203, 206n2; on Tiwa pueblos, 202–3
Castaño de Sosa expedition: ceramic typology, 298, 299; in Cañon Blanco, 230; no use of crossbows, 39; route of, 214
Caxcán-speaking Indians, 50
Caxtole (New Mexico), 201; possibly LA 50241, 200
Cebolleta Canyon (New Mexico), 181
Cedros River (Sonora), 12, 130
Cedros Valley (Sonora), 140, 141, 153
Cempoala (pueblo, New Mexico), 201, 203
Ceramics: Aztec IV, 55; Aztec Polychrome (Texcoco Black/Red), 55; Biscuitware, 299; Brown ware,151; cajete form, 298; cazuela form, 298; chicubit (chiquihuit) form, 298, 299; comal form, 298, 201; Coronado expedition form, 296–301; earthenware (losa) form, 297; Fort Walton types, 105 (*see also* Ceramics, Fort Walton types); jarra form, 297; jarro (olla) form, 297, 298; jicara form, 298, 301; Majolica types, 103 (*see also* Ceramics, Majolica types); Mesoamerican typology, 313; olive jar, 55–56, 103, 106; Polychromes (*see* Ceramics, Polychromes); puki form, 298; Red-on-brown ware, 151; Rio Grande Glazeware, 206n3, 287, 301 (*see also* Ceramics, Rio Grande Glazeware); St. Johns Black-on-red, 166, 167; San Carlos Buff, 166; San Miguel ware, 157 (*see also* Ceramics, San Miguel ware); Santa Cruz Red-on-buff, 167; seventeenth-century Spanish colonial assemblage, 302; shell-tempered wares (west Mexico), 56; textured wares, 151 (*see also* Ceramics, textured wares); tinaja form, 298; utility ware, 295 (*see also* Ceramics, utility ware); White ware (*see* Ceramics, White ware)
Ceramics, Fort Walton types, 105; Fort Walton Incised, 105; Fort Walton Punctated, 105, *108;* Lake Jackson Plain, 105
Ceramics, Majolica types, 103; Caparra Blue, 106; Columbia Plain, 106
Ceramics, Polychromes: Chihuahua Polychrome, 162, 167; Fourmile Polychrome, 162, 167; Gila Polychrome, 162, 167, 168; Tabira Polychrome, 299
Ceramics, Rio Grande Glazeware, 206n3, 287, 301; Espinoso Glaze/red, 291–93; Espinoso Glaze/yellow, 291–93; Espinoso Polychrome, 291–93; found at Abó Pass, 289, 291; found at Arenal (LA), 293; found at Cochiti, 289, 293; found at Gran Quivira, 292; found at Jimmy Owens Site, 310; found at Jemez, 299; found at LA5, 292; found at LA70, 292, 293, 294, 301; found at LA6455, 292; found at LA50529, 293; found at LA50527, 293; found at LA54147, 210, 211, 216; found at Las Humanas, 289, 290, 292; found at Montgomery Site, 275; found at Pecos, 288–89, 292, 298; found at Picuris, 299; found at Tunque Pueblo (LA240), 292, 293; found at Zia, 293; found in Albuquerque area, 293; found in Galisteo Basin, 293, 298, 299; found in lower Rio Abajo, 289, 290, 299; found in Salinas area, 289, 291, 299; found on southern Plains, 295; Glaze A, 289, 290, 291, 302; Glaze A Polychrome, 289; Glaze A Red, 289, 296; Glaze A Yellow, 289; Glaze B, 289, 291, 302; Glaze C, 273, 289, 291–92, 295–96, 300, 302; Glaze D, 289, 290, 292–94, 295–96, 300, 301, 302; Glaze E, 288,

291, 292–94; Glaze E as diagnostic, 301–3; Glaze F, 288, 290, 292–93, 293–94, 301–2; Kotyiti Glaze/red, 293–94; Kotyiti Glaze/yellow, 293–94; Kotyiti polychrome, 293–94; Kuaua Glaze-polychrome, 292; Largo Glaze/red, 289–91; Largo Glaze/yellow, 289–91; Largo Glaze-polychrome, 289–91; Pecos Glaze IV, 292; Pecos Glaze V, 293–94, 298; Pecos Glaze-polychrome, 312; Pottery Mound Polychrome, 289, 291; Puaray Glaze-polychrome, 293–94; rim forms, *290;* San Juan Glaze-polychrome, 299; Sanchez Glaze/red, 291; Sanchez Glaze/yellow, 291; Sanchez polychrome, 291; sequence, 288–96; Tiguex Glaze-polychrome, 292, 293–94; Trenequel Glaze-polychrome, 293–94

Ceramics, San Miguel ware, 157; San Miguel Red, 156; San Miguel Brown, 156

Ceramics, textured wares, 151; Alma Incised, 151; Casas Grandes Incised, 151; Convento Incised, 151; Playas Red Incised, 151

Ceramics, utility ware, 295; Edwards Plain, 274; found at Jimmy Owens Site, 315; Jeddito, 274; Rio Grande Plainware, 273; Tierra Blanca Plain, 273, 274, 275

Ceramics, White ware: Chupadero Black-on-white, 299, 301; Jemez, Black-on-white, 299; Mesa Verde Black-on-white, 298; Sankawi Black-on-cream, 299; Tabira Black-on-white, 299, 301; Vadito Black-on-white, 299

Cerro Alamo (Sonora), 85

Cerro de Tuxpán (Colima), 305

Chain mail: dating, 7; found at Blanco Canyon, 266; found at Martin site, 106; found at Paint Creek Site, 248; found at Saxman Site, 248; found near Happy Canyon, 316; found on Kiowa Indian, 248

Chama River (New Mexico), 269

Chamisal (LA 22765, New Mexico), 196, 201, 202, 203, 208n10

Chichilticale (Sonora or Arizona), 28, 35–36, 64, 67–68, 71; bighorn sheep at, 171; comparison of theories concerning location, 119–21; Gila River location, 35; identified with Casa Grande, 117; identified with Haby Ranch Ruin, 159; identified with 76 Ranch Ruin, 158, 159; Nahuatl name, 170–71; north of Arizona-Sonora border, 120–21; not mentioned by Marcos de Niza, 119; on Gila or Salt Rivers, 120–21; on expedition's return route, 251; "port" of, 67, 68, 81, 120; possibly settled by renegades from Cíbola, 120; possibly visited by Marcos de Niza, 168, 169; "red house," 119, 170–71, 172–73; region and town, 159; south of Arizona-Sonora border, 119; "thorny trees disappear," 119, 171; what is referred to by the name, 119; where the coast turns west, 32–33, 120

Chicoria Pueblo (New Mexico), *205*

Chiricahua Mountains (Arizona), 117

Cíbola, 49, 122, 123, 140–41, 158; arrival of Estevan, 190; arrival of Marcos de Niza, 76; connections with Sonora, 72, 84; death of Estevan at, 64, 85–86, 170, 190, 193; description of by Castañeda, 94; first town of described by fray Marcos, 86, *87;* gold not present at, 67; identified with Zuni pueblos, 86; Indians of, 297; language barrier, 190, 193–94; name derived from Zuni word *ciwolo,* 188; native of in Sonora, 85; received news of Spaniards before Coronado expedition, 189; Seven Cities of, 3, 85; trading center, 173, 189; turquoise at, 65, 189. *See also* Zuni

Cicúye (New Mexico), 182, 183, 185, 186, 221, 224–25, 226, *227,* 228, 232n3, 255. *See also* Pecos

Cielo Complex, 276

Cimarron River, *234*

Cita Canyon (Texas),

Ciudad Guzmán (Jalisco), 306. *See also* Zapotlán

Clifton (Arizona), 89, 122

Clothes hook (found at LA 54147), 211, *213*

Cochiti (New Mexico), *178*

Cocoraqui River (Sonora), 130

Coins found at Martin Site: Portuguese ceitils, 106; Spanish maravedis, 106

Colima (Colima), *305, 306,* 309; barrancas of, 238, 304–8, *305,* 314

Colima (province), *305*

Colonia Morelos (Sonora), 140

Colorado Plateau (Arizona), 123

Colorado River, *113, 138*

Columbus, Christopher, 48

Comales, Mesoamerican style, 54, 55, 217, 218

Comanche Springs (New Mexico), *178*

Compostela (Nayarit), 26, 27, 31, 50, 67, 74, 75, *112,* 115; arrival of Marcos de Niza at, 76

Comu (Sonora), 144

Cona (Province, Texas), 28, 280, 282, 316; as an event, 242–44; described by Castañeda, 282; location of, 242, 257, 283

Conchos River. *See* Río Conchos

Conicari, Conicarit (Sonora), 116–17, 126–27, 133

INDEX

Coofor (New Mexico, Alcanfor), 204, 228; site of Coronado expedition's winter quarters, 5, 181, 199, 209–19; suggested as Santiago Pueblo, 43, 199
Copper technology in central Mexico, 42
Corazones (Sonora), 32, 133–34, *138,* 140, 145, 147, 155, 156; base camp established by Luna y Arellano here, 134; Cabeza de Vaca given deer hearts here, 78, 134; described by Cabeza de Vaca, 78, 155; described by Marcos de Niza, 78; identified with Ures, 78, 140, 170; in middle Cedros Valley, 140–41; named by Cabeza de Vaca, 134; reached by Vázquez de Coronado, 4
Corazones, Valle de los (Sonora), 132
Corodéhuachi (Sonora), 134
Coronado expedition, 204; arrival at Hawikuh, 192–94; arrived in Quivira, 6, 247–49; "attacked" in bad pass, 192; ceramics of, 296–301; composition of, 3, 5–6, 49–50; corridor of route, 28; departed from Tiguex for Quivira, 5; distances traveled, 258–59; documents of change focus, 32; documents of criticized by scholars, 139; documents of postdate expedition, 31; documents of underutilized, 173; elusiveness of route, 25–26, 30–31; erected bridge over Río de Cicúye, 220–32, 244, 286n3; erection of cross, 249; failure of, 7, 31; followed coastal plain north of Culiacán, 150; forecast of artifactual impact at Chichilticale, 175; guides of, 229; importance of archeology to determination of route, 30–31, 147; importance of study of route, 144–45; indigenous military gear used by most European members, 52; livestock accompanying, 3; lost on the Llano Estacado, 256, 257; material culture of, 47–57, 300, 301, 310–11; need for critical edition of documents of, 36; possible campsites, 209–19, 276, 287, 296–97, 307–8; priests remain in Tierra Nueva, 251; relations with native peoples, 5–6, 48, 192–94; relevance to modern life, xi–xii; return of chosen thirty, 249–51; return route of from Tierra Nueva, 244, 249, 258; returned to New Spain, 7, 251; route from Cíbola to Río de Cicúye, 179–86; route from Cicúye to the Río de Cicúye bridge, 220–32; route from Compostela to Cíbola ,115–23; route from Corazones to Cíbola, 4; route from Río de Cicúye Quivira, 235–51; route from Río de Cicúye to the barrancas, 5–6; route from the barrancas to Quivira, 6; route from Tiguex to Río de Cicúye, 6, 182–86; route studied by National Park Service, 1; route through Sonora, 137–46, *138,* 150; route markers, 231; servants and slaves accompanying, 3; use of arquebuses, 39; use of crossbows, 39, 40–44; use of guides, 228; value of narrative accounts of, 26; winter quarters of, 181, 209, 214

Cortés, Hernán: accusation that Marcos de Niza was liar, 69; conquest of Mexico, 63; requisition of copper crossbow boltheads, 42; use of crossbows, 38

Cow Creek (Kansas): location of cross erected by expedition, 249

Crosbyton (Texas), 310

Crossbow (ballesta): decline in use, 39, 106; historic use of, 38–39; parts, 39–40; peculiar to Coronado expedition in Upper Southwest, 48–49, 217; technology of, 39–40; types, 39–40

Crossbow boltheads (dart points or quarrels), 39, *41,* 83, *312, 313;* copper, 40, 44–46, 310–11; as diagnostic of Coronado expedition, 39, 48–49, 226; dimensions, 40; found at Hawikuh, 40, 43, 218; found at Jimmy Owens Site, 46, 281, 310–11; found at Kuaua or Puaray, 44, 218; found at LA 326, 218; found at Mann-Zuris Site, 218; found at Martin Site, 40, 106; found at Pecos, 40, 43, 218, 226; found at Piedras Marcadas, 44; found at San Felipe , 40; found at Santa Elena, 40; found at Santiago Pueblo, 43; found in New Mexico, 40; found in Rio Grande pueblos, 40; found in Texas, 40; iron, 42, 44, 311; morphology, 40–42, 43, 44–45; possibly found at Comanche Springs, 44; production methods, 44, 46; requisition by Hernán Cortés, 42

Crossbow bolts, *41;* dimensions, 40; morphology, 40

Crosses, left as route markers by expedition, 5

Culiacán (pueblo, New Mexico), identified as Chamisal (LA 22765), 196, 201–2

Culiacán. *See* San Miguel de Culiacán

Cumupas (Sonora), 144

Cushing, Frank Hamilton, 86; criticized as embellishing Zuni stories, 188–89

Dahlia (New Mexico), *227,* 230
Datil (New Mexico), 180
Day, A. Grove: on Marcos de Niza, 61; on route to Quivira, 246; on route to Tiguex, 181; reconstruction of Coronado expedition route, 27, 115, 121

de la Vega, Garcilaso, 99
de las Casas, Bartolomé, 69
de l'Isle, Guillaume, 100
De Soto, Hernando. *See* Soto, Hernando de
De Soto expedition, 26, 97–99; arrival at Anhaica Apalache, 98; composition of, 98; departure from Anhaica Apalache, 99; end of, 99; fate of Indian bearers used by, 99; forecast of material culture assemblage, 104; importance of research on route of, 96–97; included pigs, 107; landfall at Tampa Bay, 98; material culture of, 311–13; relations with native peoples, 99–100; times of march, 228; use of crossbows, 38, 39
Dellenbaugh, Frederick, on location of bridge over Río de Cicúye, 185, 224
Despoblados, 72, 85, 89, 118, 119, 120, 121–23, 158, 169, 170, 171
Di Peso, Charles: efforts to delineate the Coronado expedition route, 32; on location of Chichilticale, 171; on route of Coronado expedition through Sonora, 115–18, 122, 137, 140–41
Díaz, Melchior (or Melchor), 71, 119, 148; forecast of artifactual impact of at Chichilticale, 174; ignored by researchers, 35–36; interviewed natives of Chichilticale, 169–70; return from Chichilticale, 67; sent to reconnoiter to north, 3, 64, 120, 123; spent winter at Chichilticale, 120; provided support of Marcos de Niza's report, 67, 72, 175
Dinwiddie Pueblo (Arizona), 168
Diseases, European: impact on native populations, 109, 139, 145, 146, 157; measles, 145; pneumonia, 145; references in Jesuit anuas for Sonora, 145; smallpox, 139, 145; spread in advance of mission frontier, 139, 145; typhus, 145
Donoghue, David: route hypothesis across Plains, 237–38
Double Mountain Fork Canyon (Texas), 239
Dowa Yalanne (New Mexico), *90*, 90–91, *91*, 93, 180, *191;* location of Kiakima, 86, 91–92
Duncan (Arizona), 122
Duncan Site (Oklahoma), 274

Eagle Pass (Arizona), 122, 123, *160*, 164, 168, 171, 173, 174
Edwards Complex (Oklahoma), 285, 288, 295, 302
El Corvillo (pueblo, New Mexico), 197, 200; possibly LA 50241, 200

El Fuerte (Sinaloa), 116
El Morro-Malpaís area (New Mexico), 27, 28, 180
El Turco (Turk), 267, 279, 285–86n2, 314, 317; accompanied Hernando de Alvarado to Buffalo Plains, 4; described Quivira as wealthy land, 4; discussion of activities, 20; guide of Coronado expedition, 6; Pawnee Indian, 4; said to have conspired to lead Spaniards astray, 5; told of gold jewelry held by Bigotes and the Cacique, 4
Escobar, Francisco de, 93
Espejo, Antonio de, 190
Espejo expedition, 202, 204, 206, 206n2, 207n5, 208n13; ceramic typology, 298, 299, 301; native contact, 268; no use of crossbows, 39; route of, 214, 230
Estancia Basin (New Mexico), 200
Estevan de Dorantes, 3, 64; accompanied Cabeza de Vaca, 85; arrival at Cíbola/Hawikuh, 194; black slave, 84; death of at Cíbola, 64, 86, 170, 190; described as man with "Chili lips," 91; from Azamora, Morocco, 188; gourd, token of power, 190; instructed by Marcos de Niza to keep to the west, 81; killed as slave spy, 190, 193; made demands at Cíbola, 190; place in history 189–90; sent by viceroy with Marcos de Niza, 84; went ahead of fray Marcos, 85
Eureka Springs Ranch (Arizona), 168
Extremadura (Spain), 97

Flint, Richard, on Coronado expedition indicators, 217
Flint, Richard and Shirley Cushing, on Pecos River bridge, 184–86
Florence (Arizona), 118
Flores, Dan, on the Caprock canyons, 236
Florida Mission Period, 103
Floydada (Texas), 310
Floydada Country Club Site (Texas), 313, 315; possible Coronado campsite, 313–14
Ford (Kansas), 250
Fort Apache (Arizona), 122
Frailes, Rock of the (Sonora), 136
Franciscans, 139
Fronteras, (Sonora). *See* Corodéhuachi

Galestina Canyon (New Mexico), 90, 91
Galisteo Basin (New Mexico), *178*
Galisteo/Calisteo Pueblo (New Mexico), 182, *205*

INDEX 355

Galiuro Range (Arizona),122
Gallegos, Hernán, on pueblos of Rio Grande Subregion, 199
Gallinas River (New Mexico), *178*, 186, *223, 227*, 230, 309
Garnsey Site (New Mexico), 275
Garza Complex, 273, 275–76, 284, 295, 303, 309, 312, 315, 316; identity of, 285; lithic association, 265; location of sites, 260–61
Garza Site (Texas), 261, 275
Gila River (Arizona, New Mexico), 4, 8, 35, 75, *113*, 117, 118, 121, *138*, 159, *160*, 171, 174
Glorieta Mesa (New Mexico), *178*, 184, 186, 226, *227*, 229
Goat Hill Site (Arizona), 173
Goodwin Baker Site (Oklahoma), 274
Gooseberry, 254, 281
Gran Desierto (Sonora), 80
Grape, 242, 253, 254–55, 257
Grape Creek Site (Texas), 275
Grasshopper Site (Arizona), 162
Great Bend Aspect/Focus, 295, 300
Great Bend of Arkansas River (Kansas), 26, 124, 246
Great Plains. *See* Buffalo Plains
Griddles, from LA 54147, 55, 217–18
Grosella. *See* Gooseberry
Guadalajara (Jalisco), 305
Guagarispa (Sonora), 134
Guaraspi (Sonora), 155; identified as Ispa, 141
Guasave (Sinaloa), 116
Guisamopa (Sonora), 117
Gulf of California, 32, 35, *112*, *113*, 122, *138*, *149;* latitude of head of, 81
Guthrie (Arizona), 122
Gutiérrez de Humaña, Antonio: native contact, 269; route of, 214
Guzmán, Diego, 116
Guzmán, Father Diego, 143

Habicht-Mauche, Judith, on native groups of the Southern Plains, 295, 310
Haby Ranch Ruin (Arizona), 159, *160*, 167
Hackett, Charles Wilson, on location of Alameda, 181
Hailstorm, 257, 287, 314, 315
Hallenbeck, Cleve: opinion that Marcos de Niza lied, 61, 71–72; suggested inland route for Marcos de Niza, 71
Halona/Halona:wa (New Mexico), 86, *191*. *See also* Zuni

Harahey, 285
Harrington, John P., on Teyas, 272
Haury, Emil, on location of Chichilticale, 158–59, 164, 168
Havana (Cuba), *xv,* 98
Hawikuh (New Mexico), *xiv–xv,* 37, 38, 52, *88, 89,* 92, 122, *178, 191;* crossbow boltheads found at, 40, 43, 310–11; largest of the "cities of Cíbola," 85; location described, 86–88; one of "cities of Cíbola," 86; people from all Zuni pueblos gathered there, 193–94; reached by Vázquez de Coronado, 4; seat of the "lord of Cíbola," 85; "smoke signals" approaching, 193–94; suggested as first city of Cíbola, 86–87, 188; suggested as sponsoring solstice ceremony in 1540, 192; trading center, 72. *See also* Zuni
Hawley Ellis, Florence, on ceramic typology, 299
Haxa, 256
Hemlock Canyon (New Mexico), 91; possibly Mullen Canyon, 91
Hermosillo (Sonora), 80, *112, 113, 149*
Hernandes Creek (New Mexico), 284
Hewett, Edgar L., on location of bridge over Río de Cicúye, 224
Hickerson, Nancy P., on Jumanos, 277
Hill, Frank, on route to Quivira, 246
Himmerich y Valencia, Robert, on route to Pecos River, 232n4
Hodge, Frederick W., 52; excavated Hawikuh, 86; on location of bridge over Río de Cicúye, 185, 224; on location of Quivira, 247; on route to Quivira, 246; proposed route for Coronado expedition across Arizona, 118; Querecho derived from Towa word, 268; suggested Hawikuh as first city of Cíbola, 86
Hofman, Jack, on ceramic chronology, 288
Hohokam, 65, 72, 151
Holden, William C.: on Cona, 242; on location of bridge over Río de Cicúye, 185; on return to Tiguex, 251; on Teya ranchería, 239–40; route hypothesis, 185, 236–38
Horseshoe nails, 281, 311
Horseshoes, 281, 311
Huachuca Mountains (Arizona), 171
Huépac (Sonora), 135, *142*
Hughes, Jack T., on weather in Texas Panhandle, 255

Ibarra, Francisco de, 116, 117, 140, 148, 156
Inman, Henry, on location of Quivira, 247
Isleta (New Mexico), 28, 202

Isleta del Sur (Texas), 277
Ispa (Sonora): identified as Arizpe170; identified as Guisamopa, 117; identified as Guaraspi, 141
Ivitachuco (Florida), 98

Jack plate, found at LA 54147, 211, *213*
Jala (Nayarit), *366*
Jalisco, 50, 51, 53
Janover-Achi, Genoverachi (Sonora), 136
Jaramillo, Juan de, 50, 318, discussion of expedition's route, 256; on Chichilticale, 170–71; on direction of march, 184, 232n3; on erection of cross, 249; on lack of water, 318; on march from Coofor to Cicúye, 183, 228; on march from Matsaki to Rio Grande, 228; on Quivira, 248; on Río de Cicúye, 221; on time of march, 228
Jemez Mountains (New Mexico), 269
Jesuits, 139, 156; established permanent missions among Ópata, 143, 156; facilitated spread of disease, 157
Jilotlán (Jalisco), 305
Jimmy Owens Site (Texas), *xiv–xv;* crossbow boltheads found at, 46; possible Coronado campsite, 314
Jones, B. Calvin, 102; research on Florida mission system, 102–3
Jones, Paul A.: Coronado expedition route hypothesis, 235; on chain mail, 248; on location of bridge over Río de Cicúye, 185–86
Jumano Indians, 267; identified as Tanoan, 277; identity of, 272, 277–79; language of, 278; related to Suma, 272

Kayenta Anasazi, 173
Kelley, Jane Holden, on Cona as an event, 243
Kempton, Willet, on ceramic typology, 297
Keres (Indians/province, New Mexico), 202
Keresan Pueblos, Quirix, 182
Ketchipawa/Kechiba:wa (New Mexico), 86, 93, *191*, 194. *See also* Zuni
Kiakima/Kyaki:ma (New Mexico), 86, *91, 178*, 188, *191*, 194; as first pueblo of Cíbola, 10–11, 86, 92, 94; "black Mexicans" arrived at, 92, 188–89; location described, 88. *See also* Zuni
Kiatuthlanna (ruin, Arizona), 162
Kidder, Alfred V., on ceramic chronology, 288–89, 293
Kino, Eusebio, 67, 81, 145
Kiowa Indian, wearing coat of mail, 248
Ko:thluwala:wa (Arizona), *191,* 192

Kuaua (New Mexico), 52, *178;* crossbow bolthead possibly found at, 44
Kuykendall (ruin, Arizona), *160,* 168, *169;* dating, 168
Kwakina/Kwa'kin'a (New Mexico), 86, *191. See also* Zuni

LA 54147 (New Mexico), *xiv–xv,* 52, 106; armored vest fragment from, 210, 211; artifacts from, 211, *212*, 217; as Mexican Indian encampment, 216; ceramics from, 210; dating of, 213; discovery of, 209; discussion of, 209–19; excavation of, 210–11, *212;* Mesoamerican comal fragments from, 54–55; obsidian blade fragment from, 53, 210, 211; possible occupants of, 254–55; sheep bone from, 210, 211, 214; tent depressions at, 210, 211, *212,* 217; Texcoco-style point from, 54, *56;* winter quarters of Coronado, 209–19
LA 326 (New Mexico), 210; artifacts from, 217–18; identity of, 215; location of, 215
La Florida, 97, 188
La Junta (New Mexico), *227,* 230, 231
La Junta de los Ríos (Texas, Mexico), 267, 276
La Mora (Sonora), 143
La Palma (pueblo, New Mexico), identified as Corrales (LA 288), 202
La Tescalama (Sonora), 128
Ladera del Sur (LA 50257, New Mexico), 200–201, 204
Laguna de Chapala (Jalisco), *305*
Lake Iamonia (Florida), 101
Lake Jackson (Florida), 100, 101, *102*
Lake Lafayette (Florida), 101
Las Delicias del Sur Site (Sonora), 143, 155
Las Trincheras (Sonora), 76, 77, 82, *149*
Las Vegas (New Mexico), *178*
League, Spanish: difficulties for researchers, 140–41; variation in, 207n6
Lee, Betty: archeological survey of Sulphur Springs Valley, 165
Lees, William B., on Spanish colonial artifacts in Kansas, 247
León, Luis de, 50
Leyva de Bonilla, Francisco: native contact, 269; route of, 214
Lithics: Alibates chert, 273, 274, 285; Edwards Plateau chert, 265; Fresno point, 273, 275; Garza point, 265, 275; Harrell point, *56,* 273, 275; Lott point, 275; obsidian, 274, 275, 285n1; obsidian blade, 313; Perdiz point, 275; piki-stones, 298; stone discs as

INDEX

lids, 299; Talco-like point, 273; Tecovas chert, 274; Texcoco point, 217; Washita point, 273, 275
Little Colorado River (Arizona), *113*, 121, 122, 123, *191*, 192
Little Deer Site (Oklahoma), 274
Llano Estacado (Texas, New Mexico), *xiv–xv*, 28, *234*, 267, 279, 295–96, 309, 314, 317; archeology of, 260–61; barrancas of, 252–66; 304, 307; botany of, 260; geology of, 259; hydrology of, 260; physiography of, 259; pottery break on, 287; reached by Coronado expedition, 6; trails of, 255
Lochiel (Sonora), 118
López de Cárdenas, García, 314; advance guard for Coronado, 216; at Coofor, 215; established winter quarters on Rio Grande, 5; led expedition to the Colorado River, 5; left Coronado expedition, 6; returned to expedition, 7
López, Diego: encounter with buffalo, 256; lost on the Llano Estacado, 256
Lorencio, Father Juan, 145
Los Despoblados (New Mexico): possibly Ladera del Sur (LA 50257) and Ladera Pueblo (LA 50259), 200
Los Guajolotes (New Mexico), 201; possibly Isleta (LA 724), 201
Los Lingos Canyon (Texas), 316
Los Silos (New Mexico), 219
Lubbock Lake Site (Texas), 275
Luna y Arellano, Tristán de, 130, 134; led main body of Coronado expedition to Cíbola, 5; founded San Gerónimo de las Corazones, 5
Luna (New Mexico), 122

Macana. *See* Obsidian, swords and lances
Magdalena (Sonora), 82
Maigua (LA 716, New Mexico), 201, 203
Malpaís (pueblo, New Mexico), 201; identified as Puaray, 201
Manso Indians, *268*, 276, 277, 278
Manson, Joni L.: on entrance of Coronado expedition into U.S., 123; on location of Chichilticale, 121; on route from Cíbola to Tiguex, 180; on location of Vacapa, 123
Manzano Mountains (New Mexico), *178*
Marata (Arizona or New Mexico), 174
Marcos de Niza, fray, 116; accompanied by central Mexican and Piman-speaking Indians, 3; age at time of journey to the north, 70–71; appointed by viceroy to reconnoiter the north, 3, 62, 84, 188; attacked conquistadores'

357

treatment of Indians, 69; came within sight of Cíbola, 86; career of, 62; importance of route of, 62, 73; instructed to send messages to viceroy, 74; missing documents of, 175; motivation for exaggeration, 66–67; northward route of, 76–80; possible route of, 3, 73–82, 148; possibly stopped at Chichilticale, 168–69; question of whether he reached Zuni, 3, 61; questions of veracity, 64–72, 82–83; Ramusio's edition of the *Relación*, 64; rate of travel, 73; reaction of soldiers to, on entering Cíbola, 67; received news from Estevan in form of crosses, 188, 190; *Relación*, 64, 65, 66, 76, 81; return from Cíbola, 67, 73–76; route through Sonora, *138*; rumors precipitated by, 67; side trip to the Gulf of California, 80–82, 85
Marijilda (ruin, Arizona), *160*
Marshall, Michael P., on ceramic chronology, 293, 302
Martin Site (Florida), *xiv–xv*, *102*, 109–10; artifact assemblage from, 105–6; crossbow boltheads found, 40; hypothesized to be Anhaica Apalache, 104; identified as part of large Late Fort Walton village, 107; identified as Anhaica Apalache, 109; importance of study of, 109–10; possibility of evidence of Narváez expedition, 104
Martínez, Enrico, 1602 map of New Mexico, 204, *205*
Mátape (Sonora), 135, 155
Matsaki/Matsa:kya (New Mexico), 86, 93, *191*, 228. *See also* Zuni
Maxilla of pig found at Martin Site, 107
Mayo Valley (Sonora), 125
Mazocahui (Sonora), 140
McClellan Creek (Texas), 239
McNary (Arizona), 123
Mechitiltic (Jalisco), *305*
Medina de la Torre (pueblo, New Mexico), identified as Kuaua (LA 187), 202
Méndez, Father Pedro, 156
Mendoza, Antonio de (viceroy of New Spain), 2, 50, 51, 63; alleged conspiracy with Marcos de Niza, 70; described pottery, 297, 299; dispatched Marcos de Niza and Estevan, 3, 188; instructed Marcos de Niza to send messages, 74; rival of Cortés, 69–70
Mera, Harry P., on ceramic chronology, 288–89, 291–92
Mesilla (pueblo, New Mexico), *205*; identified as Pur-e Tu-ay (LA 489), 204

Messillos Pueblo (New Mexico), 205
Metates, Mexican slab, 54; found at LA 54147, 211
Mexicalcingo (New Mexico), 197, 201
Mexico-Tenochtitlán (Mexico City), *xiv–xv,* 27, 205, 305; arrival of Marcos de Niza at, 76; compared with Cíbola, 66; conquest of (1521), 38
Michoacán, 50
Middle Rio Grande Subregion, *198,* 204; correlation of pueblo names and archeological site numbers, 196–97; stability of settlement, 204
Mixtón War (rebellion), 5, 6, 51; affect on Coronado expedition, 4; native accoutrements in, 51
Mochila, Mochilagua, Mochil (Sonora), 135, 144
Mochopa (Sonora), 136
Mogollon Rim (Arizona), 93, *113,* 117, 121, 122
Moho Pueblo (New Mexico), 207n4, 302; attack on, 181; Coronado campsite at, 214
Montgomery Site (Texas), 275, 312, 315; material culture of, 275; possible Coronado campsite, 314
Morales. *See* Mulberries
Morlete, Juan de, route of, 214
Morris, John, on Cona, 282; on Southern Plains vegetation, 319
Mota y Padilla, Matías de la, description of land between Pecos and Querechos, 255
Muchaque Valley (Texas), 239
Mulberries, 242, 253
Mulberry Canyon (Texas), 239
Mullen (Pié) Canyon (New Mexico), 90
Mututicachi, Motuticatzi (Sonora), 135

Naco (Sonora), 121
Nahuas, 50, 56, remained in Pueblo world, 7; Mexica (Tenocha), 3, 50, *51,* 56; Tlatelolcans, *50;* Tlaxcalans, 3, *52,* 56
Nails: caret-head, 311, 315; from LA 54147, 106, 211, *213;* from Martin Site, 106, *108*
Narváez, Pánfilo de, 98; did not bring pigs, 107; fate of expedition led by, 2; in Apalachee, 107; use of crossbows, 38
Natanes Plateau (Arizona), 123
National Trails System Act, 1
Navidad (Jalisco), *305*
Nebame (Sonora), identified as Corazones, 117
Nébome (Indians, Sonora), 143
Nevado de Colima (Jalisco), *305*

Nicaragua, 118
Nochistlán (Aguascalientes), 306
Nompe (pueblo, New Mexico), 201; identified as Maigua (LA 716), 201
North Concho River, 242, 246, 263, 264
Nuestra Señora de Dolores (pueblo, New Mexico), 208n12
Nueva Galicia, 3
Nueva Sevilla (pueblo, New Mexico), 205
Nuño de Guzmán, Beltrán, 2, 63, 116; found Spanish goods in trade as far north as Río Mayo, 78; informed of wealthy towns to north, 63, 66, 84; slave raids by, 189
Nuri Chico Valley (Sonora), 140
Nuts, 253; in Blanco Canyon, 260

Obregón, Baltasar de, 141; description of Señora Valley, 141, 143, 144, 155, 268–69
Obsidian (ixtle): blades (navajas) from LA 54147, 53, *54,* 210, 211; blades (navajas) from Padre Island, 53; core, 53, *55;* core from Oklahoma, 53; decline in use of swords and lances, 54; swords and lances, 53, 313; swords and lances peculiar to Coronado expedition in Upper Southwest, 49, 217; swords and lances used by Coronado expedition, 53
Ojio (Arizona), *138*
Oñate, Juan de, 93, 202, 206n2, 214
Oñate expedition, 206; campsites of, 214; in Cañon Blanco, 230; native contact, 269; no use of crossbows, 39; route of, 214
Ópata (Indians, Sonora), 154, 155; devastated by disease, 145–46; hierarchical settlement system, 143; identified with Serrana Culture, 155; Jesuits established permanent missions among, 143; lack of correspondence between explorers' and missionaries' accounts, 139; large, sophisticated population in 1540, 137; puddled adobe structures, 143; 227 prehistoric and early historic sites in Río Sonora Valley, 143
Opodepe (Sonora), *149*
Oroz, fray Pedro, 50

Padilla, fray Juan de: accompanied Hernando de Alvarado to Buffalo Plains, 4; death of, 7; remained in Quivira, 7
Paint Creek Site (Kansas), *234;* artifacts from, 248
Painted Indian woman, 245
Palo Duro Canyon (Texas), 28, *234,* 237, 238, 239, 240, 243, 260, 262, 279, 282, 310, 316

INDEX

Palo Duro Creek (Texas), 243
Palomares (pueblo, New Mexico), identified as Santiago (LA 326), 202
Patrico (Sonora), 144
Pátzcuaro (Michoacán), 305
Pecos Indians: as guides, 184, 229; farming the Pecos River Valley, 229
Pecos Plot, 5
Pecos Pueblo (New Mexico), *xiv–xv,* 28, 37, 38, 52, *178, 205, 223,* 279; as established point on route, 226; crossbow boltheads found at, 40, 43, 310–11; description of, 183; identification of, 226; hostility toward Coronado expedition, 5–6; pottery found at, 288–89; trading party from at Cíbola, 4
Pecos River, Río de Cicúye (New Mexico), 6, 27–28, *178, 227, 234,* 267, 319; known as Río Salado, *245;* location of, 184, 229; location of bridge across, 220–32, 309, 314; reports of crossing points, 227–28. *See also* Río Pecos
Pérez de Luxán, Diego
Pérez de Ribas, Andrés, 144
Pérez de Villagrá, Gaspar, 202
Peru, 98
Petatlán (Sinaloa), 78, 251
Pete Creek Site (Texas), 275
Peterson, John, et al: on location of Teya sites, 243; on route to Quivira, 246
Phoenix (Arizona), 118
Picuris Pueblo (New Mexico), *205*
Piedras Marcadas (LA 290, New Mexico), 44, 202, 203
Pietown (New Mexico), 180
Pima (Indians, Sonora), 149, 155; confined to dry northwest, 149
Pima Bajo, 149, 155
Pimería Alta, 81
Pinacate Mountains (Sonora), 82, *113, 149*
Pinal Mountains (Arizona), 117
Pinaleno Mountains (Arizona), 118, 122, 123, 168
Piro (province, New Mexico), 200
Piro language, 273, 277–78
Pitic (Sonora), *138*
Pizarro, Francisco: conquest of the Inca by, 63; use of crossbows, 38, 39; influence of Pizarro's Inca conquest on climate in 1539 Mexico, 3; relation with Hernando de Soto, 97
Plains Indians, as guides, 250
Plumasano Wash (New Mexico), 180
Pochteca tradition (central Mexico), 55; extending to New Mexico pueblos, 72
Point of Pines (ruin, Arizona), 173

Pointing Face (New Mexico), 189, *191*
Polveron Phase (Arizona), 167
Ponida (Sonora), 135
Ponsitlán (New Mexico), possibly LA 778, 200
Puala de los Martires. *See* Puaray
Puaray/Puala (New Mexico), 201, 202, 203, 214; crossbow bolthead possibly found at, 44; identified as LA 717, 202; Oñate campsite at, 214; southernmost of the pueblos of Tiguex, 201; suggestion of shift in location during sixteenth century, 202–3
Pueblo de la Cruz (New Mexico), also known as Arenal, 207n4
Pueblo del Cerco (New Mexico), also known as Moho, 207n4
Pueblo Nuevo (New Mexico), possibly LA 778, 200
Pueblo Viejo Ruins (Arizona), 168
Pueblos del Valle de Puará, 204, *205*
Puerto de Luna (New Mexico), 185
Puerto/Puerta del Sol (Sonora), 140, 150, 155
Pur-e Tu-ay (LA 489, New Mexico), 197, 204

Querecho Indians, 267, *268,* 296, 297, 309, 314; contacted by Coronado expedition, 236; contacted by Espejo, 268; identified as Apache, 269, 271–72; identified as Vaqueros, 269; identified with eastern Apaches, 6; identified with Tierra Blanca sites, 261; in Canadian River drainage, 268; location of camp of, 250, 255
Quesería (Colima), 306
Quiburi (Sonora), 118
Quitaque Canyon (Texas), *234,* 241, 263, 282, 307, 316, 318, 319
Quitovac (Sonora), 135
Quivira (Kansas), 49, 279, 301, 314; location of, 5, 184, 240, 245–49, 267, 295, 301, 309, 315; said to be wealthy land, 4

Railroad Pass (Arizona), 118
Rainbow Spring (New Mexico), *191*
Ranjel, Rodrigo, 99
Relación del Suceso, 121, 141; discussion of barrancas, 256, 258, 310; discussion of expedition route, 184, 227, 309, 314, 317
Rhodes, Diane Lee: on crossbow boltheads, 218; on magnetic declination, 246–47
Rice County (Kansas), 52; sites of, *xiv–xv. See also* Paint Creek Site; Tobias Site
Riley, Carroll L.: on entrance of Coronado expedition into U.S., 123; on location of

Alameda, 181; on location of Arenal, 181; on location of Chichilticale, 121; on location of Coofor, 181; on location of Vacapa, 123; on route from Chichilticale to Cíbola, 123; on route from Cíbola to Tiguex, 180
Río Altar (Sonora), 130, 148; evidence of Trincheras Culture on, 154
Río Apamila (Colima), 304
Río Batepito (Sonora), 117, 119, 140
Río Bavispe (Sonora), *112*, *113*, 117, 120, 130, 137, 140, 148, *149*, 150; evidence of Serrana Culture on, 153
Río Bravo. *See* Rio Grande
Río Cedros (Sonora), 130, 150; evidence of Serrana Culture on, 153
Río Chico (Sonora), 130
Río Coahuayana (Colima), 304
Río Concepción (Sonora), 148
Río Conchos/de las Conchas (Chihuahua), *205*, 268
Río de Cicúye. *See* Pecos River
Río de la Madalena. *See* Canadian River
Río de las Balsas, 221
Río de las Palmas (Texas, Tamaulipas), 98, 229
Río de Nombre de Dios (Chihuahua), *205*
Río de Santiago (Nayarit), *112*, 220
Río de Señora (or Senora, Sonora), 7, 129; identified as Río Yaqui, 117
Río del Norte. *See* Rio Grande
Río El Naranjo (Colima), 305, 306
Río Evora de Mocorito, identified as Río Petatlán, 116
Río Fronteras (Sonora), 150; evidence of Serrana culture on, 153
Río Fuerte (Sinaloa), 28, 63, 76, *112*, *138*, *149*, 150; identified as Arroyo de los Cedros, Río Mayomo, and Río San Miguel, 116; return route of expedition on, 251
Rio Grande (New Mexico), *178*, 202, 203, 204, 267; known as Río Bravo, *205;* known as Río de Guadalquivir, 200; known as Río de Nuestra Señora, 199; known as Río del Norte, 200, *205;* shift of channel, 207–8n10; winter quarters on, 221
Rio Grande pueblos (New Mexico), 28, 38, 48, 195, 269; crossbow boltheads found at, 40; difficulties in identifying, 206n3; location of, 243–44
Río Lachimí (Sonora), identified with Río Yaqui, 116–17
Río Magdalena (Sonora), 76, 82, *138*, 148, *149;* evidence of Trincheras Culture on, 154
Río Mátape (Sonora), 77, 78, *112*, *113*, *149*

Río Mayamo (Sinaloa), 116
Río Mayo (Sonora), 28, 76, *112*, 130, *149*, 150, 251
Río Moctezuma (Sonora), 130, 150; evidence of Serrana Culture on, 153
Río Mulatos (Sonora), 131
Río Nexpa (Sonora, Arizona), *160*, 170, 175
Río Oera (Sonora), 117
Río Pecos (New Mexico), location of bridge across, 184–86, 309. *See also* Pecos River
Río Petatlán (or Petatla, Sinaloa), 116
Río Puerco (New Mexico), *178*
Río Purificación (Colima), 304
Río Sahuaripa (Sonora), 150
Río Salado. *See* Pecos River
Río San Bernardino (Sonora, Arizona, New Mexico), 117, 119, 137, 140
Río San Miguel (Sonora), 80, 81, 82, 148, 154; compared with Río Sonora, 81–82; evidence of Serrana Culture on, 153; headquarters of Kino's Pimería Alta, 81; turquoise and bison hides from Cíbola, possible, 81
Río San Pedro (Sonora, Arizona), 4, 82, 83, 85, 89, *113*, 115, 118, 120, 121, 122, 131, 137, *138*, 140, *149*, *160;* identified as Río Nexpa, 170
Río Santa Cruz (Sonora), 131
Río Seco Basin (Sonora), 154
Río Sinaloa (Sinaloa), 78, *112*, 116, *149*, 251
Río Sonora (Sonora), 4, 28, 80, 81–82, 83, *112*, *113*, 118, 131, *138*, 140, *149*, 150; compared with Río San Miguel, 81–82; evidence of Serrana Culture on, 153–54; turquoise and bison hides from Cíbola, possible, 81
Río Sonora Culture (Serrana), defined by Monroe Amsden, 150
Río Tecoripa (Sonora), 84
Río Tuxpán (Colima), 305, 306
Río Yaqui (Sonora), 35, 63, 77, 78, 84, *112*, *113*, 117, 131, *138*, 139, 143, *149*, 150
Road from Colima to Compostela, *305*
Rodeo (New Mexico), 117
Rodríguez/Chamuscado expedition, 202, 204, 206, 207n5; ceramic typology, 298, 299; native contact, 268–69; no use of crossbows, 39
Rodríguez, fray Agustín, 298, 299; route of, 214, 230
Rodríguez Cabrillo, Juan: voyage of, 26; use of crossbows, 38
Rosales. *See* Rosebush

Rosebush, 253, 281; in Blanco Canyon, 260
Rowe Mesa (New Mexico), 6, 186
Running Water Draw (Texas), 239, 283

Safford (Arizona), 158, 168, 171, 173
Sahuaripa (Sonora), *149,* 155
Salado pueblo ruins (Arizona), 167–68
Salinas pueblos (New Mexico), *178*
Salome Creek (Arizona), 121
Salt Fork of the Red River (Texas), *234,* 239
Salt River (Arizona), 77, 93, *113,* 118, 120, 121, 122, *138*
Sama (pueblo, New Mexico), 205
San Agustín (Florida), *xiv–xv*
San Bernardino Valley (Sonora, Arizona, New Mexico), 115, 117, 119
San Carlos River (Arizona), 123
San Cristóbal Pueblo (New Mexico), 205
San Felipe Pueblo (New Mexico), 202, 205
San Francisco River (Arizona, New Mexico), 4, 122, 123
San Francisco Site (LA 778, New Mexico), 200
San Gabriel (New Mexico), 205
San Gerónimo de los Corazones (Sonora), 140, 141; founded by Luna y Arellano, 5; Indian uprising at, 7; location moved, 6; Pedro de Tovar sent to, 5
San Ildefonso Pueblo (New Mexico), 205
San José River (New Mexico), 181
San José Site (Sonora), 143, 153, 156
San Juan Bautista (pueblo, New Mexico), identified as Casa Colorado (LA 50261), 204
San Juan del Río (Querétaro), 205
San Juan Espanatica (Jalisco), *305*
San Juan Pueblo (New Mexico), 205
San Luis de Talimali (Florida), 100, *102*
San Luis de Xinyaca (Florida), 100
San Marcos Pueblo (New Mexico), 205
San Mateo (pueblo, New Mexico), 201
San Mateo Mountains (New Mexico), *178*
San Miguel de Culiacán (Sinaloa), *xiv–xv,* 27, 32, 36, 53, 67, *112,* 116, *138,* 139, 300; advance party under Vázquez de Coronado leaves, 4; arrival of Coronado expedition at, 4; arrival of Marcos de Niza at, 76; departure of fray Marcos and Estevan from, 84; founded, 2; return of expedition to, 251
San Pedro (pueblo, New Mexico), identified as Piedras Marcadas (LA 290), 202
San Pedro River. *See* Río San Pedro
San Pedro Valley (Sonora, Arizona), 115, 119, 122, 123, 125, 128, 132, 168, 173

San Simón Creek (Arizona), *160*
San Simón Valley (Arizona), 118, 171
Sánchez Chamuscado, Francisco, 199
Sánchez Chamuscado, Francisco, expedition: ceramic typology, 298, 299; native contact, 268; no use of crossbows, 39; route of, 214, 230
Sandal-making awls, 56
Sandals (alpargates), 56
Sandia Mountains (New Mexico), *178,* 203
Sandia Pueblo (New Mexico), 203
Sangre de Cristo Mountains (New Mexico), *178,* 269
Santa Ana Pueblo (New Mexico), 205
Santa Bárbara (Chihuahua), 205
Santa Catalina Pueblo (New Mexico), 201
Santa Clara Pueblo (New Mexico), 205
Santa Cruz River (Arizona), *113, 149*
Santa Cruz Valley (Arizona), 115, 123
Santa Elena (South Carolina), *xiv–xv*
Santa Fe (New Mexico), *178*
Santa Rosa (New Mexico), *178*
Santa Teresa Mountains (Arizona), 122, 123
Santiago Pueblo (New Mexico, LA 326), 16, 52, 205, 321; crossbow boltheads found at, 43, 310
Santo Domingo Pueblo (New Mexico), 202, 205
Satechi (Sonora), 135
Sauer, Carl: opinion that Marcos de Niza lied, 72; route of Coronado expedition through Arizona, 122–23; route of Coronado expedition through Sonora, 137; suggested inland route for Marcos de Niza, 70
Saxman Site (Kansas): chain mail from, 248
Sayopa (Sonora), 77, 140
Sayula (Jalisco), *305*
Schroeder, Albert H., 35; critique of route hypothesis, 262–63; on LA 326, 215–16; on LA 54147, 210, 216; on location of bridge over Río de Cicúye, 185, 225; on location of Chichilticale, 120–21; on route through Texas Panhandle, 243; on Teyas, 272; proposed routes of fray Marcos and Coronado expedition, 118–19
Senecú/Calicu Pueblo (New Mexico), 205
Senoquipe (Sonora), 128
Señora Valley (Sonora), 32, 128, 139, 140; densely populated in sixteenth century, 141, 146; described by Castañeda, 143–44; described by Obregón, 144; devastated by disease, 145–46; occupied by scattered rancherías in seventeenth century, 145

Serrana (province/zone, Sonora), 148, *149;* Batuco identified by Riley, 153; Cumupa identified by Riley, 153; Guaraspi identified by Riley, 153; Oera identified by Riley, 153; Sahuaripa identified by Riley, 153; Señora identified by Riley, 153

Serrana Culture: characteristics of, 150–51; expansion of interrupted by Spaniards, 155; hypothesized Casas Grandes connection of, 154–55; identified as Ópata, 157; most information concerning from upper Río Sonora Valley, 152; one-story surface structures typical, 153; organic temper in ceramics, 156; pithouses, 152; spindle whorls, 151; suggestion that large sites are still occupied, 155–56; traditions within, 150–51. *See also* Río Sonora Culture

76 Ranch (Arizona), *xiv–xv, 113, 160, 161, 163, 164, 165,* 168, *169,* 175; ceremonial room at, 162; dating of, 167; description and dimensions of, 163–64, 172; excavation of by William Duffen, 158, 159–60, 161–63; late Salado site, 158; material culture of, 162; mealing bins at, 162; occupation consistent with description of Chichilticale, 167; one-story adobe ruin, 161–62; plain, corrugated, and polychrome ceramics at, 162; present condition and extent of, 163–67; recent heavy sheet runoff at, 166–67; sherd statistics, 166; suggested as Chichilticale, 158

Sevilleta (LA, New Mexico)

Shepard, Anna O., on ceramic chronology, 288, 293

Shine, Michael, on location of bridge over Río de Cicúye, 224

Shu'la:witsi (Zuni fire god), *193*

Sierra Anchas (Arizona), 121

Sierra de los Ajos (Sonora), 128–29

Sierra de San José (Sonora), 129

Sierra de San Luis (Sonora), 117

Sierra Madre Occidental (Sonora, Sinaloa), 122

Silver Lake (Texas), *234,* 263

Simpson, James H.: errors in route proposals, 117; on location of bridge over Río de Cicúye, 224; proposed route of Coronado expedition along Santa Cruz Valley, 117; route hypothesis, 236–37

Sinaloa de Leyva (Sinaloa), 116

Sinoquipe (Sonora), 129

Slaughter Ranch, *113,* 117; suggested as Coronado expedition's crossing into modern U.S., 117

Snow, David H., ceramic chronology, 216

Sobaipuri (Indians of Sonora), 118, 120

Socorro (New Mexico), 180

Socorro Basin (New Mexico), 199

Socorro Pueblo (New Mexico), *205*

Solomon (Arizona), 168

Sonoita/Sonoyta (Sonora), 135

Sonora, eastern, topography of, 148

Sonora River. *See* Río de Señora

Sonora Valley (Sonora), 31, 121, 128, 137, 139–40; *142,* 146, 155, 156, 170; archeological survey of, 142–44; evidence of Serrana Culture in, 152; evidence of Trincheras Culture in, south of Banámichi, 153; return route of expedition through, 251

Sonoytac (Sonora), 136

Soto, Hernando de: appointment to explore Florida, 2–3, 98; attempt to find Coronado, 245; biographical sketch, 97–98; death of, 99

South Plains (Texas), 47

Soyopa (Sonora), 135

Spanish terms, spelling of, *xii–xiii*

Spanish-colonial-era objects ignored by early archeologists, 52–53

Spielmann, Katherine, on Southern Plains village sites, 296

Spur, 316

Spur Lake (New Mexico), 122

St. Johns (Arizona), 121, 189, *191,* 192

Steen, Charlie, suggested route of Marcos de Niza up Santa Cruz Valley, 117–18

Stephenson, W. H., on route to Quivira, 246

Stevens Ranch Site (Arizona), 119

Straight pin, found at LA 54147, 211

Stray Horse Creek (Arizona), 122

Suaqui Grande (Sonora), 85

Sulphur Springs Valley (Arizona), 83, 158, 159, *160,* 162, 165, 166, 167, 168, *169,* 171, 172, 173, 174, 321

Suma Indians, *268;* identity of, 272, 276; language of, 278

Suya (Sonora), identified as Señora of Francisco de Ibarra, 117

Suya Valley (Sonora), 129, 140

Swanton, John R., 100

Tabas (Kansas), 28; death of El Turco at, 248–49; location of, 249

Taiban Creek/Spring (New Mexico), 244

Tallahassee (Florida), 100, 101, *102*

Tallahassee Red Clay Hills (Florida), 101

Tampa Bay (Florida), 98

INDEX 363

Tanoan language, 277, 278, 285
Taos (New Mexico), 28, 195, *205,* 269
Tapalpa (Jalisco), 305
Taracahitan languages, 278; area conforms to region of live streams in Sonora, 149, 155; Eudeve, 149, 150; Jova, 150; Ópata, 149, 150; Mayo, 149, 150; recent intrusion of speakers into Pima- Tepehuan area, 154; Tarahumar, 149; Warihio, 149, 150; Yaqui, 149
Tarascans, *xi,* 2; remained in Pueblo world, 7; with Coronado expedition, 3, 50, 51, 56
Tatham Mound Site (Florida), 109
Taxumulco (New Mexico), possibly Be-jui Tu-ay (LA 81), 201
Taylor Site (Oklahoma), 274
Techado Mesa (New Mexico), 180
Tecoripa (Sonora), 85
Tepehuan language, 154
Termino de Puala (New Mexico), 200; identified as Sevilleta site, LA 774, 200
Tesar, Louis, made survey of Leon County, Florida, 100–101
Tesocoma (Sonora), identified as Corazones, 117, 141
Teya Indians, *268,* 296, 297, 309–10, 315, 316, 317; as guides, 258, 279; besieged Cicúye, 182; ceramics, lack of, 303; described by Castañeda, 270–71; described by Vázquez de Coronado, 269–70; description in *Relación del Suceso,* 270; description in *Relación Postrera,* 271; discussion of ethnic/linguistic affiliation, 271–72; enemies of, 280; identified as Apache by Harrington, 272; identified as Caddoan by Baugh, 272; identified as Jumano by Bandelier, 272; identified as related to Piro-Tompiro, 6, 273; identity of, 243, 267–86; location of camp, 240; possible Coronado campsite in Teya territory, 287, 314; relation with Garza Complex, 260, 275–76; use of dogs by, 270–71
Tiburon Island (Sonora), 136
Tierra Blanca Complex, 273–74, 275, 295, 303, 309, 316; location of sites, 260–61
Tierra Blanca Draw (Texas), 319
Tierra Nueva, *xiv–xv,* defined, xi
Tiguex/Southern Tiwa (province, New Mexico), 47, 53, 199, 201, 300, 303; burned and abandoned, 5; comprised of twelve or thirteen pueblos, 199; identified with southern Tiwa pueblos, 5; lack of no-man's-land between Tutahaco and Tiguex, 200; pueblos of, 201–4; 207nn4–5; return of expedition to, 318; war in, 5, 47–48, 181
Tijeras Arroyo (New Mexico), 202
Tijeras Canyon (New Mexico), 203
Tijeras Pueblo (New Mexico), *178*
Tipotia Pueblo (New Mexico), *178*
Tiwa language, 277–78
Tlajomulca (Jalisco), *305*
Tobias Site (Kansas), *234*
Tomatlán (New Mexico), 201; possibly Valencia (LA 953), 201
Tompiro language, 272, 277, 278
Tonila (Jalisco), 307
Tonque (New Mexico), *178*
Tonto Creek (Arizona), 121
Totonteac (Arizona or New Mexico), 145
Tovar, Pedro de: moved San Gerónimo, 6; sent to command San Gerónimo de los Corazones, 5
Toyah Focus, 276
Trails and trade routes (Indian and historic), 101, 121; as key to determining the Coronado expedition route, 123; "barefoot trail," 192, 193; from Casas Grandes to Sahuaripa, 140; including Chichilticale as a stop, 159, 170; linking Zuni and Sonora, 123; to buffalo plains, 230
Tres Alamos Wash (Arizona), 120
Trincheras Culture (Sonora), 153–54; core area in Altar and Magdalena Valleys, 154; extended into Arizona, 154; man-made clearings in malpaís, 153; named for hillside terraces, 153
Trujillo Formation, 259
Trujillos (pueblo, New Mexico), 207n7
Tucson (Arizona), *113, 118, 149*
Tucsonimo (Arizona), *138*
Tucumcari Peak (New Mexico), 185, *234,* 261, 314; location of Querecho camp, 265
Tule Canyon (Texas), 17, *234,* 238, 279, 282, 307, 310, 316, 319; location of Teya camp, 240
Turk. *See* El Turco
Tusayan Anasazi, 173
Tutahaco (province, New Mexico), 199; comprised of eight pueblos, 199; identified with Piro pueblos, 5–6; lack of no-man's-land between Tutahaco and Tiguex, 200; visited by Coronado, 180–81

Úbeda, Juan de, 7
Udall, Stewart, on Marcos de Niza, 61
Udden, Johan August, on location of Quivira, 247

Ulloa, Francisco de, report of latitude of head of Gulf of California, 81
Undreiner, George J., suggested route of fray Marcos in Sonora and Arizona, 118, 120, 148
United States De Soto Expedition Commission, 121
Ures (Sonora), *112, 113,* 135–36, *149;* identified with Corazones, 77, 155
Ures Canyon (Sonora), 129
Uto-Aztecan language family, 272, 276
Uva. *See* Grape

Vacapa (Sonora), *138;* Abra three days south, 80; description by Castañeda, 79; discussion of location of, 76–80, 84–85; identified with Suaqui Grande or Tecoripa, 84–85; in the Altar-Magdalena drainage, 123; language change south of, 78; on Yaqui or Mátape Rivers, 78; Piman name, 76
Valencia (LA 953 , New Mexico), 201, 204
Valle Chimal (New Mexico), *227, 273*
Vázquez de Ayllón, Lucas, 98
Vázquez de Coronado, Francisco, 116, 148; appointed governor of Nueva Galicia, 3; injured in fall, 6–7; planned to return to Quivira, 6; return to Mexico City, 251; sent main body of expedition back to Rio Grande from barrancas, 6; sent out exploring parties from Zuni, 4; unaware of Estevan's death as of July 1539, 75–76; visited Tutahaco, 5
Veracruz (Veracruz), *xv*
Verjuice, 241, 354, 257, 281
Vierra, Bradley J., on Coronado expediton encampments, 297; on LA 54147, 181
Villarasa (pueblo, New Mexico), 202; identified as Alameda (LA 421), 201, 202, 207–8
Vizcaíno, Sebastián, 48
Volcán de Colima (Colima), *305,* 305

Wagner, Henry, on Marcos de Niza, 74–75
Wagstaff, Robert M.: criticism of Bolton's route through Arizona and Sonora, 122; on first barranca, 242; on route to Quivira, 246
Watche (LA 677, New Mexico), 201, 203
Wedel, Mildred Mott: on El Turco, 317; on location of Tabas, 249
Wedel, Waldo R., on location of Quivira, 248
Wheeler Complex (Oklahoma), 273, 274–75, 285n1, 288, 295, 300; identity of, 275
White Mountains (Arizona), *113,* 118, 121
Whitmer (ruin, Arizona), *160,* 168, *169*

Wichita (Indians, Kansas): linguistics of, 249; settlements of, 255
Williams, J. W.: critique of route hypothesis, 263–65; on vegetation on the Llano Estacado, 241–42, 253, 260
Winchester Mountains (Arizona), *160*
Winship, George P.: on location of bridge over Río de Cicúye, 224; on location of Quivira, 247; on nuts, 253; route hypothesis across Plains, 237

Ximena (New Mexico), 182

Yakimi/Lachimi (Sonora), 31
Yaqui Valley (Sonora), 129
Yavapai (Arizona), 120
Yécora (Sonora), 136
Yellow House Canyon/Draw (Texas), *234, 239,* 258, 276, 281, 284, 307, 310, 318; not second barranca, 265–66
Ysopete/Isopete, 267, 285–86n2, 314; guide of Coronado expedition, 6, 229, 255; left in Quivira, 250; protested direction of march, 240; Wichita Indian, 6
Yunqueyunque (New Mexico), 297
Yupaha (Florida), 99

Zacatecas (Zacatecas), *245*
Zacoalco (Jalisco), *305*
Zapotlán (Jalisco), *305. See also* Ciudad Guzmán
Zia/Sia/Chiah (New Mexico), 28, 179, 182, *205*
Zumárraga, Juan de, 66; account of Marcos de Niza's report by, 65–66; attacked conquistadores' treatment of Indians, 69, 70; relationship with Marcos de Niza, 61–62
Zuni (New Mexico), 27, 38, 77, *87,* 89, *113,* 121, *138, 178, 191;* arrival of Vázquez de Coronado at, 4; bow priest, 190, 193; cornmeal line drawn by bow priest, 193; return route of expedition through, 251; solar observations at, 66; solstice ceremony at, 66, 192–93; trade from south, 189. *See also* Halona; Hawikuh; Kiakima; Kechipawa; Kwakina; Matsaki
Zuni Buttes (New Mexico), *191*
Zuni Canyon (New Mexico), 180
Zuni Mountain (New Mexico), *178*
Zuni Plateau (New Mexico), 122
Zuni River (Arizona, New Mexico), 4, 86, 89, 118, 121, 122, 123, *178, 191,* 192

www.ingramcontent.com/pod-product-compliance
Lightning Source LLC
Chambersburg PA
CBHW022026290426
44109CB00014B/766